D1363631

CHRISTIAN FAITH AND GREEK PHILOSOPHY
IN LATE ANTIQUITY

SUPPLEMENTS TO

VIGILIAE CHRISTIANAE

Formerly Philosophia Patrum

TEXTS AND STUDIES OF EARLY CHRISTIAN LIFE AND LANGUAGE

EDITORS

J. DEN BOEFT — R. VAN DEN BROEK — A.F.J. KLIJN
G. QUISPEL — J.C.M. VAN WINDEN

VOLUME XIX

Professor Christopher Stead

CHRISTIAN FAITH AND GREEK PHILOSOPHY IN LATE ANTIQUITY

Essays in Tribute to

GEORGE CHRISTOPHER STEAD

Ely Professor of Divinity, University of Cambridge (1971-1980)

In Celebration of his Eightieth Birthday
9th April 1993

EDITED BY

LIONEL R. WICKHAM AND CAROLINE P. BAMMEL
ASSISTED BY ERICA C.D. HUNTER

E.J. BRILL
LEIDEN · NEW YORK · KÖLN
1993

The paper in this book meets the guidelines for permanence and durability of the Committee on Production Guidelines for Book Longevity of the Council on Library Resources.

Library of Congress Cataloging-in-Publication Data

93-19426
CIP

ISSN 0920-623X
ISBN 90 04 09605 1

CONTENTS

PREFACE

Friends and pupils of Christopher Stead join together here to offer a tribute to him on his 80th birthday. Born 9th April 1913 he came to King's College, Cambridge in 1931 and read first Classics and then Philosophy (called in those days at Cambridge 'Moral Science'). After a spell as fellow of King's College he was ordained, and in 1949 became Chaplain at Keble College, Oxford. In 1971 he was made Ely Professor of Divinity (the last to hold that office) and in conjunction with it was a residentiary canon of Ely Cathedral till his retirement 13 years ago. He has continued with some occasional university teaching and remains a tireless joint-president of the Senior Patristic Seminar, at which he has benefitted numerous speakers by his kindly but penetrating criticisms and delighted participants by his scholarly precision and ever youthful sense of humour (most memorably perhaps on the occasion of the delivery of the paper "The Arian Controversy: A new Perspective").

Over the years he has come to occupy a special place in the esteem and affections of those who have laboured in the portion of the Lord's vineyard marked out as the study of the fathers of the Church. The range and depth of his personal contribution are amply attested by the list of publications which have illuminated many and various aspects of the discipline. It is a contribution which continues to be fruitful, not only in his own hands but by the stimulus to thought, and encouragement to persevere, he has given to others. For all this we are grateful, and in wishing him many happy returns of the day we add our hope that he will not lay down his pen but give us still more reason for gratitude in the years to come.

A collection of essays cannot do justice to all the facets of the ancient Church which he has concerned himself with. The heading under which we have brought these together signals the area he has made specially his own: the relation, sometimes of hostility, sometimes of symbiosis, between the life of faith as it was lived in the ancient Church and the wisdom of the philosophers. His own training has guided him to that area. For one who attended the classes of Moore and Wittgenstein in Cambridge in the 30's and 40's of the century, could not but be made acutely aware of the problems involved and see the overriding importance of clarity and truthfulness both in their statement and in their proposed resolution. His own discussions have always been critical examinations in which the worth of the arguments, no less than their pedigree, has been exposed for consideration. It has been his own special gift to render intelligible the technical elaborations of insights which have their rationale elsewhere than in the technique itself and to capture truths in danger of loss from the inexpertise of their expression. The approach has never been iconoclastic, nor has it ever been obseqious. Those who read his papers on Athanasius and Gregory of Nyssa will find sharp things said about the quality of the saints' arguments. They will not go away feeling that the saints were not worth reading: rather, that the issues themselves have been made clearer. We hope that these essays we here present may have something of this same approach or we are no true friends of the beloved colleague to whom we dedicate them. Our best wishes to you Christopher on your birthday.

Acknowledgements

The editors publicly record their debt not only to the contributors but especially to Dr. Erica C.D. Hunter for her invaluable assistance in preparing this volume for the press. The efforts of Mrs J. O'Dell and Miss Anna Maria Marino of the Office at the Faculty of Divinity are also not to be forgotten. We thank too the managers of the Bethune-Baker Fund for a subvention towards the cost of the publication.

Lionel R Wickham
Caroline P H Bammel

ABBREVIATIONS

OF MAJOR SERIES AND PRIMARY EDITIONS

AAWG.PH	Abhandlungen der k. Akademie der Wissenschaften zu Berlin
ACO	Acta conciliorum oecumenicorum
AE	Basil. *Adversus Eunomium*
AKG	Arbeiten zur Kirchengeschichte
AnGr/SFT	Analecta Gregoriana/Series facultatis theologicae
BByzE	Bibliothèque byzantine. Études
BFPUL	Bibliothèque de la faculté catholique de théologie de Lyon
BGrL	Bibliothek der griechischen Literatur
BHTh	Beiträge zur historischen Theologie
BTH	Bibliothèque de théologie historique
ByA	Byzantinisches Archiv
CA (Osborne)	Athanasius. *Contra Arianos*
CA (Rtter)	Dionysius Areopagita. *Corpus Areopagiticum*
CC	Origen. *Contra Celsum*
CChr.SL	Corpus Christianorum- Serie Latina
CE	Basil. *Contra Eunomium* II
CH	Dionysius Areopagita. *De Coelesti Hierarchia*
conf.	Augustine. *Confessiones*
CPG	Corpus Patrologia Graeca
CSCO	Corpus scriptorum Scriptores Syri
CSEL	Corpus scriptorum ecclesiasticorum Latinorum
CUFr	Collection des universités de France
DAR	Gregory of Nyssa. *De Anima et Resurrectione*
DBCD	Augustine. *De Baptismo contra Donatistas*
DCD	Augustine. *De Civitate Dei*
DDC	Augustine. *De Doctrina Christiana*
DHO	Gregory of Nyssa. *De Hominis Opificio*
DN	Dionysius Areopagita. *De Divinis Nominibus*
DSDM	Augustine. *De Sermone Domini in Monte*
ECSD	Augustine. *Epistola ad Catholicos de Secta Donatistarum*
EH	Dionysius Areopagita. *De Ecclesiastica Hierarchia*
EKK	Evangelisch-katholischer Kommentar zum Neuen Testament
Ep	Dionysius Areopagita. *Epistulae*

FChLDG	Forschungen zur christlichen Literatur- und Dogmengeschichte
FGTh	Forschungen zur Geschichte der Theologie und des innerkirchlichen Lebens
FKDG	Forschungen zur Kirchen- und Dogmengeschichte
GCS	*Theodores Anagnostes*
HAW	Handbuch der Altertumswissenschaft
HDG	Handbuch der Dogmengeschichte
H.E.	Eusebius. *Historia Ecclesiastica*
LWQF	Liturgiewissenschaftliche Quellen und Forschungen
MTh	Dionysius Areopagita. *De Mystica Theologia*
NAWG	Nachrichten (1884-1893: von) der Gesellschaft der Wissenschaften (1884-1893: zu) in Göttingen
NGWG	Nachrichten (1941-1944: von) der Akademie der Wissenschaften in Göttingen
NPNF	A select library of the Nice and post-Nicene (Christian) fathers
OECT	Oxford early Christian texts
PG	Patrologia Graeca (Migne)
PhA	Philosophische Abhandlungen. Frankfurt
PL	Patrologia Latina
PLRE	Prosopography of the Later Roman Empire
PTS	Patristiche Texte und Studien
PUCSC.F	Pubblicazioni della universita cattolica del Sacro Cuore. Contributi. Scienze filosofiche
SC	Sources chrétiennes
SGKA	Studien zur Geschichte und Kultur des Altertums
SGTK	Studien zur Geschichte der Theologie und Kirche
TBT	Theologische Bibliothek Töpelmann
TC	Traditio Christiana
Theol (P)	Théologie. Paris
Theoph.	Theophaneia
ThH	Theologisch tijdschrift
TU	Texte und Untersuchungen zur Geschichte der altchristlichen Literatur
UCPCP	University of California publications in classical philology
WdF	Wege der Forschung

PAULINE EXEGESIS, MANICHAEISM AND PHILOSOPHY IN THE EARLY AUGUSTINE

C.P. BAMMEL

Augustine tells us that after the 'conversion' effected in him by the perusal of Platonist books he turned to the writings of the apostle Paul and found confirmation there of the truth he had perceived. This information is given not only in the *Confessions* (7.21 *auidissime arripui ... prae ceteris apostolum Paulum ... et inueni quidquid illac uerum legeram, hac cum conmendatione gratiae tuae dici*), but also in the earlier *Contra Academicos* (2.2.5 *titubans properans haesitans arripio apostolum Paulum ... perlegi totum intentissime atque castissime. tunc uero quantulocumque iam lumine adsperso tanta se mihi philosophiae facies aperuit ...*).[1] Paul however was also the apostle of the Manichees. Augustine was not merely combining Platonist insights with a return to his childhood religion,[2] he was also replacing his earlier Manichaean reading of Paul with a new 'Platonising' understanding.[3]

The aim of this paper[4] is to examine firstly the Manichaean use of Paul which is likely to have been familiar to Augustine during his Manichaean period and secondly the new understanding apparent in his ear-

---

[1] Cf. also *De Beata Vita* 1.4, where he speaks of the Christian scriptures in general: lectis autem Plotini paucissimis libris ... conlataque cum eis, quantum potui, etiam illorum auctoritate, qui diuina mysteria tradiderunt, sic exarsi ... On these passages cf. John J. O'Meara, "Arripui, aperui, et legi", *Augustinus Magister. Congrès International Augustinien*, Paris, 21-24 Septembre 1954, 59-65.

[2] Cf. *Contra Academicos* 2.2.5: *respexi tamen, confitebor, quasi de itinere in illam religionem, quae pueris nobis insita est et medullitus inplicata; uerum autem ipsa ad se nescientem rapiebat.*

[3] Cf. *Contra Academicos* 1.1.3: *ipsa (philosophia) me penitus ab illa superstitione ... liberauit; Contra Academicos* 3.20.43: *apud Platonicos me interim, quod sacris nostris non repugnet, reperturum esse confido.* In *Confessions* 7.21 Augustine states that on his rereading of Paul the supposed internal contradictions and disagreements with the law and prophets disappeared.

[4] It supplements a paper on 'Augustine, Origen and the Exegesis of St. Paul' (now published in *Augustinianum* 32 (1992), 341-368) which I delivered at the Oxford Patristic Conference in 1991 and also at the Patristic Seminar in Cambridge, where Christopher Stead kindly commented on it.

liest writings after his conversion and to relate this to the change in the structure of his philosophical approach. The writings considered will be those up to and including the *De Moribus Ecclesiae Catholicae et de Moribus Manichaeorum,* which is the first explicitly anti-Manichaean treatise and also the first to make extensive use of Pauline quotations.[5] Since we have no Manichaean writings composed by Augustine I will use his anti-Manichaean writings as evidence for the kinds of views he was familiar with as a Manichee himself.[6]

The Use of Paul in African Manichaeism as known to Augustine

Augustine[7] has preserved a considerable amount of Manichaean material in his anti-Manichaean writings, in particular the *Contra Faustum,* where he quotes Faustus' book against the Catholic Christians in full,[8] the *Contra Adimantum,* in which he summarises Adimantus' attack on the law and the prophets point by point, and the records of his debates at Hippo with Fortunatus and Felix.[9] In addition Augustine' *Opus Imperfectum* reproduces part of the *Epistle to Menoch* suposedly by Mani, which had been quoted by Julian.[10]

---

[5] Maria Grazia Mara bases her article 'Agostino e la polemica antimanichea: il ruolo di Paolo e del suo epistolario', *Augustinianum* 32 (1992), 119-143, on later writings of Augustine than those considered here.

[6] On Augustine's Manichaeism cf. e.g. Henry Chadwick, 'The attractions of Mani', in *Compostellanum* 34.1-2 (1989), 203-222, reprinted in *Heresy and Orthodoxy in the Early Church* (Aldershot 1991), Erich Feldmann, 'Christus-Frömmigkeit der Mani-Jünger', in ed. Ernst Dassmann and K. Suso Frank, *Pietas. Festschrift für Bernhard Kötting* (Münster 1980), 198-216. On Augustine's early acquaintance with the bible cf. A.-M. la Bonnardière, 'L'initiation biblique d'Augustin', in *Saint Augustin et la Bible* (Paris 1986), 27-47.

[7] F. Decret gives a table of Pauline references by Fortunatus, Faustus and Felix in his *Aspects du Manichéisme dans l'Afrique romaine* (Paris 1970), 171-2, and gives a fuller discussion than is possible here of the use of Paul by Manichaeans in Africa in 'L'utilisation des Épîtres de Paul chez les Manichéens d'Afrique' in J. Ries etc., *Le Epistole Paoline nei manichei, i donatisti e il primo Agostino* (Rome 1989), 29-83.

[8] Faustus, who provides the fullest account of African Manichaean teachings, was much admired by the Manichees with whom Augustine had associated (according to *Confessions* 5.6.10).

[9] The following references to these writings are to the edition by J. Zycha (Vienna 1891).

[10] On this epistle cf. G. J. D. Aalders, 'L'Épître à Menoch, attribuée à Mani', *Vigiliae Christianae* 14 (1960), 245-9.

Adimantus and Faustus make clear the scriptural basis on which the Manichees relied in attacking the 'Jewish superstition' and 'Semi-Christianity'[11] of their Catholic opponents. The Old Testament is the property of the Jews, the repository of alien promises (*Contra Faustum* 10.1, p.310.10 ff., 18), its prophecies did not refer to Jesus (*Contra Faustum* 12.1, p.329.1 ff.). Adimantus' list of its contradictions with the New Testament make clear the gulf between its teachings and the Christian Gospel. To accept the Gospel however means not a literal belief in all that is written in it but obedience to its precepts (*Contra Faustum* 5.1-2, p. 271.13-15, 272.8-11). The Gospel accounts were written not by Jesus himself or his apostles, but long after by certain unknown 'semi-Jews', who attached the names of apostles or followers of apostles to their own compositions (*Contra Faustum* 32.2, p.761.17-22, 33.3, p.788.16-23). This critical view of the Gospels must give greater weight to Paul. Mani's own letters imitate the style of Paul, and the use of the Acts of Paul contributes to his favourable image.[12] On the other hand both Gospels and Pauline Epistles have been interpolated (*Contra Faustum* 18.3, p.491.27 ff.)[13] and Paul himself wrote as one with imperfect knowledge. Faustus quotes *2 Corinthians* 5.16-17 and *1 Corinthians* 13.11 to show Paul's progress from an old and inferior confession to a new and better one (*Contra Faustum* 11.1, pp.313-4). Manichees are taught by the Paraclete which parts of the New Testament are to be accepted and which rejected (*Contra Faustum* 32.6). Thus Felix argues in his debate with Augustine that the promised Paraclete only came in the person of Mani and was not yet present in Paul, who claims only to know in part (*1 Corinthians* 13.9; *Contra Felicem* 1.2, p.802, 1.9, p.811).

Adimantus' proof of the incompatibility of Old and New Testaments is based primarily on Gospel verses, but Paul also plays an important role. *1 Timothy* 6.16 and 1.17 are of central importance[14] as showing that God dwells in unapproachable light and is invisible, unlike the Old

---

[11] Faustus in *Contra Faustum* 1.2, p.251.23.

[12] On Mani's own attitude to Paul cf. J. Ries, 'Saint Paul dans la formation de Mani', in J. Ries etc. (*op. cit. n.7*), 7-27, and F. Decret, *ibid*, 29-40, Hans Dieter Betz, 'Paul in the Mani Biography', in ed. Luigi Cirillo, *Codex Manichaicus Coloniensis* (Marra editore Cosenza 1986), 215-234.

[13] Faustus gives alternative explanations of Pauline verses he dislikes (*Romans* 1.3, *1 Timothy* 4.14 ff., *Titus* 1.15), suggesting that they are either spurious or represent an earlier incorrect view or must be explained differently (*Contra Faustum* 11.1, pp.313-4, 30.1, p.748, 31.1, p.756).

[14] Faustus also appeals to *1 Timothy* 6.16 at *Contra Faustum* 20.2, p.536.12-13.

Testament 'demon of the Jews'[15] (*Contra Adimantum* 10, p.134.19-20 and 28, p.187.21-2), and *1 Corinthians* 14.33 as showing that he is a peace-loving God, not one who delights in battles (*Contra Adimantum* 20, p.179.9-11). *Colossians* 1.15-16 is used to contrast the creation through Christ with that described in *Genesis* 1 (*Contra Adimantum* 1, p.116.9-15). The Manichaean dualist anthropology, according to which God is author only of the good soul, not of the body and the 'fleshly' soul,[16] can be supported by *1 Corinthians* 15.50 ('flesh and blood will not inherit the kingdom of God'),[17] and Adimantus sets this verse against the Old Testament understanding that 'the soul of flesh is blood' (*Deuteronomy* 12.23, *Contra Adimantum* 12, p.138.8-23). The rejection of the Old Testament law with its prescription of circumcision and observance of days, years and seasons is confirmed by Paul in *1 Corinthians* 7.18-19, *Galatians* 5.12, and *Galatians* 4.10-11 (*Contra Adimantum* 16, p.161.10-17, 162.4-6, 13-15). For the Manichaean vegetarianism and refusal to drink wine, so contrary to the spirit of *Deuteronomy* 12.15 ff., Adimantus can appeal to *Romans* 14.21 and *1 Corinthians* 10.21 (*Contra Adimantum* 14, p.148.1-11).

In rejecting the Old Testament Faustus appeals to the example of the apostles and in particular to Paul's rebuke of the Galatians for their reversion to circumcision and to servitude to the 'weak and beggarly elements' (*Galatians* 4.9). To accept the Old Testament would be to abandon Christ's gift of liberty and to put on the yoke of bondage from which he freed us (*Galatians* 5.1, *Contra Faustum* 8.1, pp.305-6). Even the Catholics ignore most parts of the Old Testament, regarding them, in Paul's words of *Philippians* 3.8, as dung, claims Faustus (*Contra Faustum* 32.1, p.761.3). The contents of the Old Testament are alien and both Old and New Testaments forbid the coveting of alien goods (*Exodus* 20.17, *Romans* 7.7, *Contra Faustum* 10.1, p.310). Moses is to be rejected because he cursed 'everyone who hangs on a tree' (*Deuteronomy* 21.13); and that this really does refer to the crucifixion of Christ and subsequent Christian martyrs is shown by Paul in *Galatians* 3.13 (*Contra Faustum* 14.1, p.404.2-7). Christians should serve Christ alone,

---

[15] This designation is used by Faustus, *Contra Faustum* 18.2, p.491.6; cf. also 25.1, p.726.6-9 (the god of Abraham, Isaac and Jacob just one among many gods).

[16] Cf. the *Epistle to Menoch* quoted by Julian in Augustine, *Opus Imperfectum* 3.174-6, ed. M. Zelzer (Vienna 1974), 475f., and Augustine, *De Duabus Animabus* 1 and *Retractationes* 15 on the *De Duabus Animabus*.

[17] Quoted also by Fortunatus in Augustine, *Contra Fortunatum* 19, p.97.6-7.

following Paul, who said 'Our sufficiency is of God, who has made us suitable ministers of the New Testament' (*2 Corinthians* 3.5-6, *Contra Faustum* 15.1, p.417.5-9).

Faustus' view of the relationship between Judaism and Christianity is expressed most forcefully in his exposition of *Romans* 7.2-3. These verses show that those who unite themselves to Christ without previously repudiating the author of the law commit spiritual adultery. This applies particularly to Jews, who should regard their god as dead when converted to belief in Christ. A gentile who gives up his idolatry and then worships both the god of the Hebrews and Christ is no different from a woman who after the death of one husband marries two others (*Contra Faustum* 15.1, p.417.12-418.5).

Faustus' negative attitude to the Old Testament is apparent in his explanation of Paul's statements about the law in the Epistle to the Romans. He distinguishes three kinds of laws, firstly the law of the Hebrews referred to as the 'law of sin and death' in *Romans* 8.2, secondly the law of the gentiles, referred to as the 'natural law' in *Romans* 2.14-15, and thirdly the 'law of the spirit of truth in Christ Jesus' of *Romans* 8.2 (*Contra Faustum* 19.2, p.497.17-25). The law which Jesus came to fulfil was not the Jewish law, but more ancient precepts ('thou shalt not kill, thou shalt not commit adultery, thou shalt not bear false witness'), which had been promulgated in early times among the nations by Enoch, Seth and other righteous men (*Contra Faustum* 19.3, pp.498-9). This ancient law was corrupted by the Hebrew writers who infected it with their disgusting precepts about circumcision and sacrifices (*Contra Faustum* 22.2, pp.591.15-592.3).

Similarly, in Faustus' view, there are three kinds of prophets, the prophets of the Jews, the prophets of the gentiles, referred to by Paul in *Titus* 1.12, and the prophets of the truth, referred to in *1 Corinthians* 12.28 (cf. also *Ephesians* 4.11; *Contra Faustum* 19.2, pp.497-8). Faustus does not think that the Hebrew prophets prophesied Christ, but if they did know and foretell Christ the criminal nature of their lives would mean that Paul's words in *Romans* 1.21 about the wise men of the gentiles would apply to them (12.1, pp.329-30).

Faustus supports the Manichaean belief in two principles, God and 'Hyle' or the devil, by a reference to *2 Corinthians* 4.4, explaining that Paul calls the hostile substance 'the god of this age', because its worshippers call it 'god' (*Contra Faustum* 21.1, p.569.11-18). He applies *1 Timothy* 6.16 to God the Father, as dwelling in unapproachable light and *1 Corinthians* 1.24 to the Son, asserting that, since the Son is twofold, as God's power and God's wisdom, his power dwells in the sun and his wisdom in the moon (*Contra Faustum* 20.2, p.536.11-17).

Faustus' understanding of anthropology and of conversion is illuminated by Pauline verses which contrast the old man and the new man. Paul makes clear that there are two men (in each person) which he calls outer and inner (*2 Corinthians* 4.16, *Romans* 7.22, *Ephesians* 3.16), earthly and heavenly (*1 Corinthians* 15.47-9) and old and new (*Romans* 6.6, *Ephesians* 2.15, *Ephesians* 4.22-4, *Colossians* 3.9-10) (*Contra Faustum* 24.1, pp.717-21). It is not the outer, earthly or old man, but the inner, heavenly and new man that is formed by God according to his own image, and it is not at our first carnal birth that God thus creates us but at our conversion and rebirth in the spirit (*Ephesians* 4.22-24 and *Colossians* 3.9-10). At the time of this new birth we put off differences of sex, race and status, and are made one in the likeness of Christ (*Colossians* 3.11; *Galatians* 3.27-8). Paul refers to this second birth in *Galatians* 4.19, *1 Corinthians* 4.15, and, speaking of himself, in *Galatians* 1.15-16 (*Contra Faustum* 24.1, pp.717-721). In describing Manichaean spiritual worship Faustus states that he regards himself as the rational temple of God, alluding to Paul's words in *1 Corinthians* 3.16, *2 Corinthians* 6.16 and *Romans* 12.1 (*Contra Faustum* 20.3, p.537.17-18). Also Pauline is Faustus' view of the Manichaean church as the bride of Christ (*Contra Faustum* 15.1, p.416.8, cf. *Ephesians* 5.25-7, *2 Corinthians* 11.2, *Romans* 7.4).[18]

In his debates with Fortunatus and Felix Augustine attempts to press home his argument against the Manichaean position, that, if God is incorruptible, there can have been no reason for him to have sent souls, which consisted of part of his own substance, to be corrupted by evil. Against this Fortunatus and Felix assert Manichaean dualism and attempt to explain Manichaean anthropology, appealing not infrequently to Pauline verses for proof or illustration. Felix, in arguing that there is a power independent of God, which wars against God, quotes *Romans* 8.7 concerning the *prudentia carnis*, *2 Corinthians* 4.4 on the *deus saeculi huius*, and *2 Corinthians* 12.7-9 on the *angelus satanae* (*Contra Felicem* 2.2, p.830). The power which holds us in captivity and

---

[18] An example of Manichaean misuse of Paul is the adaptation of *Galatians* 3.13b at *Contra Faustum* 20.2, p.336.21, to apply to the Manichaean teaching of the *Jesus patibilis* (*omni suspensus ex ligno*). Cf. on this Ludwig Koenen, 'Augustine and Manichaeism in Light of the Cologne Mani Codex', in *Illinois Classical Studies* 3 (1978), 178-9, and, for another example of Manichaean adaptation of Paul, 179 n. 101 (*Galatians* 3.13a).

from which Christ came to save us is not a power of God, since the curse uttered against everyone who hangs on a tree, from which Christ freed us, as described by Paul in *Galatians* 3.13, is surely not spoken by a power of God (2.10, p.839).[19] Fortunatus makes fuller use of Pauline quotations. When challenged by Augustine as to why God sent us here, he quotes *Philippians* 2.5-8 and states that he understands this not only of Christ, but also of the descent of human souls and their liberation from 'this death, which is alien to God' (7, p.87.20-88.10). Maintaining that there are two opposed substances in this world (14, p.91.5-18), he quotes *Ephesians* 2.1-18 to support his view of the soul's captivity in the evil substance and reconciliation to God through Christ (16, p.92.17-93.13). *Ephesians* 2.3 ('we were by nature children of wrath') is there-fore said of the body. The word 'enmity' in *Ephesians* 2.16 shows that there is indeed a substance opposed to God, which 'enmity' Christ 'killed' when he freed our souls from it (16, p.95.9-21). Thus, whereas Augustine, quoting *1 Timothy* 6.10,[20] claims that the root and source of all evils is in human sinful desire (*Contra Fortunatum* 21, pp.100-101), Fortunatus maintains that human sinful desire is only a small portion of the evil present in the whole world (*Contra Fortunatum* 21, p.102). That the human soul sins not by its own will but under compulsion from the substance opposed to God is shown by Pauline verses describing the hostility of the flesh to God, its lusting against the spirit, and the law in our members which leads us captive to the law of sin and death (he quotes *Romans* 8.7, *Galatians* 5.17, and *Romans* 7.23-25 combined with *Galatians* 6.14b, *Contra Fortunatum* 21, p.103).[21] Souls were sent forth against the hostile substance in order to subject it by their sufferings. That evils are present not just in human bodies but in the whole world is shown by Paul's words in *Ephesians* 6.12[22] about our struggle not only

---

[19] Other Pauline verses quoted by Felix are *Romans* 3.4 (*omnis homo mendax, solus deus uerax*) used as an argument for relying on his scriptures (*Contra Felicem* I.6, p.808.9) and *1 Corinthians* 13.9, as showing that the Paraclete was not in Paul (*Contra Felicem* I.9, p.811.5-8).

[20] In the Latin version of this verse used by Augustine and Fortunatus (*radix omnium malorum est cupiditas*) the special reference of the Greek to the desire for money has disappeared.

[21] Cf. also Augustine's own description in *Confessions* 5.10.18 of his earlier Mani-chaean view that *non esse nos qui peccamus sed nescio quam aliam in nobis peccare naturam* (remiscent of *Romans* 7.17 and 20).

[22] Fortunatus' quotation alters the word order and omits *in caelestibus* .

against flesh and blood, but against the powers of darkness (*Contra Fortunatum* 22, p.107).[23]

During his period as a Manichaean hearer Augustine will have become familiar with Manichaean psalms similar to those preserved in the Coptic Manichaean Psalm-book from Egypt.[24] The Pauline allusions in these Psalms[25] include references to the 'old man' (3.31, 167.23-4) and the 'new man' (46.18, 88.2, 150.29), to the impediments against doing good caused by the flesh (135.11-12, cf. *Romans* 7.18),[26] to the god of this Aeon (56.31, 172.26-7; cf. *2 Corinthians* 4.4) and the rulers (?) of this Aeon (4.17; cf. *1 Corinthians* 2.8; cf. also the probable reference to *Ephesians* 6.16, 'the darts of the [evil one]', at 64.4-5). At 194.3 Christ's putting on the likeness of man is described with an allusion to *Philippians* 2.7. Pauline themes concerning law, commandments and judgement recur in these Psalms and the Pauline picture of the Christian life as a race is frequent.[27]

African Manichaeism and Philosophy

In the time of Augustine's youth Manichaeism was better equipped to answer philosophical objections to Christianity than was African Catholic Christianity. This aspect of Manichaeism can be illustrated from the work of Faustus. Although Faustus' *capitula* are written in answer to Catholic questions directed against Manichaeism they in fact present a religious system which meets and disarms many of the pagan criticisms of Christianity. This is not necessarily to claim that Faustus himself had elaborated his arguments in response to Platonist attacks. It may rather be the case that he inherited a tradition of argumentation which had been developed earlier by Manichees, Marcionites and Gnostics aware of

---

[23] As well as the Pauline verses mentioned above, Fortunatus also quotes *Romans* 9.20 as a response to Augustine's question why God sent us here (*Contra Fortunatum* 26, p.109.8-9). At *Contra Fortunatum* 16, p.95.13-14, he refers to Paul's description of his own ancestry in *Romans* 11.1.

[24] Cf. Feldmann (*op. cit. n. 6*), 207 ff.

[25] The following examples refer to the page and line numbers in *A Manichaean Psalm-Book*, Part II, ed. C. R. C. Allberry (Stuttgart 1938). A number of other Pauline verses are listed in Allberry's index, p.48*.

[26] Cf. also on the flesh the reference to *1 Corinthians* 15.50 at 121.9, and on the body that to *2 Corinthians* 5.6 at 135.21.

[27] Cf. Allberry's index (*op.cit. n. 25*) p.48* under *1 Timothy* 4.7; also pp.3* and 5* under ἐντολή and νόμος.

pagan philosophical objections to Christianity.[28] Since Porphyry's more detailed attack against the Christians does not survive, our fullest information about the features which Platonist philosophers found objectionable in Christianity comes from Celsus. In what follows therefore Faustus' position will be compared chiefly with Celsus' criticisms.[29]

An obvious point for attack on the Christians was their reliance on their own and the Jewish scriptures, and it was here that Porphyry went much further than Celsus. In this respect Faustus simply accepts and takes over the pagan criticisms. Thus he takes a negative view of Moses and the patriarchs and prophets (12.1, p.330.11-18, 14.1, pp.401-4, 22.1-5, pp.591-5, where however he suggests that the Old Testament stories may be slanders), he rejects the Old Testament (4.1, p.268, 15.1, pp.415-8), and its prophecies of Christ (12.1, pp.328-30, also 13.1, p.378.8, referring to pagan reactions to circular arguments about the witness of the prophets to Christ and vice versa), he attacks the genealogies of Jesus in Matthew and Luke (3.1, pp.261-2, 7.1, pp.302-3), and he asserts the unreliability of the Gospels (32.1-2, pp.760-2).

The particularity of the Christian view of salvation history, which Celsus found offensive,[30] is largely done away with by the rejection of any special role for Judaism (*Christianam nouitatem Hebraicae uetustati non misceo*—8.1; 9.1; 10.1, pp.305-6, 307 and 310; the god of Abraham the god only of the circumcised—25.1, pp.725-6; gentile prophets are more relevant to gentile converts—13.1-2, pp.377.20-2, 378.25-379.6; cf. also the more positive view of the *lex gentium* in 19.2, pp.497f.),[31] also by the Manichaean doctrine of the 'cosmic Jesus' (20.2, p.536.19-23), as well as by the fact (not mentioned by Faustus) that reincarnation gives repeated chances of salvation for the individual soul.

The Catholic attachment to the body, shown in the doctrines of incarnation and resurrection, is found particularly disgusting by Celsus.[32] This however is abandoned by the Manichees, since they view the fleshly nature as evil, and adopt a docetic Christology (29.1, p. 744.1-5).

---

[28] Cf. W. H. C. Frend, 'The Gnostic-Manichaean Tradition in Roman North Africa', *Journal of Ecclesiastical History* 4 (1953), 13-26, especially 20-22.

[29] As quoted in Origen, *Contra Celsum* , ed. P. Koetschau (Leipzig 1899).

[30] Cf. e.g. 5.41 (no special divine favour towards the Jews), 4.2-3, 6-7 and 6.78 (objections to the particularity of the incarnation), 3.71 and 6.53 (the Christian view implies unjust favouritism and incompetence in God's dealings with the human race), 4.23 (the arrogance of Jews and Christians).

[31] On Manichaean universalism cf. Decret (*op cit. n.7*), 39-40.

[32] Cf. 3.41-2, 7.13, 5.14, 8.49.

Another feature of Christian teaching which Celsus dislikes is the way it deals with the problem of evil—he states that 'In the existing world there is no decrease or increase of evils either in the past or in the present or in the future' (4.62), and rejects the idea of the devil (6.42) or that God 'inflicts correction on the world' (4.69), though he allows that the question is a difficult one (4.65) and that pagan myths 'hint at a sort of divine war' (6.42) and suggests that evils inhere in matter (4.66) and that the body is not made by God (4.52). It is here that Faustus claims complete originality for the Manichees, since the Manichaean belief in two principles, God as the origin of all good things, and 'hyle' as the origin of evil, separates them fundamentally both from pagans, who believe in a single principle as the source of all things, and from the Catholic Christians, who are merely a schism of paganism in this respect (20.3-4, pp.537-8). All these features together with the Manichaean spiritual worship (20.3-4, pp. 537.15-538.18), Christ-centered piety, and radical obedience to the Gospel precepts (5.13, pp.271-4) must have given Manichaeism considerable appeal.

In those of Augustine's early writings which are considered in the next section he not only gave evidence of his own philosophical dedication and developed a non-dualist explanation of the problem of evil on the basis of Christian Platonism, he also attempted to demonstrate the providential role of the Christian church and its teachings, showing that Catholic understanding of the Old Testament was far different from what the Manichees supposed and that even the doctrines of incarnation and resurrection could be accepted.

Augustine's earliest writings after his conversion

Augustine's *Confessions* tell us of his realisation at Milan, aided by Ambrose's sermons and the Platonist books, that God is incorporeal, unchangeable and the source of all existence, that his creation is good, and that evil is not a contrary substance but a turning away of the will from God.[33] His reading of Paul, according to *Confessions* 7.21.27, made him realise the need for divine grace to bring freedom from the power of sin[34] and healing that he might see and hold on to the divine vision. The *Confessions* were written from a position of hindsight in which later in-

---

[33] *Confessions* 7.16.22.
[34] He quotes *Romans* 7.22-5 and alludes also to other Pauline verses.

sights are not always clearly separated from the account of Augustine's spiritual and intellectual development before and after his conversion.[35] Augustine's earliest extant works, which were composed after his conversion during his retreat with his friends at Cassiciacum before his return to Milan for his baptism,[36] show him less immediately concerned with the exposition of new anti-Manichaean insights than with the refutation of the Academic position that truth is unattainable and the demonstration that his own search for truth is in accordance with the highest philosophy, that of Plato himself and Plotinus.[37] It is only in the more personal or biographical passages that hints of his newly found Christian faith are given.[38] In addition to his general assertions that all is governed by divine providence[39] he shows awareness of divine gui-

---

[35] The difference between the picture given by the *Confessions* and that of the dialogues written at Cassiciacum is caused not only by the changes in Augustine's perception between 386 and 397, but also by his different position and expectations about his readers (recently retired professor of rhetoric, or Christian bishop). There has been much debate about how great this difference is; earlier contributions to the question are conveniently described by John. J. O'Meara, 'Augustine and Neo-platonism', *Recherches Augustiniennes* 1 (1958), 91 ff., and by Eckard König, *Augustinus Philosophus. Christlicher Glaube und philosophisches Denken in den Frühschriften Augustins* (Munich 1970), 9 ff., who warns against false assumptions that Augustine must have been *either* a Christian *or* a Platonist during this period. For a well balanced account of Augustine's development cf. Henry Chadwick, *Augustine* (Oxford 1986),15 ff.

[36] The order of Augustine's works is more or less apparent from his *Retractationes*. Those looked at here are the *Contra Academicos, De Beata Vita, De Ordine, Soliloquia* (all written at Cassiciacum), *De Immortalitate Animae* (written at Milan), and *De Quantitate Animae* and *De Moribus Ecclesiae Catholicae et de Moribus Manichaeorum* (written, or at least started, at Rome). The exact dating of the *De Moribus Ecclesiae Catholicae et de Moribus Manichaeorum* is controversial and it may be that Augustine made some later additions to Book 1 and only wrote Book 2 after his return to Africa; cf. John Kevin Coyle, *Augustine's "De Moribus Ecclesiae Catholicae"* (Fribourg 1978), 66-98. In what follows the first three of these works are quoted from the edition by Pius Knöll (Vienna 1922), the following three from that by Wolfgang Hörmann (Vienna 1986). There is no modern critical edition of *De Moribus Ecclesiae Catholicae et de Moribus Manichaeorum.* It is quoted here from the Maurist edition, Volume 1 (Paris 1836), which is reprinted in PL 32. Coyle, *op. cit.,* 277 ff., reprints the Maurist text of Book 1 from PL and supplies a commentary.

[37] *Contra Academicos* 3.17.37 ff. and especially 3.18.41 ff.; cf. *Solil.* 1.4.9. In *De Ordine* 2.20.53 however Alypius praises Augustine's teaching as agreeing with that of Pythagoras. In the *Confessions* Augustine mentions his inclination towards the Academic philosophers at 5.10.19 (during the account of his stay at Rome) and 5.14.25.

[38] In his *Confessions* 9.4.7 Augustine states that Alypius was unwilling that the name of Christ should be included in the writings composed at Cassiciacum.

[39] Cf. *Contra Academicos* 1.1.1, *De Ordine* 1.1.1-2, 1.5.14, 2.1.2 etc.

dance in his own spiritual journey and those of his friends.[40] Divine revelation is necessary in the search for truth[41] and the acceptance of authority must supplement reason[42] not only for the uneducated but also as an entrance door or cradle for those intending later to proceed by the aid of reason.[43] He alludes to Christian truths in philosophical language and refers to Christian teachings, scriptures and sacraments as *mysteria* [44] and *sacra.* [45] In the *Contra Academicos* Augustine writes of himself at the beginning of Book 2 and the end of Book 3. He is seeking truth with the greatest concentration and is confident of reaching his destination. His perception of divine guidance behind Romanianus' assistance in this quest is more a matter of faith than of reason.[46] In his return to his childhood religion and perusal of Paul it was that religion which was drawing him to itself.[47] He accepts the authority of Christ but desires to grasp truth by the power of reason as well as that of belief.[48]

At the beginning of the *De Beata Vita* (1.4-5) Augustine again gives a brief account of his spiritual history, making special mention of his debts to Ambrose and to his addressee Theodorus.[49] The dialogue itself is given an overtly Christian ingredient by the participation of Augustine's mother Monica. His conclusion to the work (4.34-5) on the happiness to be sought in the knowledge of God contains Christian overtones (allusion to *1 Corinthians* 1.24, quotation of *John* 14.8, Trinitarian lan-

---

[40] Cf. *Contra Academicos* 1.1.3 (especially his prayers on behalf of Romanianus), *De Beata Vita* 1.1 (end) and 1.4, *De Ordine* 1.4.10 (using a line from the *Aeneid*), 1.8.22-3, 1.11.33.

[41] Cf. *Contra Academicos* 3.5.11 and 6.13 (in non-Christian language: *numen aliquod ... solum posse ostendere homini, quid sit uerum*).

[42] *Contra Academicos* 3.20.43, cf. *De Beata Vita* 1.4 (quoted below n.44), *De Ordine* 2.5.16. In so far as it is applied to the uneducated masses Augustine's use of this theme agrees with what he himself reports about Porphyry; cf. O'Meara (*op. cit. n. 35*), 102 ff.

[43] *De Ordine* 2.9.26.

[44] *Contra Academicos* 2.1.1 (end), *De Ordine* 2.5.15-16, 2.9.27, 2.16.46; cf. *De Beata Vita* 1.4 (*illorum auctoritas qui diuina mysteria tradiderunt*).

[45] *Contra Academicos* 3.19.42, 3.20.43 (end), *De Ordine* 2.9.27.

[46] *Contra Academicos* 2.2.4: *... quod quaero intentissimus ueritatem ... tu animasti ... cuius autem minister fueris, plus adhuc fide concepi, quam ratione conprehendi.*

[47] *Contra Academicos* 2.2.5: *ipsa ad se nescientem rapiebat.*

[48] *Contra Academicos* 3.20.43: *non credendo solum sed etiam intellegendo.* On the relation between the two in the early Augustine cf. König (*op. cit.* n.35), 131 ff.

[49] For Ambrose cf. also 4.35, where Monica quotes an invocation of the Trinity from one of his hymns.

guage), which are greeted by Monica with an invocation of the Trinity and an appeal to faith, hope and love (cf. *1 Corinthians* 13.13) as the path to this knowledge.

In the *De Ordine* the partners in the dialogue maintain that God rules all things in order despite the problem of apparent evil. Various approaches to this problem are suggested—the partial nature of the human viewpoint (1.1.2, like looking at one stone only in a mosaic pavement, 2.4.11 ff., 2.7.24, 2.19.51), the need for the contrast of opposites within the order of the universe (1.7.18), the justice of God distinguishing between the virtuous and the wicked and giving to each their due (1.7.19 and 2.7.22)—and the idea of evil as a negation seems perhaps to be hinted at in what is said about darkness and stupidity (2.3.10)—but the reader is left feeling that there are still many questions to be answered about the origin of evil (cf. especially 2.17.46). While insisting on the great value of a training in the liberal arts for those seeking divine truth, Augustine also asserts the compatibility of true philosophy with Christian teaching on the Trinity and Incarnation (2.5.16), and praises the divine authority which reveals itself in the Christian religion (2.9.27). The piety of the participants in the dialogue, represented most strikingly by Licentius, whose conversion from poetics to philosophy it celebrates, is shown in their prayers and psalm-singing (1.8.21-3, 2.20,52); at 1.10.29 Augustine describes his own almost daily weeping and prayers to God for his wounds to be healed.

The *Soliloquies,* in which Augustine expresses his longing for knowledge of God and the soul and seeks a definition of truth and an answer to the question whether the soul is immortal, is given a religious direction by the prayers which introduce its various sections and which show Augustine's sense of complete dependence on God (1.1.1 ff., 2.1.1, 2.6.9). The long and beautiful prayer which opens the work, much of it biblically inspired, is however confessed by Augustine to be put together not from what he already knows but from material collected and memorised from various sources, in which he has put his faith as far as he could (1.4.9, cf. 1.2.7). Here, as elsewhere, Augustine shows a strong awareness of the need for cleansing, healing and trust in divine mercy if the eyes of the soul are to seek the vision of God (1.6.12, 1.9.16 ff., 1.15.30).

The Pauline quotations and allusions in the dialogues written at Cassiciacum are not at all plentiful, but they are linked to some of the most important themes of Augustine's thought of this period, his attitude to philosophy and the capacity of human reason to approach divine truth, the preference for a philosophy compatible with Christianity rather than one linked with loose moral teachings or paganism, the divine providential care shown in the recall of human souls by means of the incarnation of God's son, who is his power and wisdom, the soul's exile from God and path back to the divine vision through faith, hope and love.[50] Augustine refers to *1 Corinthians* 1.24 for its description of God's son as *ipsa summi dei uirtus atque sapientia* in *Contra Academicos* 2.1.1, and there is an allusion to the same verse (a favourite one with the Manichees) in *De Beata Vita* 4.34.[51] In addition he alludes to *Colossians* 2.8 in *Contra Academicos* 3.19.42 as well as in *De Ordine* 1.11.32 (the rejection by *sacra nostra* or the divine scriptures of the philosophy of this world, but not of true philosophy).[52] Augustine's reading of Paul, in particular the well-known passage in *Philippians* 2.5 ff., surely lies behind his philosophically couched references to the incarnation at *Contra Academicos* 3.19.42[53] and *De Ordine* 2.9.27.[54] In the optimistic view which he takes in the *De Ordine* of the progress attainable by reason he may have the beginning of the Epistle to the Romans in mind (*Romans* 1.20, 2.14-15)—this is confirmed by what seems to be an allusion to *Romans* 2.15 in *De Ordine* 2.8.25 (*ipsa dei lex ... in sapientes animas quasi transcribitur*), and by his quotation of *Romans* 1.20 in *Confessions* 7.17.23.[55] In the opening prayer at the beginning of the *Soliloquies* a number of Pauline allusions refer to the divine victory over contrary forces. Augustine may have been thinking of *Romans* 8.37 and its

---

[50] On these themes and their relationship to the Platonism of Porphyry as later described by Augustine cf. O'Meara (*op. cit. n.35*), 104-111.

[51] *accepimus autem etiam auctoritate diuina dei filium nihil esse aliud quam dei sapientiam.* Cf. also *De Quantitate Animae* 33.76: *uirtutem dei atque sapientiam.*

[52] Cf. also the fuller quotation of this verse at *De Moribus Ecclesiae Catholicae* 21.38 and at *Confessions* 8.2.3 and the discussion by Coyle (*op. cit. n. 36*), 113 ff.

[53] *animas ... numquam ista ratio subtilissima reuocaret,* nisi summus deus populari quadam clementia diuini intellectus auctoritatem usque ad ipsum corpus humanum declinaret atque summitteret, *cuius non solum praeceptis sed etiam factis excitatae animae redire in semet ipsas et resipiscere patriam ... potuissent.*

[54] *auctoritas diuina* ipsum hominem agens ostendit ei, quo usque se propter ipsum depresserit ... *doceat enim oportet et factis potentiam suam et* humilitate clementiam *et praeceptione naturam, quae omnia sacris, quibus initiamur, secretius firmiusque traduntur.* Cf. also *De Ordine* 2.5.16: *quantum autem illud sit, quod hoc etiam nostri generis corpus tantus propter nos deus adsumere atque agere dignatus est, quanto uidetur uilius, tanto est clementia plenius ...*

[55] Cf. Pierre Courcelle, *Recherches sur les Confessions de saint Augustin* (Paris 1950), 175-7, also below p.17 on the quotation of *Romans* 1.25 in *De Quantitate Animae* 34.77.

context when he wrote *Deus, per quem uincimus inimicum* (1.3).[56] The words *Deus, per quem mors absorbetur in uictoriam* (1.3) are clearly derived from *1 Corinthians* 15.54,[57] and the proximity of this allusion makes it likely that a reminiscence of *1 Corinthians* 15.53 lies behind the following words *Deus qui nos ... eo, quod est, induis.* Later in the same section there is an unmistakable allusion to *Galatians* 4.9 (*Deus, per quem non seruimus infirmis et egenis elementis*).[58]

The triad of *1 Corinthians* 13.13, faith, hope and love,[59] is appealed to as the necessary foundation in the search for God at the conclusion of *De Beata Vita* (4.35, in the mouth of Monica, following an invocation of the Trinity) and *De Ordine* 2.8.25. The same triad plays a more important role in Book 1 of the *Soliloquies.* It appears twice in Augustine's opening prayer, once in an invocation (1.1.3, *Deus, cui nos fides excitat, spes erigit, caritas iungit*) and once in a prayer for the increase of these virtues that he may return to God (1.1.5), and then again later in 1.13.23, characterising the path of those who are able to approach wisdom without detours (*His credere, sperare, amare satis est*). In the central section, 6.12-7.14, faith, hope and love are explained as necessary for the healing of the eyes of the soul, that it may look towards God and may desire this vision. Faith and hope however are no longer necessary when the vision has been attained, whereas love is thereby increased, although it is only after the impediments of the mortal body have been laid aside that security of possession renders hope and faith superfluous. Augustine does not quote Paul explicitly in this passage, but he clearly has in mind *1 Corinthians* 13.8-13. In addition *Romans* 8.24 lies behind his words in 1.7.14: *Fides quare sit necessaria, cum iam uideat? Spes nihilominus, quia iam tenet. 2 Corinthians* 5.6-8 confirms not only the idea that faith is necessary as long as we are in the mortal body, but also the view of this mortal life as a journey in a foreign country separated from our true home (*quamdiu sumus in corpore peregrinamur a Domino*),[60] something central to Augustine's religious attitude not only in his later

---

[56] He quotes this verse elsewhere with the rendering *superuincimus,* rather than the Vulgate *superamus;* cf. the apparatus criticus to *Romans* 8.37 in J. Wordsworth and H. J. White, *Nouum Testamentum Latine* 2.1 (Oxford 1913), 107.

[57] Augustine quotes this verse in *Confessions* 9.4.11 in his account of his stay at Cassiciacum.

[58] In his *Commentary on Galatians* Augustine understood this verse of pagan religion. It could also be that he has the Manichaean worship of the sun and the moon in mind here too.

[59] On this triad in Neoplatonism cf. König (*op. cit. n.35*), 59 ff.

[60] The verb *peregrinari* is used by Augustine in *De Beata Vita* 1.2 (*a sua patria*

works but already in the Cassiciacum dialogues. The *Contra Academicos,* the earliest of these dialogues, is permeated by the idea of the search for truth as a journey which cannot reach its final destination during this mortal life (cf. in particular Augustine's use of this metaphor at 1.1.1 (sea voyage), 1.4.11, 2.2.5 (of himself: *respexi tamen, confitebor, quasi de itinere in illam religionem* ...), 2.9.22, 3.2.3 (sea voyage), 3.14.30 and 3.15.34), and the same picture of the voyage to the harbour of philosophy, which here is shown to differ for different individuals, is fully developed and applied to Augustine's own wanderings in the opening sections of the *De Beata Vita* (1.1-5).[61] In the two passages of the *Soliloquies* already referred to Augustine depicts himself as a runaway slave who needs faith, hope and love as his journey money for his return journey to God (1.1.5), and takes up again (from the beginning of the *De Beata Vita*) the idea of differing paths towards wisdom, combining it with the view that faith, hope and love form the most direct path.

There are only indirect references to Manichaeism in Augustine's earliest works. Thus in *Contra Academicos* Augustine mentions his own liberation from superstition (1.1.3) and his hopes for Romanianus in this respect (2.3.8). In *De Beata Vita* (1.4) he alludes to his earlier adherence to persons who thought that physical light is to be worshipped and that God and the soul are corporeal. In *De Ordine* 2.17.46 he includes some arguments against characteristic Manichaean views in a passage raising questions about the origin of evil (*quid enim potuit deo nocere mali nescio qua illa natura? si enim dicunt non potuisse, fabricandi mundi causa non erit; si potuisse dicunt, inexpiabile nefas est deum uiolabilem credere, nec ita saltem, ut uel uirtute prouiderit, ne sua substantia uiolaretur; namque animam poenas hic pendere fatentur, cum inter eius et dei substantiam nihil uelint omnino distare*).[62] The opening prayer of the *Soliloquies* is generally anti-Manichaean and more particularly in the emphasis in 1.2 that evil does not exist and that the whole creation with its better and its lower parts is in harmony, and in the statement in 1.4 that nothing has true existence apart from God.

---

peregrinari); cf. also *De quantitate animae* 31.63: *illo secretissimo et tranquillissimo mentis habitaculo, a quo nunc, dum haec incolit, peregrina est.* For later quotations of this verse cf. for example the index of scriptural passages in the edition of the *Enarrationes in Psalmos* in CCL 40 (1956), 2251. *Hebrews* 11.13-16 may also lie behind the use of this imagery; cf. Robert J. O'Connell, *St. Augustine's Early Theory of Man* (Cambridge Mass. 1968), 75.

[61] Augustine of course also has the wanderings of Aeneas in mind in this passage.

[62] Cf. *Confessions* 7.2.3 (Nebridius' argument against the Manichees).

After his return from Cassiciacum to Milan but before his baptism Augustine composed the *De Immortalitate Animae*. Perhaps the most purely philosophical of his works and one which Augustine himself later found obscure, it shows clearly the new structure of his thought that was to be so important in his later anti-Manichaean argumentation. The power which creates and preserves the whole physical universe, itself incorporeal, is the source of existence in everything that exists (7.14). That Truth, which is supreme being and the source of truth and existence in individual true things, has no opposite, since the opposite of existence is non-existence, i.e. does not exist (12.19). The soul, itself incorporeal and occupying an intermediate position between the highest being and corporeal creation (15.24), has wisdom through conversion towards the source of its being and may lose wisdom through turning away from this source, in which case it tends towards nothingness, but does not perish (12.19 and 7.12). There are no clear biblical quotations in this work, but it is perhaps not too fanciful to see a reminiscence of *Romans* 8.35 ff. behind the passage in 5.11 where Augustine asks by what power the soul can be separated from that supreme Reason which gives it life and concludes that neither any bodily force nor any other soul can do this.

During his stay at Milan Augustine began a series of treatises on the liberal arts, of which only the *On Music* survives. Book 6 of this work contains interesting discussion of the habit-forming power of sin based on *2 Corinthians* 5.6-8 (6.5.14 and 6.11.33) and a passage on the joy of contemplation of God in the afterlife quoting *1 Corinthians* 15.53, *Romans* 8.11 and *Philippians* 1.23-4 (6.15.49). Since however Augustine only completed the work after his return to Africa, it will not be discussed here.

It was during his stop at Rome on the way back to Africa after his baptism that Augustine wrote (or started to write)[63] his first anti-Manichaean work, the *De Moribus Ecclesiae Catholicae et de Moribus Manichaeorum*. During the same stay at Rome he also wrote the *De Quantitate Animae* and began the *De Libero Arbitrio,* whose second and third books he completed later when he was a priest at Hippo. The *De Libero Arbitrio* will not be considered here.[64] The *De Quantitate Animae* continues the philosophical approach of the earlier dialogues and is mainly

---

[63] See above n.36.

[64] Pauline quotations are confined to the third book, which was written later; cf. the index in the edition by W. M. Green (Vienna 1956),155.

occupied by arguments against a corporeal view of the soul. This of course can be seen as anti-Manichaean, since the Manichees thought of the soul as consisting of a fine substance.[65] There are obvious pieces of anti-Manichaean polemic at 33.71, where Augustine attacks the view that plants have souls with the power of sensation and therefore feel pain and see and hear, and 34.77, where he denies that the heavenly bodies are superior to the nature of the human soul.[66] The influence of Augustine's recent baptism is apparent in a number of references to the teachings and scriptures of the Catholic Church, some of which are accompanied by Pauline quotations. At 3.4 Augustine praises the fact that the 'mysteries' teach that the soul which wishes to be restored to the likeness of God should despise all bodily things and renounce this material world, since there is no other means of salvation, renewal (*renouatio*) or reconciliation to its creator. This renewal is described at 28.55 with an appeal to the divine scriptures and allusions to *Ephesians* 4.22,24, *Colossians* 3.9-10, and *2 Corinthians* 3.18 (putting off the old man and becoming a new man, and being renewed according to the image of God). It involves withdrawal from the body by means of reason and knowledge, since the more the soul descends to the level of the senses the more it makes a man similar to a brute beast.[67] The last part of the *De Quantitate Animae* (33.70 ff.) consists of an account of the seven steps or levels of the soul's activity, ascending from its life-giving function, shared even with plants, to its final destination in the vision and contemplation of Truth. The fourth step is that of the moral purification of the soul, when it follows the authority and advice of wise men, believing that God speaks through them, and entrusts itself to divine assistance (33.73; cf. also 34.78 on the need for strength and piety at this step in order to investigate and understand the contents of the many writings of the church). When we have ascended these levels we will recognise how true those things are which we are commanded to believe (including the resurrection of the body, the incarnation, virgin birth and other miracles of the Gospel story) and how healthful the nourishment

---

[65] Cf. for example 30.61: the soul is not spread through the body like blood.

[66] The Manichees venerated the sun and moon according to Augustine, *Epistle* 236.2 (*solem etiam et lunam ... adorant et orant*).

[67] 18.54. I suspect that behind this passage lies an understanding of the fall based on *Psalm* 48 (49).13 and 21 (*homo cum in honore esset non intellexit, comparatus est iumentis insipientibus et similis factus est illis*), such as is found in Origen, *Commentary on Romans* 2.5 (ed. C. P. H. Bammel (Freiburg, 1990), 116, ll. 73-9, from which the above quotation of the verse is taken).

given us by the Mother Church. Augustine here appeals explicitly to the metaphor used by Paul in *1 Corinthians* 3.2, the milk lovingly given to the infants in Christ who are not yet ready for solid food.[68] There are two Pauline allusions in the next section (34.77), where he states that the Catholic Church hands down that no creature is to be worshipped but only the creator (cf. *Romans* 1.25), from whom, through whom and in whom are all things (*Romans* 11.36). Augustine's concluding summary to the *De Quantitate Animae* (36.80-81) presents a picture of a divinely regulated universe in which the soul's endowment with free will does not allow it to disturb the divine order. The soul has indeed torn itself away from God by sin and has rightly been thrust into this mortal existence, but it has not been abandoned by God, it can exercise virtue even here, and every punishment and reward assigned to it contribute to the beauty and harmony of the whole.

The *De Moribus Ecclesiae Catholicae et de Moribus Manichaeorum* is strikingly different from Augustine's earlier treatises, firstly in the directness of its attack on the Manichees and secondly in its ample use of biblical quotations and proof-texts. In this work Augustine sets out to defend the Old Testament scriptures against the Manichees and to show the superiority of Christian continence based on love to Manichaean superstition (1.2). The central part of the work is a demonstration based on rational argumentation that true happiness is to be found in the love of God (3.4 ff.) and an explanation of the four cardinal virtues (15.25 ff. and 19.35 ff.). Though the Manichees agree on the prime importance of love of God and one's neighbour they do not accept that it is on these two commandments that all the Law and the Prophets hang (28.57, 29.59 ff.).

In reading the *De Moribus Ecclesiae Catholicae* one becomes aware how much the structure of Augustine's thought has changed since his own Manichaean period. The insights of the various writings he had composed since his conversion are now put together in an anti-Manichaean context. The Manichees had regarded God as spread through space and corruptible. Augustine emphasises God's incorporeality and incorruptibility. The Manichees had separated Old and New Testaments and had made a division in their perception of the material world between the realm of light and the realm of darkness. Augustine sees all being as God's creation and human history including both Testaments

---

[68] On this imagery in Augustine cf. also O'Connell (*op. cit. n.60*), 77-9, with references also to *1 Thessalonians* 2.7 and *Hebrews* 5.11-14.

and the world-wide expansion of the Christian church as part of one divine providential plan for fallen humanity. Whereas the Manichees had confused the creator and his creation in supposing the human soul to be part of God, Augustine emphasises that the human soul or mind is not of the same nature as God; though created in the divine image it is able to fall and only becomes like God when subjected to him. Whereas the Manichees based their claims on the supremacy of reason and expected conversion to result in instant perfection, Augustine now realised that daily renewal of the inner man was necessary and that the ascent from worldly desires to the purifying love of God was only possible for those nourished at the breast of the universal church and accepting the authority of the church's scriptures.[69]

Throughout the work Augustine makes abundant use of Paul. Pauline proof-texts are used along with texts from the Gospels and from the Old Testament[70] to support the main contentions about the supremacy of love of God[71] and neighbour,[72] to illustrate the exposition of the four virtues, and to refute superstitious ideas about pollution caused by meat, wine or marital relations. Thus in the section on temperance (19.35 ff.) Augustine quotes *1 Timothy* 6.10 as showing that the root of all evils is desire (for lower things), *2 Corinthians* 4.18 to show that we should set our hearts not on visible, temporal things, but on what is unseen and eternal, *Galatians* 1.10 as rejecting fame, *Colossians* 2.8 as rejecting the desire for superfluous knowledge, and *Romans* 12.2 as rejecting the love of things of this world in general and showing that one becomes like that which one loves. This section also includes a digression on the fall and

---

[69] One can read Augustine's invocation of the Catholic Church at 30.62 as a summary of these anti-Manichaean insights: *merito, ecclesia catholica, mater Christianorum uerissima, non solum ipsum Deum, cuius adeptio uita est beatissima, purissime atque castissime colendum praedicas; nullam nobis adorandam creaturam inducens ... et ab illa incorrupta et inuiolabili aeternitate ... excludens omne quod factum est ... neque confundens quod aeternitas, quod ueritas, quod denique pax ipsa distinguit, nec rursum separans quod maiestas una coniungit; sed etiam proximi dilectionem atque caritatem ita complecteris, ut uariorum morborum, quibus pro peccatis suis animae aegrotant, omnis apud te medicina praepolleat.*

[70] This use of parallel texts is his main defense against the Manichaean attacks on the Old Testament; cf. 1.2; also 10.16-17 (the Catholic understanding of the law and prophets is different from what the Manichees think), 29.59-61 (attack on the Manichaean claim that the New Testament is interpolated).

[71] Cf. 8.13 ff., 11.18 ff., where *Romans* 8.28, 35-6 and 38-9 are expounded in detail, also 16.26 quoting *Romans* 8.35 and 28,18.34 quoting *Ephesians* 3.17-18 and 26.50 quoting *Romans* 8.28.

[72] 26.50 quoting *Romans* 13.10.

on Christian renewal (see below). In the section on fortitude (22.40 ff.) Augustine quotes *Romans* 5.3-4, in that on justice (24.44) he alludes to *Romans* 1.25 (that one should worship the Creator only, and not the creation) and in that on prudence (24.45) he quotes *1 Corinthians* 5.6 as enjoining caution. In his description of Catholic ascetics[73] he states that they follow the authority of Paul in maintaining themselves by the work of their hands (33.70, cf. *1 Corinthians* 4.12, *Ephesians* 4.28, *1 Thessalonians* 4.11, *2 Thessalonians* 3.10). They do not reject particular types of food as polluted (33.71) remembering that to the clean all things are clean (*Titus* 1.15, to which Augustine adds *1 Corinthians* 6.13 and 8.8), and that love must be given priority (Augustine here quotes and expounds *Romans* 14.21, 2-4, 6 and 12-15, and *1 Corinthians* 6.12).[74] They allow the drinking of a little wine for the sake of one's health, following Paul's admonition to Timothy (*1 Timothy* 5.23), and they devote themselves more assiduously to piety than to physical exercise, following *1 Timothy* 4.8. In countering the Manichaean view that baptised persons should not marry or have possessions Augustine quotes at length from Paul as both demonstrating the ideal for the strong and allowing the lower level for the weaker members of the community (35.78-80, quoting *1 Corinthians* 6.11-7.7 and 7.14).

The various themes of the work are illustrated, argued or developed with reference to Pauline verses. Augustine quotes *Romans* 11.36 in support of the Catholic doctrine of the Trinity, that Father, Son and Holy Spirit are one God (14.24 and 16.29) and argues for the divinity of the Holy Spirit on the basis of *Romans* 5.5 and 8.20 (13.23; cf. 16.29). Christ is shown to be the power of God and the wisdom of God by *1 Corinthians* 1.24, a favourite verse both of the Manichees and the early Augustine (13.22 and 16.27).[75] That the human mind is created and not of the same nature as God is shown by Paul's use of the phrase *alia creatura* in *Romans* 8.39 (12.20). Augustine points to the danger that if the human mind does not recognise the gulf between itself as a creature and its Creator its pride and presumption may cause it to fall away, whereas if it desires lower things, it may become stupid and wretched

---

[73] According to Coyle (*op. cit. n.36*), 93-8, all this part of the work may be a later addition.

[74] Cf. John Burnaby, *Amor Dei* (London 1938), 91: 'perhaps nothing in the *De Moribus* is more noteworthy than the extent to which in its last chapters Augustine has for his portraying of the Christian life absorbed the spirit of St. Paul'.

[75] The sections on the Trinity in which these quotations occur may be later additions according to Coyle (*op. cit. n.36*), 241-259.

and be separated from the love of God by its affection for the material world (12.20-21)—he seems here to have *Romans* 1.21 ff. in mind as well as the passage in *Romans* 8 to which he refers directly. The dangers of desire for lower things are again emphasised in a later section (19.35-6) with a quotation of *1 Timothy* 6.10 and a reference to the story of Adam's disobedience in paradise as indicating that the sin of the soul is of this kind. This mystery is also hinted at by Paul's words in *1 Corinthians* 15.22 (loosely quoted as 'In Adam we all die and in Christ we shall all rise').[76] When Paul warns us to put off the old man and put on the new (cf. *Colossians* 3.9-10, *Ephesians* 4.22-4) he refers to Adam, who sinned, as the old man and the man whom the Son of God assumed in the incarnation as the new man. *1 Corinthians* 15.47-9 and *2 Corinthians* 4.16 show the same thing, that we should despise the snares of the body and turn all our love to the invisible realm, so as to be renewed in God. Augustine quotes *2 Corinthians* 4.16 again in the final section (35.80), where he attacks the Manichees for expecting immediate perfection of baptised Christians, whereas Paul speaks of a daily renewal and gradual progress. This renewal can also be seen in terms of becoming like God or being conformed to God rather than to this world (13.22)—Augustine here alludes to *Romans* 12.2 and quotes *Romans* 8.29 (cf. also 16.29, where he quotes the same verse again).

It represents a change over against Augustine's earlier philosophical dialogues that in the *De Moribus Ecclesiae Catholicae* he discusses the divine providential plan in the guidance of human history and the relationship of the Old Testament and New Testament dispensations. Here too Pauline verses play a role. When man had fallen from the divine laws through his desire for mortal things, says Augustine (7.12), divine providence did not desert him but showed both severity in punishment and mercy in salvation (surely an allusion to *Romans* 11.22) and provided a path by means of the separation of the patriarchs, the bond of the law, the predictions of the prophets, the mystery of the incarnation, the witness of the apostles, the blood of the martyrs, and the inclusion of the gentiles.[77] God himself in his mercy (27.54) sent medicine for the sins of the human race (28.55) and gave the two Testaments as a rule of discipline (28.56). The Old Testament is more characterised by coercion working through fear, the New Testament by instruction working

---

[76] On the fall cf. also 7.12 and 22.40 (*corpus homini grauissimum uinculum est, iustissimis Dei legibus, propter antiquum peccatum*).

[77] Even heresies have a role to play; cf. 17.30 quoting *1 Corinthians* 11.19.

through love—or in the words of the apostles bondage and liberty (cf. *Galatians* 4.24 ff., 5.1). Augustine takes up this distinction between fear and love (cf. *2 Timothy* 1.7, *Romans* 8.15, *1 John* 4.18) in a later section (30.64), in which a quotation of *1 Corinthians* 15.56 ('the sting of death is sin, but the strength of sin is the law') is followed by the kernel of Augustine's later exegesis of *Romans* 7.7 ff.—the awareness of the scorned precept slays the sinner; the attempted performance of works under the law is in vain, when lust lays waste the mind and is restrained by fear of punishment rather than being overwhelmed by love of virtue.

In the *De Moribus Ecclesiae Catholicae* Augustine develops his earlier emphasis on the role of the Church and on the need for the acceptance of authority as a step on the path to knowledge. Authority should precede reasoning, just as love precedes knowledge (2.3 and 25.47; cf. also 7.11 and 14.24). The Christian scriptures are validated by the testimony of churches spread throughout the whole world (29.61). The Catholic Church provides teaching adapted to the various levels of its recipients and regulates social relations (30.62-3, including an allusion to *Romans* 13.7), nourishing those who are still infants at the breast (10.17 and 30.64; cf. Augustine's use of this metaphor drawn from *1 Corinthians* 3.2 in the *De Quantitate Animae*) so that they may be led to perfect manhood (10.17 quoting *Ephesians* 4.13) and so that death may be swallowed up in victory (30.64 quoting *1 Corinthians* 15.54-5). In appealing to the Manichees to give a hearing to the teachers of the Catholic Church Augustine quotes *Ephesians* 3.14-19 as showing that this is where the Christian faith is to be found (18.33-4).

The *De Moribus Manichaeorum* uses fewer Pauline citations and is more limited in its subject matter. A discussion of the nature and source of evil (the corruption of created beings, which are good only by participation in supreme Goodness, their falling away from true existence and tending towards non-existence) is followed by an attack on Manichaean teachings and pseudo-asceticism. Augustine uses one Pauline quotation in arguing against the Manichaean view of the soul as part of God (11.22; in this case *Galatians* 5.13 would imply that part of God is in bondage), and a number of Pauline quotations in showing what Paul's purpose was in recommending abstention from meat and wine (14.31-35; *Romans* 14.21, *Romans* 13.14, *Romans* 14.1-15.3, *1 Corinthians* 8.4-13, *1 Corinthians* 10.19-25, *1 Corinthians* 10.28–11.1).

At a later date (by around 396) Augustine's understanding of Paul was to undergo certain striking developments, which might perhaps cause one to wonder whether he was reverting to a more pessimistic out-

look owing something to his earlier Manichaeism.[78] In the period immediately after his conversion his reading of Paul supported a Christian
Platonism which was derived not only from his own reading of Platonist
books[79] but also from Christian teachers and laymen at Milan.[80] The
most important Pauline contribution to this Christian Platonism is the
emphasis on love (faith, hope and love characterising the soul's path to
the divine vision, love of things that are unseen versus desire for wordly
things, love of God and love of neighbour), and on the renewal of the
inner man in becoming conformed to or like the creator. Pauline verses
are used to support an 'other-worldly' religious attitude which a modern
reader would be unlikely to regard as Paul's main message.[81] In addition
Augustine's view of the church as a mother providing suitable sus-
tenance to those of different levels is based on Paul.[82] Although he continues to quote or allude to individual Pauline verses favoured by the
Manichees (for example *1 Corinthians* 1.24, *Philippians* 2.5-8, *Galatians* 4.9),[83] it seems that his Manichaean understanding of Paul has
'gone underground'. Only in the works composed at Rome after his
baptism do major Manichaean Pauline themes begin to resurface and be
reworked. The cluster of Pauline verses which refer to the two men
(old/new, outer/inner, earthly/heavenly) in each individual and to the renewal of the inner man according to the image of God are central both

---

[78] Cf. pp.349 ff. and pp.352 ff. of the article cited above n. 4. On the general
question cf. Alfred Adam, 'Das Fortwirken des Manichäismus bei Augustin', *Zeit-
schrift für Kirchengeschichte* 69 (1958), 1-25, reprinted in *Sprache und Dogma*
(Gütersloh 1969), 141-166, Frend (*op. cit. n.28*), Johannes van Oort, 'Augustine and
Mani on concupiscentia sexualis', in ed. J. den Boeft and J. van Oort, *Augustiniana
Traiectina* (Paris 1987), 137-152.

[79] On some of the agreements and differences between Augustine and the Platonists he read cf. John J. O'Meara, *The Young Augustine* (London 1954), 143 ff. and
(*op. cit. n.35*), 104-111 (comparing what Augustine later says about Porphyry with
Augustine's own views), Chadwick (*op. cit. n.35*), 30 ff.

[80] Cf. in particular Pierre Courcelle, *Late Latin Writers and their Greek Sources*
(Cambridge Mass. 1969), 131 ff. and 171-189, especially 181-2, and (*op. cit. n.55*) on
the influence of Ambrose, Manlius Theodorus and Simplician on Augustine; also
Prosper Alfaric, *L'Évolution intellectuelle de saint Augustin* (Paris 1918), 372 ff., and
John J. O'Meara, *The Young Augustine,* 116 ff. On Augustine's Christian Platonism
cf. also Henry Chadwick, 'Christian Platonism in Origen and Augustine', in *Orige-
niana Tertia* , ed. Richard Hanson and Henri Crouzel (Rome 1985), 228 ff., reprinted
in *Heresy and Orthodoxy in the Early Church* (Aldershot 1991), item XII.

[81] See above, pp.14 ff.16-17,20.

[82] See above pp.17,21.

[83] See above pp.5, 13 and 20, 6, 7 and 13, 4 and 14.

for Manichaean anthropology and for Augustine's new and very different Platonising understanding of Christian progress.[84] Augustine's defense of the role of the Old Testament law contains a critical element
based on Paul (the contrast between bondage and liberty of *Galatians*
5.1 etc.)[85] and shared with the Manichees, and he begins already at
Rome to work out a new understanding of *Romans* 7.7 ff., a key passage
both for the Manichaean dualist approach and for his own later Pauline
exegesis.[86] It is perhaps characteristic of Augustine that an initial enthu-
siasm for and preoccupation with new insights and new influences is
followed by a resurgence and attempted incorporation of earlier attitudes.[87] It has only been possible above to touch on the very beginning
of this process.

---

[84] See above pp.7,16-17 and 20.

[85] See above pp.4 and 21.

[86] See above pp.7 and 21.

[87] I tried to show this with regard to one particular example on pp. 359 ff. of the
article cited above n. 4.

CHRISTIAN AND ROMAN UNIVERSALISM IN THE FOURTH CENTURY

HENRY CHADWICK

Adherence to Christianity was no doubt a matter of religion rather than political calculation to the emperor Constantine the Great. But there is an element of unreality to the old contrast between the saintly emperor 'canonised', so to speak, by a grateful Church and the ambitious, power-hungry military commander who, in Burckhardt's eyes, could not have decided to worship the God of the Christians unless he had carefully calculated that this would be to his political advantage. Calculation or no, he needed something the Church could provide, namely legitimation. There is paradox in this. For the emperor, already under question for usurpation in 306, to be identified with a body so un-Roman as the Church cannot prima facie have assisted him in acquiring wider recognition of his legitimacy. Might rather than any form of right had been decisive in his meteoric rise of 306. His admission to the second tetrarchy with the rank of Caesar was accepted by Galerius in 307 surely in recognition of the legions which Constantine commanded. Any reluctance that Galerius may have felt would have been far stronger if, following the opinion of T.D.Barnes, Constantine's identification with Christianity was already a public fact as early as 306.[1] In 312 the lightning war against Maxentius made necessary the justification that a religious ideology could provide, and he won the battle *instinctu divinitatis,*

---

[1] T.D. Barnes, *Constantine and Eusebius* (Harvard University Press 1981). Lactantius (*De mortibus persecutorum* 24.9 and in the addition of 324 to *Div. Inst.* 1.1.13) says that Constantine's first act on being invested with the purple was to restore freedom of worship to the Christians. This text is insufficiently explained away by Barnes' critics, e.g. Thomas Grünewald, *Constantinus Maximus Augustus: Herrschaftspropaganda in der zeitgenössischen Überlieferung* [Historia Einzelschriften, 64] (Stuttgart 1990), 80. I am not able to follow Barnes in his refusal to find any tendency to tolerate non-Christian cults or any syncretism in Constantine, and would be inclined to discern polemic against syncretism with sun-cult in Eusebius' interpretation of the Logos as the Sun (*Laus Const.* 6.19-20). Averil Cameron's remarks (*Journal of Roman Studies* 83 (1983), 197) are surely judicious.

mentis magnitudine, as the triumphal arch would declare.[2] The anonymous orator who in 313 delivered a panegyric in his honour included cautious words about the divine power which had moved Constantine to launch his attack 'against the advice of men, against the warnings of the haruspices'. The panegyrist felt sure that the amazingly successful Constantine possessed a private line of communication to 'that divine mind which delegates the care of us to inferior divinities and deigns to disclose himself to you alone'.[3] The highest god was on his side; and none knew more about the worship of the highest than the Church.

That Constantine did not identify himself with the Church to impress the citizens of the empire seems certain. Eusebius of Caesarea's oration for Constantine's thirtieth anniversary mentions the way in which scornful people laughed at him for supporting the Church.[4]

Constantine both consulted the haruspices and ignored their advice: it encapsulates the ironic problem of his religious allegiance. To consult them and then to do the opposite of what they told him was a kind of assertion that he had a higher power to guide him, namely the 'supreme Creator of the world who has as many names as there are peoples', and whose preference among these names we humans cannot know—a power immanent in the visible world and transcendent beyond and above it.[5]

The audience for an imperial panegyric in 313, or for that matter in 321, was largely pagan, and the terms used by the panegyrist cannot be squeezed to force the conclusion that not only the emperor but the selected singer of his praises was already Christian. The panegyric of 313 nevertheless presupposes that Constantine was a man for whom the highest deity had a grand purpose to fulfil, and that to achieve this end he needed special protection.

The God of the Biblical record was held in awe and respect by pagan intellectuals. Porphyry himself praised the piety of the ancient Hebrews in worshipping 'the great and true God who is terrible even to the other deities', and thought it correct to distinguish among the inferior powers benevolent angels in the ethereal realm from the daimones inhabiting the air whose benevolence could not be taken for granted.[6] Nothing in the panegyric of 313 goes beyond what Porphyry could have approved.

---

[2] Dessau, *Inscriptiones Latinae Selectae* 694.
[3] *Paneg. Lat.* 12.2.4.
[4] *Laus Const.* 11.3, 224,15 Heikel.
[5] *Paneg. Lat.* 5,26.
[6] Cited by Augustine, *De civitate Dei*, [= *DCD*] 20.24.1; 10.9.

Indeed Porphyry himself wrote words which indirectly might have influenced Constantine away from a syncretism of Christianity with the worship of the unconquered Sun. Porphyry is quoted by Augustine as declaring on the authority of the Chaldean oracles that the rites of the sun and moon, acknowledged to be the principal divinities among the gods, are incapable of purifying a man.[7] Porphyry felt sure that there must be some universal way of salvation, valid for every soul, but could not identify it.[8]

In the fourth century there were potent attractions, for an emperor trying to hold things together, in a religious policy which accepted all cults not obviously immoral as equally valid ways of venerating the deity. In the last book of Apuleius' *Metamorphoses*, Isis informs Lucius at his initiation into her mysteries that she is the one divinity 'worshipped under different forms, with a diversity of rites, and under many names by the entire world'. A list of goddesses follows, concluding with the Egyptian claim that Isis is her true name.[9] That all religions follow different routes but aspire to attain one and the same destination was a widespread view, receiving from Symmachus its most famous formulation during the argument with Ambrose over the altar of Victory, but also found elsewhere as a conventional pagan opinion.[10] In the east Themistius urged the mystery of God, impenetrable by the human mind, to be the ground for mutual toleration; the fact of religious diversity is for Themistius evidence of the relative character of all human religious assertions.[11]

The Christians found it impossible to take an optimistic evaluation of any form of pagan cult. The gods of the heathen nations are 'daimonia',

---

[7] *DCD* 10.23.

[8] *DCD* 10.32.

[9] Apuleius, *Metam.* 11,5.

[10] Symmachus, *Relatio* 3.10 (p. 40 ed. Barrow, 1973); Augustine, *ep.* 104.12 (Nectario); Porphyry in Eusebius, *Pr. Evang.* VIII 9.10 and XIV 10.

[11] Themistius, *or.* V addressed to Jovian in 364, tells the emperor, confronted by high tension between pagans and Christians in the aftermath of Julian and by frenetic rival factions in the Church demanding his support, that because the essence of religion lies in freedom of conscience, state authority is useless; that because there are many different ways to God who actually likes diversity, controversy is coterminous with religion; and that a policy of religious toleration will help to keep the newly found peace with Persia. (Had Constantius regarded his eastern wars as imposing Christian civilization and stopping the Persian custom of incestuous marriages?) Themistius receives a masterful study from G. Dagron in *Travaux et Mémoires* 3 (1968) 1-242, and is edited by G. Downey (Teubner edition, 1965).

declared the Psalmist (96.5).[12] In Christian eyes polytheistic worship was, like sorcery, hanky-panky with evil spirits. Christians were glad to discover in pagan writers of the third century, like Cornelius Labeo and even Porphyry, that in the pantheon of polytheism some of the powers are not friendly tribal spirits but malevolent forces who have to be placated and propitiated.[13] The Christians did not wish to mix their myths. Augustine was not enthusiastic when a priest of Cybele assured him that Attis, the kindly god nursing his sheep, was a Christian now.[14]

Religion is simultaneously the most uniting and the most dividing force in human society. Roman society had a large number of local cults, and the maximum of social cohesion was achieved by serene toleration. Augustine once drew a sharp contrast between the cohesiveness of a society that juxtaposed a large number of polytheistic cults, each with incompatible myths which no one took very seriously, side by side with the quarrelsome Christians, whose rancour and mutual hatred had devastating effects on North African social relations.[15] Donatist and Catholic were utterly agreed in being wholly negative to pagan cult. Before the rabid bands of Donatist Circumcellions turned their ferocity on Catholic churches and clergy, they acquired a fearsome reputation by their unstoppable charges on the orchestral players providing music for pagan festivals.[16]

---

[12] Cited by Origen, *contra Celsum* 3.3 and 37; 4.29; 7.65; especially 7.69 where Origen proves his point from the magical spells that compel a god to reside in his or her image. On this art I gather some of the principal texts in my note on *contra Celsum* 5.38. Cf. also Augustine, *DCD* 21.6.1. For rejection of the Christian thesis that all pagan cult is sorcery cf. Themistius V 70b. He even defends Maximus of Ephesus, VII 99d ff., whose magical skills had enthralled the emperor Julian. Pagans protested to Augustine that they worshipped angels, not demons: *En. in Ps.* 85.12.

[13] Labeo in Augustine *DCD* 2.11; 3.25; 8.13; Porphyry, *De Abstinentia* 2.58, and as quoted by Philoponus, *De opificio mundi* 4.20. Porphyry was also willing to grant that when gods inspired oracles, that was a compulsion imposed upon them by magic (Eusebius, *Pr. Evang.* 5.8 and 6.5).

[14] *Tract. in ev. Joh.* 7.6: a priest of Attis used to say *Et ipse pileatus Christianus est.* Did he mean that a temple of Cybele had lately been transformed into a church, on the analogy of Jerome, *ep.* 107.2 *Iam et Aegyptius Serapis factus est Christianus.* Augustine did not so understand him. Ambrosiaster (*Quaest.* 84.3, CSEL 50 p. 145) reports a pagan opinion that the Christian Good Friday memorial was plagiarised from the expiation spring ceremony of Attis and Cybele, and therefore that both religions were saying the same thing.

[15] *De utilitate ieiunii* 9 (PL.40.712-713; CChr.SL 46.237-238).

[16] Augustine, *ep.* 185.12; *Sermo* 62.17; *c. Gaudentium* I 28, 32; 38,51. Augustine grants that some Circumcellion attacks were directed against very bad people: *ep. ad Cathol. de unit. ecclesiae* 20.54, commenting that it is unwise to use illegal means to

Therefore, a Christian universal religion could not possibly be achieved by treating all cults as equally valid, all equally relative.

Constantine had a strong consciousness of possessing a mission from the highest God.[17] The intercession of the Church's bishops would be potent to secure heavenly favour for his military ventures and for the prosperity of his empire. Dissensions in the Church, on the other hand, were not only socially divisive on earth but also vexatious to heaven. The squabbles in North Africa and then at Alexandria were a source of distress and alarm that the displeasure of heaven would be provoked, with grim consequences for the defence of the frontier, the avoidance of famine and plague, and all the many threats to the survival of his rule. Pagan opinion was to interpret his adhesion to Christianity as a flight on the part of a guilt-ridden conscience, haunted by the memory of dreadful acts of inhumanity, especially the murder of Crispus and Fausta in 326.[18] Constantine needed absolution before he died to show that the highest deity had not only been the cause of his political success but also accepted him among his Friends.[19] So in its own way the quest for absolution by baptism at the end of his life was also a contribution to his search for legitimacy. God had forgiven him even if some human beings had not.[20]

But by his adhesion to the Church, Constantine identified himself with a society which did not think of itself as bound to the particularity of the Roman empire. His 'conversion' was hailed by his Christian panegyrist Eusebius of Caesarea in terms of fulfilling Old Testament prophecies that the earth would be filled with the glory of the Lord as

---

deter illegal acts. Compromise with paganism was not a Donatist characteristic (*En. in Ps.* 88, ii, 14). A degree of rivalry between Catholic and Donatist seems presupposed by *c. Gaudentium* I 38,51: *pagani quorum certe ubi potuistis templa evertistis et basilicas destruxistis, quod et nos fecimus.*

[17] Eusebius' oration in honour of his thirtieth year as emperor mentions his pride in being 'God's servant (7.12). The self-consciousness appears strongly in the bizarre letter to Arius and his supporters where Constantine tells God 'I am your man' : H.G. Opitz, *Urkunden zur Geschichte der arianischen Streites*, (document 34), 71,20. In *Vita Constantini* I 25 Constantine's campaigns against Germans on the Rhine and then in conquering Britons are fought to impose civilised gentleness, the savage and ineducable being expelled.

[18] Zosimus II 29,3-4.

[19] For Constantine as admitted to the circle of God's Friends cf. Eusebius, *Laus Const.* 2.3 p. 119,7 Heikel.

[20] The erection at Constantinople of the Church of the Apostles as a mausoleum for himself and his dynasty provided a Christian version of Alexander the Great's apotheosis as the Thirteenth god: John Chrysostom, *Hom. in 2 Cor.* 26.5 (PG 61.581 f.).

the waters cover the sea.[21] Could it be that the Christian emperor's role was not simply to ensure that, under the right worship of the true highest Deity, there would be security and prosperity for the Roman world but, further, to diffuse the values of a Christian society, governed under the rule of law to which every citizen had equal access,[22] beyond the frontier to embrace all the barbarian peoples? Could it then be that the economic, political and military success of the empire was destined by providence to be an instrument in the service of an ultimately spiritual end of which the prime agency would be the ecclesia catholica? This universal Church did not sacrifice its universality by being anchored to a visible and ordered community structured round an episcopate with focal points of authority in its great sees, and perhaps in particular in the cathedra Petri at Rome. Among jurists it was established convention to hold that, in all the diversities created by local decisions, one could be confident of having a sound basis for action if one inquired how the matter in question had been decided in the city of Rome.[23] So too a Christian Roman emperor could come to see in the episcopate, focussed in the great patriarchates and especially in the Roman see, an agency for maintaining discipline in an international order.

Ancient polytheistic religion was attached to particular places and peoples. Notoriously the Christian Church was distinctive in ancient society for being a body emancipated from attachment to ethnic divisions. Unhappily it turned out to be harder to stop civil war within the Church than to quell it in the secular world. The Donatist schism in Africa was assuredly a civil war.[24] In 313 it cannot have been a foregone conclusion that the see of Rome, with the churches north of the Mediterranean, and ultimately the emperor himself were going to support Caecilian rather than Donatus. It may simply have been inconceivable in 314 that the

---

[21] On the importance of the universal expansion of the Church in fulfilment of prophecy, see H. Berkhof, *Die Theologie des Eusebius von Caesarea* (Amsterdam 1939), 49 f.

[22] Ambrose, *Hexaemeron* V 21.66. Ambrose generally has a less pessimistic portrait of the justice administered in the courts than one finds in, e.g., John Chrysostom or Augustine who are frank and sharp about the prevalence of bribery. But Ambrose was aware that the powerful often put improper pressure on judges (*De officiis* II 24,125) and that prisoners in chains may be innocent men (*in Ps.* 118.20.23, CSEL 62). He could write that every secular dignity is under the power of the devil (*in Luc.* iv.28). Themistius (I 14d, 15a) also stresses equality before the law as crucial to Roman civilization.

[23] *Digesta* I 3.32 (Salvius Julianus).

[24] *Bellum civile:* Augustine, *c. Gaudentium* I 19,21.

Council of Arles would come to a conclusion other than that the Pope's council of the previous year had been right. Donatus' appeal from the two councils to the emperor himself met with frustration, and thereafter the government had a long and peculiarly intractable schism on its hands.

***

The ideological background of Constantine's vision of himself and of the Church lies in much earlier attitudes within the Church. In the Pauline epistles, as in *Romans* 13 and 2 *Thessalonians* 2, the Roman empire was understood to have a providential part to play in the divine plan for human history. It is presupposed in the Acts of the Apostles that the apostle Paul's final arrival in Rome, after a reasonably successful mission to the intellectuals in Athens, has symbolic significance.[25] Melito of Sardis was to see the pax Romana as divinely granted to foster the progress of the Christian mission.[26] But mission is always intimately bound up with unity, and the Christians did not find unity easy to preserve. Augustine was sadly to record that the mutual hatred between Donatist and Catholic in North Africa was driving many of the recently converted peasants back to their old polytheistic ways.[27]

In the seventies of the second century, the anti-Christian pamphleteer and Platonic philosopher Celsus made observations about the Christians which prima facie appear contradictory and antithetical. He was aware that round the body which he calls 'the great Church', or 'those of the multitude',[28] there was a large penumbra of sects in utter disagreement not only with the great Church but with one another. 'They attack one another with dreadful and unrepeatable terms of abuse; they are willing to make not the least concession to reach agreement, but hold one another in total detestation.'[29] The sects to which Celsus refers turn out to be the followers of Marcion, and various gnostic groups about which he

---

[25] How deep the significance is portrayed in Acts by the narrative of successive hindrances to his arrival in Rome which the apostle surmounts—the storm and the snake-bite being only the most dramatic.

[26] Melito in Eusebius, *H.E.* IV 27.7-11.

[27] Augustine, *ep.*20*Divjak (CSEL 88.105). How recent the evangelization of Numidia was can be judged from Aug. *En. in Ps.* 96.7: 'Everyone present had a pagan grandfather or greatgrandfather.'

[28] Origen, *contra Celsum* [= *CC*] 5.59 and 61.

[29] *CC* 63.

was reasonably well informed—Valentinians, Ebionites, Simonians, Carpocratians, and Ophites, the last named being noteworthy for adapting a Mithras liturgy to their syncretistic purposes. On the other hand, 'the great Church' of the majority is presented by Celsus as a tightly coherent body whose most striking characteristic is 'agape', the mutual love bonding the Christians together 'more powerfully than an oath'.[30] This coherence struck Celsus as a phenomenon calling for some explanation, since on the face of it such unity was a most surprising thing, and indeed on closer examination he suggested it was no more than a façade. For what Celsus could not discern in the church was any serious principle of religious authority. Because they are a breakaway body from the national religion of the Jews, a spirit of dissidence and fissiparousness is inherent in their very being. By instinct, by the law of their origin, the Christians are people wanting to defy authority.[31]

It is a leading theme in Celsus' political and religious ideology that ethnic religious cults possess an authority to be respected, even if, as he thought was the case with Judaism, some of the attitudes and practices are bizarre and highly peculiar.[32] Christianity is distinctive as a religion in ignoring ethnic frontiers. Therefore to Celsus it appears to be essentially a *stasis*,[33] a revolt, a conscious counter-culture of barbarian origin (and how barbaric Celsus will demonstrate in some detail), scornful about great Greek literature and philosophy.[34] The scorn reflects the low level of education in the community. Moreover, the Christians appear dangerously alienated from giving proper support to the emperors, to the laws of the empire, to the defence of the frontier against the attacking barbarian tribes whose sole aim is to burn and destroy.[35] Above all, they seem outrageous in their negative attitude to the gods, the givers of all fertility on the land[36] and of all military success for the legions.

Celsus asks the Christians to abandon their dangerous innovations and to resume a stand upon the old paths of polytheism, philosophy, and due respect for public office. They appear to treat as their authorities

---

[30] *CC* 1.1.

[31] *CC* 5.33 and 51. Celsus (3.9) was acutely aware that the Christians would be horrified if they succeeded in converting everybody.

[32] *CC* 5.25. In 5.41 Celsus mocks the Jews for arrogantly thinking their religion superior to that of others.

[33] *CC* 3.5; 5.33; 8.2; 8.49.

[34] *CC* 1.9.

[35] *CC* 8.73 and 75.

[36] *CC* 8.55.

sacred books of the ancient Hebrews, full of obscurities and even absurdities (like the seven days of creation) which only sophisticated allegories can twist to give a rational meaning.[37] On such a frail foundation their exegetes, not surprisingly, merely succeed in producing a mass of inconsistent doctrines.

In these circumstances, Celsus discerns within the great Church a seething debate with parties forming 'each with its own leader'. And yet this condition of somewhat acrimonious debate internal to the Church is in amazing contrast to the unanimity of their initial history. 'When they were beginning, they were few and of one mind; but since they have spread to become a multitude, they are divided and rent asunder, and each wants to have his own party.' The result is that now 'the only thing they seriously have in common is the name of Christian, which they are unwilling ever to abandon'.[38] But this name covers an astonishing diversity of opinions.

At the time when Celsus was writing, the emperor Marcus Aurelius was busy making an example of the poor Christians in the Rhône valley at Lyons, subjecting the Church there to ferocious and inhuman attack.[39] Celsus felt that persecution must be the external force imparting coherence to so heterogeneous a body. The cohesive power holding Christians together must be nothing other than the pressures of a hostile society surrounding them. Celsus has no misgivings about the emperor's policy of drastic harassment. Persecution to death is the appropriate penalty for those who insult the images of the gods, and the magistrates who impose the death penalty are only the instruments of divine vengeance.[40] At the root of the unity manifested by the Christians there lies but a single cause, 'the fear of outsiders'.[41]

Nevertheless, Celsus also knows that the squabbling Christians nurse a dream of incredible unity. Among them he finds an alarming ambition to conquer society, to become 'masters of the world',[42] to convert emperors to their faith and so to be the instruments of a providential design which is to 'unite under a single law the inhabitants of Asia, Europe, and Africa', including in this monolithic polity 'not only Greeks but the

---

[37] *CC* 1.27; 4.37; 6.60.
[38] *CC* 3.10 and 12.
[39] Eusebius, *H.E.* V.1.
[40] *CC* 8.41.
[41] *CC* 3.14.
[42] *CC* 8.69.

most remote barbarians'.[43] In other words, the normal barriers of ethnic difference and divergent cultural levels are, for the Christians, to be transcended. What is particularly strange is that the Christians do not think their dream will be realized through a military conquest, and yet their vision of a supra-national United Nations includes a large role for the Roman emperor. Celsus has heard Christians—a community known to have its reservations about war and military service—asserting that were the emperor to become a Christian, the thorny problems of defence would be altogether transformed.[44] The cause of the empire would then be defended, not by the unsatisfactory gods of the polytheistic tradition, but by the one true God. And his minister would be a believing Christian world-ruler uniting not merely the existing empire but all races of humanity under a benevolent polity, turning the *res Romana* into a theocratic world-state with centralised universal control to restrain crime and sin and to fill the inhabited world with the knowledge of the Lord.

This kind of language confirmed the pagan's worst anxieties. Were any such nightmarish scenario ever to be realized, would not the barbarians merely pour across the Rhine and the Danube and the Euphrates, destroying civilization unhindered?[45] The notion that Christianity has the potential to contribute to the social cohesion and prosperity of the empire is dangerous nonsense and fantasy. If the Church's internal coherence depends on external persecution, is it not implicit that the removal of harassment with the coming of a Christian emperor will only open the flood-gates of latent dissension and mutual intolerance which Celsus has detected in this ambitious community? In a word, nothing seemed to Celsus less likely to impart consolidation and strength to civilized society (i.e. the empire) than a fulfilment of the Christian aspiration to conquer and to bond together Roman and barbarian under one polity and moral code.

Celsus could see in polytheism a principle essentially tolerant of religious diversity. He liked to quote Herodotus who long ago saw diversity of moral and religious custom to be instinctive among the variety of the human race, where 'each tribe thinks its own customs the truest and the best'. Against biblical monotheism, inherited by the Jews and Christians from Moses the magician and sorcerer, Celsus laid down that 'each

---

[43] *CC* 8.72.

[44] *CC* 8.69. Cf. Scriptores Historiae Augustae *Probus* 20, 4-5.

[45] *CC* 8.68. The fifth-century barbarian invasions were blamed on the Christians by pagans (e.g. Aug. *ep.* 111 and especially 138.9 ff. to Marcellinus).

nation makes no mistake in observing its own laws of worship'.[46] To respect tribal diversity is to affirm polytheism, the cults of which are essentially local and regional. A cosmopolitan Christian monotheism is essentially intolerant and asks for an unrealizable degree of uniformity.

It follows for Celsus that the Jews were merely inconsistent. If they upheld their own customs on the principle that Moses was legislating only for his own race as instructed by the God of the Jews, there would be no ground for reasonable criticism, however peculiar their practices might be. But Celsus found it strange of the Jews to maintain an ethnic form of worship and at the same time to affirm a monotheism which, as they understood it, entailed the invalidity of all other cults which were no more and no less tribal than their own.[47]

Celsus' hostile but informed portrait of the Christian mind of his time shows how even in the second century there was a blueprint in the Church for the Constantinian revolution. In reply to him Origen (writing about 248) defended the hope of an eventual universal unity of all souls, but conceded that 'for those still in the body' it is 'probably' impracticable and will not be realized until the life to come.[48] In a much earlier work[49] Origen contrasted the large variety of human law codes, Greek and barbarian, each valid for its own limited race and region, with the one universal law under which all Christians are happily united. Moreover, in his Commentary on the epistle to the Romans, Origen understood both magistrates and bishops as complementary instruments for restraining transgression of divine moral law. The secular magistrate, he says, is God's minister to punish such elemental crimes as murder, adultery, theft, homosexual assault, that is 'the greater part of God's law', whereas bishops have to see to the finer points and must correct more private moral failures.[50] Here even so ascetic and world-renouncing a writer as Origen could echo the language of a blueprint for a coming Christian society in which magistrates and bishops would engage in a cooperative enterprise of social control.[51]

---

[46] *CC* 5.34 and 41. Herodotus was also congenial to the programme of toleration advanced by Themistius (II 27d).

[47] *CC* 5.41.

[48] *CC* 8.72.

[49] *De principiis* 4.1.1.

[50] *Comm. in ep. ad. Rom.* 9.28 (PL 14.1228).

[51] Jerome (*in Michaiam* I 2.9-10 p. 457 Vallarsi) regarded the cooperation of bishops and magistrates as repressing the legitimate human concerns of the poor.

The success of the bishops, however, would inevitably depend on the maintenance of unity in the Church. In answering Celsus Origen sharply dismisses as malicious the suggestion that Christian unity is the result of external hostility. But in other works addressed to a Christian readership or audience, he can be found expressing nostalgia for the old days when under persecution one could be sure of the authenticity and integrity of believers, contrasting that with the secularity and compromise which have now come to invade the community, with clergy of low quality and many laity repairing to the Church's weekly eucharist only very inter-mittently.[52] Origen records that some converts apostatized soon after their baptism because of their disillusion with the dissension and faction in the churches.[53] Conflict seemed endemic. Yet 'if only the Church were really united, the walls of Jericho would fall'.[54] 'Those who con-quer on the battlefield may lose all if they then fall to quarrelling'.[55]

The double concern for unity and mission becomes prominent with Constantine the Great.

Constantine's concern for the inter-related themes of Christian mission and Christian unity is writ large in the writings of Eusebius of Caesarea. Eusebius' panegyrical language about his hero, both in his *Laus Constantini* (including his speech for Constantine's thirtieth an-niversary) and in the unfinished *Vita Constantini*, has not improved his reputation with modern historians. Funerary or royal panegyrics of any age tend to reticence about the dark side. In antiquity too panegyrists were notorious for being less than wholly veracious.[56] But it is certain that no panegyrist ascribes to his living imperial hero attitudes other than those he would wish to possess. The oration of 336 offers an ideo-logical programme for a universal world order bonded and led by a Christian Roman monarch. It moves a step beyond the emperor's *Oratio ad sanctos* (I assume the text is an official translation of a Latin dis-course, designed to imply that no emperor responsible for persecuting worshippers of the true God can be deemed to possess legitimacy). In the *Oratio* the emperor explicitly claimed that his mission from God is

---

[52] Among many texts cf. Origen, *Hom in Num.* 10.2; *Hom in Jerem.* 4.3; *Hom. in Gen.* 10.1; 11.3; *Hom. in Levit.* 9.5.

[53] *Comm. in ep. ad Rom.* 9.41.

[54] *Hom. in Jesu Nave* 7.2.

[55] *Hom. in Num.* 26.2.

[56] Plotinus V 5.13.14; Augustine, *conf.* VI 6,9 comments that mendacity was re-garded by the audience as a virtue in such circumstances. There was no praise for a panegyrist who told the truth.

to convert the entire empire to the right religious faith.[57] In Eusebius'
Vita Constantini the point is made indirectly as the panegyric passes
(apparently without betraying any awareness of the contradiction) from
praise of Constantine's toleration to an account of his moves against pagan cult, the latter being given a moral justification. In the oration of
336 the emperor is emphatically told that legitimate sovereignty depends on true religion, and no pagan ruler can be legitimate (4.1; 5.3)
The argument rebuts critics of Constantine's liquidation of successive
superfluous colleagues, who did not share his faith. Indeed, the emperor's special divine calling is manifest in his liking for the title 'God's
Servant' (7.12). Polytheism stimulates national dissensions and is productive of conflict (9.2; 13.9; 16.2). We meet here the Christian theme
that error is associated with diversity, truth with unity. The authentic religion of peace is bringing such conflicts to an end (8.9).

Through a monarchical government, which is the image and earthly
counterpart of God's heavenly monarchy (4.3, p. 203.17 Heikel), all
peoples in North, South, East and West, can now live under a single law
(10.6).[58] The acknowledgement of one God brings recognition of the
unity of all humanity (16.3). By the universal power of Rome, the
knowledge of the one God is diffused (16.4). So the sign of the cross
protects Roman power (9.8), and through this agency there will be
brought to completion what is in part already achieved, namely, the
uniting of all nations in a single polity with freedom and security of
travel anywhere (16.6). So on the Lord's day all tribes and peoples will
offer a united worship to the one true God (17.13-14). The universal
moral law brings an end to idolatry, defiled by the barbaric custom of
human sacrifices (13.7; 16.10), cannibalism, incest and the gross homosexual practices and harlotry at the temple of Aphaca in Phoenicia, lately dismantled by Constantine's express order (8.5-6; *Vita Constantini*
III 53). The attack on pagan cult is justified by concern for morality.

---

[57] Eusebius, *Laus Constantini* 11.1 (p. 223 Heikel), i.e. in the opening chapter of
the treatise which Eusebius attached to his oration of 336.

[58] Themistius also sees the emperor as God's counterpart (n. 61 below) and therefore the bond uniting East and West in a single harmony of soul and judgement (XV
198b). The Christians thought this required one religion. The theme appears in Eusebius, *Pr. Evang.* I 4.6f. (picking up a theme from Bardaisan of Edessa), and VI 6.70 f.;
Dem. Evang. I 2.14. The distinguished monograph of T.D. Barnes, *Constantine and
Eusebius* (1981), treats Eusebius with much understanding and sympathy, especially
on this last point. Augustine (*DCD* 18.22) writes of God's design to unite the whole
world in a single respublica enjoying peace under one system of law. Cf. *conf.* XIII
34,49.

The ideological vision in the *Vita Constantini* is less universalist and more specifically Roman than that in the Tricennalian oration. The stress lies on the supremacy of the Roman empire as the home of law and civilization, acknowledged by the stream of barbarian ambassadors pouring into Constantine's court with their gifts and tribute—Britons, Scythians, Sarmatians, Blemmyes, Indians, Ethiopians—all remote barbarians untouched by high culture and respect for legal institutions. It must be doubtful whether Constantine's letter to Sapor, telling the Great King that the Persian capture of Valerian in 258 was caused by his persecution of the Christians, and that he is now commending them to the king's protection,[59] would have had the effect intended. The Persians would have observed that the Christianization of Armenia had brought the Armenians under strong Roman influence and authority. Although Constantine said not a word to suggest that a contiguous kingdom with a large Christian population might one day be incorporated within a wider orbis Christianus et Romanus, it would not have been difficult for the Persian king to envisage this possibility and to dislike the prediction.

Eusebius is surely correct in portraying Constantine as moving to the judgement that his one empire should come to have one law, one religion. The universalist ideal, however, could still be accepted by those who did not want pagan cult suppressed and felt the programme of suppression to be socially divisive and bad for the empire.[60] Themistius was to be their spokesman. He fully accepted the universalist language of a world empire; of an emperor who is the earthly image and counterpart of the divine monarch[61] and whose heart, as 'the Assyrians' said (i.e. *Proverbs of Solomon* 21.1), is in the hand of God;[62] of God as the source of all legitimacy and the Giver of victory to the emperor's armies.[63] Themistius was very aware of the mounting immigration of barbarians, especially the Germanic tribes of the north, into the empire, and of the crucial decision of Constantine in 332 to incorporate the Goths within the empire by making them foederati with responsibility to defend the frontier.[64] As the immigrants increased in number and became indis-

---

[59] Eusebius, *Vita Constantini* IV 9-13. The letter has an undercurrent of threat, especially in the opening observations that Constantine's zeal for true religion has overthrown tyrants.

[60] Themistius V 70b. The reference to Empedocles in this passage was explained by Petavius as Themistius' coded name for Christ.

[61] Themistius I 9b, cf. XI 143a.

[62] Themistius VII 89d, XI 147c, XIX 229a.

[63] Themistius XI 143a, XIX 229a. Victory: II 39a.

[64] Themistius VIII 119c. Date: Mommsen, *Chronica Minora* I 234.

pensable for the army, tension rose. The frontier was no longer an effective barrier, and in 375 the Danube defences crumbled, with consequences leading to the catastrophic defeat of Valens and the Roman legions in 378 at the battle of Adrianople, leaving the road to Constantinople wide open. Themistius interpreted the emperor's universalist ideology to entail the conclusion that war on the frontier was a mistake,[65] and that the barbarians should be peacefully settled and turned into good Romans.[66] The barbarian tribes he once compares to the *thumos* in the Platonic soul, a vast emotional force which needed to be harnessed for constructive ends by being made subordinate to reason and law.[67] They are to be Romanized, which for Themistius must involve making them more than helots to do the inferior and menial jobs and means that they will have a serious stake in Roman society.

Romanization, however, means incorporation in a society that enjoys equality before the law and at the same time affirms freedom of worship and conscience in religion. There are many paths to God, who is pleased to see much disagreement about theology and religion since it is an indirect testimony to the mystery and transcendence of the divine.[68]

Themistius' understanding of imperial universalism was not generally shared. In Ambrose and Synesius we meet Christians who deplored the weakness of the government towards the barbarian immigrations and who thought the emperor was neglecting his first duty, the defence of the frontier. The barbarians threatened civilisation and public order, and the Church was a buttress of order in society. The experience of the Gothic invasion of the Balkans in the 370s was one of cruel inhumanity. Ambrose regarded the invaders as showing no mercy and no spark of human feeling, unless their prisoners could command a price in the slave market.[69]

Nevertheless Ambrose was sure that the pax Romana made possible the spread of the gospel far beyond the frontier, the mission of St. Thomas in India and of St. Matthew in Persia, and adds: 'All have learnt by living under the authority of a single earthly imperium to confess in

---

[65] Themistius VI 75d, XVI 212a, especially X.

[66] Themistius XIII 166c. Themistius claimed Jovian a true son of the Constantinian dynasty, in effect a new Constantine reestablishing the line after Julian's death (V 70d), but needing to be less bellicose.

[67] Themistius X 131c.

[68] Themistius V passim.

[69] Ambrose, *De officiis* II 15, 71.

faithful words the rule of a single almighty God.'[70] He could tell Gratian (much as Themistius could also) that he was Augustus not of one race alone but of the entire world.[71]

The universal extension of the Christian gospel becomes fused in fourth century ideology with the limitless claim to authority by the Roman emperors of the age. Already in the third century 'ruler of the world' (*kosmokrator*) is attested in inscriptions as an imperial title for Caracalla and Gordian.[72] Ammianus Marcellinus, however, felt it to be absurd vanity that the emperor Constantius liked to sign himself *totius orbis dominus*.[73] In contrast, Themistius was normally content to say that the emperor ruled over 'almost all the world'.[74]

The immigration of the Germanic tribes transformed the empire and in the West substituted several small barbarian kingdoms—which Augustine thought a much more satisfactory form of organization for government than the huge unwieldy Roman empire.[75] The Christians did not think the barbarians fell outside the kingdom of God.[76] But incorporation in the ecclesia catholica was also integration into a society respectful of Roman law. As civil authority declined under the hammer blows of barbarian invasion, bishops emerged as the defenders of their flock and so of their cities. Bishops, Augustine once remarked, are becoming *principes super omnem terram*,[77] in an international Church

---

[70] *In Ps.* 45.21.3 (CSEL 64.344).

[71] *De fide*, prol. 1 (CSEL 78.4). Cf. Themistius XIII 163c, 169b.

[72] E. Peterson, *Heis Theos* (Göttingen 1926), 173 n. 1.

[73] Amm. Marc. XV 1.3. John Matthews, *The Roman Empire of Ammianus* (1989), 235 comments that 'Ammianus' objection is a curious one. Apart from its triviality as an instance of the point of principle at stake, he must have known that the style to which he refers was commonplace in imperial pronouncements of the times'. He later (431) explains it from XX.3.12 where Ammianus again writes of the earth as tiny in comparison with the whole universe.

[74] Themistius XIII 169b; XVIII 217 cd; XIX 227b.

[75] *DCD* 4.15.

[76] Augustine (*DCD* 20.11) rejects the exegesis of Gog and Magog attacking the holy city (Apoc. 20) to mean northern barbarians invading the empire, as in Ambrose, *De fide* II 16; Jerome, *Heb. Qu. Gen.* 10.2, PL 23. 1009; *in Ezech.* XI praef., PL 25,1, 341.

[77] *En. in Ps.* 44.32. Augustine could speak of the empire as being 'Christian by God's mercy' (*De gratia Christi et de pecc. orig.* II 17.18) and even of *imperium Christianum* (*c. Faustum* 22.60). But for him the saeculum was at a great distance from God. 'The emperors have become Christian, the devil has not' (*En. in Ps.* 93.19). His estimate of the actualities of the empirical Church is one of individual failures on a dreadful scale, striking among such bishops as Antoninus of Fussala.

which embodied unity and universality through the episcopate that transcended all frontiers whether ethnic or imperial.

For the Greek east the linchpin of order, and the embodiment of unity and universality, was seen in the emperor at Constantinople, and that ideal is already present in Themistius' pages in the 370s. In the Latin West the stronger sense of reserve towards interference by government in the independence of the Church left the path open for the authority of the Roman see, enhanced further as barbarian invasion and the dangers of travel made episcopal synods harder to hold. The Eusebian and Constantinian dream of a universal society acknowledging a single law and one authority came to be realized in the western Church in a manner distinct from that of the east.

EINE PSEUDO-ATHANASIANISCHE OSTERPREDIGT (CPG II 2247) ÜBER DIE WAHRHEIT GOTTES UND IHRE ERFÜLLUNG

HUBERTUS R. DROBNER

1. *Überlieferung, Autor und Datierung*

Unter den Werken des Athanasius steht eine lange Osterpredigt mit dem Titel *De passione et cruce Domini* (PG 28, 185-249), die auch in syrischer und armenischer Version erhalten ist.[1] Die bei Migne abgedruckte Edition der Mauriner B. de Montfaucon und J. Lopin (1698) zählte sie zu den *Dubia*,[2] K. Hoss (1899) verteidigte dagegen ihre Echtheit,[3] während V. Hugger sie (1919) mit überzeugenden Gründen als unecht erwies und nach Palästina nicht viel später als zu Ende des 4. Jh. einordnete: "A. kommt als Verfasser der Homilie nicht in Betracht. Der Verfasser ist ein in Palästina wohnender, großer Verehrer des Heiligen, der dessen Schriften mit seltenem Eifer studiert und geplündert hat. ... Aber zur Gewißheit können wir beim dermaligen Stand unseres Wissens ebensowenig gelangen, wie über die Abfassungszeit. Doch dürfte sie nicht weit über das 4. Jahrhundert hinausgehen" (S. 741).[4] M. Geerard schloß sich seiner Auffassung an.[5] Da aber der pseudo-athanasianische sog. *Sermo maior de fide* (CPG II 2803) die Predigt zitiert,[6] hängt ihre

---

[1] R.W. Thompson, *Athanasiana Syriaca III* [CSCO 324] (1972), 89-138 [Text], 153-9 [Fragmente]; [CSCO 325] (1972), 61-96, 107-12 [Übersetzung]; R.P. Casey, 'Armenian Manuscripts of St. Athanasius of Alexandria', *Harvard Theological Review* 24 (1931) 43-59.

[2] B. de Montfaucon and J. Lopin, *Sancti patris nostri Athanasii ... opera omnia quae extant ...*, 3 vols. (Paris 1698).

[3] K. Hoss, *Studien über das Schrifttum und die Theologie des Athanasius auf Grund einer Echtheitsuntersuchung von Athanasius contra gentes und de incarnatione* (Freiburg 1899), 96-103.

[4] V. Hugger, 'Mai's Lukaskommentar und der Traktat *De passione* athanasianisches Gut?', *Zeitschrift für Katholische Theologie* 43 (1919), 732-41.

[5] M. Geerard, *Clavis Patrum Graecorum II* (Turnhout 1974), 45 f.

[6] Vgl. E. Schwartz, 'der s.g. *Sermo maior de fide* des Athanasius', *Sitzungsbe-*

Datierung von dessen Einordnung ab. Er gilt üblicherweise nicht als von Athanasius verfaßt. A. Stülcken definierte den Autor generell als 'Antiochener aus der Mitte des 4. Jh.',[7] E. Schwartz präzisierte diese Identifikation dahingehend, daß er Eustathius von Antiochen († um 345) als Verfasser vorschlug,[8] F. Scheidweiler Markell von Ankyra († um 374).[9] Lediglich H. Nordberg (1962) verteidigte die Echtheit des *Sermo*.[10] M. Simonetti vermutete zuletzt mit aller nötigen Vorsicht Didymus von Alexandrien († 398) als möglichen Verfasser, jedenfalls stamme das Werk aus alexandrinischem Umfeld Mitte des 4. Jh.[11] Als Datum der Abfassung geht man aufgrund der betont nizänischen Theologie, die aber noch nicht die Entwicklung nach 356 zu kennen scheint, von den Jahren 325 bis 350 aus.[12] Die vorliegende pseudo-athanasianische Osterpredigt muß danach jedenfalls vor 350 entstanden sein.

2. *Die Erfüllung der Schrift und die Schuld der Juden*

Die Predigt beginnt, wie oft üblich, mit einer kurzen Rekapitulation des soeben vorgetragenen Evangeliums:

> "[1] Und als sie zu dem Platz namens Golgotha kamen, was 'Schädelstätte' bedeutet, gaben sie ihm Wein zu trinken mit Galle vermischt. Und nachdem er gekostet hatte, wollte er nicht trinken. Als sie ihn aber gekreuzigt hatten, verteilten sie seine Kleider, indem sie das Los warfen; damit das vom Propheten Gesagte erfüllt würde: Sie verteilten meine Kleider unter sich, und über mein Gewand warfen sie das Los. Und sitzend bewachten sie ihn dort. (*Matthäus* 27.33-36) Und so weiter." [185 B]

Der Schluß "und so weiter" weist darauf hin, daß es sich wohl um die Anfangssätze des in der Liturgie verlesenen Evangeliums handelt, so

---

richte der Bayerischen Akademie der Wissenschaften, Philosophisch-philologisch und historische Klasse 1924,6 (München 1925), 12, 32, 43.

[7] Vgl. A. Stülcken, 'Athanasiana. Litterar- und dogmengeschichtliche Untersuchungen', *Texte und Untersuchungen* 19/4 (Leipzig 1899), 28-40.

[8] Vgl. Schwartz (*op. cit. n. 6*), 57-63.

[9] Vgl. F. Scheidweiler, 'Wer ist der Verfasser des sog. *Sermo maior de fide*?', *Byzantinische Zeitschrift* 47 (1954), 333-57.

[10] Vgl. H Nordberg, 'Athanasiana I', *Societas Scientiarum Fennica. Commentationes humanarum litterarum* 30/2 (Helsinki 1962), 57-71.

[11] Vgl. M. Simonetti, 'Ancora sulla paternita dello ps. atanasiano 'Sermo maior de fide', *Vetera Christianorum* 11 (1974), 333-43.

[12] *Ibid* 336.

daß also nicht die ganze Leidensgeschichte nach *Matthäus* (ab 26.17) vorgetragen worden war. Da die Predigt im weiteren Verlauf des öfteren aus der Passion nach *Matthäus* bis hin zum Vers 27.54 zitiert, erstreckte sich der Perikopentext vermutlich zumindest bis dorthin. Der vor allem in Bibelhandschriften palästinensischer Herkunft sowie bei Eusebius vorkommende, wohl aus *Johannes* 19.24 eingewanderte Zusatz in Vers 35 "damit das vom Propheten Gesagte erfüllt würde: Sie verteilten meine Kleider unter sich, und über mein Gewand warfen sie ein Los"[13] veranlaßt den folgenden langen und weitschweifigen Diskurs zur Frage der göttlichen Wahrheit, der fast ein Drittel der gesamten Predigt ausmacht [1-10: 185-204]. V. Hugger urteilt darüber: "Nach diesem durch 8 Spalten sich hinziehenden Gemisch verschiedener Gegenstände, die unter sich keinen inneren Zusammenhang und mit dem vorangestellten Schrifttext wie dem hohen Fest gar nichts zu tun haben, beginnt die mystische Erklärung einzelner Züge aus dem Leiden des Herrn" (S. 736). Nun ist bei der Lektüre der Predigt nicht zu leugnen, daß es der Autor offensichtlich wenig versteht, präzise und straff zum Thema zu sprechen, man wundert sich aber dennoch, wie er sich über eine so weite Strecke die Aufmerksamkeit seiner Hörerschaft mit einer bloßen Abschweifung hätte erhalten können, ohne etwas die Gemeinde grundsätzlich sehr wohl Interessierendes zu erörtern.[14]

Einen ersten Hinweis darauf gibt der Prediger selbst nach Zitation vieler Bibelstellen, wobei er seine Weitschweifigkeit bemerkt zu haben scheint, die den Hörer das eigentliche Ziel konnte aus den Augen verlieren lassen:

"[8] Und was ist mir der Nutzen des vielen? Nichts gibt es, was Gott sagt und unerfüllt bleibt... Denn siehe, auch das, was vor langer Zeit vom Herrn gesagt wurde, ... sehen wir jetzt in den Evangelien erfüllt... Er selbst wurde die Erfüllung des Gesetzes und der Propheten... [9] Viele, die die Evangelien annehmen und hören 'Damit die Schrift erfüllt wurde', glauben, daß das Geschehen wegen nichts anderem geschehen sei als damit die Schrift erfüllt wurde; und daraus schlossen sie, daß die

---

[13] Vgl. Nestle-Aland, *Novum Testamentum Graece* (Stuttgart 1979), 83 app. crit. So schon Hugger (*op. cit. n. 4*), 740 f.

[14] Ich verkenne nicht, daß es vermutlich zu allen Zeiten Prediger gab, die an ihrer Gemeinde vorbeiredeten und diese die Predigt nur ertrug, weil sie nicht allein zur Predigt, sondern zur Eucharistiefeier gekommen war. Dann aber wird nicht nur jeder Interpretationsversuch hinfällig, sondern solange dafür keine eindeutigen Beweise vorliegen, muß man m. E. Prediger und Gemeinde sachgemäße Intention und Verhalten unterstellen.

Täter nicht nur unschuldig seien, sondern vielmehr des Lobes würdig, weil sie nicht als Sünder, sondern als Diener der Schrift handeln; denn die Worte der Propheten wären nicht wahr geworden, wenn es nicht ihre Taten gegeben hätte." [197 B-200 A]

Den Anstoß für den langen ersten Teil der Predigt gab also offenbar die Deutung "damit die Schrift erfüllt werde". Daraus zogen anscheinend auch Christen, "die die Evangelien annehmen", den Schluß, daß dann die Juden am Tod Jesu nicht nur unschuldig seien, sondern als gehorsame Werkzeuge zur Erfüllung der Vorsehung Gottes sogar des Lobes würdig. Wie naheliegend und alt diese Interpretation der entsprechenden Bemerkungen der Evangelien war, zeigt ein Blick in die erste erhaltene Osterpredigt, die Paschapredigt des Melito von Sardes (ca. 160-170). Dort verteidigen sich die Juden gegen den Vorwurf des Gottesmordes mit dem Argument: "weil er leiden [sterben] *mußte*".[15] Bereits Justin hatte in seinem 'Dialog mit dem Juden Trypho' dieser Entschuldigung widersprochen.[16] Da wir über die Gemeinde, vor der die Predigt gehalten wurde, nichts wissen, kann nicht entschieden werden, ob man hier von einem bereits traditionellen innerchristlichen Interpretationsproblem oder von einer aktuellen, aus der Auseinandersetzung mit den Juden entstanden Frage ausgehen muß. Sollte die Predigt allerdings wie der sie zitierende *Sermo maior de fide* aus einer Stadt wie Alexandrien stammen, die eine große jüdische Diasporagemeinde aufwies, wäre letzteres ohne weiteres vorstellbar.

3. *Gottes Wahrheit-Sein*

Philosophisch und theologisch aufschlußreich ist die Analyse dessen, wie der pseudo—athanasianische Autor das Problem der Vereinbarkeit von Vorherverkündigung des Leidens Jesu und Schuld der Juden löst. Er macht dazu zwei Schritte: Kap. 1-7 erörtern zunächst grundsätzlich Gott als die Wahrheit, Kap. 8-10 wenden dann deren Erkenntnisse auf den Fall der Juden an. Da sich der Prediger Paulus als erste Autorität erwählt hat (1-185 C: 'es genügt auch allein der Apostel'), knüpft er an

---

[15] Vers 544 Perler: ὅτι ἔδει αὐτὸν παθεῖν. Vers 529 Hall entscheidet sich allerdings für die Lesart: ὅτι ἔδει αὐτὸν ἀποθανεῖν.

[16] 95,2-3; 141,1. Vgl. O. Perler, *Méliton de Sardes, Sur la Pâque et fragments. Introduction, texte critique, traduction et notes* [SC 123] (Paris 1966), 178; S.G. Hall, *Melito of Sardis, On Pascha and Fragments. Texts and Translations* [OECT] (Oxford 1979), 41.

Hebräer 6.18 an 'es ist unmöglich, daß Gott lügt'. Diese Unmöglichkeit zur Lüge liege in der Natur Gottes begründet, ebenso wie die Lügenhaftigkeit des Menschen seiner Natur entspreche. Lüge als die Verkehrung des Wahren in sein Gegenteil setze nämlich logischerweise sowohl die Existenz der Lüge außerhalb der Wahrheit als auch Veränderung voraus. Nur ein veränderliches und teilbares Wesen könne also lügen. Veränderlich sein aber bedeute geschaffen sein, einmal vom Nichtsein zum Sein verändert worden zu sein, wie es *Römer* 4.17 ausdrücke: 'der das nicht Seiende zum Sein ruft'. (Dieses Zitat ist zwar in stringenter Logik nicht haltbar, weil es gleichsam schon dem Nicht-Seienden eine Existenz zuspricht, die dann verändert wird, kommt aber der Argumentation des Predigers entgegen.) Wenn also Gott ungeschaffen sei, sei er *per definitionem* auch unveränderlich, wie z. B. *Malachi* 3.6 bezeuge: 'Seht, seht, daß ich es bin und ich mich nicht geändert habe', und könne deswegen seiner Natur nach nicht lügen.

> "[2] Gott aber ist wahr, nicht als ob er nicht lügen würde; denn es gibt nichts Gegensätzliches zu ihm; auch nicht, wie ein Mensch einem anderen das Wahre bezeugt; denn er ist niemandem Rechenschaft schuldig; sondern wie einer, der die Wahrheit selbst schafft, existiert der Vater des Herrn, der spricht: 'Ich bin die Wahrheit' (*Johannes* 14.6)." [188 B]

Grundlage der Antwort des Predigers ist also die Unterscheidung zwischen der Wahrheit als *Sein* und der Wahrheit als *Tun*. Gott *ist* die Wahrheit und deswegen *tut* er sie notwendigerweise, wobei dieses Tun nicht in seiner Willensentscheidung begründet liegt, sondern in seinem Sein. Die Unmöglichkeit der Lüge widerspricht deswegen auch nicht dem Begriff der Allmacht Gottes. Gott *kann* selbstverständlich alles *tun*, da die Lüge aber in seinem Sein, das Wahrheit *ist*, nicht *existieren kann* (zumindest nicht gemäß dem aristotelischen Widerspruchsprinzip), ist sie in Gott und für Gott auch unmöglich. Der Prediger vermeidet mit diesem Wahrheitsbegriff aus dem Sein Gottes den Irrtum der Nominalisten, die die Frage, ob Gott lügen könne, aufgrund des Begriffs seiner Allmacht grundsätzlich bejahen mußten, weil sie Wahrheit und Lüge beide auf die Stufe der *Tätigkeiten*, nicht des *Seins* Gottes stellten.

Daß der Prediger bei all diesen Überlegungen durchaus nicht sein eigentliches Ziel aus den Augen verloren hat, erweist der kurze Zwischensatz:

> "[2] Denn es logen die Juden gegen den Heiland, und als sie vorgaben, das Gesetz zu halten, sprachen sie nicht die Wahrheit, sondern übertraten das Gesetz gegen den, der es gegeben hatte, und wirkten Tod

anstelle der Gnade für den Herrn. Sie wurden dann freilich verworfen, und den Tod, den sie lügnerisch gegen den Herrn geführt hatten, den zogen sie wahrhaft auf sich selbst herab." [188 BC]

4. *Der Eid*

Diese Bemerkung führt den Prediger zum abschreckenden Beispiel des Ananias und der Sapphira (*Apg* 5.1-11), die ihr Gott gegebenes Versprechen nicht halten wollten, ihn deshalb belogen und dafür mit dem Tode bestraft wurden. Damit beginnt nach den philosophisch-theologischen Überlegungen zu Gott als der Wahrheit deren moralisch-praktische Nutzanwendung: was ein Mensch Gott versprochen habe, gehöre nicht mehr ihm selbst, sondern Gott. Das einfache Wort des Christen müsse daher so zuverlässig wie ein Eid gelten, so daß kein Schwur mehr nötig sei:

> "[5] Was muß man also tun? Nicht mehr, als daß unser Ja ein Ja sei und unser Nein ein Nein; und überhaupt nicht zu lügen. Denn indem wir so die Wahrheit sagen, mögen wir auch darin den wahren Gott nachahmen." [192 CD]

Die Vielzahl der Worte, Bibelzitate und Beispiele, die der Prediger zu dieser Aussage anführt, dürfen hier beiseite stehen. Für den Gottesbegriff wichtig wird nämlich das Problem, das sich aus der Forderung ergibt, keinen Eid zu leisten, um die Wahrheit Gottes nachzuahmen. Denn mehrfach spricht die Bibel davon, daß Gott selbst schwöre:

> *Genesis* 22.16: "Ich schwöre bei mir selbst—Spruch Jahwes" (zu Abraham beim Opfer Isaaks).

> *Psalm* 88.50: "Wo sind deine Erbarmungen von alters her, o Herr, die du David zugeschworen hast in deiner Wahrheit?"

> *Psalm* 109.4: "Es schwor der Herr, und nicht wird es ihn reuen: Du bist Priester auf ewig nach der Ordnung Melchisedeks."

Auch dieses Problem löst der Prediger aufgrund des Wesens Gottes und des Eides. Der Eid setze voraus, daß der Mensch etwas Höheres, Heiligeres als sich selbst zum Zeugen der Wahrheit anrufe. Das sei bei Gott unmöglich, da es nichts Größeres als ihn gibt. Deswegen "schwöre" Gott bei sich selbst, was dann aber kein Eid genannt werden könne, weil dies die Definition des Eides nicht erfülle, sondern nur ein kräftigerer Ausdruck für die Wahrheit seiner Worte sein könne.

5. *Christus, die Wahrheit*

Danach schweift die Predigt auf den Fall Ninives ab, wo sich doch die Verheißung des Herrn scheinbar nicht erfüllt hat. Dabei hilft aber die Formulierung der LXX (*Jona* 3.4) ἔτι τρεῖς ἡμέραι καὶ Νινευῒ καταστρα-φήσεται, da καταστρέφειν 'zerstören', aber auch 'umwenden' heißen kann. Und 'umgewendet', d. h. bekehrt, hat sich die Stadt ja. Hier scheint der Prediger nun doch zu merken, daß er mit seinen Ausführungen vom eigentlichen Ziel weit abschweift und stellt schließlich die oben zitierten Frage nach dem Sinn seines Diskurses:

> "[8] Und was ist mir der Nutzen des vielen? Nichts gibt es, was Gott sagt und unerfüllt bleibt... Denn siehe, auch das, was vor langer Zeit vom Herrn gesagt wurde, ... sehen wir jetzt in den Evangelien erfüllt... Er selbst wurde die Erfüllung des Gesetzes und der Propheten." [197 B-D]

Diese christologische Aussage, daß in der Person Christi selbst die Erfüllung der Verheißungen erschienen ist, erschließt sich auf dem Hintergrund der ersten Überlegungen zum Sein Gottes als der Wahrheit, die er mit seinem Sohn gemeinsam ist, so daß dieser sagen kann 'Ich bin die Wahrheit' (*Johannes* 14.6). Christus erfüllt nämlich nicht nur durch sein *Tun* die atl. Typoi und Prophetien, sondern notwendigerweise durch sein *Sein*. Denn derselbe Gott, der in seinen Prophetien aufgrund seiner Natur unmöglich lügt, macht in seiner Person, das heißt aufgrund seiner unwandelbaren und deswegen wahrhaftigen Natur seine Worte wahr—wobei das Wort wahr'machen' bereits irreführen kann, weil Christus die Wahrheit in Person *ist*. Er läßt durch seine Menschwerdung die Wahrheit der Prophetien erscheinen.

> "[8] Er selbst wurde die Erfüllung des Gesetzes und der Propheten. Denn was er durch sie vorherverkündet hatte, das vollbrachte er selbst in seiner Gegenwart, indem er erfüllte und sprach: 'Ich, derselbe, der gesprochen hat, bin gegenwärtig' (*Jesaja*. 52.6)." [197 CD]

Deswegen erfülle sich die Verkündigung Emmanuels durch *Jesaja* 7.14 in der Geburt Jesu aus der Jungfrau Maria, die Prophetie seines Geburts-ortes bei *Micha* 5.1 durch seine Geburt in Bethlehem, das Wort des *Zacharias* 9.9 über den auf dem Füllen einer Eselin reitenden Messias am Palmsonntag, *Psalm* 21.19 über die Teilung der Kleider und *Psalm* 68.22 über den Trunk von Essig mit Galle am Kreuz. Damit ist der Prediger zur Passionsgeschichte zurückgekehrt und zu den Juden, die durch die Kreu-zigung Christi die Prophetien wahrmachten, d. h. zu der problematischen

Formulierung des Evangeliums 'Das geschah, damit die Schrift erfüllt
werde', wodurch die Juden scheinbar entschuldigt werden.

Die nun folgende Lösung dieser Frage zeigt allerdings, wie, trotz aller Langatmigkeit und vielen Abschweifungen, zielgerichtet die Ausführungen über Gott als die Wahrheit und die daraus resultierende not-
wendige Erfüllung seiner Prophetien in der Person Jesu Christi waren.
Denn aufgrund dieses Konzeptes sind die Juden gar nicht ursächlich an
der Erfüllung der Prophetien beteiligt. Die Prophetien des AT und
Christus korrespondieren miteinander aufgrund ihrer Identität der
Wahrheit. Das Verhalten der Juden ist aber gerade nicht von den Prophetien motiviert. Sie kreuzigten Jesus, weil sie nicht an seine Got-
tessohnschaft und Sendung als Messias glauben. Ihre Handlungsmotive
sind ihr Wille zum Bösen, nicht der Gehorsam gegenüber Gott und seinen wahren Prophezeiungen. Deswegen tun die Juden lediglich, was
Gott als wahr vorausgesehen hat, ohne Glied der Wahrheitskette zu sein.
Denn das Böse als dem Göttlichen völlig fremd kann nicht zu dieser
ursächlichen Abfolge der Wahrheit gehören. Die Formulierung der
Evangelien 'Das geschah, damit die Schrift erfüllt werde' bedeutet daher nicht 'Die Juden handelten mit dem Ziel, die Schrift zu erfüllen',
sondern die Wahrheit Gottes handelte sowohl im AT als auch in Christus und erfüllte so die Schrift.

Resüme

Der erste Teil der hier besprochenen pseudo-athanasianischen Osterpredigt beantwortet also die Frage, was die Formulierung des Evangeliums
bedeuten soll 'Das geschah, damit die Schrift erfüllt werde' (*Matthäus*
27.36), woraus man schließen könnte, daß die Juden nicht nur notwendigerweise und deswegen ohne Schuld auf sich zu laden Christus
kreuzigten, sondern sogar noch dafür als Vollbringer des göttlichen
Willens gelobt werden müßten (ohne daß der Stellenwert dieser Frage in
der angesprochenen Gemeinde bestimmt werden kann). Der Prediger
holt dazu weit—und für eine klare und straffe Darstellung zu weit—aus,
insbesondere bei der Erörterung der Erlaubtheit des Eides (wobei man
gerade hier fragen dürfte, ob dieses Thema nicht ebenfalls von der
aktuellen Situation der Gemeinde veranlaßt ist).

Seine philosophisch und theologisch originelle und tiefe Prämisse:
Gott *ist* seiner Natur nach Wahrheit und handelt deswegen nur wahr.
Dieser Gott, diese Wahrheit wird in Christus Mensch und erfüllt so sei-

nem *Sein,* nicht nur seinem *Tun* nach das, was von Gott als wahr vorbereitet und vorherverkündet worden war. In dieser Wahrheitskette haben die Juden als Lügner und Übeltäter keinen Platz, weil dies dem Wesen der Wahrheit Gottes widersprechen würde. Ihre Motivation steht außerhalb der Abfolge Verkündigung-Erfüllung, ja ist ihr geradezu entgegengesetzt, wie das Böse dem Guten. Und deswegen ist auch ihr Verhalten nicht zu entschuldigen.

AUGUSTINE'S PARADOXES

GILLIAN R. EVANS

The writings of Augustine of Hippo are shot through with paradoxes. Some are incidental to an argument and serve the purpose of capturing attention. But several form the girders of a system of thought which will stand up only if they can be accepted as expressions of inherently contradictory yet somehow simultaneous truths. There can be no question but that Augustine knew what he was doing in using them. Some of his paradoxes, and his devices for resolving them, were innovatory. Nevertheless, he was drawing on a good deal of tradition, too, and we must look at that first.

Very broadly, the late antique conception of paradox contained two elements. They were *admirabilia* and they were *contra opinionem*, as Cicero puts it.[1] They are striking and can therefore be used to rhetorical effect. And they make assertions which, on first hearing at least, defy acceptance. The user may place more stress on one or the other feature. That is to say, he may primarily intend to make the reader or listener wonder, or he may chiefly mean to make him think. The paradox as a figure of thought[2] was familiar to Augustine in Scripture, through Cicero, through Zeno and Socrates, and perhaps to some degree through Aristotle's logic; though in the case of the Greeks the directness of his acquaintance may be in question. Jesus' teaching contained many paradoxes. The Kingdom is here already, yet it is to come; it is both within and outside us; it comes both gradually and suddenly. He who would save his life must lose it (*Matthew* 16.25); to him that has shall be given (*Matthew* 25.29); he who abases himself shall be exalted (*Luke* 14.11). Paul, too, bristles with paradoxical notions of sovereignty and freedom; law and grace; living through dying; strength through weakness; foolishness and wisdom.

---

[1] Cicero, *Paradoxa Stoicorum*, ed. J.Molager (Paris 1971), 55: *quae quia sunt admirabilia contraque opinionem (ab ipsis etiam paradoxa appellantur).* See also, E.B. Keller, *Some Paradoxes of Paul* (New York 1974), 8 ff.

[2] *Rhetorica ad Herennium*, ed. H. Caplan (London 1954), IV.xiii.18.

Augustine approaches such Biblical paradoxes with a view to explaining them, so that readers may see the truth they state and at the same time not be puzzled or disturbed in their faith by its form. In writing on the Sermon on the Mount, for example, he discusses 'Thy Kingdom Come'. He explains that even though it is in a sense not yet present on earth, the Kingdom may be said to have 'come' already in that it has been revealed. Thus it is both here and not here.[3] Earlier in the same study he explains the apparent contradiction between the instruction that no man should put away his wife (except for fornication), and: ' if any man come to me and hate not his father and mother and wife and children and brethren and sisters ... he cannot be my disciple' (*Luke 14.26*). By way of the explanation that in heaven there will be no such temporal relationships; and an account of the sexual relation between husband and wife which sees it as an unfortunate temporary necessity, he comes to a crucial distinction between that which is 'corruptible and mortal' in relationships in this life, and that which involves a love for the human essentials which will survive into heaven.[4] 'Blessed are ye when men shall revile you and persecute you' is, like much in the Sermon on the Mount, not merely an intellectual puzzle but a moral challenge, and Augustine responds to it accordingly by presenting an understanding which will make it possible for the reader not only to grasp it intellectually, but also to accept it emotionally and spiritually. The blessedness is within; the revilings strike only the outside of the recipient, and so they cannot diminish the blessedness.[5] Of a similar sort is the paradox of Christ the servant promising freedom to all who believe in him (*John 8.31-6*). It disturbs with its implication that this will not be an uncomplicated freedom. Again Augustine treats it, this time in the *Tractates* on John, in a way which helps acceptance as well as insight.[6]

Setting aside Zeno's mathematical and physical paradoxes, we are left with a body of classical paradox literature whose possible influence on Augustine's handling of theological paradoxes we must now briefly assess. The Socratic principles:[7] that virtue is knowledge, understanding

---

[3] Augustine, *De Sermone Domini in Monte*, [= *DSDM*] ed. A. Mutzenbecher, [CChr.SL 35] (Turnhout 1967), II.vi.20.

[4] *DSDM* I.xiv.39-40.

[5] *DSDM* I.iii.10-13.

[6] *In Johannis Evangelium Tractatus* CXXIV, ed. D.R.Willems [CChr.SL 36] (Turnhout 1954), 42.1.

[7] E.R.Dodds, *The Greeks and the Irrational* (Berkeley and Los Angeles 1951); M.J.O'Brien, *The Socratic Paradoxes and the Greek Mind* (North Carolina 1967).

and goodness separable; and that 'no one does wrong on purpose', with all its implications for Augustine's theology of the broken will, form lynch-pins of Augustine's system. But they do so not by way of direct adoption, but as a consequence of his absorption of the world of thought in which they were formed. Of Cicero's *Paradoxa Stoicorum* there is no direct evidence that Augustine had first-hand knowledge,[8] but a number of the sentiments expressed there appear in the *Academica* and the *Lucullus*, and were to some degree Stoic commonplaces. If we can think he knew the *Paradoxa* itself, he would have found there the ideas that: *quod honestum sit id solum bonum esse; in quo virtus sit ei nihil deese ad beate vivendum; aequalia esse peccata et recte facta; omnes stultos insanire; solus sapiens dives,*[9] and confirmation of the principle that a paradox is both that which causes wonder (*admirabile*) and that which goes against, or appears to go against, reasonable opinion (*contra opinionem*).[10] Cicero's paradoxes are both moral rules and metaphysical assertions, along lines which are certainly echoed in Augustine, and sometimes very closely. Equally tantalising is the possibility that Augustine had some acquaintance with the logical tradition in the closely-related area of sophistries. Aristotle treats the subject not only in the *Sophistici Elenchi*, but also, briefly, in the *De Interpretatione*.[11]

Boethius developed the implications of this particular passage at some length, using principles to be found in Greek commentary literature.[12] He produced a list of six ways in which the opposition of propositions is frustrated by a fallacy, most of which, as we shall see, Augustine himself understood and used in his explanations of paradoxes. Boethius notes equivocation, where a term is used in two different senses in a contradiction. *Cato fortis est* [physically;] *Cato non fortis est* [mentally], may both be true, although on the face of it they appear irreconcilable. The second possibility involves univocation. In *homo ambulat*, 'man' may be an individual or the human race, and so the statement may be both true and not true. *Oculus albus est* is both true (with reference to the white of the eye) and not true (with reference to another part). As well as difference of 'part' there may be difference of relation,

---

[8] H. Hagendahl, *Augustine and the Latin Classics*, 2 vols. (Gottenberg 1967), finds no direct reference to Cicero's *Paradoxa Stoicorum* in Augustine.

[9] *DSDM* 55.

[10] *DSDM* 3.

[11] *Perihermeneias*, 6.17a.34-7.

[12] On the history of the treatment of this passage after Boethius, see L.M.de Rijk, *Logica Modernorum*, 1 (Assen 1961), 24 ff.

time, or mode (for example 'potential' and 'actual').[13] It would be too much to suggest that Augustine was deliberately following formal logicians' procedures, but it seems entirely likely that a broad understanding of the ways in which paradoxes may be tested to see whether they are simply fallacies was commonplace equipment of the rhetorician.

In this area we are on secure ground. Augustine was every inch a professional in the matter of rhetoric. He was also gifted by nature with a mind which took delight in the striking patterns which may be made with language and logic. The *Rhetorica ad Herennium* sees paradox as a two-edged implement. It may involve foul practice, 'when either an honest thing is attacked or something unworthy is defended.'[14] Or it may be an antithesis, 'made up of contraries' or a *contrarium* supporting two contrary views.[15] The philosophical difficulties are not explored far in the rhetorical tradition. The emphasis is chiefly upon the effects which are to be achieved by the juxtaposition of figure of thought and figure of diction. Augustine's prose affords many examples of paradoxical notions made more striking by a play on words or a repetition or a cadence. To take a few instances from the *Confessions*:

> summus enim es et non mutaris, neque peragitur in te hodiernus dies, et tamen in te peragitur, quia in te sunt et ista omnia.[16]

> ad satiandas insatiabiles cupiditates copiosae inopiae et ignominiosae gloriae.[17]

> recolens vias meas nequissimas in amaritudine recogitationis meae, ut tu dulcescas mihi, dulcedo non fallax, dulcedo felix et secura.[18]

> non enim longe est a nobis omnipotentia tua, etiam cum longe sumus a te.[19]

Neque peragitur... et tamen peragitur; in te ... in te, in the first; *satiandas insatiabiles ... copiosae inopiae*, in the second; the bitterness of recollection leading to sweetness in the third; the puzzle of the way in which God may not be far from us although we are far from him, in the last: all demonstrate a consummate rhetorical skill and a delicate

---

[13] *Logica Modernorum*, 27 ff.
[14] *Ad Herennium*, I.iii.5.
[15] *Ad Herennium*, IV.xiii.21,25.
[16] *Confessiones*, [= *conf.*] ed. L. Verheijen, [CChr.SL 27] (Turnhout 1981), I.vi.9.
[17] *conf.* I.xii.19.
[18] *conf.* II.i.1.
[19] *conf.* II.ii.3.

sensitivity to the difference between a paradox which needs to be explained and a paradox which is to be enjoyed and indeed made more
mysterious by the way it is presented. The essence of such rhetorical
paradoxes is that they stimulate wonder. They are designed to prompt
the reader or listener to worship, to cause him to give glory to God.

That does not imply that Augustine did not sometimes see such paradoxes as requiring elucidation even when they could be classified as
also having a rhetorical complexion or dimension. We have glanced already at his handling of some of Scripture's paradoxes in this spirit. He
attacks the whole question of their rhetorical function at length in the *De
Doctrina Christiana*. There we find him setting out more or less com-
monsense rules for reading what appear to be contradictions and ambi-
guities in Scripture's treatment. These are frequently paradoxical in appearance. In the case of proper terms, there should be no ambiguity
which cannot be got round by examining the context, asking what was
the writer's intention, comparing translations, referring to the original
language.[20] Most problems arise, Augustine argues, from confusion of
literal with metaphorical senses. [21] It is important never to take a figurative expression literally.[22] If a passage seems to ascribe severity to
God or the saints, the test is to ask whether it is intended to overthrow
the dominion of inordinate desire. If so, it is to be taken literally, otherwise, figuratively.[23] On the other hand, any text which imputes seemingly wrong actions to God or the saints must be taken to be entirely figurative.[24] The reader should seek systematically for an interpretation
which establishes or fosters the rule of love in the world.[25] Any command or prohibition which seems to urge violence or wrongdoing must
be read figuratively.[26] Some commands do not apply to everyone.[27]
Some do not apply at all times.[28] It may even be that the same word does
not have the same signification in different contexts. The word 'lion'
may refer to Christ (*Revelation* 5.5) or to Satan (*1 Peter* 5.8).[29] Augus-

---

[20] *De Doctrina Christiana*, [= *DDC*] ed. G.M.Green, [CSEL, 80] (Vienna 1963),
III.iv.8.
[21] *DDC* III.i.1.
[22] *DDC* III.v.9.
[23] *DDC* III.xi.17.
[24] *DDC* III.xii.18.
[25] *DDC* III.xv.23.
[26] *DDC* III.xvi.24.
[27] *DDC* III.xvii.25.
[28] *DDC* III.xviii.25.
[29] *DDC* III.xxv.35.

tine comes down squarely in favour of the application of rhetoric to exegesis, both as an interpretative tool (where knowledge of the standard rhetorical tropes is valuable)[30] and as a source of devices to be used by the Christian preacher and author himself.[31] It can even be argued that the *Rules* of Tichonius the Donatist which Augustine introduces with approval are in part rhetorically conceived.[32]

Before we leave the question of sources of Augustine's notion of paradoxes, we ought to consider the great paradoxes of Tertullian's *De Carne Christi*. Tertullian was himself a superb rhetorician.[33] In his *De Carne Christi* he attacks the accusations of various heretics that it would be *stultus* to believe in the literal nativity of Christ and his truly becoming man.[34] Such *stulta* may be seen as the other face of *admirabilia*. They challenge belief in a similar way, and Tertullian goes on to present several paradoxes on this basis: *credibile est quia ineptum est; non pudet quia pudendum es; certum est quia impossibile.*[35] The first and last of these are epistemologically particularly interesting. Belief is balanced against absurdity; certitude against impossibility.

The paradoxes of Augustine's own maturity serve three broad purposes in his writings. There continued to be a place for those which are primarily rhetorical, that is, intended chiefly to startle and compel interest: 'my confession is silent ... but in love it cries aloud';[36] 'why do people demand to hear me confess what I am when they refuse to hear from you what they are?' '[37] 'They are your servants, my brothers, who by your will are your sons and my masters';[38] 'let me confess what I do not know of myself';[39] 'your works praise you that we may love you, and we love you that your works may praise you';[40] 'the recalling of my wicked ways is bitter in my memory, but I do it so that you may be

---

[30] *DDC* III.xix.40.

[31] *DDC* III.vi.9.

[32] *DDC* III.xxx.42 ff. See, too, P.Bright, *The Book of Rules of Tichonius: its purpose and inner logic* (Notre Dame 1988).

[33] R.D. Sider, *Rhetoric and the Art of Tertullian* (Oxford 1971).

[34] Tertullian, *De Carne Christi*, ed. J.P.Mahé (Paris 1975), I.

[35] *Ibid* IV.

[36] *conf.* X.2.2. I have used here and following the English translation of H. Chadwick (Oxford 1990).

[37] *conf.* X.3.3.

[38] *conf.* X.3.3.

[39] *conf.* X.5.7.

[40] *conf.* .XII.33.48.

sweet to me.'[41] There are metaphysical and epistemological puzzles in theology. How can the mind understand or grasp itself? Can it be big enough to encompass itself?[42] The memory retains not only memories but forgetfulness.[43] All desire the happy life they have not known. But if they have not known it, how have they known about it so as to want it?[44] Where is God to be found so that he may be learned about except in the fact that he is beyond us?[45] 'You were with me and I was not with you', Augustine cries of his unregenerate days.[46] These are mysteries which Augustine sometimes pauses to explore, as he does most extensively in the case of the paradoxes about time with which he deals in Book XI of the *Confessions*.

The third large class of paradoxes of Augustine's later years arose as he developed a system of doctrine. Justice requires the condemnation of all sinners, mercy their forgiveness. God could therefore neither condemn all men, or save them all, he concludes in the *De Civitate Dei*.[47] But he is still left with the underlying question whether God can do certain things and still be himself. Throughout his later writings he wrestles with the paradox of a Church which is both holy and full of sinners; a body of the elect known only to God and a body of members visibly identifiable by baptism. We shall come to these and other great paradoxes of Augustine's system later.

First we need to consider more closely the modes of Augustine's attempted resolution of the paradox. Some he addresses by means already relatively well-tested in the tradition, and often along lines to be laid out in Boethius' account of the handling of sophistical arguments. There is, for example, the resort to the distinction of times. An impossibility ceases to be so if we can show that time is irrelevant. That is the case for the saints who are justified by faith even though they lived before the coming of Christ; they had faith in the mystery of the incarnation which was as yet unseen.[48] In St. John's Gospel John the Baptist says 'I knew him not', but that contradicts the other Gospel account.[49] Augustine explains that the two contradictory statements refer to dif-

---

[41] *conf.* II.1.1.
[42] *conf.* X.9.15.
[43] *conf.* X.15.23.
[44] *conf.* X.20.29.
[45] *conf.* X.26.37.
[46] *conf.* X.27.38.
[47] *De civitate Dei* , [= *DCD*] [CChr.SL 47-8] (Turnhout 1955), XXI.11.
[48] *DCD* X.xxv.
[49] *John* 1.31,33-4; *Matthew* 3.14.

ferent times. When Mary visited Elisabeth John leapt in his mother's womb, and so he certainly knew Christ then; but he could also be said not to know him until he baptised him, for then there was a direct revelation that he was the Son of God.[50] There is also an attempt to use the devices of 'container and contained' or 'whole and part' in a discussion of 'He who sent me is true'. The Son is truth. Can it be that there is an inequality here? No, says Augustine, the Father is not true because he contained a part of the truth, but because he begat the whole Truth.[51] There can be a difference of *relatum*. *Romans* 6.20,22 contains the paradox that the Christian is free because he is God's servant. The freedom is in relation to sin, the service in relation to righteousness.[52] Causation may be seen to run in two opposing directions, as in the assertion that Adam did not love Eve because she was beautiful. She was beautiful because he loved her. Rather similar is the treatment of the notion that Satan did not abide in the truth because the truth was not in him.[53]

Then there is a group of methods of resolving paradoxes which play on deceiving appearance, contradictory expectations and internal inconsistencies, that is, upon the affront to reasonableness. Augustine can use the accusation of internal inconsistency as a ground for condemnation, as he does in the case of Varro's theological doctrine.[54] Deceiving appearances are rife. Demons who were created as purely rational beings are full of turbulent passions, no longer bridled by their reasons; they are not what they seem.[55] Some of the wicked wear the 'badge' of the sacraments and appear to be members of the Church although they are not.[56] The philosophers of this world call themselves lovers of wisdom, for that is how they get their name; but although they seem to defend wisdom, they are really its enemies, for they continue to recommend noxious superstitions.[57] Such persons are all living paradoxes. Closely linked to these are cases which raise contradictory expectations. Men, although they are mortal, can hope to enjoy true blessedness.[58] Angels, although

---

[50] *De Consensu Evangelistarum*, ed. F.Weihrich [CSEL 43] (Vienna 1904), II.xvi.32.

[51] *In Johannis Evangelium Tractatus CXXIV*, 39.7.

[52] *In Johannis Evangelium Tractatus CXXIV*, 41.8.

[53] *DCD* XI.xiv.

[54] *DCD* VII.xxviii.

[55] *DCD* IX.xi.

[56] *DCD* I.xxxv.

[57] *Enarrationes in Psalmos*, ed. E. Dekkers and J. Fraipont, [CChr.SL 38-30] (Turnhout 1956), VIII.6.

[58] *DCD* IX.xiv.

created for bliss, proved able to fall.[59] The gods of the pagans demand worship, but on grounds (of their criminal actions), which in themselves prove them to be unworthy of worship.[60] Augustine's method in such instances is to reveal the deception or make the contradiction explicit so that the Christian reader will not be fooled.

It may be the case that both of two apparently contradictory things or statements are true, and here we shall find, Augustine shows, either that the same word is being used in two different ways, or that God has intervened to make what seems impossible the case. In a letter to Memor of 409 Augustine says that he is bent under the load of the high honour Memor places upon him by writing, but at the same time he is raised up by his love. He elaborates. It is not by an ordinary man that he is thus raised, and made to stand erect, but by a man who is a priest of God, and so accepted by God that when he raises his own heart to God, with Augustine in it, he raises Augustine with him.[61] Augustine points to equivocation, univocation and a variety of 'modes of speaking' (*usus loquendi*) in such contexts. To take an example of each, 'I have chosen you out of the world' (*John* 15.19), says John's Gospel. Augustine makes play with *mundus*. 'If the world (*mundus*) gives you pleasure, your desire is always to be unclean (*immundus*). But if the world no longer delights you you are already clean (*mundus*)'.[62] Luke says that Herod was Tetrarch of Galilee when Jesus was baptised (*Luke* 3.1-21); Matthew says that Herod died before the baby Jesus returned from Egypt. 'These two answers cannot both be true unless we may also suppose that there were two different Herods,' Augustine observes.[63] For *usus loquendi* and *modus loquendi* dozens of instances suggest themselves, for this was a favourite preoccupation of Augustine's. A characteristic case is the puzzle of the apparent conflict between *Matthew* 8.5-13, which describes how the centurion came to Jesus on behalf of his servant, and *Luke* 7.1-10, which says that the centurion sent to Jesus on his servant's behalf. Augustine argues that 'came' is a mode of speaking, a figure of speech for approaching through another person, and that the centurion did not come in person.[64] Such scrutiny of words and their behaviour is normally designed to eliminate

---

[59] *DCD* XI.xi.

[60] *DCD* II.xiii.

[61] Letter 101, PL 33.367-9.

[62] *In Johannis Evangelium Tractatus*, 38.6.

[63] *De Consensu Evangelistarum*, II.viii.20.

[64] *De Consensu Evangelistarum*, II.xx.48-9.

the paradox by explaining one of its opposing elements in such a way that it does not contradict the other.

Augustine sometimes resorts to the explanation that both must stand, but that they may do so because God has acted directly to make it possible. God can bend the rules of nature and what appear to limited human understanding to be the rules of reason, or of right conduct. Samson brought his own death upon himself. But his act of self-destruction was divinely sanctioned. Virgins have cast themselves into rivers where they kew they would be drowned, and thus committed suicide, yet some of them are deemed martyrs by the Church. That is right, because they did it to escape violation. 'When God enjoins any action, and makes it plain that it is his will, who will say that obedience is wrong?' Augustine asks.[65] But there must be clear evidence that this is a special case, for if it were not so, others would be tempted to break the rules too. It would be sensible for everyone to kill himself as soon as he was baptised. So the paradoxical actions of the virgins and of Samson remain paradoxical except in the light of the exceptional divine dispensation which is able to make them right in God's eyes. Man's fallen nature is a paradoxical breach of natural order the other way. Created faultless and sinless, man now retains life, sense, intellect, but lacks through his own fault illumination and healing. He has ceased to be his natural self.[66] Miracles are paradoxes in nature sanctioned by God, as Augustine shows in his discussion of the manna in the wilderness and other cases.[67] The great paradox represented by God's encompassing the impossible and receiving the sinner in justice as well as in mercy stands out in this category.

Augustine also recognises paradoxes of moral dilemma. The suicidal virgin who dies to save her virtue appears again here. She is clearly in a moral dilemma. If she kills herself she commits a sin in order to avoid another, the possible pleasure she may involuntarily experience when she is raped. If she does not kill herself, she must be seen as avoiding a certain sin but at the same time allowing another equally certain sin to be perpetrated against her by another.[68] There are paradoxical moral saws, too. 'In most cases we serve others best by not giving, and would injure them by giving, what they desire.' Augustine quotes the proverb about not putting a sword in the hand of a child.[69]

---

[65] *DCD* I.xxvi-xxvii.
[66] *De Natura et Gratia*, iii.3.
[67] *DCD* X.viii.
[68] *DCD* I.xvii.
[69] Letter 104, To Nectarius, PL 33.388-91.

All these, testing though they are, are ultimately not serious problems for Augustine, because he can see his way round them, and they can be more or less satisfactorily resolved within his system. But a series of grave paradoxes are never fully resolved by him. Wicked men do many things which are against God's will. But they cannot really be against the will of an omnipotent God. So Augustine argues that they are taken up into his purposes and in fact tend towards the good ends and issues he has foreordained.[70] A string of difficulties follows. God's saints, who will his will, often prove to desire things which never happen. They may, for example, pray at his prompting for those whom God does not in fact deliver. Here we must understand, Augustine says, that God wills that they should thus will, but not the outcome for which they will, and that it is by a figure of speech that we say 'God wills' when we mean that he wills in them.[71] Here Augustine is entering, as he sees, the area of difficulty which arises in connection with divine foreknowledge and predestination: that an omnipotent God has, as it were, always already had his will. So if we say, 'it will happen if God wills', we do not mean that there is any doubt about the outcome, but only that we ourselves are ignorant of it.[72] Elegant though these devices for sidestepping the confrontation may be, Augustine never succeeds in explaining the ultimate paradox of the presence and effectiveness of the will for evil in God's world. He even asks how free will can persist in heaven, when it will be impossible to opt for sin. He points out that God is the ultimate standard of free will, and he is not able to sin, and that we therefore cannot hold that true freedom consists in the power to do evil.[73]

It was in his controversies with Donatists, Pelagians and Manichees that Augustine was forced into such unresolved paradoxical positions, because he was obliged by the exigencies of the situation to construct an account of things which denied those points in his adversaries' positions which were separating them from the Church. The complex of issues about grace, predestination, divine foreknowledge and human free will proved inseparable from the mass of difficulties about the problem of evil, as the passage we have just looked at illustrates. Augustine is left with the imperative to assert that evil is both nothing, and at the same time a force so powerful that fallen humanity is helpless against it; with

---

[70] *DCD* XXII.2.
[71] *DCD* XXII.2.
[72] *DCD* XXII.2.
[73] *DCD* XXII.30.

the need to insist that God both predetermines human destinies and respects his creatures as free beings who love him because they want to. A little apart stand the ecclesiological paradoxes engendered by the controversy with the Donatists. It is these I should like to look at briefly in conclusion.

It was the Donatists' view that the true Church is a garden sealed, a *hortus conclusus*. They drew their interpretation of this image and its fellows—the seamless garment; Noah's Ark; the enclosing net in the sea of the world; the sealed spring or well—in part from Cyprian's account of them.[74] These images have in common the notion of a Church which one must either be 'inside' or 'outside', and outside which it is impossible to 'drink' from the 'fountain' of the sacraments.[75] Within, all is shining holiness; outside, the darkness of sin.[76] Like Noah's Ark, the Church saves only those within it, and is the only means of salvation for them.[77] It is the unique vessel of salvation, for Christ can have only one Bride.[78] It cannot be divided, for it is a seamless garment.[79] It cannot change or develop.[80] It has clear distinguishing marks, which Parmenian, the Donatist Bishop of Carthage, saw as dowries of Christ's Bride: the *cathedra* which is the seat of authority of the bishop, and a sign of the unity of which he is minister: three signs of true baptism, the angel who presides, the font and its seal (*sigillum*); the altar.[81] In short, the Donatist model of corruption in the Church is a tidy one, in which there are no blurred edges, no room for uncertainty as to the validity or efficacy of the sacraments, no difficulty in identifying the members of Christ's body.

It is also strong in its emphasis on human capacity to recognise and even to define the true Church; and perhaps somewhat 'pharisaical' in its self-confidence and its reliance on a notion of 'guarantee' in the matter of getting the parameters right. What Augustine was to put forward

---

[74] Cyprian's position is well described in J.-P. Brisson, *Autonomisme et Christianisme dans l'Afrique romaine* (Paris 1958).

[75] Cyprian, Ep. lxxix.11, ed. G. Hartel [CSEL, 3] (Vienna 1868-71), 808.23.

[76] Brisson (*op. cit. n. 74*), 141.

[77] *Ibid* 145.

[78] Cf. Optatus, *De Schismate Donatistarum*, I.10, ed. C. Ziwsa [CSEL, 26] (Vienna, 1896), 11; Augustine, *Contra Cresconium*, IV.lxiii.77, *Opera Contra Donatistas*, ed. M. Petschenig [CSEL, 51-52] (Vienna 1908-10), 52.576.14.

[79] Cyprian, *De Unitate Catholicae Ecclesiae*, 7 [CSEL, 216.9].

[80] Cf. Brisson (*op. cit. n. 74*), 129.

[81] Cf. W. Frend, *The Donatist Church* (Oxford 1952, rpt. 1971), and Optatus, *De Schismate Donatistarum*, I.10 ff., II-2.

was altogether untidier, but it placed the stress on God as the agent of salvation, working as he pleases within the Church and outside it. He could not accept the Donatist equating of holiness with separation; their contrasting of purity with treason.[82] Here he was departing not only from what was in fact a very ancient and Biblical idea of the Church as a body of Christ's people who ought to keep themselves unspotted from the world; he was also moving away from the position of his contemporary Ambrose of Milan, which had tended towards seeing the Church as a force in the world which will purify and transform, not setting itself apart but engaging with the world.

Augustine was attracted by the paradox of the view he found in the *Book of Rules* of the Donatist Tichonius (himself condemned within his own sect for the opinion). Tichonius read many contradictory statements in Scripture, where what appears to be the same thing is cursed in one place and blessed in another. *Isaiah* 45.3-4, for example, says that God will reveal himself; *Isaiah* 29.13, that he will not be recognised. Tichonius offers an explanation in terms of the bipartite nature of the Church which is signalled in the *Song of Songs* (1.5), 'I am dark and beautiful'. He saw in the Church the mystery of the bringing together in one body of saint and sinner.[83] Augustine became convinced that it would be presumption to try to separate the wheat from the chaff in the Church before God's own time came for doing so, for it is not given to man to know who is saved; and that therefore the Church must be understood not as a pure, but as a mixed body.[84]

This line of thought necessitates the embracing of a further paradox: if the visible Church is thus a mixed body of saints and sinners, that cannot be understood to be the case with the mystical and invisible body of those God alone knows to be his own. So we have both a 'true Church' which is 'impure' and a 'true Church' which is 'pure' and holy, existing one within the other in some ultimately perhaps indefinable relation.[85] So Augustine is left with the unresolved paradox that the 'true' Church is a mixed and partly impure community, and also pure and holy.

---

[82] Cf. Optatus, *De Schismate Donatistarum*, I.21 and Augustine, *Contra Litteras Petiliani*, I.xvii.18, [CSEL, 52], 14.

[83] Cf. P.Bright, *The Book of Rules of Tichonius; its purpose and inner logic* (Notre Dame 1988),.63 ff.

[84] Augustine, *Contra Epistulam Parmeniani*, I.vii.12 and I.ix.15, 31-5 ed. M. Petschenig [CSEL, 51] (Vienna 1908) . See too G. Bonner, 'The Church and the Eucharist in the Theology of St. Augustine', *Sobornost* 7 (1978), 448-61.

[85] P. Batiffol, *Le catholicisme de s. Augustin*, 2 vols. (2nd ed., Paris 1920), I, 266.

Augustine went a significant step further here. He was able to envisage a communion in parts, an interpenetration of the true Church
with that which is not the Church truly or fully. He argued in his book
on baptism against the Donatists that the Donatists are in communion
with the Catholic Church at all points where they are in agreement with
it; they are in schism at the points where they disagree. Individual Christians may be partly in schism (that is, in those points at which they differ
from the Catholic consensus), and partly in unity with the Catholic
Church (I.i.2). That means that the Donatists are not wholly out of communion with the Catholics, and for this reason too their baptism need
not therefore be regarded as invalid. 'In virtue of that which belongs to
the true Church in each of them', they may administer and participate in
the true sacraments (I.x.14).

Augustine also had a good deal to say about the ways in which the
Church may be both one and many, and about the manner of the communion of the many churches in the one. The primary idea that the one
Church is somehow the 'source' or 'origin' of the many, appears in
Cyprian. He uses the familiar images of the Trinity in a manner appropriately modified to make them apply to the Church. The sun emits many
rays, but it is one light; a tree has many branches, but one trunk standing
on a firm root; many streams flow from a single spring, where 'numer-
ousness' appears in the plenitude, but unity is preserved in the source.[86]
It was of the first importance to Cyprian that the Church's unity should
be seen in this way in its relation to and dependence upon the unity of
God. But there remains the substantive difference that whereas in God
the plurality of the Persons does not diminish or alter or add to the unity
of the Godhead, in the Church the model is that which is found in all
creation, of the many multiplying from the one. Yet of all creatures the
Church is unique in being united with God himself in Christ. Augustine
seeks to find a way to express this type of plurality which is unique to
the Church.

It had from the first been accepted that the one Church might be fully
the Church in each place.[87] The many local churches remained one

---

[86] Cyprian, *De Unitate Catholicae Ecclesiae*, 5, 213-4.

[87] That paradox of being fully one in many exemplifications was to be developed
strongly in the West in the Middle Ages in connection with the doctrine of tran-
substantiation. A number of authors of the eleventh and twelfth centuries stress the
fact that the same body of Christ *unum et idem numero* is present in every local
Eucharist. See *The Works of Gilbert Crispin*, ed. A.S.Abulafia and G.R.Evans (Oxford
1986), Index.

Church in this way, and no breach of communion was implied in their plurality. Nevertheless, there could be complicating factors of nationalism or tribalism or some other form of claim to regional identity and autonomy. There seems to be some such compounding sense in the case of the Donatists[88] and Augustine saw its dangers to communion. He argues instead for a view of plurality in communion which resolves the whole into, as it were, conceptual parts or elements, some of which may be maintained in communion even where others are not. This, as we have seen, enables him to say that a Christian is in unity and communion with the Catholic Church at some points even if not at others.[89] On the other hand, he would not consider such a Donatist or other heretic or schismatic to be 'in' the Church. The Church's claim to an autonomy which makes it somehow self-sufficient for salvation is, paradoxically for Augustine, precisely an indication that salvation is not to be found there.

He explains what he means with some care in a letter he wrote about the Donatist sect for his people, seeking to meet a pastoral need for a clear account of the difference between the Donatist position and their own.[90] The catholic Church is the whole Church (*secundum totum*). Members of Christ are joined to one another by the love of unity (*per unitatis caritatem*) and they are united because they belong to the same Head who is Christ Jesus. No one who is not a member of Christ in this way can have Christ's salvation.[91] Those who dissent from the Head, even if they appear to be the Church in every respect, are not in the Church. Those who hold everything Scripture says, but who do not communicate with the unity of the Church, are not in the Church. Those who are in some error of faith dissent in such a way that their communion is not with the whole Church everywhere, but with some separated part. It is clear that these are not in the catholic Church.[92] It is thus possible not to be in the Church, and so not to obtain salvation, by a breach of faith or of communion, and also by loyalty to a 'part' of the Church (*pars separata*) which identifies itself as a distinct ecclesial entity over against the universal Church. The weight of 'over against' is crucial here, for the ecclesial distinctness of churches not so identifying themselves is at war with their being in union with the universal Church. Au-

---

[88] Discussed by A.H.M.Jones,'Were ancient heresies national or social movements in disguise?' *Journal of Theological Studies* 10 (1959), 280-98.

[89] *De Baptismo contra Donatistas*, [= *DBCD*] I.i.2-ii.3, [CSEL, 51], 146 ff.

[90] *Epistola ad Catholicos de Secta Donatistarum* [= *ECSD*] ii.2, [CSEL, 52], 232.

[91] *ECSD* ii.2, 232.

[92] *ECSD* ii.2, iv.7, 238-9.

gustine develops the point in the *Contra Epistulam Parmeniani*. He stresses that the Christians in the local Church of Africa must see themselves as joined in unity with the Church spread throughout the world (*toto orbe diffusa*) 'by communion' (*per communionem*).[93] The Donatist position is ecclesially untenable, because it cannot sustain that principle.

The test of universality is thus crucial for Augustine. How can the Donatists be right when they stand against 'so many Churches throughout the world?' he asks.[94] In a correspondence on the question of catholicity with Honoratus, a local Donatist bishop in 398, he argues that while the Catholics can clearly claim to be in communion with the universal Church, the Donatists must hold to the unlikely view that Christ allowed his whole Church on earth to disappear, preserving it only in Donatism.[95] The Donatists also have to say that the prophecy of the universal Church has been fulfilled and no longer applies.[96] There must be extraordinary special pleading to sustain the Donatist case.

So we find Augustine putting himself in the paradoxical position of, on the one hand, making a case for partial communion or degrees of communion, and, on the other, maintaining that only in full communion within the one and universal Church can salvation be found. This contradictory position is at its most challenging in connection with baptism. Augustine thought the practice of rebaptism of those baptised outside the Catholic Church a greater threat to communion than the acceptance of such baptisms as valid (provided they had been administered in the name of the Trinity.) The emphasis here was upon the once-and-for all character of the forgiveness of baptism. We have seen that that seemed to Augustine wholly non-negotiable, and to be so clearly the act of God that it could safely be left to divine power to act even through unworthy or heretical or schismatic ministers, when his name was invoked for the purpose of baptism. The Church has its unity in Christ; its communion is with him; and so those baptised into his body are in some measure in communion with him, whatever the context and circumstances of their baptism.

The stress here is quite different from Tertullian's. He put purity first, and defined communion in the Church as consisting in the union of those purified. The true Church is without spot or wrinkle; no impure

---

[93] I.i.1, [CSEL, 51], 19-20.

[94] *Contra Epistulam Parmeniani* ed. M. Petschenig (Leipzig 1908)*ECSD* ii.2, I.ii.2, 20-1.

[95] See Batiffol (*op. cit. n. 85*),145 and *Contra Epistulam Parmeniani*, I.ii.3, p.22.

[96] *Ibid.*

person can have the Holy Spirit, and so it is impossible for an unworthy minister, or one not in the Church, to administer baptism at all,[97] for such a notion is nonsense. Baptism can therefore somehow persist validly wherever it is found, even outside the catholic Church.[98] In a similar way, the one God can be worshipped outside the Church, and the one faith held, by which we confess Christ to be the Son of God, the faith for which Peter was called blessed, even by those who are not in the Church.[99] Acts says as much (17.23).'He whom you have been worshipping without knowing it, I announce to you'.[100] The difference is that those who worship in ignorance and outside the Church, like those who are baptised outside the Church, act *inutiliter*, without profit, instead of *salubriter*, to their salvation.[101] Augustine, then, seeks to resolve his paradox by arguing that that which is real baptism or real faith or real worship, becomes efficacious for salvation only when it is within the one catholic Church. Those who join the Donatists, clearly understanding that they are becoming members of a sect which distinguishes itself from the catholic Church, do so aware that there must be some uncertainty about what they are doing, because they know that the Donatist position is a minority position. They therefore cannot join in full confidence of salvation.[102] But their faith, worship and sacraments are not entirely outside communion if it remains true that by returning to the Catholic fold the Donatists can obtain salvation without otherwise changing their position or actions.

It is unclear here exactly what Augustine deemed a Church-dividing issue other than the fact of the will to separate. He recognises the difficulty that views other than his own about baptism and communion have been held within the Catholic Church, 'in the unity of the Church itself', by those whose membership of the Body of Christ is not to be doubted.[103] This was manifest in Cyprian's time, when 'greater importance and praise were attached to unity' than to uniformity of opinion.[104] Difference of view on the question of rebaptism was not allowed to divide

---

[97] *De Pudicitia*, 18, PL 2.1069 and *De Baptismo* 8 and 15, ed. A.Reifferscheid and O.Wissowa [CSEL, 20] (1890).

[98] *De Baptismo* I.xiv.22,.

[99] *Contra Cresconium*, I.xxix.34, [CSEL, 52], 353.

[100] *Contra Cresconium*, I.xxix.34, [CSEL, 52], 353.

[101] *Contra Cresconium*, I.xxix.34, [CSEL, 52], 353.

[102] *DBCD* I.iv.5 ff.,.150.

[103] *DBCD* VII.i.1, 341 ff.

[104] *DBCD* V.vii.8, 268-9.

the Church then, and, as Augustine sees it, it is highly praiseworthy that Cyprian and his episcopal colleagues loved unity so deeply that they continued in unity and communion even with those they believed to be betraying the truth. And, significantly, they did not deem themselves polluted by them.[105] Here, again, there would seem to be an attempt to hold together a doctrine of degrees of communion or partial communion, with a strong assertion of the view that only within the single communion of the one Church can salvation be found.

Augustine certainly saw the force of the notion that some things may be permissible in an emergency situation which would otherwise be disorderly acts or provisions; he also clearly held that division in the Church constitutes the supreme emergency. In his book on the correction of the Donatists, he tells the story of two men together in a house which is falling down. The great need is to save the house. The opposition in his mind lies between those who 'create schism' and 'set altar against altar' and those who seek peace and unity,[106] as he himself tried in practice to do. For those with the *votum unitatis* some living with paradoxes will be necessary. The acceptance of Donatist baptism as valid, if not efficacious, is one of them; allowing that God may hold within his Church both those who are truly his own and those who will prove to be weeds at the harvest is another, with its concomitant acceptance that the Church in this world cannot be pure.

What, then, are we to say in sum about Augustine's paradoxes? First that he was not afraid of the paradoxical. His rhetorician's training and his natural liking for the startling and challenging encouraged him to enjoy the contemplation of intellectual impossibilities. Secondly we can say that while never profoundly original at a technical level in his resolutions of paradoxes, he is endlessly inventive in making them work for him theologically and homiletically. Their obstinate outlines greatly help to form his landscape. They are always there to be got round or to be placed in advantageous positions. And he left the legacy of a taste for such puzzles to a western Latin-speaking world whose temper of mind might otherwise have made less of them and been the duller for it throughout the Middle Ages.

---

[105] *DBCD* VII.iii.2, 343 ff.

[106] *Psalmus contra Partem Donati*, [CSEL 51], 3.14-7; *Contra Litteras Petiliani*. II.lxviii, 153 ff., [CSEL, 52], 99 and cf. Batiffol *(op. cit. n. 85)*, I, 137-8.

BASILIUS VON CAESAREA UND DAS *HOMOOUSIOS*

REINHARD M. HÜBNER

In diesem kleinen Beitrag geht es nicht darum, das schon so häufig be-
handelte Verständnis der trinitätstheologischen Begriffe *homoousios*
und *mia ousia* bei Basilius nochmals in extenso darzulegen.[1] Vielmehr
soll auf einige bisher unbeachtet gebliebene Widerspüche in der basilianischen Interpretation des *homoousios* hingewiesen und versucht werden, die Ursache dieser Widerspüche aufzuzeigen. Vorausgesetzt wird
dabei die Echtheit des Briefwechsels zwischen Basilius und Apolinarius
(*ep.* 361-364), die G. L.Prestige und vor allem H. de Riedmatten m.E.
überzeugend erwiesen haben.[2] Da Basilius das Wort *homoousios* ebenso

---

[1] Vgl. dazu A. M. Ritter, *Das Konzil von Konstantinopel und sein Symbol. Studien
zur Geschichte und Theologie des II. Ökumenischen Konzils* [FKDG 15] (Göttingen
1965), 270-293; R. Hübner, 'Gregor von Nyssa als Verfasser der sog. Ep. 38 des Basilius. Zum unterschiedlichen Verständnis der *ousia* bei den kappadozischen Brüdern',
in *Epektasis. Mélanges patristiques offerts au Cardinal Jean Daniélou*, publiés par J.
Fontaine et Ch. Kannengiesser (Paris 1972), 463-490; M. Simonetti, *La crisi ariana
nel IV secolo* [Studia Ephemeridis 'Augustinianum' 11] (Roma 1975), 401-434. 511-
525; F. Dinsen, *Homoousios. Die Geschichte des Begriffs bis zum Konzil von Konstantinopel* (381), Diss. theol. Kiel 1976, 155-167 (dieses Kapitel über das *homoousios* der Kappadozier bedeutet mit seiner undifferenzierten Behandlung der drei Theologen eher einen Rückschritt gegenüber einem bereits erreichten Forschungsstand); A.
M. Ritter, 'Zum Homousios von Nizäa und Konstantinopel. Kritische Nachlese zu
einigen neueren Diskussionen', *Kerygma und Logos. Festschrift Carl Andresen*, hg.
von A. M. Ritter (Göttingen 1979), 404-423; G. C. Stead, 'Individual Personality in
Origen and the Cappadocian Fathers' (1981), in Ders., *Substance and Illusion in the
Christian Fathers* (London 1985), XIII, 170-191; M. Simonetti, 'Genesi e sviluppo
della dottrina trinitaria di Basilio di Cesarea', *Basilio di Cesarea, la sua età, la sua
opera e il Basilianesimo in Sicilia*, Atti del congresso internazionale, Messina 3-6 XII
1979, vol. I (Messina 1983), 169-197; A. de Halleux, 'Personnalisme ou essentialisme
trinitaire chez les Pères cappadociens?', *Revue théologique de Louvain* 17 (1986),
129-155, bes. 144-148.

[2] G. L. Prestige, *St Basil the Great and Apollinaris of Laodicea* (London 1956);
H. de Riedmatten, 'La correspondance entre Basile de Césarée et Apollinaire de Lao-
dicée I, II', *Journal of Theological Studies* N.S. 7 (1956), 199-210 und 8 (1957) 53-
70; zustimmend: J. Gribomont, 'Esotérisme et Tradition dans le Traité du Saint-Esprit
de Saint Basile', *Oecumenica* 2 (1967), 22-56, hier 27[23]; E. Mühlenberg, *Apollinaris*

wie das Wort *theos* in keinem schriftlichen Zeugnis ausdrücklich für den Heiligen Geist verwendet,[3] geht es demnach hier ausschließlich um seine Deutung der Homouseität von Vater und Sohn.

Basilius kommt an vier Stellen seiner ersten beiden Bücher gegen Eunomius,[4] in einer Homilie[5] und in zwölf Briefen,[6] wenn ich mich nicht irre, also bei insgesamt siebzehn Gelegenheiten, auf das *homoousios* zu sprechen. Bei dieser Zahl ist nicht berücksichtigt, daß das Wort dabei mehrmals auftauchen kann. Mitgerechnet wurde hier *ep.* 140, in der das *homoousios* lediglich innerhalb des Zitats der *fides Nicaena* erscheint. Nicht mitgerechnet wurden die neun Briefe, in denen zwar der Glaube von Nicaea erwähnt wird, und zwar so, daß daraus die unbedingte Zustimmung des Basilius zu seinem integralen Wortlaut hervorgeht, das *homoousios* aber nicht ausdrücklich genannt wird.[7] Die letztgenannten Briefstellen (zuzüglich *ep.* 140) sind für die Erkenntnis der basilianischen Deutung des *homoousios* ohne Belang. Das gilt auch

---

von Laodicea, [FKDG 23] (Göttingen 1969), 3; Simonetti (*op. cit. n. 1*), 416[53], und viele andere; ablehnend aufgrund der (scheinbar entgegenstehenden) Autorität der Aussagen des Basilius: Y. Courtonne, *Un témoin du IVᵉ siècle oriental. Saint Basile et son temps d'après sa correspondance* (Paris 1973), 225. Zweifel an der Echtheit äußert P. J. Fedwick, 'A Chronology of the Life and Works of Basil of Caesarea', in: Ders. (Hg.), *Basil of Caesarea: Christian, Humanist, Ascetic. A Sixteen-Hundredth Anniversary Symposium I* (Toronto 1981) 6. Seine Bedenken habe ich auszuräumen versucht, siehe *Die Schrift des Apolinarius von Laodicea gegen Photin (Pseudo-Athanasius, contra Sabellianos) und Basilius von Caesarea* [PTS 30] (Berlin 1989), 198[8].

[3] Daß Basilius sich dagegen im Gespräch in diesem Punkte deutlich geäußert hat, bezeugt Gregor von Nazianz, *or.* 43,69 (PG 36,589 A-C); vgl. H. Dörries, *De Spiritu Sancto. Der Beitrag des Basilius zum Abschluß des trinitarischen Dogmas* [AAWG. PH 39] (Göttingen 1956), 23-28; B. Pruche, *Basile de Césarée. Sur le Saint-Esprit* [SChr 17 bis] (Paris 1968), 79-110. Nicht ursprünglich ist, wie J. Gribomont (*op. cit. n.2*), 37[69] mitteilt, das Wort *homoousios* (innerhalb der Formel βαπτίζομεν εἰς τριάδα ὁμοούσιον) in dem an Mönche gerichteten Glaubensbekenntnis des Basilius, *de fide* 4 (PG 31, 688A). In *ep.* 214.4,15-22 (II 205 f. Courtonne) bezieht jedoch Basilius das *homoousios* implizit auch auf die dritte göttliche Person, wenn er es als Ausdruck für die Einheit der Gottheit der Hypostasen von Vater, Sohn und Heiligem Geist nennt.

[4] Basil., *adv. Eunom.* I 20 (PG 29,556 C); II 4 (580 B); II 10 (589 A); II 19 (613 C).

[5] Basil., *hom.* 24.4, *c. Sabell., Arium et Anom.* (PG 31, 608A).

[6] Basil., *ep.* 9; 52; 90; 125; 140; 159; 214; 226; 236; 244; 263; 361.

[7] Basil., *ep.* 51.2; 91; 92.3; 113; 114; 128.2; 204.6; 258.2; 265.3. In den Briefen 52, 125, 140, 159, 214, 226, 244 ist von Nicaea und zugleich vom *homoousios* die Rede. Zum Rang des Konzils und Glaubens von Nicaea im Denken des Basilius siehe H. J. Sieben, *Die Konzilsidee der Alten Kirche* [Konziliengeschichte, hg. von W. Brandmüller, Reihe B, Untersuchungen] (Paderborn, München, Wien, Zürich 1979), 207-230 passim.

von den drei Briefen, in denen das nizänische Stichwort zwar in verschiedenem Zusammenhang fällt, aber nicht interpretiert wird.[8]

Diese relativ hohe Zahl von Textstellen allein zeigt schon, daß Basilius zu Recht als ein Verteidiger des Glaubens von Nicaea gilt. Dennoch ist, wenn man die Zeugnisse im einzelnen betrachtet, nicht zu übersehen, daß Basilius dem *homoousios* anfänglich zögernd, ja sogar mißtrauisch gegenüberstand und noch keinen rationalen Weg sah, es mit seinen trinitarischen Vorstellungen in Übereinstimmung zu bringen. Das ergibt sich jedenfalls aus seiner frühesten Stellungnahme, dem Brief 361 an Apolinarius, der, wie H. de Riedmatten glaubhaft gezeigt hat, aus der Zeit nach seinem verlegenen Rückzug vom Konzil von Konstantinopel (360) stammt.[9] In diesem Brief bittet Basilius den Apolinarius, den er wahrscheinlich im Jahre 357 während seiner Informationsreise durch die monastischen Zentren in Syrien kennengelernt hat,[10] um Auskunft über einen unanstößigen Gebrauch des Wortes *homoousios* in der Theologie. Da heißt es:

> Bislang haben wir mit Dir über die dunklen Stellen in der Schrift korrespondiert, und wir freuten uns über das, was Du zur Antwort schicktest und was Du verspraschst. Jetzt aber ist uns *eine noch größere gedankliche Schwierigkeit* (μείζων... ἡ φρόντις) *in noch größeren Dingen* aufgekommen, zu deren Lösung wir niemanden unter den Zeitgenossen haben, den wir als solchen Vertrauten und Führer anrufen könnten wie Dich, den uns Gott als einen Menschen geschenkt hat, der im Denken und Reden korrekt und zugleich leicht erreichbar ist.

---

[8] Basil., *ep.* 90.2; 244.7.9; 263.3.

[9] H. de Riedmatten (*op. cit. n.* 2), 59 f.; vgl. S. Giet, 'Saint Basile et le Concile de Constantinople de 360', *Journal of Theological Studies* N.S. 6 (1955), 94-99; L. R. Wickham, 'The Date of Eunomius' Apology: A Reconsideration', *Journal of Theological Studies* N.S. 20 (1969), 231-240, hier 235-237. Auch Th. A. Kopecek, *A History of Neo-Arianism II* (Cambridge, Mass. 1979), 362, entscheidet sich für die Zeit nach dem Konzil von Konstantinopel 360.

[10] Vgl. Basil., *ep.* 1,22 (I 4 Courtonne); *ep.* 223.2,20-23 (III 10 C.); hierzu J. Gribomont, 'Eustathe le Philosophe et les voyages du jeune Basile de Césarée', *Revue d'histoire ecclésiastique* 54 (1959), 115-124. Am Ende des Briefes 361 grüßt Basilius "die Brüder", d.h. Asketen, die mit Apolinarius zusammen sind, und erwähnt, daß Gregor (von Nazianz) sich bei seinen Eltern befindet (und nicht bei Basilius in der pontischen Einöde), setzt also voraus, daß Apolinarius auch über die asketischen Aspirationen des Gregor unterrichtet war: *ep.* 361,39-43 (III 222 Courtonne); *ep.* 363,1 (III 224 C.) redet Basilius den Apolinarius als "Bruder" an, ebenso wie Apolinarius in *ep.* 364,1 (III 225 C.) den Basilius. "Mönche (*monazontes*) des Bischofs Apolinarius" waren 362 auf dem Konzil in Alexandrien anwesend: Athan., *tom. ad Antioch.* 9 (PG 26,808 A).

Weil nun die, die alles durcheinanderrühren und die ganze Welt mit Diskussionen und Untersuchungen angefüllt haben, das Wort *ousia* verworfen haben, da es den göttlichen Worten fremd sei,[11] sei so gütig und zeige uns, wie es die Väter gebraucht haben und ob (auch) Du es nirgendwo in der Schrift gefunden hast. (…) Sodann gib uns doch bitte eine möglichst breite Erläuterung über das *homoousios* selbst (dessentwegen sie meines Erachtens dies alles ins Werk setzen und die *ousia* völlig verwerfen, damit für das *homoousios* nur ja kein Platz mehr bleibt): welche Bedeutung es hat und wie es in gesunder Weise von denen ausgesagt werden könnte, bei denen es weder ein gemeinsames übergeordnetes Genus gibt, noch ein zuvor vorhandenes stoffliches Substrat, noch eine Abtrennung des ersten in ein zweites. Also, auf welche Weise man den Sohn dem Vater *homoousios* nennen muß, ohne daß man auf eine der genannten Vorstellungen verfällt, setze uns bitte ausführlich auseinander.

Wir haben nämlich bisher folgende Auffassung vertreten: Als das, als was zum Beispiel die *ousia* des Vaters verstanden werde, müsse unbedingt auch die des Sohnes verstanden werden; wenn man folglich die *ousia* des Vaters als geistiges, ewiges, unerzeugtes Licht bezeichnet, wird man auch die *ousia* des Einziggeborenen als geistiges, ewiges, gezeugtes Licht bezeichnen. Für einen solchen Begriff scheint mir aber der Ausdruck 'unterschiedslos gleich' (ἡ τοῦ ἀπαραλλάκτως ὁμοίου φωνή) jedenfalls besser als der des *homoousios* zu passen. Denn da es zwischen 'Licht' und 'Licht' keinen Unterschied hinsichtlich eines Mehr und Minder gibt, beide gleichwohl nicht identisch sind, weil sich ein jedes von ihnen in einer eigenen Umschreibung der *ousia* befindet, wird man sie, glaube ich, wohl richtig als der *ousia* nach genau und unterschiedslos gleich bezeichnen.

Ob man also diese Begriffe in der Erörterung beibehalten soll, oder ob man an ihre Stelle andere und bessere setzen soll, das (entscheide) als ein weiser Arzt (habe ich Dir doch das enthüllt, was ich im Herzen trage), heile das Kranke, stärke das Schwache, stütze uns in jeder Weise! …[12]

---

[11] Im Bekenntnis des Konzils von Konstantinopel (360) heißt es (bei Athan., *de syn.* 30,8: II 259,12-16 Opitz): "Es wurde beschlossen, das Wort *ousia*, das von den Vätern in schlichtem Sinn benutzt wurde, dem Volk aber unbekannt war und deshalb Anstoß erregte, vor allem weil auch die Schrift es nicht enthält, zu beseitigen und es künftig überhaupt nicht mehr zu erwähnen, weil auch die göttlichen Schriften nirgends etwas von einer *ousia* des Vaters oder Sohnes verlauten lassen."

[12] Basil., *ep.* 361,2-13.15-39 (III 220-222 Courtonne). Eine kritische Edition des Briefwechsels hat auch H. de Riedmatten (*op. cit. n.2*), 202 ff. gegeben. Ich zitiere nach Courtonne, weil diese Ausgabe leichter zugänglich ist, und verweise nur bei Abweichungen auf de Riedmatten.

Zunächst ergibt sich aus diesem Brief, daß für Basilius sowohl der Vater
als auch der Sohn jeder eine mit dem anderen nicht identische *ousia* in
einer eigenen Umschreibung ist.[13] *Ousia* meint hier eindeutig das ein-
zelne konkrete Seiende oder Individuum, das Basilius auch als *hypostasis* bezeichnet. So hat auch Apolinarius in seiner Antwort den Basilius verstanden.[14] Vater und Sohn sind also zwei *ousiai* oder Hypostasen. Von einer Distinktion der beiden Begriffe *ousia* und *hypostasis*
und ebenso von der Formel 'eine einzige *ousia*—drei Hypostasen', die
ja die Distinktion voraussetzt, ist Basilius noch weit entfernt. Von diesem Standpunkt aus bedeutet für ihn die durch das Nicaenum auferlegte
Verpflichtung, Vater und Sohn *homoousios* zu nennen, eine unüber-
windliche Schwierigkeit.

Basilius sieht drei Möglichkeiten, eine Homouseität von zwei miteinander nicht identischen *ousiai* auszusagen, und alle diese drei Möglichkeiten scheiden nach seinem Urteil in der Theologie aus, weil sie
unweigerlich zu einem nicht mehr akzeptablen Gottesbegriff führen.
Man könne (erstens) die gemeinsame *ousia* (= das *homoousios*) von
Vater und Sohn nicht im Sinn eines allgemeinen, übergeordneten Gat-
tungsbegriffs verstehen.[15] Diese Möglichkeit wehrt Basilius in seiner
etwa fünfzehn Jahre später entstandenen Schrift de Spiritu Sancto noch
entschiedener ab. Dort nennt er es Wahnsinn und Gottlosigkeit anzunehmen, "der Gott des Alls werde wie ein Allgemeinbegriff, der nur der
Vernunft erkennbar ist und in keinerlei Hypostase das Sein hat, auf die
Subjekte aufgeteilt."[16] Eine weitere Begründung für seine Ablehnung
gibt Basilius nicht, aber sie liegt auf der Hand: Wer die gemeinsame
ousia von Vater und Sohn als abstrakten Gattungs- oder Artbegriff interpretiert, landet konsequent bei einem Tritheismus. Auch Gregor von
Nazianz weist mit dieser Begründung eine solche Deutung der Homouseität zurück.[17]

Eine gemeinsame *ousia* von Vater und Sohn, so fährt Basilius fort,
könne auch (zweitens) nicht "ein zuvor vorhandenes stoffliches Sub-

---

[13] Vgl. Basil., *ep.* 361,24-33 (III 221 Courtonne).

[14] Apolin., *ep. ad Basil.* = Basil., *ep.* 362,4 f. (III 222 Courtonne): Οὐσία μία οὐκ
ἀριθμῷ μόνον λέγεται ὥσπερ λέγεις, καὶ τὸ ἐν μιᾷ περιγραφῇ ...

[15] Basil., *ep.* 361,19 f. (III 221 Courtonne): ἐφ' ὧν οὔτε γένος κοινὸν ὑπερκείμενον...

[16] Vgl. Basil., *de Spir. S.* XVII 41,16-25 (394 ²Pruche); Zitat 18-21 ... τὸν Θεὸν
τῶν ὅλων ὥσπερ κοινότητά τινα, λόγῳ μόνῳ θεωρητήν, ἐν οὐδεμιᾷ δὲ ὑποστάσει τὸ
εἶναι ἔχουσαν, εἰς τὰ ὑποκείμενα διαιρεῖσθαι; dazu Hübner (*op. cit. n. 1*), 472

[17] Gregor. Naz., *or.* 31,15 (304 Gallay, SChr 250).

strat" sein.[18] Diese zweite Interpretation lehnt er ebenfalls an späterer Stelle, vor allem *adv. Eunomium* I 19 und *ep.* 52, mit starken Worten ab und erklärt dabei ausführlicher, was er meint. Er will in der Theologie den Gedanken ausschließen, die gemeinsame *ousia* sei eine vorhandene Stoffmasse, die auf die aus ihr Stammenden aufgeteilt werde,[19] so daß die aufgeteilte Substanz *(ousia)* die Bezeichnung der Konsubstantialität *(homoousiou)* denen mitteile, in die sie aufgeteilt worden sei. Eine solche Vorstellung treffe z.B. für das Kupfer und die aus ihm geschlagenen Münzen zu, sagt Basilius; aber zu glauben, Gott-Vater und Gott-Sohn sei eine *ousia* vor- oder übergeordnet (οὐσία πρεσβυτέρα, ὑπερκειμένη), sei eine Blasphemie. Außerdem sei das, was aus einem einzigen stamme, verschwistert (ἀδελφά).[20]

Es ist nicht schwer festzustellen, woher diese Deutung des *homoousios* stammt. Basilius hat sich hier einen der Einwände zu eigen gemacht, den die Homoiusianer, wie uns Hilarius bezeugt, in einem während dogmatischer Verhandlungen in Sirmium (358) verlesenen, den Unterschied von *homoiousion* und *homoousion* behandelnden Brief vorgetragen haben.[21] Jedoch scheint er sowenig wie Athanasius, der den

---

[18] Basil., *ep.* 361,20 f. (III 221 Courtonne): ... οὔτε ὑλικὸν ὑποκείμενον προϋπάρχον,...

[19] Basil., *adv. Eunom.* I 19 (PG 29,556 A): Εἰ μὲν τὸ κοινὸν τῆς οὐσίας οὕτω νοήσας εἶπεν, ὡς ἐξ ὕλης προϋπαρχούσης διανομήν τινα καὶ καταδιαίρεσιν εἰς τὰ ἀπ' αὐτῆς νοεῖν, οὔτ' ἂν αὐτοὶ καταδεξαίμεθα τὴν διάνοιαν ταύτην· μὴ γένοιτο!

[20] Basil., *ep.* 52.1,28-40 (I 134 f. Courtonne). Die crux interpretum *ep.* 52.2,15 f. (I 135 C.), wo Basilius das Gegenteil von dem zu sagen scheint, was er eben gesagt hat und sonst sagt, nämlich daß Geschwister *nicht homoousia* seien, ist wohl nur durch Konjektur zu lösen: Οὐ γὰρ <ὡς> τὰ ἀδελφὰ ἀλλήλοις ὁμοούσια λέγεται (scil. nennen wir Vater und Sohn *homoousios*). Vgl. Apolin., *ep. ad Basil.* = Basil, *ep.* 362,52-54 (III 224 C.): Οὗτος ὁμοούσιος (...) οὐχ ὡς τὰ ὁμογενῆ, οὐχ ὡς τὰ ἀπομεριζόμενα. Vgl. Basil., *hom.* 24.4 (PG 31,605 B): Ὅταν δὲ εἴπω μίαν οὐσίαν, μὴ δύο ἐξ ἑνὸς μερισθέντα νόει, ἀλλ' ἐκ τῆς ἀρχῆς τοῦ πατρὸς τὸν υἱὸν ὑποστάντα, οὐ πατέρα καὶ υἱὸν ἐκ μιᾶς οὐσίας ὑπερκειμένης. οὐ γὰρ ἀδελφὰ λέγομεν. Ähnlich *ep.* 226.3 (s. Anm. 28).

[21] Hilar., *de syn.* 81 (PL 10,534 A): De homousio vero, quod est unius essentiae, tractantes, primum idcirco respuendum pronuntiastis, quia per verbi hujus enuntiationem substantia prior intelligeretur, quam duo inter se partiti essent. Vgl. ebd. 68 (525 C): Est praeterea error hic tertius, ut cum unius substantiae Pater et Filius esse dicatur, significari existimetur substantia prior, quam inter se duo pares habeant: ac sic tres res sermo significet, substantiam unam, et duos unius substantiae velut cahaeredes.Auch Marius Victorinus kennt und bekämpft diesen Einwand der Homoiusianer, siehe sein *adv. Arium* I 29,7-10 (270 Henry-Hadot, SChr 68): Nunc autem supra, infra, in ὁμοουσίου perversionem, nihil aliud dicis quam quod istud dicentes, necesse sit confiteri substantiam praeexistere et sic ex ipsa patrem et filium esse. Dazu P. Hadot, ebd., Introduction 32-38, und P. Hadot–U. Brenke, *Christlicher Platonismus. Die theologi-*

Einwand ebenfalls wiederholt diskutiert,[22] von diesem aus unmittelbarer
Kenntnis des Schriftstücks der Homoiusianer zu wissen, denn er bringt
ihn mit der angeblichen Verwerfung des *homoousios* durch die Synode
von Antiochien (268) in Zusammenhang, auf der Paulus von Samosata
abgesetzt wurde.[23] Von dem in diesem Punkte sicherlich besser unter-
richteten Hilarius erfahren wir aber, daß die Homoiusianer zwar auch
dieses Synodalurteil als (zweites) Argument gegen das *homoousios*
anführten, dafür aber eine anderslautende Begründung gaben.[24] Sehr
wahrscheinlich sind die Ausführungen des Basilius Reminiszenzen aus
seinen Unterredungen mit den Homoiusianern, vor allem mit Basilius
von Ankyra und Eustathius von Sebaste, die beide an den sirmischen
Verhandlungen (358) beteiligt waren.[25] An deren Seite finden wir Basilius nach einer Mitteilung des Philostorgius auf dem Konzil von Konstantinopel (360),[26] und seine anschließenden langjährigen Kontakte
und häufigen Gespräche über Glaubensfragen mit Eustathius und dem
homoiusianischen Kreis bezeugt er selbst.[27] Dazu stimmt, daß Eustathius, der nach seinem Bruch mit Basilius um 375 den ehemaligen
Freund als *homoousiastes* betitelt, ihm gerade jene massive Deutung des
homoousios unterstellt, die Basilius immer als Gottlosigkeit von sich
gewiesen hat.[28] Noch der Makedonianer des zweiten pseudathanasia-

---

schen Schriften des Marius Victorinus (Zürich und Stuttgart 1967), 57-62, sowie in
Auseinandersetzung mit P. Hadot: W. A. Löhr, *Die Entstehung der homöischen und
homöusianischen Kirchenparteien. Studien zur Synodalgeschichte des 4. Jahrhunderts* (Witterschlick/Bonn 1986), 76-78. 88-92.

[22] Athan., *c. Ar.* I 14 (PG 26,41 A): Οὐ γὰρ ἔκ τινος ἀρχῆς προϋπαρχούσης ὁ πατὴρ
καὶ ὁ υἱὸς ἐγεννήθησαν, ἵνα καὶ ἀδελφοὶ νομισθῶσιν. Vgl. Athan., *de syn.* 45,4; 51,3 f.

[23] Siehe Basil., *ep.* 52.1,28-30 (I 134 Courtonne).

[24] Hilar., *de syn.* 81 (PL 10,534 B); zu diesem ungezählte Male verhandelten Thema siehe die Diskussion bei F. Dinsen (*op. cit. n. 1*), 41-51; dort (228) auch die vor-
aufgehende Literatur. H. Chr. Brennecke, 'Zum Prozeß gegen Paul von Samosata: Die
Frage nach der Verurteilung des Homoousios', *Zeitschrift für die neutestamentliche
Wissenschaft* 75 (1984), 270-290, hat gegen F. Dinsen wahrscheinlich machen können, daß die Behauptung, die antiochenische Synode von 268 habe das von Paulus
vertretene *homoousios* zurückgewiesen, eine homöusianische Schlußfolgerung ist.

[25] Sozomenus, *hist. eccl.* IV 13,5; 15,1; Hilar., *de syn.* 90 (PL 10,542 B); vgl. J.
Gummerus, *Die homöusianische Partei bis zum Tode des Konstantius. Ein Beitrag zur
Geschichte des arianischen Streites in den Jahren 356-361* (Leipzig 1900), 90-97;
Simonetti (*op. cit. n. 1*), 241 f.; W. A. Löhr (*op. cit. n. 21*), 76.

[26] Philostorgius, *hist. eccl.* IV 12 (64,1-7 Bidez); vgl. die Literatur oben Anm. 9.

[27] Basil., *ep.* 223.5,1-19 (III 14 Courtonne).

[28] Basil., *ep.* 226.3,5-9 (III 26 Courtonne): Οὗτοι νῦν καὶ τὴν ἐν Νικαίᾳ διαβάλ-
λουσι πίστιν καὶ ὁμοουσιαστὰς ἡμᾶς ἀποκαλοῦσι διὰ τὸ ἐν ἐκείνῃ τῇ πίστει τὸν μονο-
γενῆ υἱὸν τῷ θεῷ καὶ πατρὶ ὁμοούσιον ὁμολογεῖσθαι, οὐχ ὡς ἀπὸ μιᾶς οὐσίας με-

nischen Dialogs hält an dieser Auslegung des *homoousios* fest und lehnt es deshalb in der Theologie ab.[29] Das zeugt für eine konstante homoiusianische Tradition.

Die dritte mögliche Deutung der Homouseität zweier selbständiger *ousiai*, die Basilius in *ep.* 361 sieht und für Vater und Sohn nicht akzeptieren kann, ist die Vorstellung, daß von einem Ersten ein Zweites abgetrennt wird.[30] Daß er hierbei die gewöhnliche Hervorbringung eines Sprosses durch seinen Erzeuger im Auge hat, erkennt man leicht aus *ep.* 52.[31] In der Ablehnung dieser Interpretation des *homoousios* sind sich alle damaligen Theologen, ob Arianer, Homoiusianer oder Nizäner, einig.[32]

Eine vierte mögliche Auslegung des *homoousios*, nämlich die 'sabellianische', die zur Identität der Hypostasen des Vaters und Sohnes führt, die von den Homoiusianern an erster Stelle zurückgewiesen wird,[33] die auch Basilius von Jugend auf verabscheut und unablässig bekämpft,[34] erwähnt er in *ep.* 361 nicht ausdrücklich, schließt sie aber implizit aus, indem er von den nicht identischen, in eigener Umschreibung befindlichen *ousiai* des Vaters und Sohnes redet.[35]

ρισθείσης εἰς δύο ἀδελφά, μὴ γένοιτο. Auch die oben Anm.20 zitierte Stelle aus *hom.* 24.4 ist vor diesem historischen Hintergrund zu sehen.

[29] Ps-Athan., *c. Macedon. dial. II* (PG 28,1336 C) = 122,167 Elena Cavalcanti (ed.), *Ps.Atanasio, Dialoghi contro i Macedoniani* (Torino 1983): Ἀλλὰ τὰ ὁμοούσια ἔχουσι προϋποκειμένην οὐσίαν.

[30] Basil., *ep.* 361,21 f. (III 221 Courtonne): ...οὐκ ἀπομερισμὸς τοῦ προτέρου εἰς τὸ δεύτερον.

[31] Basil., *ep.* 52.3,9-11 (I 136 Courtonne): Οὐ γὰρ ἐμερίσθη ἡ οὐσία ἀπὸ πατρὸς εἰς υἱόν, οὐδὲ ῥυεῖσα ἐγέννησεν, οὐδὲ προβαλοῦσα, ὡς τὰ φυτὰ τοὺς καρπούς κτλ. Siehe auch *hom.* 16,3 (PG 31,477 CD–480 A); *adv. Eunom.* II 6 (29, 581 B-C = II 26,7-12 Sesboüé).

[32] Vgl. z.B. Arius, *ep.ad Alex.* 5, bei Athan., *de syn.* 16 (II 244, 18 Opitz): ... ὡς μέρος αὐτοῦ ὁμοουσίου καὶ ὡς προβολή ... ; Eunom., *apol.* 26,23 f. (70 Vaggione); Synodalschreiben der Homoiusianer von Ankyra (358) bei Epiphan., *haer.* 73,6,1; 11,4; Hilarius, *de syn.* 68 (PL 10, 525 C): Quin etiam et hujus statim erroris occurrit occasio, ut divisus a sese Pater intelligatur, et partem exsecuisse quae esset sibi filius.

[33] Vgl. die wiederholten Verwahrungen gegen eine Identität (ταὐτόν) der *ousia* des Vaters und des Sohnes im Synodalschreiben von Ankyra (358) bei Epiphan., *haer.* 73,8,8; 9,2.10; 10,2.6.8; 11,4, und die Verwerfung des *homoousios* als *tautoousios* ebd. *haer.* 73,11,11; vgl. auch Hilar., *de syn.* 81 (PL 10,534 B).

[34] Basil., *ep.* 224.2,27-36 (III 19 f. Courtonne); vgl. *ep.* 9.2; 52.3 (hier betrachtet Basilius das *homoousios* bereits als einen Schutz gegen eine Identität der Hypostase: ἀναιρεῖ γὰρ τὴν ταυτότητα τῆς ὑποστάσεως); *ep.* 125.1; 126; 129.1; 207.1; 210.3-5; 214.3; 223.6; 226.4; 236.6; 265.2.

[35] Basil. *ep.* 361,31-33 (III 221 Courtonne): Φῶς γὰρ φωτὶ μηδεμίαν ἐν τῷ μᾶλλον

Mit den aufgezählten und verworfenen Deutungen sind für Basilius
die Möglichkeiten eines Verständnisses des *homoousios* erschöpft.
Einen Ausweg aus dem Dilemma sieht er nicht und wählt deswegen, um
die Einheit von Vater und Sohn auf "gesunde Weise" zu kennzeichnen,
den Ausdruck, sie seien der *ousia* nach genau und unterschiedslos
gleich (ὅμοιον... κατ' οὐσίαν ἀκριβῶς καὶ ἀπαραλλάκτως). Die *ousia* des
Sohnes ist ebenso Licht wie die *ousia* des Vaters; der (individuierende)
Unterschied liegt nur darin, daß der eine gezeugtes, der andere unge-
zeugtes Licht ist.

Apolinarius anerkennt in seiner Antwort alle drei Einwände des
Basilius gegen das *homoousios*.[36] Aber er besteht doch darauf, daß es
eine (von Basilius ausgeschlossene) Identität (ταυτότης) der *ousia* Gottes geben müsse.[37] Er sieht sie darin, daß gewissermaßen wie von einem
Stammvater die ganze göttliche "Gattung" (γένος) und "Form" (εἶδος)
vom einzigen Prinzip (ἀρχή), dem Vater, vollständig und ohne Abtrennung dem einzigen Sproß (γέννημα), dem Sohn, übertragen wird, so daß
eine Identität in Andersheit (ταὐτὸν ἐν ἑτερότητι) gegeben ist. Die
Identität der einzigen *ousia* (= das *homoousion)* wird durch das Zeugungsverhältnis (ἀπογέννησις) garantiert; die Andersheit, durch die der
Sohn nicht mit dem Vater identisch ist, durch eine Steigerung der
Identität im Vater und eine Verminderung der Identität im Sohn.[38]

Lassen sich irgendwo Auswirkungen dieser Deutung des *homoousios* bei Basilius feststellen?

In der bekannten *ep.* 9 des Basilius an den Philosophen Maximus,[39]
die von seiner pontischen Einöde aus geschrieben ist[40] und aus etwas
späterer Zeit stammt, erklärt er: Er akzeptiere die Formel "der *ousia*
nach gleich", wenn ihr das Wort "unterschiedslos" (ἀπαραλλάκτως) bei-
gefügt werde, als bedeutungsidentisch mit dem *homoousios*, wobei aber
sichergestellt sein müsse, daß das *homoousios* in "gesundem Sinn"
verstanden werde.[41] Die vormalige Reserve gegenüber dem nizänischen
Stichwort ist hier noch deutlich zu spüren,[42] aber Basilius verwendet es

---

καὶ ἧττον τὴν διαφορὰν ἔχον ταὐτὸν μὲν οὐκ εἶναι, διότι ἐν ἰδίᾳ περιγραφῇ τῆς οὐσίας
ἐστὶν ἑκάτερον,...

[36] Apolin., *ep. ad. Basil.* = Basil., *ep.* 362,14-16. 30-33 (III 222 f. Courtonne).
[37] Siehe den Text bei Anm. 67.
[38] Apolin., *ep. ad Basil.* = Basil., *ep.* 362,14-57 (III 222-224 Courtonne).
[39] Zu dieser Figur siehe M.-M. Hauser-Meury, *Prosopographie zu den Schriften
Gregors von Nazianz* [Theoph.13] (Bonn 1960),119-121.
[40] Basil., *ep.* 9.3,29-35 (I 40 Courtonne).
[41] Ebd., 9.3,1-4 (I 39 Courtonne).
[42] Vgl. auch Basil, *ep.* 52.1,20-28 (I 134 Courtonne); *ep.* 125.1, 16-25 (II 31 C.).

nun, wie er weiter sagt, doch auch selbst, weil es ihm weniger Ansatz-
punkte für eine unorthodoxe Auslegung zu bieten scheine.[43]

Basilius bekennt sich also immer noch zur homoiusianischen Formel, zieht ihr aber die nizänische vor. Interessanterweise verwendet er
nun die Begründung, die er im Brief an Apolinarius dem Stichwort der
Homoiusianer gab, nahezu gleichlautend auch zur Deutung des nizänischen *homoousios*. Auch die Väter von Nicaea hätten dieses Wort, so
erklärt er, im Sinne der *unterschiedslosen Gleichheit* der *ousia* nach
verstanden, "wenn sie den Eingeborenen Licht aus Licht und wahren
Gott aus wahrem Gott und dergleichen nennen und konsequent das *homoousios* anschließen. Es ist ja nicht möglich, sich jemals irgendeinen
Unterschied (παραλλαγήν) zwischen Licht und Licht oder Wahrheit und
Wahrheit oder der *ousia* des Eingeborenen und der des Vaters vorzustel-
len".[44] Basilius bleibt also bei seinem alten Standpunkt. Von einer
Auswirkung der Argumentation des Apolinarius in diesem Punkte ist
nichts zu bemerken.

Die Deutung, die er ursprünglich (in *ep.* 361) vom homoiusianischen
Kennwort gab, jetzt aber auf das *homoousios* übertragen hat, kehrt auch
später in den Briefen und den Büchern gegen Eunomius mehrfach in
ähnlicher Weise wieder.[45] Dabei fällt auf, daß er zur Begründung der
Gemeinsamkeit der *ousia* gewöhnlich nicht darauf rekurriert, daß der
Sohn vom Vater gezeugt ist, sondern lediglich hervorhebt, daß zwischen
Licht und Licht, als solche betrachtet, kein Unterschied bestehe. Das
Zeugungsverhältnis bleibt dabei—anders als bei Apolinarius—außer
Betracht. Die Adjektive ἀγέννητον und γεννητόν, die das Licht des Va-
ters und das Licht des Sohnes kennzeichnen, begründen nicht etwa die
Gemeinsamkeit der *ousia*, sondern differenzieren als antithetische
Eigentümlichkeiten (ἰδιώματα) die gemeinsame *ousia* der Gottheit in
Vater und Sohn.[46] Anderseits gibt es aber durchaus Stellen, an denen
Basilius auf das Zeugungsverhältnis zu sprechen kommt. Ihre Bedeu-
tung und Tragweite soll weiter unten erörtert werden.

---

[43] Basil., *ep.* 9.3,16-18 (I 39 Courtonne).

[44] Basil., *ep.* 9.3,4-10 (I 39 Courtonne); vgl. *ep.* 361,24-34 (III 221 C.).

[45] Siehe *ep.* 52.2,6-15 (I 135 Courtonne); *ep.* 125.1,46-49 (II 32 C.); *ep.* 226.3,9-13
(III 26 f. C.). (Noch) nicht das *homoousios*, sondern die eine oder gemeinsame *ousia*
wird mit dem gleichen Gedanken in *adv. Eunom.* begründet, vgl. ebd. II 25; 26; 28
(PG 29,629 B; 632 B-D; 636 C = II 104-106; 108-110; 116-118 Sesboüé); weitere
Stellen siehe unten Anm. 57.

[46] Vgl. z.B. Basil., *adv. Eunom.* II 28 f., (PG 29,637 B–640 B = II 118-122 Sesboüé).

Auch die Rede von der *ousia* des Vaters und der *ousia* des Sohnes (also von zwei *ousiai)* ist in *ep.* 9 noch nicht aufgegeben und begegnet ebenfalls noch eine Weile, auch in *adv. Eunomium,*[47] ebenso wie die homoiusianische Formel, von der er sich meines Wissens nie distanziert hat.[48]

Daneben finden wir aber in den Büchern gegen Eunomius bereits das *homoousios,* und auch die in *ep.* 361 zurückgewiesene Identität der *ousia* ist in *adv. Eunom.* II 28 akzeptiert: "Dies nämlich sei die Natur der Eigentümlichkeiten (scil. des *agenneton* und *genneton),* daß sie in der Identität der *ousia* die Andersheit (scil. von Vater und Sohn) zeigen."[49] Die *ousia* ist hier natürlich nicht mehr wie in *ep.* 361 als konkrete Einzelsubstanz verstanden. Die Terminologie (ταυτότης, ἑτερότης) verweist deutlich auf Apolinarius,[50] ist aber ganz basilianisch verarbeitet. In der Umgebung dieser Stelle stößt man auf weitere unzweideutige Spuren der apolinareischen Antwort (*ep.* 362), wie schon der scharfsichtige Gelehrte G. L. Prestige in seiner Untersuchung des Briefwechsels bemerkt hat. Aber hier rezipiert Basilius nicht, sondern er lehnt schroff ab: Die Theorie einer gesteigerten Identität des göttlichen Lichts im Vater, einer geminderten im Sohn gilt dem Basilius als abwegig. Prestige, der die korrespondierenden Passagen aus *ep.* 362 und *adv. Eunom.* II 27 f. abdruckt, kommt zu dem Schluß: "It is difficult to resist the conclusion that in writing against Eunomius Basil had, at certain definite moments, not only his own letter (*Ep.* 361) to Apollinaris in his head—or hand—but also the letter (*Ep.* 362) which Apollinaris sent him

---

[47] Vgl. Basil., *hom.* 23.4, in *s. mart. Mamantem* (PG 31,597 C). Basilius wendet sich hier gegen eine Verschmelzung der *ousiai* (= Hypostasen) von Vater und Sohn; *ousia* im Sinne der Einzelsubstanz auch *adv. Eunom.* I 7 (PG 29,525 A.B); 13 (541 B); 26 (569 A); 27 (572 B): *ousiai;* II 3 (577 A); 6 (581 C); 11 (592 B–593 A); 13 (596 B-C); 17 (605 B). An zahlreichen anderen Stellen der Bücher gegen Eunomius, an denen Basilius von der *ousia* des Vaters und der des Sohnes o. ä., sogar von ihren *ousiai* redet, hat *ousia* den Begriffsinhalt der *hypostasis* (den das Wort bei Eunomius immer auch zugleich hat, vgl. besonders II 6: 584 A) eher verloren und meint den Seinsinhalt.

[48] Vgl. *adv. Eunom.* I 23 (PG 29,564 A = I 254 Sesboüé); II 22; 25; 31 (620 B; 621 A; 629 B; 644 B = II 88; 92; 106; 128 S.).

[49] *Adv. Eunom.* II 28 (PG 29,637 C = II 120,43 f. Sesboüé): Αὕτη γὰρ τῶν ἰδιωμάτων ἡ φύσις, ἐν τῇ τῆς οὐσίας ταυτότητι δεικνύναι τὴν ἑτερότητα.

[50] Siehe Apolin., *ep. ad Basil.* = Basil., *ep.* 362, 33-37 (III 223 Courtonne): ταὐτὸν ἐν ἑτερότητι καὶ ἕτερον ἐν ταυτότητι; vgl. das von Basilius dem Apolinarius zugeschriebene Zitat aus dem von den Eustathianern in Umlauf gesetzten Syntagma in einem Brief an Meletius, *ep.* 129.1,8-10 (II 40 Courtonne): ... ἡνωμένως τῇ ἑτερότητι νοεῖν ἀναγκαῖον τὴν πρώτην ταυτότητα, καὶ δευτέραν καὶ τρίτην λέγοντας τὴν αὐτήν.

in reply."[51] Wohl jeder, der mit der trinitätstheologischen Terminologie des Basilius einigermaßen vertraut ist und diese Stellen aufmerksam liest, wird diesem Urteil, das sich noch mit mehreren philologischen Einzelbeobachtungen stützen ließe, zustimmen können.

Angesichts der deutlichen Kritik des Basilius scheint die Aussicht, einen positiven Einfluß der *ep.* 362 auf seine Deutung des *homoousios* zu entdecken, eher gering zu sein. Aber sehen wir zu.

Das *homoousios* begegnet in *adv. Eunomium* insgesamt fünfmal, davon zweimal innerhalb einer *argumentatio ad hominem*, die für das Verständnis des theologischen Begriffs nichts austrägt.[52] Dreimal steht es im Zusammenhang trinitarischer Erörterungen, bezeichnet zweimal jedoch lediglich die Homouseität der Menschen, und nur ein einziges Mal das Verhältnis des Vaters zum Sohn.

Die Stellen, an denen die Homouseität der Menschen ausgesprochen und begründet ist, klingen zwar für unsere Ohren höchst erstaunlich, stimmen aber mit dem üblichen Verständnis der *ousia* bei Basilius durchaus überein. An der ersten Stelle, *adv. Eunom.* II 4, erläutert Basilius die Homouseität der Menschen mit dem Schriftwort *Hiob* 33.6: "Aus Lehm bist du geformt, heißt es, so wie auch ich; dieses Wort kennzeichnet nichts anderes als das *homoousion* aller Menschen."[53] Die zweite Stelle, *adv. Eunom.* II 19, lautet: "Die Menschen überragen durch die Technik ihre eigenen Werke, dennoch sind sie mit ihnen *homoousioi*, wie der Töpfer mit dem Ton und der Schiffsbauer mit dem Holz. Beide sind ja in gleicher Weise Körper und in gleicher Weise wahrnehmbar und irden."[54]

---

[51] Siehe Prestige (*op. cit. n.* 2), 24-26, Zitat S. 26.Prestige zitiert die Mauriner Ausgabe. Die von ihm verglichenen Stellen aus *adv. Eunom.* II 27 f. stehen PG 29,636 A. B. C–637 A. B. C = II 114,37 f. 116,49-54. 118,10-14.27 f 31-120,37.43 f. Sesboüé.

[52] Basil., *adv. Eunom.* II 4 (PG 29,580 B = II 20-22 Sesboüé): "Denn die Natur der Dinge folgt nicht den Bezeichnungen, sondern die Bezeichnungen sind ersichtlich später als die Dinge. Denn wenn dies wahr wäre, dann müßte das, was dieselben Bezeichnungen hat, auch eine und dieselbe *ousia* haben. Demnach wären die Menschen, weil ja die in der Tugend Vollkommenen der Bezeichnung Gottes gewürdigt sind, mit dem Gott des Alls konsubstantial (*homoousioi*)"—*Adv. Eunom.* II 10 (PG 29,589 A = II 38 Sesboüé): "Aber dieser Allerweiseste, der sein ganzes Leben den eitlen Künsten gewidmet hat (scil. Eunomius), schämt sich nicht zu behaupten, das Wort 'Erzeugnis' (*gennema*) bezeichne die *ousia* des Eingeborenen selbst. Welchen Unsinn diese Behauptung enthält, betrachte: Wenn nämlich die *ousia* Erzeugnis ist, und umgekehrt, was Erzeugnis ist, auch *ousia* ist, dann sind folglich alle Erzeugnisse miteinander konsubstantial (*homoousia*)."

[53] *Adv. Eunom.* II 4 (PG 29,580 B).

[54] *Adv. Eunom.* II 19 (PG 29,613 C).

Es haben also, nach diesen Texten zu urteilen, für Basilius alle körperlichen Dinge (einschließlich der Tiere und Menschen) eine einzige, identische *ousia*. Das wird durch andere Aussagen bestätigt.[55] Die *ousia* ist hier das (stoffliche) Substrat (ὑλικὸν ὑποκείμενον), ein Begriff, der sich am zwanglosesten in Analogie zur stoischen unqualifizierten oder erst teilweise qualifizierten *ousia* verstehen läßt und den Basilius analog auch für das Sein der trinitarischen Hypostasen verwendet. Danach ergibt die *ousia* zusammen mit den jeweiligen Eigentümlichkeiten die (erkennbare) individuelle Hypostase.[56] Wo Basilius diese Anwendung macht, taucht zur Bestimmung des gemeinsamen Seinssubstrats von Vater und Sohn auch wieder jene bereits aus dem Brief an Apolinarius (*ep.* 361) bekannte Überlegung auf, daß sich das Licht, das der Vater ist, vom Licht, das der Sohn ist, nicht unterscheide.[57] Basilius ist sich also bislang ziemlich treu geblieben. Das Zeugungsverhältnis von Sohn und Vater, das Apolinarius zur Begründung ihrer Homouseität herangezogen hatte, erwähnt Basilius nicht.

Es läßt sich jetzt auch erklären, warum er diese Begründung nicht aufnimmt. Für ihn haben alle körperlichen Dinge eine einzige *ousia*; das heißt aber, daß die Menschen auch mit nicht von ihnen Gezeugtem (wie Holz, Lehm) *homoousioi* sind. Das Zeugungsverhältnis drückt demnach in seinen Augen nicht das Eigentümliche der Homouseität aus und kann daher zu ihrer Begründung und Erklärung nicht genügen.

Wenn sich Basilius bei der Bestimmung der *ousia* bislang so treu bleibt und das *homoousios* oder die "gemeinsame *ousia*" konsequent im selben Sinn interpretiert, so ist eine Abweichung an anderer Stelle umso auffälliger. Hat er in *adv. Eunom.* II 4, II 19 und II 28 erklärt, daß Lehm, Holz, Mensch, alle körperlichen Dinge eine einzige *ousia* haben, so scheint er in *adv. Eunom.* II 32 das Gegenteil vorauszusetzen.

---

[55] Vgl. *adv. Eunom.* II 28 (PG 29,637 C). Daß bei Basilius das *homoousios* ebensoviel bedeutet wie τὸ κοινὸν τῆς οὐσίας (o.ä.), μία οὐσία, μία καὶ ἡ αὐτὴ οὐσία, ἡ αὐτὴ οὐσία, ἡ τῆς οὐσίας ταυτότης, ergibt sich leicht z.B. aus einem Vergleich von *ep.* 361 und *adv. Eunom.* I 19 f., II 4; 10; 28.Eine ganz entsprechende, ausdrücklich als nichtaristotelisch bezeichnete Auffassung der *ousia* vertritt der Makedonianer im 2. pseudathanasianischen Dialog (PG 28,1336 C–1337 A = 122,161-187 E. Cavalcanti).

[56] Vgl. *adv. Eunom.* I 15. 19; II 4. 28, dazu meine in Anm. 1 zitierte Untersuchung S. 470-482. Vgl. C. Stead, *Philosophie und Theologie I. Die Zeit der Alten Kirche* (Stuttgart 1990), 127: "... es hat den Anschein, daß zumindest Basilius dazu neigte, mit dem Begriff *ousia* stoische Hintergedanken zu verbinden."

[57] *Adv. Eunom.* I 19 (PG 29, 556 A-B = I 240-242 Sesboüé); II 25; 28; 29 (629 B; 637 B-C; 640 A-B = II 104-106; 120; 122 S.).

In einer Argumentation gegen Eunomius führt er dort aus, daß man, wenn man einmal zur Erläuterung des Verhältnisses von Vater und Sohn Beispiele aus dem menschlichen Bereich heranziehen wolle, finden werde, "daß wir nicht aus den Werken des Handwerkers dessen *ousia* erkennen, aber aus dem Gezeugten die Natur dessen, der gezeugt hat. Denn es ist nicht möglich, aus dem Haus die *ousia* des Baumeisters zu erfassen; aber aus dem Erzeugten (*gennema*) läßt sich leicht die Natur des Erzeugers erkennen."[58]

Hier wird im Gegensatz zu dem, was sich bei Basilius bisher fand, das Zeugungsverhältnis als Erkenntnisgrund der Homouseität eingeführt; das Schaffensverhältnis wird dagegen als Erkenntnisweg ausgeschlossen. Das impliziert aber eigentlich die (im Antwortbrief des Apolinarius ausgesprochene) Auffassung, daß durch Zeugung etwas Homousisches, durch Schaffen aber etwas Heterousisches entsteht: Ein Schaffender hat mit dem Geschaffenen nicht eine gemeinsame *ousia*, ein Baumeister ist mit dem Haus nicht *homoousios*.

Basilius fährt fort:

"Wenn daher der Eingeborene ein Geschöpf (*demiourgema*) ist, so stellt er uns die *ousia* des Vaters nicht dar. Wenn er uns aber durch sich den Vater erkennen läßt, dann ist er kein Geschöpf (*demiourgema*), sondern wahrer Sohn und Bild Gottes (vgl. *Kolosser* 1.15) und 'Charakter der Hypostase' (*Hebräer* 1.3)."[59]

Was ist geschehen? Was hat den Basilius zu solcher Kehrtwendung veranlaßt? Abweichend von seiner üblichen Argumentation begründet er jetzt aus dem Zeugungsverhältnis und, mit Bezug auf *Kolosser* 1.15[60] und *Hebräer* 1.3, aus der Abbildlichkeit des Sohnes die gemeinsame *ousia* von Vater und Sohn. Hat Basilius inzwischen des Athanasius' zweiten Brief an Serapion von Thmuis in die Hände bekommen und haben ihn dessen Worte erschreckt? Sie klingen ja in der Tat so, als seien sie eigens gegen Basilius geschrieben: "Und der Schiffsbauer und der Baumeister zeugen nicht, was sie machen, sondern jeder stellt her: der eine das Boot, der andere das Haus. (…) Wie also nur ein Rasender sagen könnte, das Haus sei mit dem Baumeister, das Boot mit dem

---

[58] *Adv. Eunom.* II 32 (PG 29,648 C-D = II 136 Sesboüé).

[59] *Ibid.*

[60] *Kolosser* 1.15 wird von Basilius in *adv. Eunom.* I 18 (PG 29,552 C = I 234,5 f. Sesboüé) zitiert, ebenso II 16 (PG 29,604 C = II 64,33 S.); es wird also auch hier gemeint sein.

Schiffsbauer *homoousios*, so spricht jemand sachgerecht, wenn er jeden Sohn mit seinem Vater *homoousios* nennt."[61]

Es ist jedoch unwahrscheinlich, ja eigentlich auszuschließen, daß Basilius diese Stelle des von ihm geschätzten Athanasius gelesen und danachnoch in *adv. Eunom.* II 19 geschrieben haben könnte, der Schiffsbauer sei mit den Bauhölzern *homoousios*.[62] Weil es von der Sache her näher liegt, nehme ich an, daß es ihm inzwischen gelungen ist, einer Kopie von *de decretis Nicaenae synodi* habhaft zu werden, der Schrift aus der Zeit 350/351,[63] in welcher Athanasius erklären will, warum und in welcher Bedeutung die Väter von Nicaea das der Hl. Schrift fremde *homoousios* ins Glaubenssymbol schrieben. Es mußte ihn ja interessieren, was ein Teilnehmer der Synode zu dem ihm selbst bisher unlösbaren Problem zu sagen hatte. In *de decret.* 13 gibt es eine mit der eben aus *ad Serap.* II 6 zitierten sachlich parallele, aber im Ton nicht ganz so scharfe Ausführung:

"Wer, der gesunden Verstand besitzt, erkennt nicht, daß das, was geschaffen und gemacht wird, sich außerhalb des Machenden befindet, der Sohn aber, wie die vorhergehende Darlegung zeigte, nicht außerhalb (des Vaters), sondern aus dem zeugenden Vater existiert? Und es gründet (schafft) ja ein Mensch ein Haus, er zeugt aber einen Sohn, und es würde wohl niemand umgekehrt sagen, das Haus und das Schiff würden von dem Herstellenden gezeugt, der Sohn aber von ihm geschaffen und gemacht, noch wiederum, daß das Haus Bild des Schaffenden sei, der Sohn aber dem Zeugenden unähnlich (*anhomoios*). Sondern er wird vielmehr bekennen, daß der Sohn Bild des Vaters sei, das Haus aber ein Werk (*demiourgema*) der Technik, es sei denn einer im Verstand nicht gesund und habe die Urteilskraft verloren."[64]

Dieser Text scheint mir den Basilius zu einem Rückzug und zu einer vorsichtigen Korrektur seiner vorher geäußerten Meinung veranlaßt zu haben. Daß der Sohn aus dem Vater gezeugt und dessen Bild ist, wie Athanasius sagt, gilt jetzt als Erkenntnisgrund der (gemeinsamen) göttlichen *ousia*. Das ist freilich mehr implizit als explizit gesagt, und das *homoousios* bleibt ungenannt. *Hebräer* 1.3, bei Basilius der zweite Schriftbeleg für die Bildhaftigkeit des Sohnes, wird von Athanasius ein paar Zeilen zuvor zitiert.[65] Aber man wird doch zweifeln, ob sich *allein*

---

[61] Athanas., *ad Serap*. II 6 (PG 26,617 A-B).

[62] Chronologisch wäre eine Kenntnis dieser Schrift des Athanasius seitens des Basilius möglich. M. Tetz, 'Athanasius von Alexandrien', in *Theologische Realenzyklopädie* 4 (1979), 344, setzt sie 357/358 an.

[63] Vgl. Tetz (*op. cit. n. 62*).

[64] Athanas., *de decret.* 13,4 (II 11,24-32 Opitz); vgl. 23,1-4 (II 19,10-30 Opitz).

[65] *De decret.* 12,2 (II 10,32-11,1 Opitz).

die Lektüre von *de decretis* in *adv. Eunom.* II 32 ausgewirkt hat. Basilius hat ja jetzt—nahezu am Ende seines zweiten und wichtigsten Buches gegen Eunomius—zu einem guten Teil die von Apolinarius vertretene Position erreicht. Bestimmte Aussagen, die er wiederholt in der Schrift des Athanasius fand, mußten ihn an entsprechende bei Apolinarius erinnern und könnten ihn bewogen haben, dessen Ausführungen nochmals zu bedenken.

Athanasius sagt im zitierten Text *de decret.* 13,4, daß das Geschaffene sich außerhalb des Schaffenden befinde, und wiederholt dies in 23,1. Der Sohn aber, weil in der Schrift immerzu als "Abglanz" verkündet (*Hebräer* 1.3), sei das eigene Erzeugte (*gennema*) der *ousia* des Vaters und bewahre darin im Verhältnis zu diesem notwendig die Identität (ταυτότητα). Deswegen könnten die Christusbekämpfer über das *homoousios* nicht befremdet sein. Denn der Logos, heißt es ein wenig weiter, "ist nicht etwas Andersgeartetes (ἑτεροειδές), damit nicht etwas Fremdes und Unähnliches der *ousia* des Vaters beigemischt werde, noch ist er einfach äußerlich gleich (ἔξωθεν ἁπλῶς ὅμοιος), damit er nicht gemäß einem anderen oder gänzlich anderen Wesens (ἑτερο-ούσιος) erscheine (...). Wenn nun auch der Sohn so ist (scil. wie wesensunähnliche Dinge), so soll er ein Geschöpf sein wie wir und nicht *homoousios*."[66]

Ähnliches schreibt Apolinarius: "Die einen nämlich, welche die *ousia* in keinerlei Identität (ἐν οὐδεμιᾷ ταυτότητι) angenommen haben, tragen die Ähnlichkeit von außen heran (τὴν ὁμοίωσιν ἔξωθεν φέροντες) und weisen sie dem Sohne zu, was doch auch bis zu den Menschen möglich ist, die Gott verähnlicht sind. Die anderen aber, weil sie wissen, daß die Ähnlichkeit den Geschöpfen angemessen ist, verbinden zwar den Sohn mit dem Vater in Identität, jedoch in geminderter Identität (ὑφειμένῃ δὲ ταυτότητι), damit er nicht etwa der Vater sei oder ein Teil des Vaters (...). So ist er Gott, nicht als jener, sondern als aus jenem, nicht das Urbild, sondern Bild; dieser ist *homoousios* auf eine ganz außergewöhnliche und eigentümliche Weise ..."[67]

Die literarischen Bezüge zwischen beiden Texten sind im einzelnen hier nicht zu erörtern. Es ist deutlich, daß sich bei Apolinarius Gedanken und Begrifflichkeit des Athanasius wiederfinden. Ob Apolinarius dem Basilius zugleich mit seinem Antwortbrief auch eine Kopie der athanasianischen Verteidigung des *homoousios* mitgeschickt hat? Jedenfalls

---

[66] *De decret.* 23,2 f.; das wörtliche Zitat: (II 19,21-23.27 Opitz).
[67] Apolin., *ep. ad Basil.*, *ep.* 362,44-53 (III 223 f. Courtonne).

scheint der theologische Anfänger Basilius unter dem Eindruck der doppelten Autorität der beiden befreundeten Theologen Zeugungs- und Abbildverhältnis nochmals erwogen und geschrieben zu haben, was am Ende des Kapitels *adv. Eunom.* II 32 steht. Die Identität der *ousia* hat er in II 28 freilich erst rezipiert, nachdem er der apolinareischen Auffassung einer im Sohne geminderten Identität eine entschiedene Absage erteilt hat. Den Unterschied aber zwischen der II 32 erkennbaren *ousia*-Auffassung und seinen bisherigen Definitionen erläutert er uns nicht.

Es sind jetzt noch die oben übergangenen Stellen aus *adv. Eunomium* zu berücksichtigen, an denen Basilius das Zeugungsverhältnis erwähnt. Helfen auch sie zur Erklärung des soeben festgestellten Gesinnungswandels? Das scheint nicht der Fall zu sein. Denn es sind jene Stellen, an denen Basilius berichtet, in welcher Weise Eunomius den Vater- und Zeugungsbegriff von Gott ausschließen will, um die von den Homoiusianern aus diesem gezogenen Schlußfolgerungen zunichte zu machen.[68] In seiner Antwort übernimmt er weitgehend deren Gedanken und Formulierungen: "Es wäre nötig gewesen (...), den Begriff einer der Heiligkeit und Leidenschaftslosigkeit Gottes würdigen Zeugung zu denken, die Weise, nach der Gott zeugt, weil unsagbar und unerdenklich, beiseite zu lassen, sich aber von der Bezeichnung des Zeugens zur Gleichheit der *ousia* nach (τὴν κατ' οὐσίαν ὁμοιότητα) führen zu lassen. Indessen ist jedem, der die Sache betrachtet, klar, daß die Bezeichnungen, ich meine 'Vater' und 'Sohn', von Natur aus hauptsächlich und zuerst nicht den Gedanken körperlicher Leidenschaft hervorrufen, sondern, so wie sie für sich gesagt werden, allein die gegenseitige Beziehung (σχέσιν) anzeigen. Denn Vater ist, wer einem anderen den Ursprung des Seins gemäß der ihm gleichen Natur gewährt; Sohn aber, wer aus einem anderen durch Zeugung den Ursprung des Seins empfangen hat."[69]

Das faßt die Überlegungen zusammen, mit denen Basilius von Ankyra in der Denkschrift seiner Synode von 358 die Gleichheit der *ousia* nach zu begründen sucht.[70] An den übrigen hierher gehörigen Stellen in *adv. Eunomium* redet Basilius von τῆς οὐσίας οἰκείωσις oder τῆς φύσεως οἰκειότης oder ähnlichem und benutzt damit ebenfalls homoiusianische Begrifflichkeit.[71] Die Überlegungen der Homoiusianer führen aber nicht

---

[68] Basil., *adv. Eunom.* II 22 (PG 29, 620 A-B = II 88,2-14 Sesboüé).

[69] *Adv. Eunom.* II 22 (PG 29,621 A-B = II 90-92 Sesboüé).

[70] Vgl. das Synodalschreiben von Ankyra (358) bei Epiphan., *haer.* 73,3,1-4,4 und an anderen Stellen.

[71] Basil., *adv. Eunom.* II 6 (PG 29,581 C = II 26,17-20 Sesboüé); II 23 (624 C–625

zum *homoousios* und der Identität der *ousia,* sondern schließen sie eigens aus, indem Vater und Sohn immer als zwei *ousiai* aufgefaßt werden.[72] So gibt es auch bei Basilius dort, wo er die homoiusianischen Gedanken und Formeln aufgreift, keine Brücke vom Zeugungsverhältnis zur gemeinsamen *ousia* von Vater und Sohn. Die Gedankenreihen stehen unverbunden nebeneinander, ein deutliches Zeichen dafür, daß Basilius die verschiedenen von ihm aufgenommenen Ideen nicht in einer einheitlichen Konzeption zu integrieren vermochte.

Wenn Basilius, als er in *adv. Eunom.* II 19 schrieb, der Töpfer sei mit dem Ton, der Schiffsbauer mit den Hölzern *homoousios,* noch nicht auf die seiner dort dargelegten Auffassung diametral entgegengesetzte Meinung des Athanasius in *de decretis* gestoßen war, dann wird man nicht erwarten, daß er bereits in *adv. Eunom.* I 20, der einzigen Stelle in seiner Trilogie gegen den Anhomoier, an der er das Wort *homoousios* auf Vater und Sohn anwendet, das Zeugungsverhältnis ins Spiel bringt. Das geschieht auch tatsächlich nicht:

"Es ist nicht möglich, daß der Gott des Alls mit seinem Bilde (vgl. *Kolosser* 1.15), das zeitlos erglänzt, nicht von Ewigkeit zusammen sei und nicht eine Verbindung habe, die über die Zeit, ja über alle Äonen erhaben ist. Denn deswegen heißt er 'Abglanz', damit wir die Verbundenheit erkennen, und 'Charakter der Hypostase' (*Hebräer* 1.3), damit wir das *homoousion* erlernen."[73]

Nur die Abbildhaftigkeit, wie in *adv. Eunom.* II 32 durch *Kolosser* 1.15 und *Hebräer* 1.3 belegt, begründet hier die göttliche *synapheia* und das etwas kleinlaut hervorgebrachte *homoousion.* Auf diese beiden Schriftstellen, zugleich aber auch auf das Zeugungsverhältnis, nimmt Basilius nun auch an der einzigen Stelle seiner Homilien Bezug, an der das *homoousios* überhaupt vorkommt, nämlich in *hom.* 24.4, *contra Sabellianos, Arium et Anomoeos.* Nun ist diese Stelle nachweislich eine Kopie der entsprechenden Passage im pseudathanasianischen Traktat *contra Sabellianos.* Ich setze beide Stellen hierher.

A = II 96,56-62 S.); II 24 (625 B.C = II 98,1-4.16-100,23 S.); damit ist zu vergleichen der Brief des Georg von Laodicea bei Epiphan., *haer.* 73,19,1-5, mit der fast gleichen Formel: τῆς φύσεως τὴν οἰκειότητα (ebd. *haer.* 73,19,4).

[72] Vgl. das Synodalschreiben des Basilius von Ankyra bei Epiphan., *haer.* 73,8,3; 9,2.6 f.; 10,2.10; differenzierter schon Georg von Laodicea ebd. *haer.* 73,17,4-18,5.

[73] Basil., *adv. Eunom.* I 20 (PG 29,556 C = I 242,6-244,11 Sesboüé).

Basilius, hom. 24.4
(PG 31,605 D-608 C)

Ps-Athanasius, contra Sabellianos 6f.
(PG 28,108 B; 109 A)

Denn wo es nur ein einziges Prinzip gibt und zugleich ein einziges, das aus ihm ist, und wo es nur ein einziges Urbild gibt und zugleich ein einziges Abbild (εἰκών), da wird der Begriff der Einheit nicht zerstört. Weil der Sohn durch Zeugung (γεννητῶς) aus dem Vater stammt und auf natürliche Weise in sich den Vater abbildet, so besitzt er als Bild die unterschiedslose Gleichheit (τὸ ἀπαράλλακτον), als Erzeugtes (γέννημα) bewahrt er das ὁμοούσιον.

Wo es aber nur ein einziges Prinzip gibt und zugleich ein einziges Erzeugnis (γέννημα) aus ihm, da ist das genaueste und natürliche Bild, weil es ja auch aus ihm gezeugt ist; da ist ein einziger Gott, weil die Gottheit als vollkommene im Vater erkannt wird, und vollkommen auch im Sohn die väterliche Gottheit vorhanden ist.

Du vermagst ja doch auch durch jenes kleine Gleichnis, das die göttliche Schrift kundgetan hat, da sie Christus 'Bild des unsichtbaren Gottes' (*Kolosser* 1.15) nannte, das Gesagte zu begreifen: Meiden wir auch hier wieder das Unähnliche in dem Gleichnis, daß nämlich das Bild Gottes künstlich und anderen Wesens (ἑτεροούσιον) sei, und bekennen wir, daß es gezeugt und gleichen Wesens (ὁμοούσιος) ist.

Denn niemand, der auf dem Markt das kaiserliche Bild betrachtet und den im Bilde (Dargestellten) 'Kaiser' nennt, bekennt deswegen zwei Kaiser, das Bild und den, dessen das Bild ist; noch hat er, wenn er auf den deutet, der auf der Tafel gemalt ist, und sagt: 'Dies ist der Kaiser', das Urbild der Bezeichnung des Kaisers beraubt. (...)
Doch hier machen Holz und Wachs und des Malers Kunst das Bild vergänglich, eines Vergänglichen Nachahmung, und ein künstliches Bild eines, der selbst gemacht ist. Wenn du aber dort von einem

Gleichwohl aber sieht, wer das Bild des Kaisers sieht, den Kaiser und sagt: Siehe, dies ist der Kaiser! —und hat doch nicht zwei Kaiser gemacht (...).

'Bild' hörst, so verstehe darunter den 'Abglanz der Herrlichkeit'. Was ist 'der Abglanz' und was ist 'die Herrlichkeit'? Der Apostel erklärt es sofort selbst, indem er hinzusetzt: 'und Charakter der Hypostase' (*Hebräer* 1.3). Dasselbe also ist die 'Hypostase' mit der 'Herrlichkeit', der 'Charakter' mit dem 'Abglanz', so daß, weil die Herrlichkeit vollkommen bleibt und in nichts gemindert wird, der Abglanz vollkommen hervorgeht. Und so stellt uns das Wort des 'Bildes', wenn es gotteswürdig aufgefaßt wird, die Einheit der Gottheit dar.

Denn dieser ist in jenem und jener in diesem, insofern dieser von der Art ist wie jener, und jener von der Art wie dieser. So werden auch die zwei dadurch geeint, daß der Sohn nicht verschieden und auch nicht in einer anderen Gestalt (εἶδος) und einem fremden 'Charakter' (*Hebräer* 1.3) zu denken ist.	Wie ist dieser in jenem und jener in diesem? Insofern dieser von der Art ist wie jener, und jener von der Art wie dieser. So sind auch die zwei dadurch eins, daß der Sohn nicht verschieden, nicht abgesondert und auch nicht in einer anderen Gestalt und einem fremden 'Charakter' (*Hebräer* 1.3) zu denken ist.

Es würde eine lange Darlegung ergeben, wollte man jetzt auf die feinen theologischen Unterschiede eingehen, die bei der Benutzung desselben Materials erkennbar sind. Es ist ersichtlich, daß Basilius das einzige *homoousios* seiner gesamten Predigten zusammen mit der Begründung aus dem Zeugungs- und Abbildverhältnis (*Kolosser* 1.15 und *Hebräer* 1.3)[74] von dem meinerseits mit Apolinarius identifizierten pseudathanasianischen Autor übernimmt.[75] Eine Zurückhaltung gegenüber dem nizänischen Kennwort und seiner Herleitung aus dem Sohnschaftsverhältnis zeigt er in der Homilie, anders als sonst, nicht, was zweifellos durch die massive Übernahme aus seiner Vorlage bedingt ist. Weil sich die Spu-

---

[74] *Kolosser* 1.15 wird von Ps-Athanasius zitiert, von Basilius hier nur angedeutet, aber *hom.*24.2 (PG 31,604 B) angeführt; umgekehrt zitiert Basilius die Stelle Hebr. 1.3, die Ps-Athanasius nur andeutet, aber *c. Sabell.* 5 (PG 28,105 B) anführt. Beide Autoren haben also dieselben Schriftstellen.

[75] Siehe die Untersuchung 'Die Schrift des Apolinarius von Laodicea gegen Photin', 47-125. 197-281 (*op. cit. n. 2*).

ren der Theologie und Terminologie des apolinareischen Traktats und gerade auch des oben daraus zitierten Textstücks in naher Umgebung (I 18) der einzigen theologischen *homoousios*- Stelle der Bücher gegen Eunomius finden lassen, ist es wahrscheinlich, daß Basilius unter dem Einfluß dieser Schrift hier zum ersten Male vorsichtig die Homouseität des Sohnes mit dem Vater formuliert.[76] Dafür spricht auch der Bezug auf *Kolosser* 1.15 zusammen mit *Hebräer* 1.3, Schriftstellen, die im ersten Buch gegen Eunomius nur in I 18 und 20 vorkommen,[77] im Antwortbrief des Apolinarius (*ep.* 362) aber nicht zitiert werden. Die Verteidigung des *homoousios* durch Athanasius in *de decretis* hat Basilius zu diesem Zeitpunkt noch nicht gelesen, und in den homoiusianischen Denkschriften wird zwar *Kolosser* 1.15 mehrfach zitiert, aber nicht *Hebräer* 1.3.

Faßt man die Beobachtungen zusammen, so kann man nicht umhin festzustellen, daß das theologische Erstlingswerk des Basilius nicht aus einheitlichem Guß ist. Das ist auch eigentlich nicht zu erwarten, wenn man bedenkt, daß die "Bekehrung" des Basilius erst wenige Jahre zurückliegt und er sich seitdem zwar mit den praktischen Anweisungen der Schrift für ein christliches Leben, aber nicht genug mit den im strengen Sinn theologischen Fragen der Gotteslehre beschäftigt hat. So mußte er, um Eunomius antworten zu können, sich auf verschiedenen Seiten nach theologischem Rat umsehen. Weil er selbst noch nach einem festen Standpunkt suchte, vermochte er die unterschiedlichen Lösungen für dasselbe Problem nicht souverän zu beurteilen und in einen geschlossenen und in sich kohärenten Zusammenhang zu bringen. Homoiusianisches, Athanasianisches, Apolinareisches und aus dem Studium mitgebrachte philosophische Kenntnisse stehen zum großen Teil unverbunden nebeneinander. Die Einflüsse der einzelnen Schriften lassen sich ziemlich scharf abgrenzen, man kann manchmal die Seiten angeben, bei deren Abfassung Basilius jeweils auf einen bestimmten Text zurückgegriffen hat. So erklären sich auch die zum Teil schon seit langem bemerkten begrifflichen und sachlichen Unausgeglichenheiten und Widersprüche in seinen Ausführungen, die umso deutlicher hervortreten, je weniger Zeit Basilius zur Verarbeitung des aufgenommenen Materials hatte.[78] Bei der literarischen Analyse seines Werkes stehen wir aber

---

[76] Vgl. *Ibid* 252-255.

[77] Sie kehren zusammen, deutlich unter dem Einfluß von Ps-Athan., *c. Sabell.*, in *adv. Eunom.* II 16 f. und dann eben II 32 wieder.

[78] Einige Erläuterungen in: 'Die Schrift des Apolinarius von Laodicea gegen Photin' (*op. cit. n. 2*), 120-125. 257-268.

durchaus noch am Anfang, so daß auch das hier zum *homoousios* Dargelegte unvollständig bleibt. wird verständlich, wenn man sich vor Augen hält, daß die nachnizänische Trinitätslehre eine Lehre im Werden ist, für welche weder die vorangegangene Theologiegeschichte noch die Philosophie adäquate Kategorien zur Verfügung stellte oder stellen konnte. Nur ein durchgehender Kommentar zu den Büchern gegen Eunomius könnte umfassende und zuverlässige Auskunft bringen. Der Mangel an konsistenter Begrifflichkeit und kohärentem Denken bei den Kappadoziern, von dem hier Geehrten in vielfachen Arbeiten aufgezeigt,[79] wird verständlich, wenn man sich vor Augen hält, daß die nachnizänische Trinitätslehre eine Lehre im Werden ist, für welche weder die vorangegangene Theologiegeschichte noch die Philosophie adäquate Kategorien zur Verfügung stellte oder stellen konnte.

---

[79] Vgl. die zahlreichen Studien in dem Sammelband von G.C. Stead, *Substance and Illusion in the Christian Fathers* (London 1985); ders., 'Why Not Three Gods? The Logic of Gregory of Nyssa's Trinitarian Doctrine', in H.R. Drobner und C. Klock (Hg.), *Studien zu Gregor von Nyssa und der christlichen Spätantike,* = FS A. Spira (Leiden 1990), 149-163; und zuletzt: 'Homousios', *Reallexikon für Antike und Christentum* Lieferung 122/123 (Stuttgart 1992), 364-433, hier 423-425.

'TRAMPLE UPON ME...'
THE SOPHISTS ASTERIUS AND HECEBOLIUS:
TURNCOATS IN THE FOURTH CENTURY A.D.

WOLFRAM KINZIG

Christopher Stead's masterly contributions to the history of Arianism
need no special mention here since they are standard reading for everyone interested in the subject. One of the Arians of the first generation
was the sophist Asterius. The patriarch of Antioch, Severus, tells the
following story about him:

> ... it is related in church histories that Asterius, who was a sophist and
> author among the Arians, was often received and often returned to his
> vomit [cf. *Proverbs* 26.11 = *2 Peter* 2.22], insomuch that this ex-
> pression of his is cited in histories. He cried out lying on his face before
> everyone and saying, "Trample upon me, the salt which has lost its
> savour' [cf. *Matthew* 5.13].[1]

Severus refers to 'church histories' as the source of this anecdote. Yet in
the church histories preserved it is not attested—at least insofar as it refers to Asterius. We do find, however, in Socrates' *Church History* a
very similar story about Hecebolius, one of emperor Julian's teachers.
In 3,13 Socrates points out that Julian's policy of appointing only pagans to administrative posts induced many people to put money and
career before the true faith and to apostatise. He goes on:

> Of these was Ecebolius, a sophist of Constantinople who, accommo-
> dating himself to the dispositions of the emperors, pretended in the
> reign of Constantius to be an ardent Christian, while in Julian's time he
> appeared an (equally) vigorous pagan; and after Julian's death, he
> again wanted to be a Christian. For he prostrated himself before the
> door of the house of prayer, and called out: "Trample upon me, the salt
> which has lost its savour" [cf. *Matthew* 5.13]. Of so fickle and un-

---

[1] Sever. Ant., *ep.* VI 5,4; ed. E.W. Brooks, *The Sixth Book of the Select Letters of Severus, Patriarch of Antioch, in the Syriac Version of Athanasius of Nisibis,* 2 vols. (London 1904), I, 321 f.; transl. II, 286.

scrupulous a character was this Ecebolius, throughout the whole period of his history.[2]

It appears that we are dealing with the same event. Both Severus and Socrates speak about a man lying on the ground and shouting: 'Trample upon me, the salt which has lost its savour' in order to be readmitted to the Church. In the first case, however, the man is said to have been Asterius and in the second Hecebolius. The life and works of Asterius have recently been studied by the author of the present article.[3] Hecebolius, however, has not yet received much scholarly attention.[4] In what follows, therefore, I should like, first, to give an outline of Hecebolius' life; secondly, I shall examine the odd behaviour described in the story; and thirdly, I should like to ask whether the story is historical, about whom it was told originally and why it became a 'wandering story'.

I

A closer analysis of the seemingly trivial anecdote about Asterius/Hecebolius leads us to one of the most fascinating and, as it were, 'modern' phenomena of the fourth century, namely those people who, apparently without inner scruples, changed from paganism to Christianity and vice versa. In the wake of the Constantinian revolution there was a large influx of people into the Christian Church which, almost overnight, had turned out to be the new mainstay of late antique Roman society. It has

---

[2] Ὧν εἷς ἦν καὶ ὁ Κωνσταντινουπόλεως σοφιστὴς Ἐκηβόλιος. Ὅστις τοῖς ἤθεσι τῶν βασιλέων ἐπόμενος ἐπὶ μὲν Κωνσταντίου διαπύρως χριστιανίζειν ὑπεκρίνατο· ἐπὶ δὲ Ἰουλιανοῦ γοργὸς Ἕλλην ἐφαίνετο· καὶ αὖθις μετὰ Ἰουλιανόν χριστιανίζειν ἤθελε. Ῥίψας γὰρ ἑαυτὸν πρηνῆ πρὸ τῆς πύλης τοῦ εὐκτηρίου οἴκου, Πατήσατέ με, ἐβόα, τὸ ἅλας τὸ ἀναίσθητον. Τοιοῦτος μὲν οὖν κοῦφος καὶ εὐχερὴς Ἐκηβόλιος πρότερόν τε καὶ ὕστερον ἦν (PG 67, 413A-B; tr. NPNF, altered). Cf. also *Suda*, s.v. Ἐκηβόλιος which is based on Socrates.

[3] *In Search of Asterius: Studies on the Authorship of Homilies on the Psalms,* [FKDG 47] (Göttingen 1990), 14-21, 125-132. Cf. now also the doctoral dissertation by Markus Vinzent, *Asterius von Kappadokien, Theologische Fragmente: Einleitung, kritischer Text, Übersetzung und Kommentar,* Diss. Munich 1991.

[4] Cf. esp T. W. D(avids), 'HECEBOLIUS', *Dictionary of Christian Biography* II (1880), 872 f with references to earlier literature; (Otto) Seeck, 'Hekebolios 1', *Paulys Real-Encyclopädie* VII/2 (1912), 2800; Wilmer Cave Wright, *The Works of the Emperor Julian* III, (London 1923; rpt. 1961), XLVII-XLVIII; A. H. M. Jones, J. R. Martindale and J. Morris, *The Prosopography of the Later Roman Empire* I [= PLRE I] (Cambridge 1971), 409, s. v. 'Hecebolius I'.

been estimated that the number of Christians in the Latin west rose dramatically from two million at the end of the third to four to six million by the end of the fourth century.[5] In the East there may have been a rise from between five and ten million to double this figure during the same period. At the same time the overall population in the empire may have decreased from a supposed level of fifty million in A.D. 300. Figures such as these are, of course, notoriously unreliable, since we neither have any ancient statistics at our disposition nor do we know the exact development of the overall population of the ancient Mediterranean world.[6] There can, however, be no doubt that the old pagan cults lost ever more of their members to the Church.[7]

A closer look, however, raises doubts in some cases as regards the sincerity of these conversions. Ambrose, for example, mentioned those Christians 'by name only' *(nomine Christiani)* who advocated a reinstalment of the altar of Victory in the Roman Curia in 384;[8] and Augustine saw reason to give special advice as to how to treat those people who only pretended to be Christians when they sought to be admitted to the catechumenate.[9] In the first three centuries conversion to Christianity meant becoming an outsider in Roman society, suffering social pressure and even outright persecution. Morals in the Church were, therefore, broadly speaking, rather high. In the fourth century, however, especially after Constantine's victory over Licinius in 324 and his sub-

---

[5] Cf. Ludwig Hertling, 'Die Zahl der Christen zu Beginn des vierten Jahrhunderts', *Zeitschrift für Katholische Theologie* 58 (1934), 243-253; Ludwig Hertling, 'Die Zahl der Katholiken in der Völkerwanderungszeit', *Zeitschrift für Katholische Theologie* 58 (1934), 92-108; cf. also Bernhard Kötting, 'Christentum I', *Reallexikon für Antike und Christentum* II (1954), 1138-1159,1139. T.D. Barnes, 'Christians and Pagans in the Reign of Constantius', in *L''Église de l'Empire au IVe Siècle* [Fondation Hardt/Entretiens sur l'antiquité classique 34] (Vandœuvres-Geneva 1989), 308.

[6] As regards the statistical difficulties in describing the development of the overall population cf. Hertling *(op. cit. n. 5)*, A.H.M. Jones, *The Later Roman Empire: A Social, Economic, and Administrative Survey*, 2 vols. (Oxford 1964; rpt. 1986), II, 1040-1045; Alexander Demandt, *Die Spätantike: Römische Geschichte von Diocletian bis Justinian 284-565 n. Chr.* [HAW III/6] (Munich 1989), 276. On the theory of a decrease in population as a factor accelerating the fall of Rome cf. the literature surveyed by Alexander Demandt, *Der Fall Roms: Die Auflösung des römischen Reiches im Urteil der Nachwelt* (Munich 1984), 352-368. Demandt himself is rather sceptical as regards all such theories.

[7] Cf. e.g. Kötting *(op cit. n.5)*; Karl Baus and Eugen Ewig, *Die Reichskirche nach Konstantin dem Großen*, I/1: Die Kirche von Nikaia bis Chalkedon, 2nd ed. (Freiburg 1985), 189-238; Robin Lane Fox, *Pagans and Christians* (London 1986), 663-681.

[8] Cf. *ep.* 72(17), 8.

[9] Cf. *de cat. rud.* 5,9; moreover *conf.* I.11.18.

sequent increased interest in Christianity, all this changed. Now it was socially advantageous to belong to the Church which all of a sudden enjoyed imperial benevolence and support.[10] In most cases, it is true, the nature of our evidence prevents us from determining the motives for which people converted to Christianity. Moreover, as Ramsay MacMullen has convincingly argued, the term conversion itself involves considerable conceptual difficulties.[11] Nevertheless, a careful and patient analysis of the ancient sources does suggest that the phenomenon of 'half'-Christians was quite widespread.[12]

Hecebolius is a classic example of this pattern of behaviour. Unfortunately, the historical evidence as regards his life is scattered and must be carefully pieced together. His name is, of course, derived from ἑκη-βόλος (> ἑκών + βάλλω originally meaning 'attaining his aim' and in later writers 'far shooting'.[13] In Homer this word occurs as an epithet (cf. e.g. Il. 1,14.21.373 etc.) and as an independent noun (cf. e.g. Il. 1,96.110 etc.), and in both cases it designates Apollo.[14] As a name it is relatively rare. (I have found only two further bearers, who are most certainly not related to our Hecebolius.[15]). His name suggests that our Hecebolius was originally pagan. Socrates may also indicate that when

---

[10] On this phenomenon in general cf. Kurt Aland, *Über den Glaubenswechsel in der Geschichte des Christentums* [TBT 5] (Berlin 1961), 41-56.

[11] Cf. Ramsay MacMullen, *Christianizing the Roman Empire (A.D. 100-400)*, (New Haven/London 1984).

[12] Cf. the material collected in A(rthur) D(arby) Nock, *Conversion: The Old and the New in Religion from Alexander the Great to Augustine of Hippo* (Oxford 1933), 156-163; Gustave Bardy, *La Conversion au Christianisme durant les Premiers Siècles* [Theol(P) 15] (Paris 1949), 329-351; Winfried Daut, 'Die "halben Christen" unter den Konvertiten und Gebildeten des 4. und 5. Jahrhunderts', *Zeitschrift für Missionswissenschaft* 55 (1971), 171-188; Polymnia Athanassiadi-Fowden, *Julian and Hellenism: An Intellectual Biography* (Oxford 1981), 28 f.; MacMullen *(op. cit. n. 11)*, 56 f., 144 f.

[13] Cf. Henry George Liddell, Robert Scott and Henry Stuart Jones, *A Greek English Lexicon*, 9th ed. (Oxford 1940; rpt. 1985), s. v.

[14] Cf. *ibid.* and Jessen, 'Hekebolos, Hekatebolos, Hekatebeletes', *Paulys Real-Encyclopädie* VII/2, (1912), 2800-2802, 2800 f. Moreover, it sometimes also refers to Artemis; cf. *ibid* 2802 and Liddell-Scott-Jones, *(op cit. n.13)*, s. v.

[15] Cf. IG XII/7 (Amorgos-Minoa), no. 344 (M. Ἰούλιος Ἐκήβολος, perhaps second or third century); cf. P.M. Fraser and E. Matthews (eds.), *A Lexicon of Greek Personal Names*, I: The Aegean Islands, Cyprus, Cyrenaica (Oxford 1987), s.v. Cf. furthermore P.M. Fraser, E. Matthews and J.R. Martindale, *The Prosopography of the Later Roman Empire* II, [= PLRE II] (Cambridge 1980), 528: Hecebolus (probably a governor of Libya Pentapolis in the early sixth century). As to other bearers of this name cf. below.

he says that 'in the reign of Constantius he pretended to be an ardent Christian'.

This change of allegiance may have been a matter of conviction; it may, however, also have come about, because Hecebolius wanted to be appointed to one of the official teaching posts in Constantinople.[16] As Raban von Haehling pointed out, Constantius 'attempted with more determination than his father to drive out paganism from public life by legislative means'.[17] Consequently, he promoted Christians, and in particular Arians, to high administrative posts.[18] Moreover, it is well attested that Constantius frequently interfered with appointments at the school of Constantinople as in the case of Libanius and Themistius.[19] Under Constantius, 'Constantinople became the intellectual

---

[16] On the official support of the teaching of rhetoric in the fourth century cf. Henri-Irénée Marrou, *Histoire de l'Éducation dans l'Antiquité,* 6th ed. (Paris 1965), 431-450, esp. 436 f.; George A. Kennedy, *Greek Rhetoric under Christian Emperors* [A History of Rhetoric III] (Princeton, New Jersey 1983), 134 f.; Robert A. Kaster, 'The Salaries of Libanius', *Chiron* 13 (1983), 37-59, 39-41; as to the schools of Constantinople cf. *ibid,* 163-167; Fritz Schemmel, 'Die Hochschule von Konstantinopel im IV. Jahrhundert p. Ch. n.', *Neue Jahrbücher für das Klassische Altertum* 11 (1908), 147-168; Kennedy (*op cit.*), 163-167; Robert A. Kaster, *Guardians of Language: The Grammarian and Society in Late Antiquity* [The Transformation of the Classical Heritage 11] (Berkeley 1988), 126 f. Cf. also the behaviour of Hecebolius' colleague at Constantinople, Bemarchius, who, according to Libanius, praised Constantius' religious works in a *panegyricus*, even though he was a pagan (cf. *or.* 1,39). Furthermore *or.* 62,11: The rhetors received their appointments as reward for flattery. Libanius does not mention, however, that he, too, wrote a βασιλικὸς λόγος on the emperors Constans and Constantius (*or.* 59).

[17] Cf. Raban von Haehling, *Die Religionszugehörigkeit der hohen Amtsträger des Römischen Reiches seit Constantius I.: Alleinherrschaft bis zum Ende der Theodosianischen Dynastie (324-450 bzw.455 n. Chr)* [Antiquitas 3/33] (Bonn 1978), 527-536. Cf., however, the qualificatory remarks by Karl Leo Noethlichs, 'Hofbeamter', *Reallexikon für Antike und Christentum* XV (1991), 1111-1158, 1154; cf. also Karl Leo Noethlichs, *Die gesetzgeberischen Maßnahmen der christlichen Kaiser des vierten Jahrhunderts gegen Häretiker, Heiden und Juden,* Diss. Cologne 1971, 62-70; Karl Leo Noethlichs,'Kirche, Recht und Gesellschaft in der Jahundert mitte', in *L'Église de l'Empire au IVe Siècle* [Fondation Hardt/Entretiens sur l'antiquité classique 34] (Vandœuvres-Geneva 1989), 251-299, esp. 288-291.

[18] Cf. Haehling (*op cit. n. 17*), 527-536, esp. 534; Barnes (*op. cit. n. 5*), 306-321. However, Constantius' policy was not altogether consistent in this respect, since he had also to give in to the constraints of *Realpolitik*. Cf. Haehling *ibid.*

[19] Cf. Lib., *or.* 1,35.37.74.80.94 f.; Them., *or.* 2; Marrou (*op cit. n. 16*), 441; Peter Wolf, *Vom Schulwesen der Spätantike: Studien zu Libanius* (Baden-Baden 1952), 24 f., 42.

capital'.[20] At this time (around 342) Constantinople boasted a school
with distinguished teachers, among them the *grammatici* Didymus and
Nicocles of Sparta and the sophist Bemarchius. The young Libanius
taught there privately 340-342 (and again later in an official function
348-353).[21] Moreover, Libanius tells us that during this first stay at the
'new Rome' there were two further sophists there, whose names he
does not mention. One of them came from Cyzicus[22] and had with
Nicocles' help acquired the citizenship of the city. Later he seems to
have fallen out with Nicocles, for the latter attempted to gain Libanius' support in trying to ruin this man.[23] The other one was a Cappadocian[24] who had been given the position which Libanius had hoped
for: he had been appointed 'highest rhetor' (ῥήτωρ ἄκρος) by the emperor on the Senate's request.[25] Both sophists were hostile towards

---

[20] Paul Lemerle, *Le Premier Humanisme Byzantin: Notes et Remarques sur Enseignement et Culture à Byzance des Origines au Xe Siècle* [BByz.E 6] (Paris 1971);
the English translation which is slightly expanded and which is used here appeared
under the title *Byzantine Humanism—The First Phase: Notes and Remarks on Education and Culture in Byzantium from Its Origins to the 10th Century* [Byzantina
Australiensia 3] (Canberra 1986); cf. there 55 and in general 55-63; moreover, N(igel)
G. Wilson, *Scholars of Byzantium* (London 1983), 49 ff.

[21] Cf. Schemmel (*op cit. n. 16*), 151 f. and the relevant entries in PLRE I. On
Didymus cf. also Kaster (*op cit. n. 16*), 269 (no. 46); on Nicocles cf. Otto Seeck, *Die
Briefe des Libanius zeitlich geordnet* [TU 30/1-2] (Leipzig 1906), 221 f.; Wolf (*op.
cit.. n. 19*), 37-39 and n.74; Kaster (*op cit. n. 16*), 202-204, 317-321 (no. 106) and
Willy Stegemann '10) N[ikokles] von Sparta', *Paulys Real-Encyclopädie* XVII/1,
(1936), 352-356; on Libanius cf. (R.) Foerster and (K.) Münscher, 'Libanios', *Paulys
Real-Encyclopädie* XII/2, (1925), 2485-2551.

[22] No other sophist from Cyzicus seems to be known. The Diogenes mentioned by
Karl Gerth, 'Die Zweite oder Neue Sophistik', *Paulys Real-Encyclopädie* SVIII,
(1956), 719-782, 781 was in fact a *grammaticus*, not a sophist. Cf. *Fragmente der
Griechischen Historiker* III/B, 3 vols., (Leiden 1950/55), No. 474; Kaster (*op. cit. n.
16*), 398f. (no. 207).

[23] Cf. Lib., *or.* 1,31.

[24] Other famous Cappadocian sophists were e. g. Pausanias of Caesarea, Eutychia-
nus and Strategius of Caesarea; cf. Gerth (*op cit. n. 22*), Nos. 204, 92, 260.

[25] Lib., *or.* 1,35. The expression ῥήτωρ ἄκρος (= *orator/rhetor summus*?) appears
to have been an official title designating the supreme sophist in the school (a kind of
headmaster?). It is apparently not attested elsewhere. On the synonymous use of
σοφιστής and ῥήτωρ in official terminology cf. dig. 27,1,6,2 (Antoninus Pius) and
Wolf, (op. cit. n. 20), 20. For the (non-technical) usage of *orator summus* cf. the references given in *Thesaurus Linguae Latinae* IX/2 (Leipzig 1968-1981), 899, 71-73. On
the Constantinopolitan senate cf. Jones (*op. cit. n.6*), 132 f, 527; Gilbert Dagron,
Naissance d'une Capitale: Constantinople et Ses Institutions de 330 à 451, 2nd ed.
[BByz.E 7] (Paris 1984), 117-210 and Alexander Demandt (*op. cit. n.6*), 396 and n.
226. On the procedure for appointment cf. Kaster (*op .cit. n. 16*) p 39-41.

their new colleague[26] and appear to have been involved in the plot against Libanius which led to his expulsion from Constantinople.[27]

Since we know that Theodosius II expanded the school in 425 (he appointed three *oratores* and ten *grammatici* in Latin literature and five *sofistae* and ten *grammatici* in Greek literature[28]), we may assume that at the time when Hecebolius taught there it was somewhat smaller. This could mean, however, that from Libanius we in fact learn about *all* official Greek sophists who taught at Constantinople during the 340s (i.e. the man from Cyzicus, the Cappadocian and Bemarchius).[29] Hence Hecebolius was probably one of them, and there are several hints which suggest that he is identical with the anonymous Cappadocian. Around 340[30] Hecebolius became young Julian's teacher. Without doubt, only

---

[26] Cf. Lib., *or.* 1,38; as to the identity of the two sophists mentioned in this chapter I follow Jean Martin/Paul Petit (eds.), *Libanios–Discours, Tome I: Autobiographie (Discours I)* [CUFr] (Paris 1979), 38 pace A. F. Norman (ed.), *Libanius' Autobiography (Oration I)* [University of Hull Publications] (Oxford 1965), 158 who identifies them with the Cappadocian and Nicocles. Nicocles was *grammaticus*, not sophist (cf. Socr. 3,1 and Kaster (*op cit. n. 16*), 317).

[27] Cf. Lib., *or.* 1,44-47.

[28] Cf. *cod. Theod.* 14,9,3 and 15,1,53; moreover, cf. Schemmel (*op cit. n. 16*), 167; Friedrich Fuchs, *Die höheren Schulen von Konstantinopel im Mittelalter* [ByA 8] (Leipzig/Berlin 1926) 1 ff.; Louis Bréhier, 'Notes sur l'Histoire de l'Enseignement Supérieur à Constantinople', *Byzantion* 3 (1926), 73-94; 4 (1927), 13-28, esp. (1926), 82-94; Marrou (*op. cit. n. 16*), 442 f.; Kennedy (*op. cit. n. 16*), 165-167; Lemerle (*op. cit. n. 20*), 66-68.

[29] The number of sophists who were *immunes* appears to have varied between three and five, depending on the size of the city; cf. the rescript by Antoninus Pius in *dig.* 27,1,6,2. On immunity for sophists cf. Marrou (*op. cit. n. 16*), 434-436.

[30] On Julian's biography cf. Richard Klein, 'Julian Apostata: Ein Lebensbild', *Gymnasium* 93 (1986), 273-292 who lists the most important literature. The chronology of Julian's youth and education is highly controversial, since the evidence is contradictory (cf. the survey of scholarship in Kaster (*op. cit. n. 16*), 319-321). One of the main difficulties concerns Julian's exile in Fundus Macelli. Did it precede or did it follow Julian's studies at Constantinople and Nicomedia? The chronology was first put forward by Norman H. Baynes in his review of Seeck (see below) in *The English Historical Review* 27 (1912), 755-60, 758 f. and in a subsequent article, 'The Early Life of Julian the Apostate', *Journal of Hellenic Studies* 45 (1925), 251-254. It was recently defended by Kaster (*op. cit.*). Baynes assumed *two* stays at Constantinople and proposed this chronology: 339/40 studies in Constantinople with Mardonius; 342-348 exile in Fundus Macelli; 348 second stay in Constantinople: Julian studies with Nicocles and Hecebolius; 348/9 stay in Nicomedia (Kaster: late 347 or early 348 until 348 or early 349: studies with Nicocles and Hecebolius in Constantinople followed by the stay in Nicomedia). I follow, however, Eberhard Richtsteig, 'Einige Daten aus dem Leben Kaiser Julians', *Philologische Wochenschrift* 51 (1931), 428-432 who slightly modified Otto Seeck's earlier findings in *Geschichte des Untergangs der antiken Welt*

the best sophist was considered for this position. The Cappadocian, however, was appointed 'highest rhetor' *by the emperor himself* (βασι-λέως πέμποντος, Lib., *or.* 1,35). Hence he held a particularly eminent position and must, in the emperor's eyes, have been just the right man to teach his cousin. It is, therefore, highly likely that the anonymous Cappadocian and Hecebolius are identical. He was, perhaps, at that time, still young, since Libanius emphasizes that the Cappadocian had only won one rhetorical contest so far (ἐξ οἶμαί τινος ἀγῶνος ἑνός, *or.* 1,35).[31] Moreover, Libanius' hostility towards this man fits the facts very well, since we know that he thoroughly disliked Hecebolius as well and would not even mention his name.[32]

As regards Hecebolius' teaching, Socrates gives us the following account. It is probably partly based on Libanius' *Funeral Oration over Julian* (*or.* 18) and partly on one of Emperor Julian's biographies:[33]

'And Julian, when he was grown up, attended the schools at Constantinople, in the Basilica, where the schools then were. He appeared in public in plain clothes and was superintended by the eunuch Mardonius. In grammar, Nicocles the Spartan was his instructor; and from Ecebolius the Sophist, who at that time happened to be a Christian, he learned the art of rhetoric. The emperor Constantius had made this provision lest by attending lectures of a pagan teacher he would turn away to idolatry.'[34]

IV (Berlin 1911), 456-458. As opposed to Baynes and Kaster Richtsteig assumed that Julian was only *once* in Constantinople (which is the simpler hypothesis) and gave as dates for Julian's subsequent stay in Nicomedia and (indirect) contact with Libanius the years 341/2-345; for the stay in Macellum 345-351. Richtsteig's chronology, however, is not free from difficulties either.

[31] This may, however, be pure polemics. On the importance of rhetorical contests cf. Norman (*op cit. n. 26*), 157; Stefan Rebenich, 'Augustinus im Streit zwischen Symmachus und Ambrosius um den Altar der Victoria', *Laverna* 2 (1991), 55-75, 59 and n. 31. Both anonymous sophists are again mentioned in 1,38: Τὼ μὲν δὴ σοφιστὰ ἐπενθείτην, ὁ μὲν οὐδὲ ἀνθήσας ἀρχήν, ὁ δὲ ἀπηνθηκώς. ὁ μὲν γὰρ οὐδὲ παρῆλθεν εἰς τὸ δύνασθαι, ὁ δὲ ἐξεπεπτώκει (Martin/Petit 114, 9-11). The first one must be the Cappadocian. *Pace* Fritz Schemmel, 'Die Schulzeit des Kaisers Julian', *Philologus* 82 (1926/27), 455-466, 456 f., who concludes from *or.* 1,35 ὁ μὲν δὴ σεμνὸς σεμνῶς εἱστήκει that this 'fits better an old than a young man' and who, therefore, identifies Hecebolius with the man from Cyzicus. Considering Libanius' irony in this passage, I do not find this convincing.

[32] Cf. below.

[33] Cf. Franz Geppert, *Die Quellen des Kirchenhistorikers Socrates Scholasticus* [SGTK] (Leipzig 1898), 69-75, 122. Libanius cannot have been Socrates' only source, because he gives some details which are not found in Libanius (*pace* Kaster (*op. cit. n. 16*), 317).

[34] Ἰουλιανὸς δὲ αὐξηθεὶς τῶν Κωνσταντίνου πόλει παιδευτηρίων ἠκροᾶτο, εἰς τὴν

We learn from this that Julian underwent the classical three tier education, i.e. 'primary school' under the παιδαγωγός Mardonius;[35] 'secondary school' with the *grammaticus* Nicocles and, finally, 'higher education' with the σοφιστής Hecebolius who taught him the art of rhetoric.[36] At that time the school was situated in the Basilica in the east of the city and not yet on the capitol to where it moved, perhaps in 425.[37] Hecebolius was then a Christian which was one of the reasons why Constantius had chosen him. Libanius, who, when writing about Julian's youth, does not even mention Hecebolius' name, emphasizes this

βασιλικήν, ἔνθα τότε τὰ παιδευτήρια ἦν, ἐν λιτῷ σχήματι προϊὼν καὶ ὑπὸ Μαρδονίου τοῦ εὐνούχου παιδαγωγούμενος. Τῶν μὲν οὖν γραμματικῶν λόγων Νικοκλῆς ὁ Λάκων ἦν αὐτῷ παιδευτής· ῥητορικὴν δὲ παρὰ Ἐκηβολίῳ κατώρθου τῷ σοφιστῇ Χριστιανῷ τότε τυγχάνοντι. Τούτου δὲ ὁ βασιλεὺς Κωνστάντιος προενόησε μήπως Ἕλληνος διδασκάλου ἀκροώμενος πρὸς δεισιδαιμονίαν ἐκκλίνοι. Χριστιανὸς γὰρ ἦν ἐξ ἀρχῆς Ἰουλιανός (3,1 [PG 67,369A-B]; tr. NPNF, altered).

[35] As regards Mardonius' role, Socrates is not altogether clear. At least for part of the time at Constantinople, Mardonius seems to have taught Julian simultaneously with Nicocles and to have acted as his minder. About him cf. PLRE I, 558 and (W.) Enßlin, 'Mardonios (2)', *Paulys Real-Encyclopädie* XIV/2 (1930), 1658; Peter Guyot, *Eunuchen als Sklaven und Freigelassene in der griechisch-römischen Antike* [Stuttgarter Beiträge zur Geschichte und Politik 14] (Stuttgart 1980), 58, 215 (no. 67). The religious allegiance of Mardonius is a matter of debate; cf. e. g. G. W. Bowersock, *Julian the Apostate* (London 1978), 24; Athanassiadi-Fowden (*op cit. n. 12*), 14-23 (Mardonius was a pagan) *pace* Seeck (*op cit. n. 21*), 457; Enßlin (*op cit.*), 1658; Demandt (*op cit. n. 6*), 95 (Mardonius was a Christian). Cf. furthermore Augusto Rostagni, *Giuliano l'Apostata: Saggio Critico con le Operette Politiche e Satiriche Tradotte e Commentate* [Il Pensiero Greco 12] (Torino 1920), 361-370. Apart from Mardonius Julian was looked after by another eunuch whom Libanius calls σωφροσύνης φύλαξ (*or.* 18,11).

[36] As to the Roman education system cf. Marrou (*op cit. n. 16*), 389-421. The modern terms must, of course, be applied with some caution. As to the danger of false retrojections cf. Paul Speck's review of Lemerle, (*op cit. n. 20* ; French ed.), *Byzantinische Zeitschrift* 67 (1974), 385-393, 386 f. Robert Browning, *The Emperor Julian* (London 1975), is quite unclear about Hecebolius. On p. 39 he states that Julian may have studied under him in *Constantinople*; on p. 52, however, he claims that after Macellum Julian 'probably began once again to attend the lectures of Hekebolios at *Nicomedia'* (my italics).

[37] Cf. Paul Speck, *Die Kaiserliche Universität von Konstantinopel: Präzisierungen zur Frage des höheren Schulwesens in Byzanz im 9. und 10. Jahrhundert* [ByA 14] (Munich 1974), 94; Speck., review cited (n. 36), 389 and n.15; Cyril Mango, *Le Développement Urbain de Constantinople (IVe-VIIe Siècles)*, [Travaux et Mémoires du Centre de Recherche d'Histoire et Civilisation de Byzance/Collège de France/Monographies 2] (Paris 1985), 26 *pace ibid*, 30; Schemmel (*op cit. n. 16*), 151; Wolfgang Liebeschuetz, 'Hochschule', *Reallexikon für Antike und Christentum* XV (1991), 858-911, 872. As to the topographical problems which nevertheless remain cf. Lemerle (*op cit. n. 20*), 68 n.58.

point as well (*or.* 18,12) and says that Julian 'was enduring this incompetence in rhetoric because of the war waged against the altars by his teacher.'[38]

Socrates then goes on to explain that young Julian made great progress in the λόγοι which lead to his quickly becoming famous in Constantinople.[39] Since he thus had become a potential threat to the throne, the emperor decided to send him to Nicomedia, to the same city where Libanius had moved after the scandal at Constantinople. Constantius gave orders, however, that Julian should not be allowed to attend lectures by Libanius because of the latter's paganism.[40] Strangely enough, however, Libanius claims that 'the reason for the fact that he found pleasure in my oratory and yet avoided its author was that marvellous teacher of his. He had bound him with many fearsome oaths never to be or to be called my pupil and never to be enrolled on the list of my students.'[41] He, therefore, attributes this prohibition to Hecebolius rather than to the emperor.

We do not know whose account is more reliable. At first sight Libanius' version seems more likely to be correct. There were, after all, strong tensions between the rhetor of Nicomedia and his former Constantinopolitan colleague, especially if Hecebolius is identical with the anonymous Cappadocian mentioned above. These were not least due to the fact that Libanius was a pagan, and Hecebolius was briefed by the emperor to avoid everything which could encourage in his young pupil a favourable disposition towards the gods.[42] Yet why did Socrates

---

[38] ...φέροντα τὴν φαυλότητα τῶν λόγων διὰ τὸν πρὸς τοὺς βωμοὺς τοῦ διδασκάλου πόλεμον (*or.* 18,12 (Foerster II,242,3-5; tr. Norman)). Cf. also Socrates' polemical reaction in 3,32: Καὶ εἰ Ἰουλιανὸς ἦν σοφιστής, εἶπεν ἂν καὶ αὐτὸν κακὸν σοφιστὴν ὡς καὶ Ἐκηβόλιον ἐν τῷ ἐπιταφίῳ Ἰουλιανοῦ (PG 67,437C).

[39] Cf. 3,1 (PG 67,369B-C).

[40] Ἰουλιανὸς δ' ἐκωλύετο φοιτᾶν παρ' αὐτῷ διότι Λιβάνιος Ἕλλην τὴν θρησκείαν ἐτύγχανεν ὤν (1,13 (PG 67,369C-372A).

[41] Τὸ δὲ αἴτιον τοῦ τοῖς λόγοις <μὲν> χαίρειν, φεύγειν δὲ τὸν ἐκείνων πατέρα πολλοῖς καὶ μεγάλοις αὐτὸν ὅρκοις ὁ θαυμαστὸς ἐκεῖνος κατειλήφει σοφιστὴς ἦ μὴν ἐμὸν μήτε γενέσθαι μήτε κληθῆναι φοιτητὴν μήτ' εἰς τὸν κατάλογον ἐγγραφῆναι τῶν ἐμῶν ὁμιλητῶν (Foerster II, 242,16-243,3; tr. Norman). (This clearly refers to Hecebolius, not to Nicocles; *pace* Foerster and Münscher (*op. cit. n. 21*), 2490; Stegemann (*op. cit. n. 21*), 354). Johannes Geffcken, *Kaiser Julianus* [Das Erbe des Alten 8] (Leipzig 1914), 8, 129 assumes, therefore, that Hecebolius accompanied Julian to Nicomedia (cf. also Demandt (*op cit. n. 6*), 95). I find this far from convincing: if Hecebolius had been with Julian he could have controlled him without binding him by oaths.

[42] Socrates himself appears to acknowledge this when he says: Οὗτος μὲν οὖν τὴν

deviate from his source in this point? Did he suspect that Libanius tried to exonerate Constantius from certain charges which had been made against him?[43] In any case, he had other information about this matter to which he gave more credit than to Libanius' version.

Furthermore, Socrates tells us in 3,13 that Hecebolius reverted to paganism during Julian's rule. He connects this piece of information with the fact that Julian did not tolerate any Christians in the imperial household or in the provincial administration. The steadfast Christians, therefore, resigned from their offices, whereas others, 'because they preferred money and worldly honour to the true happiness, turned without hesitation back to sacrificing.'[44] Socrates' account reflects the political reality quite accurately. As Raban von Haehling showed convincingly, during his short reign Julian appointed only pagans to administrative posts.[45] Since for many people the line between the old and the new faith was blurred anyway, Hecebolius was by no means the only one who returned to the old faith. There were several lapsed Christians in Julian's administration.[46]

It could be, therefore, that Hecebolius' lapse has to be seen in connection with his being appointed governor or *praeses* of Egypt. We possess a letter by Libanius which he addressed to the Prefect of Egypt, Gerontius (*ep.* 306 Foerster). In this letter, Libanius says that some slaves had run away from their master Sebon (one of Libanius' friends) and had been found by Euodus with a certain Onesimus. He, in turn, had sent them to Hecebolius, the son of Ascholius, assuming that they would then be returned to Libanius (and probably from there to Sebon). However,

---

ὀργὴν κατὰ τῶν παιδαγωγῶν, εἰς τὸν κατ' αὐτῷ γραφέντα λόγον ἐκένωσεν. This speech is lost. Cf. Foerster and Münscher (*op. cit. n. 21*), 2527.

[43] Cf. in particular Libanius' description of the murder of Julian's relatives, which he does not directly lay at Constantius' door; cf. *or.* 18,10.

[44] Ἕτεροι δέ, ὅσοι μὴ ὀρθῇ γνώμῃ ἐχριστιάνιζον, ὅσοι [ὡς *coni. Valesius*] τὰ χρήματα καὶ τὴν ἐνταῦθα τιμήν, τῆς ἀληθοῦς εὐδαιμονίας προκρίναντες, μὴ μελλήσαντες πρὸς τὸ θύειν ἀπέκλινον (PG 67,411C-413A).

[45] Cf. Haehling (*op. cit. n. 17*), 537-547.

[46] Cf. also Greg. Naz., *or.* 4,11; furthermore Haehling (*op. cit. n. 21*), 544-546; Hanns Christof Brennecke, *Studien zur Geschichte der Homöer: Der Osten bis zum Ende der homöischen Reichskirche* [BHTh 73] (Tübingen 1988), 106 and n. 48; Noethlichs (*op. cit. n. 17*), 1154-5. Another classical case of a turncoat from that time is Domitius Modestus who also changed sides at least twice. He was the prototype of a nimble, ambitious official 'who when applying for a high administrative office aligned himself with the denomination of each individual ruler' (Haehling (*op. cit. n. 21*), 67 f.). Cf. moreover, PLRE I, 605-608.

they never arrived. Libanius, therefore, suspected that they had run away a second time and asks Gerontius to restore the law in its full force.

From one of Libanius' remarks it may appear that he did not particularly like the Hecebolius mentioned in this letter. For he comments on the fact that the slaves had not arrived yet by saying … πολλαί τε ὑπ-οψίαι κατὰ τοῦ πράγματος. If this is intended to denigrate Hecebolius it would fit well with what we know about Libanius' relationship with the sophist of the same name and would suggest their identity.[47] This would mean that Hecebolius became at some unknown date some kind of higher official (governor? *praeses?*) in Egypt.[48] He would have been appointed by Constantius, since *ep.* 306 probably dates from spring or summer 361.[49] Such an honour for a sophist is not impossible, if one considers the fact that the sophist Demetrius became governor of Phoenice some time before 358[50] and the pagan (!) rhetor and philosopher Themistius was not only adlected to the Senate of Constantinople in 355, but even made Proconsul of that city in 358-9.[51] When Julian came to power, Hecebolius wanted to retain his job and therefore decided to sacrifice.

On the other hand Libanius was on friendly terms with Ascholius, the father of this governor, as can be seen from *ep.* 615 (Foerster). The remark in *ep.* 306 must, therefore, perhaps, be understood in a different way, in which case it is rather unlikely that the Hecebolius mentioned by Libanius is identical with the sophist. In this case the latter's lapse was a consequence of the school law issued by Julian in June 362.[52]

---

[47] Cf. in this sense e.g. Seeck (*op. cit. n. 4*), 2800.

[48] Cf. *ibid.*

[49] Cf. Seeck (*op. cit. n. 21*), 378.

[50] PLRE I, 247 f. (DEMETRIUS 2).

[51] *Ibid* 890. As regards the rise of some *grammatici* cf. Kaster (*op. cit. n. 16*), 130-132.

[52] Cf. Gustave Bardy, 'L'Eglise et l'Enseignement au IVᵉ Siècle', *Recherches de science religieuse* 14 (1934), 525-549; 15 (1935), 1-27; (1934), 546. One wonders whether Socrates' wording ὁ Κωνσταντινουπόλεως σοφιστὴς 'Εκηβόλιος does not imply that under Julian he was still sophist in this city. Cf. also *Suda,* s.v. Μᾶρις where Socr. 3,12f. is abbreviated in such a way that the lapse of Hecebolius is the result of Julian's school law. Cf., moreover, above n. 2) On Julian's school law cf. *cod. Theod.* 13,3,5; *cod. Iust.* 10,53,7; *ep.* 61 (Bidez) and the testimonies collected in J. Bidez and F. Cumont, *Imperatoris Flavii Claudii Iuliani Epistulae, Leges Poemata, Fragmenta Varia* [Nouvelle Collection de Textes et Documents] (Paris/London 1922), 69-75. Cf. on the whole problem, J. Bidez, *L'Empereur Julien—Oeuvres Complètes,* I/2: Lettres et Fragments, texte révu et traduit [CUFr] (Paris 1924), 44-47; Bardy (*op cit. n. 12*) 542-549; C. J. Henning, *De Eerste Schoolstrijd tussen Kerk en Staat onder Julianus*

This law was specifically directed against the Christian sophists.[53] Julian left them a choice: either to take their teaching of the classics seriously and hence to worship the gods or to resign their posts.[54] Consequently, many Christians chose the second alternative, among them Marius Victorinus[55] in Rome and Prohaeresius in Athens, even though in the case of the latter the emperor wanted to make an exception.[56] The reason for Hecebolius' lapse may, therefore, be directly connected with this law.

Julian never mentions his teacher in his writings, unless a highly rhetorical letter in which Julian asks Hecebolius to keep on writing to him is genuine.[57]

As regards Hecebolius' later life we have no further information[58]—

---

den Afvallige, Diss. Nijmegen 1937 (unavailable to author); Glanville Downey, 'The Emperor Julian and the Schools', *Classical Journal* 53 (1957), 97-103; B. Carmon Hardy, 'The Emperor Julian and His School Law', *Church History* 37 (1968), 131-143; also (in German) in Richard Klein (ed.), *Julian Apostata* [WdF 509] (Darmstadt 1978), 387-408; Richard Klein, 'Kaiser Julians Rhetoren- und Unterrichtsgesetz', *Römische Quartalschrift für christliche Altertumskunde* 76 (1981), 73-94. Cf. also Brennecke (*op. cit. n. 46*), 105 n. 46.

[53] Iul., *ep.* 61 (Bidez 74,3-5).

[54] Orosius even claims: *Sed tamen, sicut a maioribus nostris compertum habemus, omnes ubique propemodum praecepti condiciones amplexati officium quam fidem deserere maluerunt* (adv. pag. 7,30,2 CSEL 5,510,2-4). This appears to be exaggerated. Cf. also Klein (*op. cit. n. 52*) 87 f.

[55] Cf. Aug., *conf.* 8,10.

[56] Cf. Hier., *chron.* a. 363 (Helm² 242,24-243,1); Eunap, *vit. soph.* 512 (ed. Wright).

[57] Iul., *ep* 194 (Bidez and Cumont). The authenticity of this letter is disputed e.g. by Franz Cumont, *Sur l'Authenticité de Quelques Lettres de Julien* (Gent 1889) [Université de Gand. Recueil de travaux publiés par la Faculté de Philosophie et Lettres 3], esp 15 f., 19; W. Schwarz, 'Julianstudien', *Philologus* 51 (1892), 623-653, 626 f. and note c; Geffcken (*op. cit. n. 41*), 145; Bidez (*op. cit. n. 52*), 234; Wright (*op. cit. n. 4*), XLVIII; Seeck (*op. cit. n. 4*), 2800. The authenticity is defended by Bidez and Cumont (*op. cit. n. 52*), 263f.; Kennedy (*op. cit. n. 16*), 164. Cf. furthermore E. v. Borries, 'Flavius Claudius Iulianus', in: *Paulys Real-Encyclopädie* X/1 (1918), 26-91, 80-83; PLRE I, 409.

[58] It is, of course, tempting, to assume his identity with the *praeses* (?) of Cappadocia Secunda to which Gregory Nazianzen addresses a letter in around 385 (cf. *PLRE* I, 409 (HECEBOLIUS 3)). It seems, however, that for chronological reasons this is rather unlikely, since then Hecebolius would have been at least 65 years old (assuming as latest date of birth some time around 320). According to the codex Parisinus gr. 7155 (codex C in the edition by Bidez and Cumont (*op. cit. n. 52*)) Julian's *ep.* 115 (Bidez and Cumont) is addressed to the same person as *ep.* 194 (on which cf. above), i. e. Hecebolius. In the Laurentianus LVIII,16 (L) and the Harleianus 5610 (H), however, no such address is found, and modern editors, therefore, tend to emend Ἐκηβολίῳ το Ἐδεσσηνοῖς. Cf. e. g. Geffcken (*op. cit. n. 41*), 145; Bidez and Cumont (*op.*

that is apart from the fact, to which I shall now turn my attention, that Socrates tells us how Hecebolius wanted to be readmitted to the Church.

II

When we examine the story related by Socrates and Severus in some more detail, it is important to regard its context in both these authors' works. Socrates clearly sees Hecebolius as one of those turncoats who trim their religious beliefs according to the tides. Severus, it is true, also underlines that Asterius 'was often received and often returned to his vomit.'[59] Yet at the same time he seems to regard Asterius' lying on the floor and crying as a sign of true repentance. The letter that contains the story (*ep.* VI,5,4 (Brooks), written some time between 515 and 518) deals with the problem of the monk and presbyter Mark who attempted to be readmitted to the Monophysite Church after having lapsed to the Diphysites and Massalians.[60] Severus advocates receiving Mark into the Church 'on the basis of a written document, upon his anathematizing the heresies of the Diphysites and of the Massalians, together with the impious men themselves and their impiety.'[61] The reason for this was that, during the Arian controversy, the Church had been equally indulgent towards men like the bishops Eleusinius[62] and Hosius of Corduba and Asterius himself. Hence, for Severus, Asterius' behaviour was by no

---

cit. n. 52), ad loc.; Bidez (*op. cit. n. 52*), 234, 241 and ad loc.; Wright (*op. cit. n. 4*), XLVIII; B. A. van Groningen (ed.), *Juliani Imperatoris Epistulae Selectae* [Textus Minores 27] (Leiden 1960) , *ad loc.*; Bertold K. Weis, *Julian—Briefe*, griechisch-deutsch, (Munich 1973), 186, 237; *pace* PLRE I, 409. Cf. also Borries (*op cit. n. 57*), 80-83.

[59] The saying from *Proverbs* 26.11 is traditionally used in the context of apostasy; cf. e. g. *2 Peter* 2.22; conc. Nic., *can.* 12 (Joannou 33); Bas. Caes., *can.* 44 (J. 136) etc.

[60] Cf. also *ep.* VI,5,5 (Brooks (*op. cit. n .1*)).

[61] Brooks (*op cit. n. 1*), II/2, 287; cf. also 291.

[62] This is perhaps not bishop Eleusinius of Sasima, as Brooks (*op cit. n. 1*), II, 467, s. v. 'Eleusinius' suggests, but probably the fourth century bishop Eleusius of Cyzicus. At Nicomedia in 365 he 'weakly succumbed to Valens' threats of banishment and confiscation, and declared his acceptance of the Arian creed. Full of remorse at his cowardly submission, on his return to Cyzicus, he assembled his people, confessed and deplored his crime, and expressed his desire, since he had denied his faith, to resign his charge into the hands of a worthier bishop. The people of Cyzicus, who were devotedly attached to him, refused to accept his resignation' (Edmund Venables, 'ELEUSIUS (2)', *Dictionary of Christian Biography* II, (1880), 76f., 76; cf. Socr., *h. e.* 4,6; Philost., *h. e.* 9,13).

means outrageous, but a sign of his true repentance. One does wonder,
however, why he did not express greater astonishment in this particular
case. Was a very emotional plea for readmittance to the Church perhaps
a normal occurrence when one who had lapsed repented of his offence?

A glance at the practice of penance in the fourth century provides us
with an answer to this question. In the early Church apostasy as committed by Asterius and Hecebolius was regarded as one of the gravest
sins. In the fourth century there was a widespread view that repenting
apostates were only to be readmitted to the Church at the moment of
their death.[63] In this regard the views of Basil of Caesarea on the subject
are of particular interest. For he says that apostates should 'mourn'
(προσκλαίειν) all their lives.[64] He describes this first degree of penance[65]
as follows: the penitent 'stands outside the door of the house of prayer
and asks the entering believers to pray for him, confessing his in-
justice.'[66] The parallel with the story in Socrates' version is immediately
apparent. Whereas Severus is much more general, the historian, too,
describes Hecebolius as being 'outside the door of the house of prayer'
(πρὸ τῆς πύλης τοῦ εὐκτηρίου οἴκου) and mourning. In particular, the expression ὁ εὐκτήριος οἶκος is quite striking, since it seems to reflect offi-

---

[63] Cf. Syn. Elv., can. 1; Bas. Caes., can. 5 (Joannou 103; for heretics); can. 73 (J.
150); Greg. Nyss., can. 2 (J. 209f); furthermore Dion. Alex., can. 5 (J. 15f). Cf., however, the somewhat different legislation at the Nicene Council, can. 10-12 (J. 32-34)
and the Synod of Carthage in 419 (can. 45 [J. 262]).

[64] Cf. can. 73 (Joannou 151,2).

[65] For the intricate problem of the degrees of penance (Bußstufen) cf. F. X. Funk,
'Die Bußstationen im christlichen Altertum', Kirchengeschichtliche Abhandlungen
und Untersuchungen I (Paderborn 1897), 182-209; Eduard Schwartz, 'Bußstufen und
Katechumenatsklassen', Schriften der Wissenschaftlichen Gesellschaft in Strassburg
VII (1911); which has been reproduced in: Gesammelte Schriften V (Berlin 1963),
274-362 (quoted thereafter); Bernhard Poschmann, Art. 'Bußstufen (Bußstationen)',
Reallexikon für Antike und Christentum II (1954), 814-816; Joseph Grotz, Die Ent-
wicklung des Bußstufenwesens in der vornicänischen Kirche (Freiburg 1955).

[66] ... ἔξω τῆς θύρας ἑστὼς τοῦ εὐκτηρίου οἴκου καὶ τῶν εἰσιόντων πιστῶν δεόμενος
εὐχὴν ὑπὲρ αὐτοῦ ποιεῖσθαι, ἐξαγορεύων τὴν ἰδίαν παρανομίαν (can. 56 (Joannou
144,18-221)). Cf. also can. 22 (J. 125), 75 (J. 152). Moreover Ps.-Greg. Thaum., can.
11 (J. 29); Hier., ep. 77,5 (on Fabiola): 'dissuta habuit latera, nudum caput, clausum
os. non est ingressa ecclesiam domini, sed extra castra cum Maria, sorore Moysi, separata consedit, ut, quam sacerdos eiecerat, ipse reuocaret' (Hilberg II,42,13-15). For the
third century cf. already Tert., paen. 7,10; pud. 3,5 and A. d'Alès, L'Édit de Calliste:
Étude sur les Origines de la Pénitence Chrétienne [BTH] (Paris 1914), 409-421;
Bernhard Poschmann, Paenitentia secunda: Die kirchliche Buße im ältesten Christentum bis Cyprian und Origenes. Eine dogmengeschichtliche Untersuchung [Theoph.
1; rpt. 1964] (Bonn 1940), 240 f.

cial terminology such as that found in Basil's canons.[67] It is not quite clear whether the πρόσκλαυσις as a separate degree of penance existed only in Asia Minor[68] or whether it has to be presupposed even where our sources are silent.[69] The question has no bearing on our case anyway, since both Asterius and Hecebolius appear to have come from Cappadocia.[70]

Therefore, the mourning as such was by no means unusual, but standard practice in penance at that time. What was unusual, however, was the fact that Asterius/Hecebolius *lay on the floor*. In this respect an interesting parallel is provided by an anonymous author whom Eusebius quotes in his *Church History*. He recounts how the confessor Natalius had been installed as a rival bishop to Pope Zephyrinus of Rome (198-207) by the adoptionists Asclepiodotus and Theodotus the Banker. As a result of nocturnal visions and angelic castigations, however, he felt remorse: he got up in the morning, 'put on sackcloth, and covered himself with ashes, and went with much haste, and fell down with tears before Zephyrinus the bishop, rolling at the feet not only of the clergy but also of the laity, and moved with tears the compassionate Church of the merciful Christ. But for all his prayers and the exhibition of the weals of the stripes he had received, he was scarcely admitted into communion' (5,28,12; tr. Lake).[71] In doing this Natalius exactly fulfilled the require-

---

[67] As to the 'official' flavour of the term cf. G.J.M. Bartelink, '"Maison de Prière" comme Dénomination de l'Eglise en tant qu'Édifice, en particulier chez Eusèbe de Césarée,' *Revue des Etudes Greques* 84 (1971), 101-118, 117.

[68] Thus e. g. Bernhard Poschmann, *Buße und Letzte Ölung* [HDG IV/3] (Freiburg 1951), 47; Heinrich Karpp, *La Pénitence: Textes et Commentaires des Origines de l'Ordre Pénitentiel de l'Eglise Ancienne* [TC 1] (Neuchâtel 1970), XXII. Cf., however, *const. apost.* 2,10,4; 2,18,7; 3,8,3 (on these passages Marcel Metzger, *Les Constitutions Apostoliques* III, introduction, texte critique, traduction et notes [SC 329] (Paris 1986), 102-104); conc. Trull., *can.* 87 (Joannou 223); *can.* 1, wrongly attributed to the Council of Constantinople 381 (cf. CPG 8604; ed. C. H. Turner, 'Canons Attributed to the Council of Constantinople, A. D. 381, Together with the Names of the Bishops, from Two Patmos MSS POB' PΟΓ', *Journal of Theological Studies* 15 [1913/4], 161-178, 164; on the problem of origin cf. Fr. van de Paverd, 'Die Quellen der kanonischen Briefe Basileios des Grossen', *Orientalia Christiana Periodica* 38 (1972) 5-63, esp. 27-45); Theod. Stud., *ep.* 2,49 (PG 99,1257C).

[69] Cf. Schwartz (*op. cit n. 65*), 312; Gustav Adolf Benrath, 'Buße V.', *Theologische Realenzyklopädie* VII (1981), 452-473, 458; C. Vogel, 'Penitenza I', in: *Dizionario Patristico e di Antichità Cristiane* II (1983), 2742-2746, 2745 f.

[70] For Asterius cf. Kinzig (*op. cit. n. 3*), 14 and n. 12. For Hecebolius cf. above.

[71] ...ὥστε ἕωθεν ἀναστῆναι καὶ ἐνδυσάμενον σάκκον καὶ σποδὸν καταπασάμενον μετὰ πολλῆς σπουδῆς καὶ δακρύων προσπεσεῖν Ζεφυρίνῳ τῷ ἐπισκόπῳ, κυλιόμενον ὑπὸ τοὺς πόδας οὐ μόνον τῶν ἐν κλήρῳ, ἀλλὰ καὶ τῶν λαϊκῶν, συγχέαι τε τοῖς δάκ-

ments of the *exomologesis* as set out by Tertullian.[72] The public pro-stration as part of penance is also described by other sources from the third century.[73] At that time, however, such a public display of con-trition already appears to have been exceptional.[74] One and a half centu-ries later, it certainly was.[75]

Moreover, Asterius/Hecebolius reinforced the impact of his behav-iour by shouting 'Trample upon me, the salt which has lost its savour.' What does this saying actually mean? It clearly alludes to *Matthew* 5.13: 'You are the salt of the earth; but if salt has lost its taste, how shall its saltness be restored? It is no longer good for anything except to be thrown out and trodden under foot by men.'[76] Whatever its original meaning was,[77] in the early Church Jesus' words were interpreted as re-ferring to discipleship. According to an exegesis favoured especially by Origen, the disciples, the salt of the earth, guaranteed the further ex-istence of the earth by preserving it from decomposition and decay. By

---

ρυσιν τὴν εὔσπλαγχνον ἐκκλησίαν τοῦ ἐλεήμονος Χριστοῦ πολλῇ τε τῇ δεήσει χρησά-μενον δείξαντά τε τοὺς μώλωπας ὧν εἰλήφει πληγῶν μόλις κοινωνηθῆναι (Schwartz/ Mommsen 504,2-8). On this incident cf. Paul Galtier, *Aux Origines du Sacrement de Pénitence* [AnGr/SFT A/6] (Rome 1951), 152 f.; Gustav Bardy, *Eusèbe de Césarée—Histoire Ecclésiastique. Livres V-VII,* texte grec, traduction et notes [SC 41] (Paris 1955), 77 n. 11; Poschmann (*op. cit. n. 66*), 363 f.

[72] *Paen.* 9-12; cf. the commentary in the edition by Charles Munier, *Tertullien—La Pénitence,* introduction, texte critique, traduction et commentaire [SC 316] (Paris 1984). Furthermore cf. *pud.* 5,14; 13,7.

[73] Cypr., *laps.* 35; Orig., *c. Cels.* 6,15.

[74] Cf. Tert., *paen.* 10,1.

[75] For the west cf., however, Ambrose, *paen.* 1,90; 2,96. On public penance in Milan at Ambrose's time cf. Roger Gryson, *Ambroise de Milan—La Pénitence,* texte latin, introduction, traduction et notes [SC 179] (Paris 1971), 31-50. The most famous act of penance in the fourth century and beyond was, of course, performed by the em-peror Theodosius the Great on Christmas 390; cf. Ambr., *ob. Theod.* 34 (Faller 388, 6-10): *Stravit omne, quo utebatur, insigne regium, deflevit in ecclesia publice peccatum suum, quod ei aliorum fraude obrepserat, gemitu et lacrimis oravit veniam. Quod pri-vati erubescunt, non erubuit imperator, publicam agere paenitentiam.* The last clause is suggestive as regards penitential practice. On the incident cf. Hans von Campen-hausen, *Ambrosius von Mailand als Kirchenpolitiker* [AKG 12] (Berlin/Leipzig 1929), 238-240; Rudolf Schieffer, 'Von Mailand nach Carossa: Ein Beitrag zur Geschichte der christlichen Herrscherbuße von Theodosius d. Gr. bis zu Heinrich IV.', *Deutsches Archiv für Erforschung des Mittelalters* 28 (1972), 333-370, 340. Cf. fur-thermore Sozomen, *h. e.* 7,15,5f. on public penance in Rome. Unlike in the case in question here, in Rome the shedding of tears formed part of the liturgy.

[76] Cf. also *Mark* 9.49 f. *Luke* 14.34 f.; *Colossians* 4.6.

[77] Cf. the commentaries, esp. Ulrich Luz, *Das Evangelium nach Matthäus,* 1. Teil-band: Mt 1-7 [EKK I/1,1] (Zurich etc. 1985) , 219-227.

following the example of Christ it was, therefore, actually possible to postpone the end of the world.[78] Moreover, since at least the times of Augustine, the *datio salis* had formed part of the (western) rite of the acceptance into the catechumenate.[79] It is unclear if before Augustine such a practice was already carried out. Moreover, we do not know whether this practice would have been carried out in those areas for which our sources are silent (especially in the East). If so, the words discussed here could be a direct allusion to a liturgical use of *Matthew* 5.13 during the catechumenate.[80] Be that as it may, a lapse from Christianity meant that the salt had lost its savour[81] which, if it occurred too often, could be understood to have serious implications for the preservation of the world. It is probable that Asterius/Hecebolius alludes to this understanding of *Matthew* 5.13.

---

[78] Cf. *c.Cels.* 8,70; *comm. Ioh.* 6,303; *comm. ser. Matt.* 37 (Klostermann/Benz/ Treu 70,1-5); *cat. Matt.* 90 f. On these passages cf. Henri Irénée Marrou, *A Diognète*, introduction, édition critique, traduction et commentaire [SC 33] (Paris 1951), 164- 166; Wolfram Kinzig, *Novitas Christiana: Die Idee des Fortschritts in der Alten Kirche bis Eusebius*, unpublished Habilitationsschrift, Heidelberg 1991, 443 f and n. 128. Cf. furthermore *mart. Pion.* 12,12; Cypr., *unit.* 1; *syn. Carth.* (256), 7 (Soden 254); Ioh. Chrys., *hom. Matt.* 15.6f.; ps.-Ioh. Chrys., *op. imperf. Matt.* 10.13; Theod. Mops., *frg. Mat.* 24 (Reuss 104 f.). On discipleship cf. Wolfgang Nauck, 'Salt as a Metaphor in Instructions for Discipleship', *Studia Theologica Lund u.a.* 6 (1953), 165-178. On salt in antiquity in general cf. I. Blümner, 'Salz', *Paulys Real-Encyclopädie* II/1,2 (1920), 2075-2099. On salt as metaphor in the Church Fathers cf. James E. Latham, *The Religious Symbolism of Salt* [ThH 64] (Paris 1982), 104-171. Salt as a metaphor for preservation or incorruptibility was 'by far the most universal [theme] throughout the history of salt symbolism'(p. 161).

[79] It is probably first attested in Aug., *de pecc. mer. et rem.* 2,26,42. Cf. the discussion in Franz Josef Dölger, *Der Exorzismus im altchristlichen Taufritual: Eine religiongeschichtliche Studie* [SGKA 3/1-2] (Paderborn 1909), 92-100; G. Bareille, 'Catéchuménat', *Dictionnaire de Théologie Catholique* II, (1923), 1968-1987, 1972 f.; Alois Stenzel, *Die Taufe: Eine genetische Erklärung der Taufliturgie* [FGTh 7/8] (Innsbruck 1958), 171-175; L(eo) Koep, 'Salz', Lexikon für Theologie und Kirche IX, 2nd ed., (1964), 284 f.; Elmar Bartsch, *Die Sachbeschwörungen der römischen Liturgie: Eine liturgiegeschichtliche und liturgietheologische Studie* [LWQF 46] (Münster, Westfalen 1967), 253 f., 290-305; Georg Kretschmar, 'Die Geschichte des Taufgottesdienstes in der alten Kirche', *Leiturgia* V (1970), 1-348, 72-74; Latham (*op. cit. n. 78)*, 87-103.

[80] From the sixth century onwards the interpretation of the salt given to the catechumens as preservation (Exegesis of *Matthew* 5.13?) is found quite often (cf. the references given in Dölger (*op. cit. n.* 79) 93 n. 3 and Latham (*op. cit. n. 78*) 87-96). Dölger himself, however, rejects such an interpretation of the original meaning of the *datio salis.*

[81] Cf. esp. Origen, *cat. Matt.* 90 f.

No doubt, in the imperial Church of the fourth century the behaviour by well-known figures such as Asterius and/or Hecebolius must have caused quite a stir. Severus seems to have interpreted it as a sign of true repentance; for Socrates it was just the whining of an opportunist who sees a cake turn into dough.

III

Finally I turn to the question from which we started: which story, if any, is the original? We cannot, of course entirely exclude the possibility that the anecdote was told about a whole variety of people and has, therefore, to be regarded as a literary *topos* rather than as an account of an actual event. However, it appears to me more likely that we are dealing here with a confused piece of historical information. Several reasons allow us to assume that Socrates' version[82] is at the basis of Severus' account:

1. Socrates is much more precise: as was shown above, Hecebolius belonged to a clearly definable group of penitents.
2. Severus refers explicitly to 'history books' as the source of his information.
3. He does that in such an imprecise way that he is probably quoting from memory. Such imprecision is also found in his other example, Hosius of Corduba. Severus says: 'Hosius also, the bishop of Corduba, the old man, whom Athanasius who is among the saints often called "a man of goodly old age" was often perverted and overcome by the times and again received'.[83] In fact, Athanasius calls Hosius εὐγηρότατος only once;[84] moreover, Hosius lapsed from what was later regarded as the orthodox position not 'often' but just once, namely at the council of Sirmium in 357 where, under strong pressure, he signed the Arian Second Creed.[85]

Hence it appears that Severus vaguely remembered a story about a fourth century sophist who had lapsed—and promptly confused Hece-

---

[82] It is probably based on oral tradition; cf. Geppert (*op. cit. n. 33*), 15 f., 59-65, 123; on Socrates' predilection for anecdotes cf. ibid, 16, 64 f.

[83] Brooks I, 322; II, 286 f.; cf. also VI,2,2 (B. I, 230; II, 206 f.).

[84] *Fug.* 5,1 (Opitz 71,7); another example is found in the letter by the (Eastern) synod of Serdica (342/3), in: Ath., *apol. sec.* 42,7 (Opitz 120,5).

[85] Cf. T(homas) D(aniel) C(ox) M(orse), 'HOSIUS (1)', *Dictionary of Christian Biography* III (1882), 162-174, 171 ff.

bolius with Asterius.[86] Another, and perhaps even more important, clue for this confusion is given when we compare the Greek of Socrates 3.13 as printed by Migne with its Armenian version. F.C. Conybeare pointed out that after the words ἐπὶ μὲν Κωνσταντίου διαπύρως χριστιανίζειν ὑπεκρίνατο the Armenian 'adds words equivalent to καὶ αὐτὸς 'Αρειανὸς ὤν, which must certainly have stood in the Greek text'.[87] One may ask whether Conybeare was not somewhat over-confident in attributing the addition to the original text.[88] For one wonders whether the addition is not an old gloss in which a reader explained in what sense Hecebolius actually *followed* Constantius (i.e. by becoming *Arian*), since Constantine had already favoured Christianity. Nevertheless, it may well have stood in the original text, for it fits with what we know about Socrates' views. He loathed not only the dialectics of the sophists, but also Arianism in all its versions.[89] If it is a gloss, it is in any case a very old one, because Severus' confusion is explained with much more ease if we assume that he read it in his text.

Severus' version is, therefore, nothing more than a *lapsus memoriae*.

---

[86] For Asterius cf. Kinzig (*op. cit. n. 3*), 16.

[87] F. C. Conybeare, 'Emendations of the Text of Socrates Scholasticus', *Journal of Philology* 33 (1914), 208-237, 232. The Armenian version, which was made by Philo of Tirak in 695/6, was printed by M. Ter Mowsesean, Valarshapat 1897.

[88] It is, apparently, not only missing in both Valesius' and Hussey's editions (which are based on different manuscripts), but also in the *Historia ecclesiastica tripartita* and the manuscript used for the relevant entry in the *Suda*. As to the complicated textual history of Socrates' *Church History* which is still not fully cleared up cf. Pierre Périchon, 'Pour une Édition Nouvelle de l'Historien Socrate: les Manuscrits et les Versions', *Recherches de Science Religieuse* 13 (1965),112-120 and the literature in CPG 6028. As to the Armenian translation cf. ibid and Périchon (*op .cit.*), 114-116.

[89] Glenn F. Chesnut, *The First Christian Histories: Eusebius, Socrates, Sozomen, Theodoret, and Evagrius*, 2nd ed. (Macon, Georgia 1986), 182-184. As to the role of Arian officials in the emperor's administration cf. von Haehling (*op. cit. n. 17*), 534.

AMBROSE AND PHILOSOPHY

ANDREW LENOX-CONYNGHAM

Ambrose, Bishop of Milan from 374 to 397, was unique as the only Christian who rose to high office in the early Church after being closely involved in the administration of the State as a governor. His father was probably high in the administration of the Praetorian Prefecture of the Gauls[1] and the son was well on his way to the most senior posts in the Empire when he was 'snatched from the judgement seats and brought away from the vanities of this world.'[2] It is probable that his election to the bishopric of Milan was engineered by the Emperor Valentinian I and Petronius Probus[3] rather than being instigated purely by a child's voice, as Paulinus, Ambrose's biographer, reports. Valentinian I was a Catholic Christian who was later praised by Ambrose, with some exaggeration, for his 'confession' in Julian's reign, when he had protested against being sprinkled with water by a pagan priest in the presence of the Emperor and had, temporarily, been deprived of his post in the army. However Valentinian I was an Emperor who was indifferent to religious controversy. He had, despite the protests of the orthodox, allowed Ambrose's Arian predecessor, Auxentius, to remain in possession of the see of Milan, after Auxentius had presented him with a vague confession of his own faith and denied that he had ever known Arius. The pagan Ammianus Marcellinus described Valentinian I admiringly as one who 'remained neutral in religious differences.'[4] Even so, since

---

[1] Since I place Ambrose's birth in 333/4 his father could not have been Praetorian Prefect since either someone else was Praetorian Prefect then or there was no Praetorian Prefect at that time. See A. Paredi, *Saint Ambrose: His Life and Times*, trans. M.J. Costelloe (University of Notre Dame Press 1964), 2 and 380, n. 5. The date of Ambrose's birth is discussed below.

[2] raptus de tribunalibus, abductus vanitatibus saeculi huius: *De paenitentia* II, 8, 72; CSEL 73, 192, l. 53 to 193, l. 54. [Ambrose's letters are cited according to the CSEL numbering with that of the PL in brackets.]

[3] C. Corbellini , 'Sesto Petronio Probo e l'elezione episcopale di Ambrogio', *Istituto Lombardo. Accademia di Scienze e Lettere*. Rendiconti. Classe di Lettere e Scienze Morale e Storiche, 109, fasc. I (Milan 1975), 181-9.

[4] Ammianus Marcellinus 30, 9, 5.

he was a Catholic Christian he might well have hoped, rather as Henry II hoped of Thomas Becket, that placing a sound Catholic like Ambrose, with his background of state administration, in the episcopal seat of the capital of the Empire would be a good way of ensuring harmony between Church and State.

But it was not to work out like that, even though this could hardly have been realised by Valentinian I who was to die only a year after Ambrose became bishop. If the Emperor's expectations were similar to those of Henry II, Ambrose's policy had resemblances to that of Becket. The Callinicum incident of 388, when Ambrose compelled Theodosius the Great to rescind his decree ordering the rebuilding of the synagogue which had been destroyed by the Christians of the area, showed clearly where the priorities lay in Ambrose's mind: 'Which is of greater importance, the appearance of discipline or the cause of religion? It is necessary that judgement should yield to piety.'[5] One reason for this attitude, surprising in one who had been a state administrator earlier, is probably that Ambrose regarded the Church as representing on earth that perfect society which the State itself should aspire towards. Thus it was actually in the State's interests to ensure that precedence should always be given to the interests of the Church, although Ambrose took care never to express this in so many words. A point often overlooked by those examining Ambrose's attitude to the State is that Ambrose never spoke of the rights or privileges or laws of the Church. (It is, therefore, a little misleading when Richard Klein, in his otherwise excellent study of Symmachus, speaks of the Emperor in 384, in the Altar of Victory controversy, having to give way to the 'law of the christian church',[6] an emphasis which Ambrose always seems studiedly to avoid). The phrase 'the laws of the Church' appears to be used only in one place, in which Ambrose asserts that the Church does not know how to publish them, hardly an outrageous theocratic statement![7] Ambrose's emphasis is always upon the fact of the Emperor or the State (with which the Emperor is regarded as being mystically identified) being subject to God, which could hardly be denied by any Christian. Nor could Ambrose, for his part, deny the obvious function of the State in preserving order, as his remarks on the Empire and, particularly, on the barbarian threat, make quite clear. Yet he appears strangely reserved in his attitude to the State's function of preserving order and stability. This is an interesting

---

[5] *Ep.* 1a, 11 (PL *Ep.* 40); CSEL 82/3, 167, ll. 132-4.

[6] R. Klein, *Symmachus* (Darmstadt 1971), 125.

[7] *De fuga saeculi*, 2, 8; CSEL 32/2, 168, l. 15.

ambivalence in Ambrose. Is this political ambivalence connected with his seemingly ambivalent attitude to philosophy?

Ambrose as a Kirchenpolitiker and Ambrose as a reader and user of philosophy (one could hardly describe him as a philosopher) may appear superficially to have little in common. Until about twenty five or so years ago the main emphasis of large-scale studies of Ambrose tended to be placed on his political activity. Theologically he was regarded as having little or no originality although he was admired for having taken the trouble to turn himself into a well-educated theologian through intensive study in his spare time. His interest in philosophy received little examination and was hardly mentioned. (In F. Homes Dudden's two-volume study, *The Life and Times of St Ambrose* (Oxford 1935), it is mentioned on seven out of 710 pages). Since that time, however, there has been an increasing tendency to see in Ambrose not only a theologian of far greater originality than had been admitted in the past but also a reader of philosophy who apparently had no hesitation in drawing upon pagan philosophers to 'fortify' his sermons, even though virtually all his remarks about philosophy were highly disparaging. Two of the most significant results of this interest in Ambrose's philosophical side have been Courcelle's study of Ambrose and Platonism[8] and Madec's general study of Ambrose and philosophy.[9]

Madec points out that the problem of philosophy is one which is marginal in the work and in the spirit of Ambrose[10] and that Ambrose's attitude to philosophy is an obviously ambivalent one. As Courcelle has shown, Ambrose was, however, widely read in pagan philosophy and did not hesitate to draw upon it for some of his own sermons. The most obvious example of Ambrose's interest in philosophy is his extensive use of the *Enneads* of Plotinus which has been examined by Courcelle.[11] The textual parallels are indisputable but, as Madec comments, their interpretation is more difficult and it is striking that they occur only in Ambrose's three sermons *De Isaac vel anima, De bono mortis* and *De Iacob et vita beata* and nowhere else. Courcelle maintains that the *De Isaac* and the *De bono mortis* must have been preached by 386 at the latest

---

[8] P. Courcelle, *Recherches sur les Confessions de saint Augustin*, new ed. (Paris 1968) especially Appendix IV 'Aspects variés du platonisme ambrosien'.

[9] G. Madec, *Saint Ambroise et la Philosophie* [Études Augustiniennes] (Paris 1974). C. Hill, 'Classical and Christian Traditions in some Writings of Saint Ambrose of Milan', Diss. Oxford 1979, examines the views of Madec.

[10] Madec (*op. cit. n.9*), 339.

[11] Courcelle (*op. cit. n.8*), 106-38

and would have been heard by Augustine.[12] The presence of these Plotinian elements in his works at all has aroused great interest. It had been thought by Dörrie that Ambrose was indebted to a lost treatise of Porphyry, On 'Know Yourself', in his sermon De Isaac,[13] but Pierre Hadot holds that the principal text on which Dörrie based his case (De Isaac, 6, 50) is only a summary of the Song of Songs, without any Neoplatonic signification, and that many of the texts which Dörrie considers porphyrian come from Philo or Origen, two of the authors to whom Ambrose is most heavily indebted in any case.[14] Madec points out that we cannot exclude the possibility that a Greek Father was an intermediary of these Plotinian elements[15] and that Ambrose was unaware of their Neoplatonic source. The most likely explanation, however, as Madec recognises, is simply that Ambrose had read the Enneads for himself, and this raises the question of when Ambrose is likely to have read these and, possibly, other writings of pagan philosophy.

Four letters of Ambrose are addressed to his old friend and mentor Simplician (Ep. 2, 3, 7 and 10 (PL Ep. 65, 67, 37 and 38)) whom Augustine described Ambrose as loving 'as though he were his father' and who probably instructed Ambrose before his baptism and consecration (at least, that is the usual interpretation of Augustine's description of Simplician as Ambrose's father in accipienda gratia).[16] Simplician had been a friend of Marius Victorinus, the Neoplatonic philosopher whose conversion to Christianity in the middle of the century was described to Augustine by Simplician himself.[17] Madec asks whether it may not have been Simplician who introduced Ambrose to Neoplatonism in his instruction before Ambrose's consecration or whether it was 'only later', 'seulement plus tard', that Ambrose might have come across Neoplatonism.[18] Similarly Dassmann holds that Ambrose must have come into contact with Neoplatonic ideas 'already early, (but) certainly after his

---

[12] Ibid 138, n. 2. However, Courcelle's remark, 'Prétendre que ces sermons sont postérieurs au séjour d'Augustin reviendrait donc à imaginer qu'Augustin a révélé Plotin à Ambroise. Ce qui paraît absurde,' is difficult to understand.

[13] H. Dörrie 'Das fünffach gestufte Mysterium. Der Aufstieg der Seele bei Porphyrios und Ambrosius', in Mullus. Festschrift Theodor Klauser, Jahrbuch für Antike und Christentum, Ergänzungsband 1 (1964), 79-92.

[14] P. Hadot, Compte rendu des conférences, in Annuaire de l'École Pratique des Hautes Études, Section des sciences religieuses (1965-66), 152.

[15] Madec (op. cit. n.9), 167.

[16] conf. VIII, 2, 3.

[17] conf. VIII, 2.

[18] Madec (op. cit. n.9), 170.

consecration as bishop'.[19] Carole Hill believes that it was probably not until 385-387 that Ambrose found time for the 'philosophical' study he had indicated his intention of following at the time of, or just before, his consecration.[20] None of these or other suggestions as to when Ambrose became acquainted with Neoplatonic philosophy appears to take into account the difference which the dating of Ambrose's birth is likely to make to this matter. The dating of his birth is based upon the interpretation of Letter 49 (PL *Ep.* 59) written to Severus, Bishop of Naples, in which Ambrose mentions that he is in his fifty-fourth year and refers, in *Ep.* 49, 3, to some contemporary trouble; 'we, exposed to the outbreaks of barbarians and the storms of war, are being tossed on a sea of troubles'. This has been taken to refer either to the invasion of Italy by Maximus in 387, or, according to Palanque, to a barbarian outbreak in the spring of 392 or to the occupation of Italy by Eugenius in 393/4. Most authorities are still inclined to accept one of the last two possibilities, giving the date of Ambrose's birth as either 339 or 340.[21] However, this question appears settled by Otto Faller's detailed consideration of this matter in his review of Homes Dudden's work on Ambrose.[22] Faller refers to the phrase in *Ep.* 49, 4, '*habitamus cum habitantibus Madian*', a phrase which had not been taken into account by previous writers. These words clearly imply that Ambrose was actually in Milan at the same time as the city was being occupied by the enemy troops. This could apply neither to 392, when there were no enemy troops in Milan, nor to 393/4, when Ambrose fled from Milan in the face of Eugenius. It must, therefore, apply to Maximus' invasion which sets Ambrose's birth in 333 or 334. This is also the date accepted by Paredi.[23] This straightforward chronological matter has some possible bearing on Ambrose's philosophical formation. It means that he was already about forty when he became bishop. (In the same article Faller has, again I believe conclusively, shown that the date of his consecration must be Sunday 7 December 374, and not 373). Ambrose was a member

---

[19] 'schon früh, sicher nach seiner Bischofsweihe', E. Dassmann , 'Ambrosius von Mailand' *Theologisches Realenzyklopädie* 2 (1977), 374.

[20] Hill (*op. cit. n. 9*), 174-6.

[21] Dassmann says probably 339. See (*op. cit. n. 19*), 362. M.G. Mara says 339 or 337 in the *Encyclopedia of the Early Church* 1 (translation of the *Dizionario Patristico e di Antichità Cristiane*) (Cambridge 1992), 28, but it is difficult to see what support there could be for 337.

[22] O. Faller, *Deutsche Literaturzeitung*, 59 Jahrgang, 39, 25 (September 1938), 1369-1372.

[23] Paredi (*op. cit. n. 1*), 2 and 380, n. 5.

of the Roman aristocracy, related to Symmachus, the leading pagan of
the time, and had been educated in Rome. He is likely to have practised
as an advocate in Rome before going to Sirmium probably in 365 to
serve under the new Praetorian Prefect, Volcacius Rufinus, who was re-
placed by Sextus Petronius Probus in 367. From 370 he had been Pro-
consular of Aemilia-Liguria, based on Milan. His time in Rome, therefore, would have overlapped with that of Marius Victorinus, one of the
leading Neoplatonic philosophers of the age, whose translations were
read by Augustine. Is it not likely that someone of Ambrose's vast
culture and education, together with his ability to read Greek fluently
(which would have been helped, in any case, by his five or so years in
Sirmium), would have studied the leading philosophy of the time long
before he had reached the age of forty, rather than after his consecration
as bishop? In other words, despite his Christian background, he is more
likely to have had a knowledge of Neoplatonism than of Christian
writings, apart from the Bible, before 374. He probably acquired an interest in Neoplatonism during his time in Rome where he was until the
age of about thirty-one, bearing in mind that his years in that city coinci-
ded with the time when Marius Victorinus was at the peak of his reputation. One of the devices Ambrose employed to try to escape the honour of being Bishop of Milan, Paulinus tells us, was his declared intention 'to profess philosophy', *philosophiam profiteri voluit*.[24] Courcelle has examined this phrase[25] and suggests that it was in the course of
the year before his episcopal consecration, 'in order to avoid being
elected bishop', that Ambrose made a public declaration of his interest
in 'Pythagoras, Plato and Plotinus, in other words Neoplatonism'. However, the impression we receive from Paulinus' account is that there was
only a short delay between the election and the consecration, as one
would expect, and Ambrose was, as we have seen, probably interested
in philosophy in any case more especially since Milan, where he was for
about four years as governor before becoming bishop, was a centre of
Neoplatonic studies and the residence of Chalcidius, a Neoplatonist
Christian, who wrote a commentary on the *Timaeus*. Courcelle, who
dates this commentary to 380, thinks that it was a knowledge of this
work which enabled Ambrose to make fuller use of a passage from Origen's Commentary on the Epistle to the Romans and that Ambrose also

---

[24] Paulinus, *Vita Ambrosii*, 7, 3.

[25] P. Courcelle, *Recherches sur Saint Ambroise—'Vies' Anciennes, Culture, Icono-
graphie* [Études Augustiniennes] (Paris 1973), 9-16.

became acquainted with some Platonic doctrines through Chalcidius.[26] It is not likely that Ambrose as governor in Milan would have been insulated from these Neoplatonic circles before 374.

Klaus Zelzer accepts that the phrase *philosophiam profiteri voluit* refers to connections which Ambrose must already have had to philosophy.[27] As we have seen, Madec suggests that a course in Neoplatonism may have been part of Simplician's preparation of Ambrose before his consecration as bishop. If, however, Ambrose was already acquainted with Neoplatonism, as is likely, it is more probable that Simplician's instruction was exclusively a theological one, as one would expect before an impending episcopal consecration. Certainly the four surviving letters to Simplician, already mentioned, concern only theological matters and make no reference to any interest the two men may have had in common philosophically. Augustine read Neoplatonic works in Milan, among which may have been the *De regressu animae* of Porphyry, to which he refers in the *City of God*. It is not likely that Ambrose, with his knowledge of Greek and general equipment of a more formal education than Augustine had received, would have been less well read in philosophy at the age of forty than Augustine was at the age of thirty two. Philosophy was, in the phrase often used by French writers on this subject, 'monnaie courante', legal currency, of the time and no educated Christian of Ambrose's background could have avoided it, however little he may have agreed with it. Ambrose's knowledge of philosophy, therefore, is not, in itself, a remarkable fact calling for an involved explanation, any more than it would have been surprising to have found a Christian in the former Communist bloc possessing a knowledge of Marxism. Madec speaks of finding in the spirit of Ambrose 'la rencontre and la cohabitation des deux cultures, profane et chrétienne,'[28] due respectively to his education and fervent Christian background, and in this he is likely to have been typical of many of his class.

Why, however, should Ambrose have used philosophy as he did? Plainly there was much, especially in Neoplatonism, that was compatible with Christian doctrine in any case and he may have incorporated it simply because he found it useful supporting material. But he also used it to set particular points of Christian doctrine in greater relief. Thus in the *Hexaemeron*, in whose doxography (I, 1, 1-4) we can find certain

---

[26] Courcelle (*op. cit. n. 25*), 20 and 24.

[27] K. Zelzer, 'Zur Beurteilung der Cicero-Imitatio bei Ambrosius, De officiis', *Wiener Studien*, Neue Folge, 11 (1977), 178.

[28] Madec (*op. cit. n.9*), 342.

blurred traces of the *De philosophia,* a lost dialogue of the young Aristotle,[29] Ambrose begins by opposing the teachings of pagan philosophers on the nature of the physical world in order to emphasise the Christian doctrine of God as creator. In this work Ambrose shows no more esteem for the opinions of philosophers on the physical ordering of the world than for their dialectical exercises. We also find here his basic reproach of philosophers, that they lose themselves in idle researches about the world instead of simply giving thanks to its Creator. A similar approach is also found in the *De officiis ministrorum,* Ambrose's work on Christian ethics, designed primarily for his 'spiritual sons', the clergy of Milan, and modelled upon the *De officiis* of Cicero. The *De officiis ministrorum* shares the approach of the *Hexaemeron,* but in this case Ambrose attacks the moral teachings of philosophers. The purpose of Ambrose in this work is best shown by the passage in which he opposes the philosophical discussions on the *vita beata* to the Christian doctrine of the *vita aeterna.*[30]

By his use of philosophy, therefore, Ambrose was able sometimes to set in sharper relief, and even in opposition, specific examples of Christian doctrine. But why, since he did not hesitate to use this philosophy, was he against it in the first place? There were several reasons which it would be difficult to set in any order of priority. Perhaps we should start with Ambrose's admiration of St Paul and with the negative attitude adopted by Paul in *Colossians* 2.8, where the word 'philosophy' is plainly used in a pejorative sense and refers to pagan philosophy. But Ambrose's attitude to Paul was an intensification of his attitude to the Bible generally, which was that everything worth knowing was to be found in the Bible in any case, and that was the source from which philosophers derived the most valuable parts of their teaching.[31] If only the philosophers had remained content with what they derived from the Bible!, *Utinam non superflua his et inutilia miscuissent.*[32] Ambrose was convinced of the absolute and all embracing truth of the Bible, a truth

---

[29] J. Pépin, *Théologie Cosmique et Théologie Chrétienne* (Paris 1964), 4.

[30] *De officiis ministrorum* II, 1, 3–2, 6; *Opera Omnia di Sant' Ambrogio 13,* I Doveri (Milan 1977), 184-6.

[31] This attitude is summed up well by S. Vanni Rovighi: 'Potremmo riassumere il suo pensiero in due parole: tutto quello che di vero ci dicono i filosofi si trova anche, e molto meglio spiegato, molto più chiaro e completo nei Libri sacri, quello poi che non si trova nel Libri sacri è vanità, ricerca oziosa ed inutile', 'Le idee filosofiche di Sant' Ambrogio', in *Sant'Ambrogio nel XVI centenario della nascita* (Milan 1940), 237.

[32] *De bono mortis,* 10, 45; CSEL 32/1, 741, l. 18.

revealed by the Spirit of God. Therefore the worthwhile aspects of philosophy could not be anything other than wisdom borrowed from the Bible. So when the Christian borrows from the philosophers he is only taking back what is his own; 'so those writings belong to us which are the most outstanding in the writings of the philosophers.'[33] Any judgement of Ambrose's attitude to philosophy has to take account of the overriding importance of the Bible in his spirituality; 'the truth of the Bible and the faith which responds to it constitute, in the eyes of Ambrose, the world of orthodoxy', comments Madec pertinently.[34] Philosophy was, in any case, suspect because it appeared to be so popular with heretics who had fallen into the trap of deriving their teachings from the writings of philosophers rather than from the Bible. Ambrose was not the first to denounce the collusion between dialectic and Arianism, but he certainly gave it the fullest emphasis. 'The Arians', he wrote, 'have left the Apostle to follow Aristotle.'[35]

Of all his non-Christian sources Ambrose uses none as extensively as Philo, from whose writings elements are found in the *Hexaemeron* and the *De Iacob et vita beata* and in some of his letters, but above all they are found in the five treatises *De paradiso, De Cain et Abel, De Noe, De Abraham II* and *De fuga saeculi.*. These have already been closely examined by Hervé Savon in his work on Ambrose and the exegesis of Philo.[36] On the difference between Ambrose and Philo Savon remarks: 'In this secret dialogue between Ambrose and Philo two spiritual universes are represented and opposed.'[37] As in his treatment of pagan philosophers, Ambrose often uses the teaching of Philo to bring into sharper relief some aspect of Christian doctrine. Thus the debate between Pleasure and Virtue in Philo's *De sacrificiis* , which Philo conducts in a purely earthly perspective, is placed by Ambrose in an eschatological setting with reference to the rewards and penalties of the after-life.[38]

---

[33] Nostra sunt itaque quae in philosophorum litteris praestant: *De bono mortis*, 11, 51; CSEL 32/1, 747, ll. 8-9.

[34] Madec (*op. cit. n.9*), 236.

[35] reliquerunt apostolum, secuntur Aristotelem: *Expositio psalmi 118*, 22, 10; CSEL 62, 493, ll. 18-19.

[36] H.Savon, *Saint Ambroise devant l'Exégèse de Philon le Juif,* 2 vols. [Études Augustiniennes] (Paris 1977). See also E. Lucchesi, *L'usage de Philon dans l'oeuvre exégétique de saint Ambroise* (Leiden 1977) and H. Savon, 'Saint Ambroise et saint Jérôme, lecteurs de Philon', *Aufstieg und Niedergang der römischen Welt* 21/1, ed. W. Haase (Berlin 1984), 731-59.

[37] Savon (1977) (*op. cit. n. 36*),I ,378.

[38] *De Cain et Abel* I, 4, 14: CSEL 32/1, 348-51.

It may appear surprising that in the main confrontation between Christianity and paganism in the Ancient World, between Symmachus and Ambrose in 384 over the Altar of Victory and the disendowment of paganism, pagan philosophy did not play a significant part. In his *Relatio* III, Symmachus made use of social and political arguments, together with the sacred principle of *mos maiorum*. Ambrose was prepared to take the same ground and to answer Symmachus in the same terms. But in its lack of compromise his approach was fundamentally the same as his approach to pagan philosophy, tersely summed up by his statement in Letter 73, written as a detailed reply to *Relatio* III: 'Our concerns do not agree with yours.'[39] It was exactly the same as his approach in the *De officiis ministrorum*: *Haec illi. Nos autem....*[40] Even though philosophy does not directly appear here it may have been this conflict with Symmachus which prompted the writing of the work in which Ambrose did broach the question of philosophy directly. This is the lost *De sacramento regenerationis sive de philosophia*, in which he was concerned to refute the opinions of those Platonists who claimed that Christ had derived his teachings from the books of Plato. Madec devotes the second half of his study to an examination of this work, which is known to us only from fragments derived almost entirely from Augustine. Augustine read the work during his time in Milan so it must have been written before the spring of 387, when he was baptized, and probably some time between 384 (after the controversy with Symmachus) and 386. Its title is highly significant for an understanding of Ambrose's approach to philosophy. The *sacramentum regenerationis*, for Ambrose, is baptism. In his Commentary on the Gospel according to Luke, Ambrose writes that there are three things which help man to attain salvation, the sacrament (meaning the sacrament of baptism), solitude and fasting.[41] In the *De mysteriis* Ambrose calls the baptistery *regenerationis sacrarium*.[42] How is 'philosophy' to be understood here? Generally in the thought of Am-

---

[39] Non congruunt igitur vestra nobiscum: *Ep.* 73, 8 (PL *Ep.* 18); CSEL 82/3, 38, ll. 81-2.

[40] *De officiis ministrorum* I, 9, 27-8; M. Testard, *Saint Ambroise: Les Devoirs* (Paris 1984), I, 108.

[41] tria sunt enim quae ad usum proficiunt salutis humanae, sacramentum desertum ieiunium: *Expositio evangelii secundum Lucam*, IV, 4; CSEL 32/4, 141, ll. 8-9. This occurs in the passage discussing the temptation of Jesus, who was baptised, went into the desert and fasted. In the only inaccurate reference I have found in Madec's work [(*op. cit. n.9*) 54, n. 170] his apparent reference to this passage in fact refers to *Exp. ev. sec. Lucam*, IV, 45 in CSEL 32/4, 161, l. 6.

[42] *De mysteriis*, 2, 5; CSEL 73, 90, l. 23.

brose there was a natural link between philosophy and paganism—he uses 'philosophy' to indicate the hindrances, the 'impedimenta', of which we have to rid ourselves in order to attain the vision of Christ. The only time Ambrose appears to use 'philosophy' to designate Christianity or christian asceticism is in the *De virginitate* 8, 48.[43] Is *philosophia*, however, in the title *De sacramento regenerationis sive de philosophia* to be taken in the sense in which Ambrose virtually always uses it in his surviving works, i.e. as referring to pagan philosophy? Madec maintains that it should be understood here in a Christian sense;[44] in other words for Ambrose the true philosophy is that conferred by the sacrament of regeneration, which is baptism. It is this sacrament, conferring a mystical death and burial, which enables us to be conformed to Christ; about a fragment of the *De sacramento regenerationis*, which speaks of this mystical death and burial, Madec remarks: 'Dead with Christ through baptism, a new life of the christian, a new life consecrated to the spiritual warfare in order to assure the domination of the spirit over the flesh—that, in short, is the whole spirituality of Ambrose.'[45]

It is, perhaps, above all in the emphasis of Ambrose's own work on philosophy that we can see its relevance to his ambivalent understanding of the work of the State. As we have seen, entry upon this 'philosophy' is through baptism. For the Christian baptism marked, according to Ambrose, the transition from spiritual death to life. Ambrose expressed his own high understanding of this rite in his baptismal address of which we have two written versions, one by Ambrose himself, namely the *De mysteriis*, and one by somebody else, the *De sacramentis*.[46] Ambrose's stress on asceticism probably results directly from his understanding of the consequences of baptism.[47] Baptism marks the transition from the earthly to the heavenly: 'He who passes through this font, that is, from earthly things to heavenly ... he who passes through this font does not die but rises.'[48] In Ambrose's own case, however, it marked at the same

---

[43] Madec (*op. cit. n.9*), 41.

[44] *Ibid* 279.

[45] *Ibid* 284.

[46] The *De sacramentis* was probably a series of discourses given by Ambrose and written down in shorthand; C. Mohrmann, 'Observations sur le "De Sacramentis" et le "De Mysteriis" de saint Ambroise', in *Ambrosius Episcopus*, ed. G. Lazzati (Milan 1976), I, 107.

[47] See G. Toscani, *Teologia della chiesa in sant' Ambrogio* (Milan 1974), 409.

[48] *De sacramentis* I, 4, 12; CSEL 73, 20, 1.9 and 12-13.

time his transition from Roman governor to bishop, from serving the State to serving the Church. In an interesting passage in the *De paenitentia* Ambrose refers to the time when he was serving the State, before he was called to the priesthood, as a time when he was 'lost'.[49] I believe that this passage is neither a 'rhetorical exaggeration', as Gryson thinks,[50] nor evidence of a moral lapse in his youth (or, indeed, any time up to 374), as Lamirande suggests,[51] but is simply to be taken as a reference to his secular career, particularly in the light of contemporary papal statements (which may, in any case, have been directed primarily against Nectarius of Constantinople) on those who had been in secular service before their ordination. The significance of baptism, therefore, for Ambrose, quite apart from its obvious spiritual importance for any Christian, was heightened for him by the fact that it marked this abrupt change in his own life outwardly. It is interesting also to notice that the chief of all social virtues, according to Ambrose, was justice which, he said, pertains to the society and the community of the human race[52] and that justice represents the union of other virtues.[53] Ambrose's high regard for baptism is emphasised by the fact that it was in this rite that he considered the plenitude of justice to be established, *Vide, quia omnis iustitia in baptismate constituta est.*[54] This is the first time that we find a connection between the rite of baptism and the concept of justice. Personal justice also meant, for Ambrose, man devoting himself to God, to whom man owes all that he has in any case, and, in Ambrose's case, this happened when he was baptised and devoted himself to God in the service of the Church, following the true philosophy with which he regarded baptism as synonymous. The importance of anniversaries for the Romans is well known and it would not be surprising if Ambrose had written this work to mark precisely the tenth anniversary of his own baptism in December 374 when he passed 'from earthly things to hea-

---

[49] quem perditum vocasti ad sacerdotium: *De paenitentia* II, 8, 73: CSEL 73, 193, l. 63.

[50] *La Pénitence*, ed. R. Gryson, [SC 179] (Paris 1971), 180, n. 2.

[51] E. Lamirande, *Paulin de Milan et la 'Vita Ambrosii'* (Paris/Tournai/Montreal 1983), 150 and n. 14.

[52] Iustitia igitur ad societatem generis humani et ad communitatem refertur; *De officiis ministrorum* I, 28, 130; Testard (*op. cit. n. 40*), 158.

[53] iustitia ... concordia virtutum est ceterarum: *De paradiso*, 3, 18; CSEL 32/1, 277, ll. 9-10.

[54] *De sacramentis* I, 5, 15: CSEL 73, 22, ll. 26-7.

venly,'[55] from the vanities of the world to the enduring realities of the City of God, represented on this earth by the Church.[56]

Just as pagan philosophy falls short of the true Christian philosophy, which is the regeneration conferred by baptism, so the society of the State, necessary though it is, falls short of the society of the Church, which represents the Kingdom of God. Just as pagan philosophy should be used only to serve a Christian purpose, to highlight some aspect of Christian doctrine, or to throw into sharper relief the superior teaching of the Bible, so the State should realise that its purpose, under a Christian Emperor, is to serve the Kingdom of God, to which the State owes its justification. For what other justification, in a Christian perspective, could the State possibly have? Obviously it has to maintain law and order but the law has to be a reflection of the law of God if it is to have any validity at all, and order itself has to be a reflection of the divine ordering of the universe, as depicted in Genesis. It would be unacceptable, indeed, illogical from a Christian viewpoint, for the State, in the supposed interests of maintaining a lesser order, to take measures which plainly infringe the principles of a greater order to be found in the Kingdom of God, since it is the State's primary task to bring about the realisation of that greater order in the world.

Thus for Ambrose it is the sacrament of baptism which marks the divide between pagan and Christian philosophy no less than, in his experience, between the State and the Church. But there may be another reason which explains Ambrose's ambivalence towards philosophy, a reason which owes its origin to the controversy of 384 and which was rooted in his own political experience. Ambrose was at least a fully-grown man when the pagan reaction occurred under Julian the Apostate between 361 and 363. If he was born in 333/4, he would have been in his late twenties and already well embarked on his political career in Rome, before going to Sirmium in 365. The reaction of Julian was a reaction of precisely that pagan, cosmic philosophy in a political form. Julian attempted to regenerate Roman society by founding it both on philosophy and a pagan tradition inspired by Neoplatonism.[57] One might be tempted to think that Ambrose was attempting to do the same by means of the Christian faith, but his perspective was an altogether

---

[55] See above, n. 48.

[56] Ambrose, not Augustine, was the first to understand the Church as the City of God; see *Expositio psalmi 118*, 15, 35.

[57] See J.M. Alonso-Nuñez, 'L'Empereur Julian et les Cyniques', *Les Études Classiques* LII (1984) 254-9.

wider one and, as far as the Roman state was concerned, his view of its political health was simply that it could be best ensured by promoting the Christian religion; 'for salvation' (by which Ambrose meant the political health of the Empire as well as the salvation of each person) 'is not safe, unless each person truly worships the true God, that is the God of the christians.'[58] With the possible exceptions of Hadrian and Marcus Aurelius, Julian was the emperor best educated in philosophy that Rome had seen and the hold of pagan philosophy upon him was shown by his apostasy from the Christian faith. In his funeral speech on Theodosius Ambrose described Julian as one who 'deserted the author of his salvation and surrendered himself to the error of philosophy.'[59] Ambrose may have seen in Symmachus' *Relatio* the thin end of the wedge, an attempt to preserve under a Christian emperor at least that 'tolerance' which would wait for the time when a second Julian would arise to complete the work of the first. The short-lived pagan reaction under Eugenius in 394 might have taken a fatefully much firmer hold had Valentinian II granted Symmachus' request and restored paganism to the position it enjoyed before 382.

If this could be one explanation for Ambrose's negative attitude to philosophy, shown in this case by his opposition to what he regarded as the possible political implications of Symmachus' *Relatio*, it might also help to explain the difference between Ambrose and Augustine in their attitude to philosophy. Augustine had almost certainly come across Neoplatonism first through his reading of the *libri Platonicorum*, as he mentions in the *Confessions*. Had his first acquaintance with Neoplatonism been made through the sermons of Ambrose, as Courcelle[60] and Madec[61] maintain, it seems extraordinary that he did not mention this fact. Besides, how could Augustine have recognised the specifically Neoplatonic content of these sermons in the first place, since Ambrose does not mention his source, unless he already had some knowledge of the writings of Plotinus? It is, at any rate, clear from Book VII of the *Confessions* that Neoplatonism helped to clear Augustine's mind of Manichaean debris and, at any rate as he saw it when he wrote the *Confessions*, prepared the way for his acceptance of the Christian faith.

---

[58] Aliter enim salus tuta esse non poterit, nisi unusquisque deum verum hoc est deum Christianorum ... veraciter colat: *Ep.* 72, 1 (PL *Ep.* 17); CSEL 82/3, 11, ll. 7-9.

[59] ... Julianum, qui salutis suae reliquit auctorem, dum philosophiae se dedit errori: *De obitu Theodosii*, 51; CSEL 73, 398, ll. 13-15.

[60] Courcelle (*op. cit. n.8*), 122 and 133 and (*op. cit. n. 25*), 138.

[61] Madec (*op. cit. n.9*), 15-16.

Because of his experience it is understandable that his attitude towards philosophy was more positive than that of Ambrose. Madec has suggested that one might almost say—although one would hesitate to go quite so far!—that Augustine's remark on philosophy in the *De Ordine* could be applied to Ambrose; 'Whoever thinks that all philosophy should be avoided does not want anything else for us than that we should not love wisdom'.[62] The reason for this difference may simply be that, as far as the political implications of philosophy were concerned, Ambrose was already fully embarked on his legal career in Julian's reign, whereas Augustine was only a child of eight, so the impact upon the two of the events of the time would clearly have been different. Secondly, we know of the link formed by Ambrose between philosophy and Arianism. Arianism was, in effect, a dead creed in the Empire from at least the time Augustine was in Milan (the solid support of the population of Milan, and of part of the soldiery, for Ambrose during the basilica conflict of 386 was a clear demonstration of this) and Augustine may not have had occasion in his own experience to think of a link between heresy and philosophy before Pelagianism, whose ethic, according to Jerome, commenting on Pelagius' letter to Demetrias, had its ultimate roots in popular Stoicism.[63] Finally we have to remember that Augustine's first conversion was to philosophy in the form set out by Cicero in his *Hortensius.*

The principal themes of Ambrose's approach to philosophy are found in their most consistent form in his *Expositio psalmi 118*, his theory of the borrowings of philosophers, the opposition of the Christian wisdom and that of the world or of the flesh, the collusion between heresy and philosophy, illustrated by the usual Pauline citations.[64] However much Ambrose may have drawn upon Platonic sources we find him in fundamental disagreement with the *Platonis lectores et dilectores* over the two points on which Platonic doctrine disagreed most with Christianity: the Platonic belief in polytheism and its metempsychosis. The fact that nevertheless he did not hesitate to use this philosophy is another indication of his supreme intellectual confidence which, in its turn, was based upon the massive spiritual certainties of his life. As Peter Brown has put it, Ambrose drew on the works of the pagan philosophers rather

---

[62] *De Ordine* I, 11, 32.

[63] venena ... , quae de philosophorum et maxime Pythagorae et Zenonis, principis Stoicorum, fonte manarunt: Jerome, *Ep.* 133, 1; CSEL 56, 242, ll. 4-5.

[64] Madec (*op. cit. n.9*), 85 and, for a summary of Ambrose's views on philosophy, 90-97.

as we would draw on a spiritual anthology, adapting their conclusions to make a point as an orator and as a moral teacher.[65] Jean Pépin provides an excellent summary of Ambrose's attitude to philosophy in the following words: 'un évêque que son activité pastorale n'empêchait pas de donner du temps aux lectures philosophiques, fort capable d'y faire un choix et d'agencer de façon personelle des éléments de provenances diverses, voire d'élaborer judicieusement des observations que la tradition scolaire ne lui offrait pas telles quelles.'[66]

Madec has, I think rightly, remarked that we should not play down the pejorative remarks which Ambrose makes about philosophy.[67] Madec's line has come in for criticism by, among others, Carole Hill in her dissertation[68] and by Klaus Zelzer.[69] Zelzer holds that the distinction drawn by Madec between *verba* and *res* in Ambrose's philosophical borrowings assumes an intellectual distinction in Ambrose's writings which is not in accordance with the general outlook of the ancient world and that Ambrose was influenced rather by the critical synthesis of the Alexandrian school in which both polemic and borrowings (Polemik und Nachfolge) are closely connected.[70] However this synthesis is to be found more closely in Clement of Alexandria than in Origen. Origen, whose approach to pagan philosophy was a more critical one than that found in Clement, was one of the chief sources of Ambrose's theology and it is perhaps significant that Ambrose, who supports his general attitude against philosophy with *1 Corinthians* 3.19, does not appear to be influenced by the more modified interpretation of this verse which we find in Clement.[71] Ambrose's outlook, his background, his practical experience in the service of the State before he became bishop and the importance for him of his own baptism, which happened at the same time as his consecration, all strongly militate against the likelihood of his having much interest in achieving a synthesis of pagan philosophy and Christianity in the first place, as has been claimed by Courcelle.[72] Hadot has pointed out that we find in Ambrose no important trace of what constitutes the essence of Plotinian thought, namely, passing

---

[65] P. Brown, *Augustine of Hippo* (London 1967), 88.

[66] Pépin (*op. cit. n.29*), 533.

[67] Madec (*op. cit. n.9*), 175.

[68] Hill (*op. cit. n.9*), 80-83.

[69] Zelzer (*op. cit. n.27*).

[70] *Ibid* 186.

[71] Madec (*op. cit. n.9*), 203.

[72] Courcelle (*op. cit. n.8*), 136 and 252-3.

beyond the intelligible in order to attain the One in ecstasy.[73] Ambrose's use of philosophy was probably influenced partly by a wish to show that such a synthesis was impossible because of the immense superiority of the Christian revelation. Inasmuch as he did use philosophy he seems to have neutralised it—and that was probably his intention. In a kind of religious homoeopathy, if one may so put it, it was precisely by using Platonic metaphors that Ambrose succeeded in imparting greater point to his disagreement with Platonic doctrine. Tissot's remark on the inspiration Christian authors gave Ambrose applies even more to the influence on him of philosophical sources: 'On a parfois l'impression que la lecture des modèles est avant tout, pour l'évêque de Milan, une éveilleuse d'idées: il écoute Origène, Eusèbe ou Hilaire, il enregistre et retient leurs expressions; mais pendant tout ce temps il a suivi sa propre pensée, et il arrive qu'avec les mêmes mots il construise un raisonnement assez différent, parfois même diamétralement opposé.'[74]

Verbal imitation is not to be confused with doctrinal influence and the very variety of philosophical influence on Ambrose ought to make us cautious. Ambrose passes so easily from one philosophical doctrine to another, perhaps because he refuses to attach himself to any of them. As Madec points out, if he could be a 'Platonist' one day and a 'Ciceronian' the next, is it not because he retained from his varied reading merely literary ornaments, rather than the true intellectual substance?[75] An Ambrose who would have been concerned with the academic pursuit of achieving a synthesis of Platonism and Christianity would have been a markedly different character from the formidably consistent figure who, in his writings and actions, confronts us with such disconcerting clarity. That pagan cosmic philosophy could be politically dangerous had already been shown by the Julian reaction. One might reasonably question whether anyone who was concerned with achieving a synthesis of pagan philosophy and Christianity would have had much interest in setting forth his own account of what he regarded as the true philosophy, to which presumably any synthesis would have been a rival. As we have seen, for Ambrose the true philosophy was one which could be attained only by undergoing 'the sacrament of regeneration' which was baptism. As a baptised Christian and as a Kirchenpolitiker Ambrose's use of philosophy was consistent with both his political astuteness and his belief in the towering superiority of the Christian revelation.

---

[73] Hadot (*op. cit. n.14*), 151.

[74] G. Tissot, Ambroise de Milan, *Traité sur l'Évangile de S. Luc,* (Paris 1956), 17.

[75] Madec (*op. cit. n.9*), 175.

DIE SPRACHE DER RELIGIÖSEN ERFAHRUNG BEI PSEUDO-DIONYSIUS AREOPAGITA

EKKEHARD MÜHLENBERG

Als Väter der christlichen Mystik gelten Gregor von Nyssa und das Schrifttum unter dem Namen Dionysius Areopagita. Von beiden hat man leidenschaftlich behauptet, daß ihren Darstellungen besondere religiöse Erfahrungen zugrunde liegen, mystische Erfahrungen, die ein Berühren der Gottheit oder auch Einswerden mit der Gottheit meinen.[1] Von Plotin berichtet sein Schüler und Biograph Porphyrius, daß er die Einung erstrebt und viermal erlebt habe.[2] Gregor von Nyssa sagt von sich selbst nirgends, daß er besondere religiöse Erfahrungen gemacht habe; er bestreitet ausdrücklich, daß es den Ruhepunkt der Einswerdung mit Gott gebe.[3] Proclus, der Neuplatoniker im 5. Jahrhundert, führt aus, daß die Theologie über den ersten Gott sich aus der Einung mit eben diesem Gott ergebe.[4] Und nun der sich als Christ darstellende Dionysius: Er spricht von Einung, aber muß er sie auch selbst erlebt haben? Ist seine mystische Theologie Ausfluß des Erlebnisses der Einung mit Gott? Es gibt dazu verschiedene Meinungen.[5] Sehr seltsam formuliert Walter Völker: "Ich will das ganze System von seinem Herzstück aus zu durchdringen suchen, d.h. von den geheimen mystischen Erfahrungen

---

[1] Vgl. beispielhaft Kurt Ruh, *Geschichte der abendländischen Mystik* (München 1990). Ohne weitere Begründung vermerke ich die beiden—nicht immer voneinander unabhängigen—Möglichkeiten, daß einerseits erlebte Erfahrung authentischer ist als spekulatives Denken und daß andererseits schon Erlebtes auch wieder zum Erlebten werden kann.

[2] Vita Plotini 23; Plotin habe sich an die Anweisungen aus Platos Symposium gehalten.

[3] Vgl. meinen Beitrag: 'Die Sprache der religiösen Erfahrung bei Gregor von Nyssa', in Walter Haug (Hrsg.), *Modelle religiöser Erfahrung in christlicher Tradition* (München 1992).

[4] Vgl. Theol. plat. II 11.

[5] P. Scazzoso, *Ricerche sulla struttura del linguaggio dello Pseudo-Dionigi Areopagita. Introduzione alla lettura delle opere pseudodionisiane* [PUCSC.F 14] (Milano 1967) gibt auf 164 n. 29 eine Liste derer, die für De Mystica Theologia ein persönliches Erleben des Autors behaupten (Völker, Lossky, Roques) und die es bestreiten (Puech, Hornus, Vanneste). Scazzoso selbst erklärt, daß diese Frage für die Interpretation des Traktates nicht entscheidend sei.

des Autors."[6] Demgegenüber ist zunächst festzuhalten, daß der Autor,
den ich im folgenden Dionysius nennen werde, selbst und für sich keine
geheimen Erfahrungen berichtet und keine in Anspruch nimmt. Unbe-
streitbar ist jedoch, daß seine Schriften religiöse Erfahrung beschreiben;
und wenn auch anfangs offen bleiben darf, ob es sich um erlebte Erfahrungen oder ob es sich um zu erlebende Erfahrungen handelt, so darf
doch hypothetisch ein Wechselverhältnis zwischen Erfahrung und Sprache, in der sie dargestellt wird, angenommen werden.

Die Formulierung des Themas verdanke ich dem Tübinger Germa-
nisten Walter Haug. Er bat mich im Jahre 1990 anläßlich eines Sym-
posions über "Modelle religiöser Erfahrung", über die Sprache der religiösen Erfahrung bei Gregor von Nyssa zu sprechen. Ich nahm seinen
Vorschlag gern auf, da ich selbst mir einen neuen Zugang zu dem mir
sonst wohl vertrauten Gregor versprach. Den Dionysius ebenfalls unter
diesem Thema zu untersuchen, traute ich mich erst, nachdem ich die Register für die erste kritische Textausgabe bearbeitet hatte.[7] Denn die
Aufgabe ist gewaltig, einerseits wegen der Wirkungsgeschichte, die die
Schriften des Dionysius gehabt haben, was eben nicht völlig ausgeblen-
det werden kann, andererseits wegen der Forschung über Dionysius,
die—abgesehen vom Wuchern der Forschungsliteratur überhaupt—sich
unter anderen Formulierungen mit diesem Thema schon beschäftigt hat.
Denn nachdem im Jahre 1895 in zwei Veröffentlichungen die Abhän-
gigkeit des Dionysius von dem Neuplatoniker Proclus nachgewiesen
wurde, befaßte man sich insbesondere mit seiner Sprache, um das Pseudonym zu lokalisieren. So nannte Hugo Koch den Titel seiner Mono-
graphie von 1900: *Pseudo-Dionysius Areopagita in seinen Beziehungen
zum Neuplatonismus und Mysterienwesen. Eine literarhistorische Untersuchung.*[8] Und 1967 erschien Piero Scazzoso, *Ricerche sulla struttura del linguaggio dello Pseudo-Dionigi Areopagita. Introduzione alla
lettura delle opere pseudodionisiane.*[9] Schon Hugo Koch stellte sich die
Frage, ob Begriffsapparat und Sprache, die Dionysius so offensichtlich

---

[6] *Kontemplation und Ekstase bei Pseudo-Dionysius Areopagita* (Wiesbaden
1958) S. III. Erst 217 wird der Ausdruck noch einmal aufgenommen.
[7] Corpus Dionysiacum I u. II, [PTS 33 u. 36) (Berlin 1990/91). Ich zitiere nach
dieser Ausgabe mit Kapiteleinteilung und Seitenangabe DN = De Divinis Nominibus,
ed. B.R. Suchla; CH = De Coelesti Hierarchia, EH = De Ecclesiastica Hierarchia, ed.
G. Heil; MTh = De Mystica Theologia, Ep = Epistulae ed. A.M. Ritter.
[8] H. Koch, *Pseudo-Dionysius Areopagita in seinen Beziehung zum Neuplatonismus und Mysterienwesen* [FChLDG Bd. 1 Heft 2 u. 3] (Mainz 1900).
[9] Refer Scazzoso (*op. cit. n. 5*).

von Proclus übernommen hatte, auch eine Basis in christlicher Erfahrung des Autors haben. Und Koch resümiert, daß die Sprache die des
Neuplatonikers Proclus, jedoch der Gedanke biblisch sei (und wohl
auch bleibe).[10]

Ich werde in zwei Schritten auf das Thema zugehen. Ich will zuerst
nach einer Sachdefinition von religiöser Erfahrung bei Dionysius
suchen, dann in einem zweiten Teil mich der Sprache zuwenden, in der
religiöse Erfahrung ausgedrückt wie auch mitgeteilt wird.

I. *Was ist eine religiöse Erfahrung?*

Ich möchte nicht unklar lassen, wonach ich bei Dionysius suche. Deswegen sollen einige Formulierungen über religiöse Erfahrung an den
Anfang gestellt werden. Ich schlage vor, religiöse Erfahrung zu bestimmen als Empfindung von Gegenwart Gottes, Wahrnehmung der Präsenz
des Göttlichen, d.h. als Gotteserfahrung. Es ist unentbehrlich, den Namen und Begriff Gott für religiöse Erfahrung zu beanspruchen, um die
religiöse Erfahrung von Welterfahrung und allgemeiner Wirklichkeitserfahrung zu unterscheiden. Und insofern Wirklichkeitserfahrung das
dialektische Gegenmoment zu Selbsterfahrung ist, setzt Gotteserfahrung auch Selbsterfahrung voraus; das genannte "Voraussetzen" soll an
dieser Stelle nicht mehr aussagen, als daß bei Gotteserfahrung eine
Selbsterfahurng eingeschlossen ist. Daß das, was religiöse Erfahrung
bestimmt, Gott genannt wird, heißt so viel wie die Erfahrung einer
Macht, die größer ist als das Selbst; es ist in logischer Analyse weiterhin
zu folgern, daß das Erleben der Macht, die Gott genannt wird und
größer als das Selbst ist, auch erfahren wird als von dieser Macht selbst
herbeigeführt und als von dieser Macht beherrscht. Damit ist auch gegeben, daß die Wirklichkeit, mit der das Selbst dialektisch verbunden ist,
als von der "Gott" genannten Macht beherrscht wird.[11]

Meine Formulierungen sind gedrängt und bedürften gewiß weitläu-
figer Begründungen. Aber das mag genügen; den Vorwurf der Simpli-
fizierung brauche ich nicht zu fürchten. Jedoch könnte eingewendet
werden, ob Dionysius nicht überall und fast in jedem Satz seiner Schriften so spreche und also "Einung mit Gott" die Definition der dionysi-

---

[10] Koch (*op. cit. n. 8*), 258.
[11] Meine Formulierungen sind nicht unabängig von William James, *The Varieties
of Religious Experience* (1902).

schen Schriften sei, so daß der erste Teil meiner Aufgabe sich erledigt hätte. Allgemeinheiten helfen selten weiter. Ich werde die Passagen bei Dionysius genauer untersuchen, wo ausdrücklich religiöse Erfahrung beschrieben wird. Es sind die biblischen Gestalten Mose und Paulus, dazu sein eigener Lehrer. Dionysius verweist auf die biblischen Gestalten wie auf Modelle. Es darf deswegen davon ausgegangen werden, daß deren Erfahrung Paradigmata religiöser Erfahrung sind.

1. *Mose (MTh I.3)*

In der Schrift "Über die mystische Theologie" steht nach der einleitenden Anrede die Feststellung, daß es sich in der Theologie um Verneinungen und Bejahungen handele und daß sich Verneinung und Bejahung nicht widersprächen, also kataphatische und apophatische Theologie ein gleiches Recht hätten. Dazu wird eine grundsätzliche Beschreibung von Gotteswort (θεολογία) und von Evangelium hingestellt. Diese Beschreibung ist einer autoritativen Quelle entnommen; Dionysius sagt: "So heißt es bei dem göttlichen Bartholomäus". Als dem Bartholomäus entnommen soll gelten: "Die Theologie ist umfangreich und ganz kurz, und das Evangelium ist weitschweifig und groß und zugleich knapp zusammengedrängt." Dionysius überträgt diese Aussagen in seine eigene Sprache und formuliert so: "Die gute Ursache von allem ist wortreich und zugleich wortkarg und sprachlos." Ein scheinbarer Widerspruch liegt vor; der jedoch löst sich auf, wenn man sich die ontologische Stellung des ersten Prinzips, d.h. Gottes, vergegenwärtigt. "Die gute Ursache von allem" (ἡ ἀγαθὴ πάντων αἰτία) liegt auf einer Stufe jenseits des Seins von Allem, ist aber geoffenbart in dem, was sie ist. Und nun wird Dionysius beredt; mit Verben der Bewegung beschreibt er: Die wahre Natur der "guten Ursache von allem" ist geoffenbart denen, die "durchqueren" (τοῖς ... διαβαίνουσι), die "übersteigen" (τοῖς ... ὑπερβαίνουσι), die "zurücklassen" (τοῖς ἀπολιμπάνουσι). Nachdem sie sich vorwärts und aufwärts und nach jenseits bewegt haben, treten sie ein "in das Dunkel" (εἰς τὸν γνόφον εἰσδυομένοις). Der Ausdruck "Dunkel" als der Ort, wo die Wanderer und Kletterer ankommen, ist dem biblischen Bericht über des Mose Aufstieg zum Sinai entnommen (*Exodus* 20.21). Dionysius vermerkt die biblische Referenz.

Der nächste Schritt im Argument des Dionysius ist der Übergang zur Moseserzählung. Dionysius gibt eine Kurzfassung der biblischen Geschichte. Nimmt man die Verben als Leitfaden, so wird zunächst ein

Reinigen und Trennen, dann ein Hören und Sehen betont. Es folgt ein
weiteres Trennen und schließlich das Ankommen auf dem Gipfel.[12] Alle
Handlungen des Mose werden als Aufstieg gedeutet, d.h. die Reinigung,
das Hören und Sehen, die Trennung. Impliziert ist die Begegnung mit
Gott , die sich beim Ankommen "auf dem Gipfel der göttlichen Aufstiege" ereignet (ἐπὶ τὴν ἀκρότητα τῶν θείων ἀναβάσεων φθάνει). Jedoch
schränkt Dionysius die Erwartung, daß Mose hier auf dem "Gipfel der
göttlichen Aufstiege" Gott begegne, sofort ein. Mose begegnet nicht
Gott selbst (Κὰν τούτοις αὐτῷ μὲν οὐ συγγίνεται τῷ θεῷ ...). Das Verb
συγγίνεται ist vieldeutig. Seine Bedeutung reicht von "treffen" über
"sich zusammentun mit" bis zu "intimen Beziehungen".[13] Ich schlage
vor, hier "sich vereinigen mit" zu übersetzen. Denn die Beschreibung
dessen, was Mose bei seiner Ankunft auf dem "Gipfel der göttlichen
Aufstiege" widerfährt, wird weitergeführt: "Und dort vereinigt er sich
nicht mit Gott selbst, er schaut auch nicht ihn—Gott ist ja unsichtbar—,
sondern den Ort, an dem er sich befand (... οὗ ἔστη)."

Eigentlich endet hier die biblische Erzählung; das Element "Ort"
stammt zwar aus *Exodus* 33.20-23, aber auf die dortige Folge läßt sich
Dionysius nicht ein, sondern beläßt es bei *Exodus* 20.21: "Mose ging in
das Dunkel, οὗ ἦν ὁ θεός." Diesen Vers hatte er auch vor seiner Einfüh-
rung des Mose zitiert. Aber für Dionysius endet die Erzählung nun doch
nicht mit dieser abschließenden Feststellung, sondern das Handeln des
Mose erscheint jetzt geteilt in zwei Handlungen. Erst also "betrachtet
Mose den Ort, an dem sich Gott befand." Dann aber, ausdrücklich τότε,
befreit sich Mose von allem Sichtbaren und von den Sehorganen, er
schließt seine Augen, auch seine geistigen Augen, und tritt in das Dunkel ein. Dort im Dunkel, jenseits der sinnlichen und der geistigen Sinne,
"gehört er ganz dem Transzendenten (πᾶς ὢν τοῦ πάντων ἐπέκεινα)", gibt
sich in den, der alles umfaßt, auf, "ist mit dem Unerkennbaren ... vollkommen vereint und erkennt über die Vernunft hinaus dadurch, daß er
nichts erkennt".[14]

---

[12] Καὶ γὰρ οὐχ ἁπλῶς ὁ θεῖος Μωϋσῆς ἀποκαθαρθῆναι πρῶτον αὐτὸς κελεύεται καὶ
αὖθις τῶν μὴ τοιούτων ἀφορισθῆναι καὶ μετὰ πᾶσαν ἀποκάθαρσιν ἀκούει τῶν
πολυφώνων σαλπίγγων καὶ ὁρᾷ φῶτα πολλὰ καθαρὰς ἀπαστράπτοντα καὶ πολυχύτους
ἀκτῖνας· εἶτα τῶν πολλῶν ἀφορίζεται καὶ μετὰ τῶν ἐκκρίτων ἱερέων ἐπὶ τὴν ἀκρότητα
τῶν θείων ἀναβάσεων φθάνει. (143, 17–144,3).
[13] Vgl. Plotin, Enn. VI 9, 7, 21 u. 11, 32.
[14] ...πᾶς ὢν τοῦ πάντων ἐπέκεινα καὶ οὐδενός, οὔτε ἑαυτοῦ οὔτε ἑτέρου, τῷ παντελῶς δὲ ἀγνώστῳ τῇ πάσης γνώσεως ἀνενεργησίᾳ κατὰ τὸ κρεῖττον ἑνούμενος καὶ τῷ
μηδὲν γινώσκειν ὑπὲρ νοῦν γινώσκων. (144, 12–15).

Das ist also die religiöse Erfahrung des Mose, sicher eine paradigmatische religiöse Erfahrung. Die Erfahrung endet in der Einung— ἐνούμενος heißt es—, aber sie wird in Stufen zerlegt und begann mit einem Befehl Gottes (κελεύεται, p. 143, 18). Worin besteht die Endstufe? Sie besteht nicht in einem Verlust des Bewußtseins, jedoch im Aufgeben des Selbstbewußtseins. Aber auch diese Antwort ist noch nicht richtig; denn Dionysius verliert das Subjekt, dem die Einigung widerfährt, nicht aus dem Auge und bewahrt ihm noch eine Art von Wissen oder Erkennen. Mir scheint, daß nur ein Punkt in dem ganzen Bericht klar ist; das ist die ontologische Stellung dessen, mit dem die Einigung stattfindet. Die ganze Wanderung von Aufsteigen und Sich-Trennen und Zurücklassen muß der Einung notwendig vorangehen, um eben Gott jenseits von allem zu qualifizieren. Gott ist ὁ πάντων ἐπέκεινα; mit diesem Ausdruck ὁ πάντων ἐπέκεινα ersetzte Dionysius das biblische ὁ θεός von *Exodus* 20.21 (p. 143, 17). Dadurch gab er schon im voraus zu erkennen, wie das Ziel der Aufstiege zu bestimmen ist. Logische, oder besser rationale Folgerichtigkeit erfordert, daß es eine Gegenwart Gottes in den unteren Stufen des Seins gibt, ja ein Gewahren der Gegenwart Gottes in allem Sichtbaren und Intelligiblen. Wenn eine Gegenwärtigkeit Gottes überall vorausgesetzt werden kann, dann kann auch eine Einung mit dem, dessen Gegenwärtigkeit es ist, vorgestellt werden. Was ich nun ein Erfordernis rationaler Folgerichtigkeit nannte, hat Dionysius in Parenthese auch tatsächlich eingefügt (p. 144, 5-9). Um sicherzustellen, daß eine Einung mit Gott, der "jenseits von allem ist", stattfindet, kann Dionysius Gott nicht vollkommen von der Wirklichkeit trennen, die Mose durchwandert und übersteigt. Andernfalls würde Mose irgendwo ankommen, aber eben nicht genau bei dem, der "jenseits von allem" ist, der "die gute Ursache von allem" ist.

Zweifellos hat Gregor von Nyssa die entscheidende Interpretation von des Mose Aufstieg und vor allem vom Sehen Gottes in dem Dunkel geliefert.[15] Aber bei Gregor findet sich die Endstufe der Einung mit Gott nicht. Gregor begnügt sich mit dem Ergebnis, daß Mose Gottes Unerkennbarkeit erkennt, und diese Erkenntnis begleitet weiteren Fortschritt,

---

[15] Vgl. Gregor von Nyssa, De Vita Moysis II (82, 4–89, 14 Musurillo), wo es von Mose heißt: καταλιπὼν γὰρ πᾶν τὸ φαινόμενον, οὐ μόνον ὅσα καταλαμβάνει ἡ αἴσθησις ἀλλὰ καὶ ὅσα ἡ διάνοια δοκεῖ βλέπειν ἀεὶ πρὸς τὸ ἐνδότερον ἵεται ἕως ἂν διαδύῃ καὶ τῇ πολυπραγμοσύνῃ τῆς διανοίας πρὸς τὸ ἀθέατόν τε καὶ ἀκατάληπτον κἀκεῖ τὸν θεὸν ἴῃ. ἐν τούτῳ γὰρ ἡ ἀληθής ἐστιν εἴδησις τοῦ ζητουμένου καὶ ἐν τούτῳ τὸ ἰδεῖν ἐν τῷ μὴ ἰδεῖν, ὅτι ὑπέρκειται πάσης εἰδήσεως τὸ ζητούμενον οἷόν τινι γνόφῳ τῇ ἀκαταληψίᾳ πανταχόθεν διειλημμένον. (87, 1-9).

ja wird zum Stimulus für einen unendlichen Fortschritt.[16] Der formale Grund dafür, daß Gregor des Mose Aufsteigen nicht in der Erfahrung der Einung im "Dunkel der Unerkennbarkeit" enden läßt, liegt auf der Hand: Gregor folgt der weiteren Geschichte des Mose, die ja in *Exodus* 20.21 auf dem Berge Sinai nicht endet, so daß der Eintritt in das "Dunkel der Unerkennbarkeit" nicht die letzte Erfahrung des Mose ist. Konsequenter jedoch erklärt Gregor den undendlichen Fortschritt in seinem Kommentar zum Hohenlied. Dort verhindert das Thema ἔρως die Einung mit Gott, weil ἔρως seinem Wesen nach unersättlich und nicht zu befriedigen ist. Warum geht Dionysius über Gregor hinaus? Auf diese Frage werde ich weiter unten zurückkommen.

2. *Paulus (DN IV 13)*

Ein weiteres Paradigma religiöser Erfahrung ist der Apostel Paulus. Dionysius bezieht sich auf Paulus in dem Zusammenhang des göttlichen Namens "Liebe", in Kapitel IV 7 eingeführt. Dionysius will zeigen, daß Gott als Liebe besser durch sein griechisches Äquivalent ἔρως als durch das biblische ἀγάπη zu charakterisieren ist. Er stellt das Wesen von göttlichem Eros, d.h. dem Gott eigenen Eros dar und betrachtet eine seiner Eigenschaften, nämlich daß sie ekstatisch sei. Diese Eigenschaft ist schon in der Etymologie von Schönheit, die Gott ist, beschlossen (vgl. DN IV 7, p. 151, 9 sq).[17] Denn Dionysius erklärt daß καλόν sich aus καλεῖν herleite, also das Schöne zu sich hinrufe.[18] Aber Dionysius ver-

---

[16] Als Auslegung von Ex. 33.20-23 schreibt Gregor von Nyssa über den Aufstieg: μηδενὸς δὲ ὄντος ἄνωθεν τοῦ τὴν ὁρμὴν ἐπικόπτοντος (ἑλκτικὴ γὰρ πρὸς ἑαυτὴν ἡ τοῦ καλοῦ φύσις ἐστὶ τῶν πρὸς ἐκείνην ἀναβλεπόντων) ἀεὶ πάντως ὑψηλοτέρα ἑαυτῆς γίνεται τῇ τῶν οὐρανίων ἐπιθυμίᾳ συνεπεκτεινομένη τοῖς ἔμπροσθεν, καθώς φησιν ὁ ἀπόστολος, καὶ πάντοτε πρὸς τὸ ὑψηλότερον τὴν πτῆσιν ποιήσεται. ποθοῦσα γὰρ διὰ τῶν ἤδη κατειλημμένων μὴ καταλιπεῖν τὸ ὕψος τὸ ὑπερκείμενον, ἄπαυστον ποιεῖται τὴν ἐπὶ τὸ ἄνω φορὰν ἀεὶ διὰ τῶν προηνυσμένων τὸν πρὸς τὴν πτῆσιν τόνον ἀνανεάζουσα (De vita Moysis II, 112, 16–25 Musurillo). Vgl. In Cant. Hom. XII (352, 6–357, 2 Langerbeck).
[17] ...ὡς πάντα πρὸς ἑαυτὸ καλοῦν, ὅθεν καὶ κάλλος λέγεται... Vgl. Bernhard Brons, *Gott und die Seienden. Untersuchungen zum Verhältnis von neuplatonischer Metaphysik und christlicher Tradition bei Dionysius Areopagita* [FKDG 28] (Göttingen 1976), 227-229.
[18] Zu Plato, Phaedrus 250 d, sagt Proclus: ἐτύμως γάρ, εἴτε διὰ τὸ καλεῖν εἰς ἑαυτὸ κέκληται καλὸν εἴτε διὰ τὸ κηλεῖν καὶ θέλγειν τὰ πρὸς αὐτὸ δυνάμενα βλέπειν, ἐραστόν ἐστι κατὰ φύσιν· διὸ καὶ ὁ ἔρως πρὸς τὸ καλὸν ἄγειν λέγεται τὸ ἐρῶν (In Alc.

folgt diesen Gedanken nicht weiter, nachdem er ἀγάπη durch ἔρως ersetzt hat. Eros führt vielmehr ein neues Element in das göttliche Schönsein ein; es benennt ein besonderes Motiv in Gottes Gutsein. Denn nach Dionysius ist Liebe als Eros nicht ausschließlich das Band, das den Seienden innewohnt und sie mit der transzendenten Ursache ihres Seins verbindet. Vielmehr ist Eros Aktivität, die der transzendenten Ursache selbst zueigen ist. Und indem Dionysius Eros auf Gott selbst überträgt, versucht er auch das ekstatische Wesen des Eros auf Gott zu übertragen.[19] Dionysius gibt deutlich zu erkennen, daß dies ein sehr gewagtes Unternehmen ist (p. 155, 14; 159, 9). Ich habe den Kontext soweit referiert, da die Bewertung für den Stellenwert des Verweises auf Paulus davon abhängt. Das ekstatische Wesen göttlicher Liebe wird zuerst erwiesen durch das liebende Verlangen, welches das Universum durchzieht. Ein Sonderfall, der dies beweist, ist Paulus. Denn Paulus sagt von sich selbst in *Galater* 2.20: "So lebe nun nicht mehr ich, sondern es lebt Christus in mir." Dionysius zitiert den Vers in der Betonung, die ich in meiner Übersetzung wiederzugeben versuche.

Das Argument des Dionysius setzt mit einer allgemeinen Feststellung ein: "Der göttliche Eros ist aber auch ekstatisch und läßt nicht zu, daß die Liebenden sich selbst angehören, sondern nur den Geliebten" (p. 158, 19 sq). Das soll wahr sein, was sich an dem Bande zeige, welches das Universum zusammenhält. Es ist die Fürsorge, die πρόνοια, die Gemeinschaft bewirkt und die Rückwendung zur transzendenten Ursache verursacht. Nachdem Dionysius das allgemeine Prinzip benannt hat, sozusagen die metaphysische Regel, führt er den Apostel Paulus ein. Denn, so läuft das Argument, weil es im Universum diese allgemeine Regel gebe, deswegen sage der Apostel Paulus mit Recht: "So lebe nun nicht mehr ich, sondern es lebt Christus in mir." Paulus dient als Beispiel für die allgemeine Regel. Aber gleichzeitig soll Paulus der allgemeinen Regel natürlich ihre Richtigkeit bescheinigen.

Zwei Momente charakterisieren die Erfahrung des Paulus. Erstens wurde Paulus von göttlicher Liebe ergriffen. Und zugleich mit der göttlichen Liebe, die von ihm Besitz ergriff, erfaßte ihn auch die ekstatische Macht der göttlichen Liebe.[20] Was aber widerfuhr nun dem Paulus nach

---

328, 11-14). Vgl. W. Beierwaltes, *Proklos. Grundzüge seiner Metaphysik* [PhA 24] (Frankfurt[2] 1979), 307 Anm. 17.

[19] Vgl. Plato, Phaedrus 249 c 8 und Plotin, Enn. VI 9, 11, 23.

[20] Vgl. Proclus über den Eros: τὸ γὰρ εἰς ἑαυτὸν ἐπιστρέφειν τὸν ἐρώμενον καὶ ἀνακαλεῖσθαι καὶ συλλέγειν οἰκεῖόν ἐστι τοῖς ἐνθέοις ἐρασταῖς· μέσην γὰρ οὗτοι τάξιν ἀτεχνῶς ἐνστησάμενοι τοῦ τε θείου κάλλους καὶ τῶν δεομένων τῆς παρ' αὐτῶν

seinem eigenen Zeugnis? Die allgemeine Regel stellte fest: "nicht zulassend, daß die Liebenden sich selbst angehören, sondern nur den Geliebten." Paulus sagt: "So lebe nun nicht mehr ich, sondern es lebt Christus in mir." Zwischen diese beiden Aussagen hat Dionysius die triadische Dynamik des Universums gestellt, d.h. Providenz, Gemeinschaft und Rückkehr. Wenn eine der Bewegungen, die das Universum durchziehen, auf Paulus übertragen werden kann, so kann es nur die letzte sein, die Rückkehr (ἐπιστροφή). Aber dabei ist ein Unterschied zu beachten, und dieser Unterschied ist das zweite Moment, das ich herausstellen möchte. Die Erfahrung des Paulus durchschneidet die zirkulare und mehr oder weniger in sich selbst ruhende Bewegung des Universums. Nach des Paulus eigenen Worten ist es Christus, der in ihm lebt. Dionysius ist an Christus überhaupt nicht interessiert, sondern nur an dem unbedingt Letzten, an Gott. Paulus ist nicht unschuldig daran, daß Dionysius den Verweis auf Christus übersieht und für ihn gleich Gott einsetzt. Denn Dionysius weiß wie aus einer Konkordanz, daß das Wort, auf das es in seinem Zusammenhang ankommt, von Paulus an anderer Stelle benutzt wird. Ekstatisch ist das Stichwort, von dem Dionysius ausgegangen war. Paulus benutzt das Wort in *2 Korinther* 5.13, wo er sein eigenes Verhalten gegenüber den Korinthern beschreibt: "Denn wenn wir in Verzückung geraten sind, so geschah es für Gott; sind wir aber bei Sinnen, so sind wir's für euch." So lesen wir den Text, nicht jedoch Dionysius. Der bezieht den Dativ "für Gott" (θεῷ) auf das Verb, so daß eine dem Dionysius gemäße Übersetzung lauten müßte: "Paulus ist in Verzückung geraten (ἐξεστηκώς) und hat sich Gott ausgeliefert." In anderen Worten: Paulus verhält sich nicht verzückt um Gottes willen, sondern Gott wohnt ihm ein, so daß er, Paulus, nicht mehr sein eigenes Leben lebt; aber auch Gott ist "aus sich herausgetreten".

Das *erste* Moment ist des Paulus Passivität, göttliche Liebe ergreift Besitz von ihm. Dieses Moment entspricht dem anfänglichen Befehl Gottes bei Mose. Das *zweite* Moment ist der Austausch der Leben insofern, als der Ursprung der göttlichen Liebe durch das Adjektiv "göttlich" mit Gott identifiziert wird und dann dieser Ursprung als ein aktiv Liebender dargestellt wird. Ich denke nicht, daß Dionysius die Heil-

---

προνοίας, ἅτε δὴ τὸν ἔρωτα τὸν θεῖον ἀποτυπούμενοι, συνάγουσι μὲν εἰς ἑαυτοὺς τὴν τῶν ἐρωμένων ζωὴν καὶ συνάπτουσιν ἑαυτοῖς, ἀνάγουσι δὲ μεθ᾽ ἑαυτῶν ἐπὶ τὸ νοητὸν κάλλος ἐπαντλοῦντες, ὥς φησιν ὁ ἐν τῷ Φαίδρῳ Σωκράτης, εἰς τὴν τούτων ψυχὴν ὅσα ἂν ἐκεῖθεν ἀρύτωνται. εἰ τοίνυν ὁ ἐρωτικὸς τῷ ἔρωτι κάτοχός ἐστιν, ἐπιστρεπτικός τις ἂν εἴη τῶν εὖ πεφυκότων εἰς τὸ ἀγαθόν, ὥσπερ δὴ καὶ ὁ ἔρως, καὶ ἀνακλητικός (In Alc. 26, 12–27,3).

staten durch Jesus Christus im Sinne hat, wie es in der Textausgabe durch den Verweis auf *2 Korinther* 5.15 angedeutet wird; Dionysius hat sich der gebräuchlichen Sprache der Platoniker angeschlossen. Der Kontext war offen genug, um einen Verweis auf das Evangelium ("Christus ist für uns gestorben," *2 Korinther* 5.15) einzuflechten, wenn es gemeint sein sollte. Gottes Liebe ergreift Paulus, so daß Paulus das Leben dessen, der ihn liebt, sich zu leben sehnt (ζῶν ... τὴν τοῦ ἐραστοῦ ζωὴν ὡς σφόδρα ἀγαπητήν). Abgesehen von dem Zitat *Galater* 2.20 enthält der Abschnitt nichts, wofür es bei Proclus nicht Äquivalente gibt.

Ich fasse zusammen: Wenn Mose und Paulus Paradigmata für religiöse Erfahrung sind, dann ist das Subjekt religiöser Erfahrung sich erstens einer Aktivität bewußt, die es ergreift als ein Objekt, und zweitens auch bewußt des Wesens der Aktivität, deren Ursprung von der sinnlich wahrnehmbaren und intelligiblen Wirklichkeit unterschieden ist, sogar unterschieden vom eigenen Selbst des Subjektes und doch Gott als die Ursache aller Wirklichkeit.

3. *Der Lehrer (DN II 9)*[21]

Ich füge noch den einen Bericht hinzu, den Dionysius von seinem "berühmten Lehrer", wie er sagt, in II 9 des Traktates "Über die göttlichen Namen" gibt. Der Verweis auf seinen Lehrer ist aus zwei Gründen in die Einleitung zum Traktat aufgenommen. Erstens will Dionysius sagen, daß alles, was über Christologie zu lehren ist, in einer autoritativen Quelle enthalten ist, und zweitens will sich Dionysius aller weiteren Fragen zu diesem Thema entledigen. Der erste Grund ist ein durchgehendes Thema bei Dionysius; denn alles, was er weiß, führt er auf Offenbarung zurück, wie sie vorliegt in den göttlichen Worten der Bibel oder in der Überlieferung göttlicher Lehrer. Trotzdem sieht sich Dionysius veranlaßt, das Buch, auf das er verweist, durch seinen Schreiber zu beglaubigen. Es sieht so aus, als trage der Name des Autors keine eigene Autorität; genannt wird er in diesem Zusammenhang nicht. Und es erscheint der Name Hierotheus auch nur zweimal im ganzen Schrift-

---

[21] B. Brons, *Sekundäre Textpartien im Corpus Pseudo-Dionysiacum? Literarkritische Beobachtungen zu ausgewählten Textstellen* [NAWG Phil.-hist. Kl. 1975, 5] hat gezeigt, daß der Abschnitt DN III 2-3 im Kontext schlecht verankert ist und sowohl sprachlich wie auch inhaltlich auffällige Besonderheiten aufweist. Aber es scheint mir nicht möglich zu sein, ihn als Nachtrag eines Redaktors auszuscheiden. Ich übergehe ihn; Neues zum Thema religiöser Erfahrung trägt der Abschnitt nicht bei.

tum.[22] Also wird der Autor eingeführt durch eine Beschreibung der Weise, wie er zu dem Wissen gelangte, das er in dem genannten Buch "Theologische Grundlehren" darstellt. Drei Quellen werden genannt, um ihn nicht als den Erfinder von Neuem, sondern als den treuen Überlieferungsmittler erscheinen zu lassen. Die erste Quelle sind die heiligen Schreiber, d.h. abgekürzt die Bibel. Die zweite Quelle ist methodisches und gelehrtes und unermüdliches Forschen in der heiligen Schrift. Die dritte Quelle ist Inspiration. Es heißt: ἐμυήθη = es wurde ihm enthüllt. Die Frage ist: Wie? Die Enthüllung ist von Gott verursacht. Dionysius sagt: "aufgrund irgendeiner göttlicheren Inspiration" (ἔκ τινος ἐμυήθη θειοτέρας ἐπιπνοίας). Der Akt der Enthüllung, der nach der benutzten Vokabel auch soviel heißt wie Einweihung, umfaßt zwei Elemente.[23] Zuerst ist vom Lernen die Rede, ein Lernen, durch das ein Faktum oder ein gesprochenes Wort erfaßt wird. Dieses Element bedarf keiner weiteren Erläuterung. Das andere Element kommt aus Erfahrung als einem Widerfahrnis. Der Text sagt: "das Göttliche erleiden" (παθὼν τὰ θεῖα). Aber klar ist dabei noch nichts, außer daß die Gegenüberstellung von μαθών–παθών letztlich auf Aristoteles zurückgeht und von den Neuplatonikern benutzt wurde, um zwischen dem diskursiven Denken und der intuitiven Erkenntnis der absoluten Wahrheit zu unterscheiden.[24] Die Sprache des Dionysius lehnt sich an das neuplatonische Verständnis an, und die Fortsetzung lautet: "das Göttliche erleidend und aus Sympathie mit dem Göttlichen, wenn ich so sagen darf, er in einer unlehrbaren und mystischen Einung und Glauben vervollkommet wurde."

---

[22] Der Lehrer wird mit dem Namen Hierotheos genannt DN 139, 18 und 143, 8; vgl. Anm. 21.

[23] ...εἴτε καὶ ἔκ τινος ἐμυήθη θειοτέρας ἐπιπνοίας οὐ μόνον μαθὼν ἀλλὰ καὶ παθὼν τὰ θεῖα κἀκ τῆς πρὸς αὐτὰ συμπαθείας, εἰ οὕτω χρὴ φάναι, πρὸς τὴν ἀδίδακτον αὐτῶν καὶ μυστικὴν ἀποτελεσθεὶς ἕνωσιν καὶ πίστιν. Καὶ ἵνα τὰ πολλὰ καὶ μακάρια θεάματα τῆς κρατίστης ἐκείνου διανοίας ἐν ἐλαχίστοις παραθώμεθα, τάδε περὶ τοῦ Ἰησοῦ φησιν ἐν ταῖς συνηγμέναις αὐτῷ θεολογικαῖς στοιχειώσεσιν (DN 134, 1-6).

[24] Vgl. Jeanne Croissant, *Aristote et les mystères* [BFPUL fasc. LI] (Liège/Paris 1932), 150 ff. Die Bezugsstelle wird als De philosophia frg. 15 geboten. Mit *Hebräer* 4.14 ff hat Dionysius gar nichts zu tun. Zu vergleichen ist vor allem Proclus, *In Rempublicam* II 108, 17-30 (Kroll): αἱ τελεταὶ ... συμπαθείας εἰσὶν αἰτίαι ταῖς ψυχαῖς περὶ τὰ δρώμενα τρόπον ἄγνωστον ἡμῖν καὶ θεῖον· ὡς τοὺς μὲν τῶν τελουμένων καταπλήττεσθαι δείματων θείων πλήρεις γιγνομένους, τοὺς δὲ συνδιατίθεσθαι τοῖς ἱεροῖς συμβόλοις καὶ ἑαυτῶν ἐκστάντες ὅλους ἐνιδρῦσθαι τοῖς θεοῖς καὶ ἐνθεάζειν (108, 18-24). Das Testimonium zum Aristotelesfragment bei Synesius, Dio VIII gibt die für Dionysius wichtige Gleichsetzung: οὐ μαθεῖν τι δεῖν, ἀλλὰ παθεῖν καὶ διατεθῆναι, δηλονότι γενομένους ἐπιτηδείους. Dazu vgl. EH II (68, 21–69, 2).

Rorem[25] hat argumentiert, daß hier an die Liturgie zu denken sei: Ich stimme ihm zu, aber aus einem anderen Grund als dem, den er vorträgt, nämlich wegen der Sprache, was ich in Teil II ausführen werde. Teilnahme des Lehrers an der Liturgie der Kirche führte den Lehrer zur Einung mit dem Göttlichen. Solch eine Einung ist nicht lehrbar; sie widerfährt einer Person.[26] Offensichtlich sind mit der Einung Visionen verbunden, wobei hier nicht gesagt wird, ob sie in der Einung selbst sich ereignen oder ihr folgen. Jedenfalls kann der Vollkommene davon sprechen, wie es sein Lehrer in seinem Buch "Theologische Grundlehren" getan hat.

Aus diesem Text ergeben sich drei neue Elemente für religiöse Erfahrung. Das erste Element ist relativ unbestimmt durch die Vorstellung von Inspiration angedeutet; es ist eine besondere Form göttlicher Kausalität. Das zweite Element ist der verschlüsselte Hinweis auf eine psychologische Vorbereitung oder ethische Haltung, die für die Einung mit Gott vorausgesetzt wird; das ergibt sich aus den Paralleltexten zu μαθών–παθών. Und das dritte Element ist die Implikation, klarer als im Fall des Mose, daß etwas gesehen wird, was für Mitteilung benutzt werden kann.

II. *Die Sprache religiöser Erfahrung*

Ich wende mich jetzt einer Beschreibung der Sprache, in der religiöse Erfahrung beschrieben wird, zu. Ich bin mir wohl bewußt, daß ich den größten Teil der Texte übergangen habe, aber ich denke, daß ich die Texte gut genug kenne, um gegen Einwände gewappnet zu sein. Die moderne Forschung hat gezeigt, daß Dionysius starke Anleihen bei der Sprache der neuplatonischen Philosophen macht; besonders frappierend ist die Nähe zu Proclus. Ich wähle ein paar Beispiele aus den Texten, die ich im Teil I analysiert habe. Diese Basis ist gewiß schmal, aber umso

---

[25] Paul Rorem, *Biblical and Liturgical Symbols within the Pseudo-Dionysian Synthesis* [Studies and Texts 71] (Toronto 1984), 133-135.

[26] Vgl. die Überlegung bei Plotin, Enn. VI 9,4: Ὑπὲρ ἐπιστήμην τοίνυν δεῖ δραμεῖν καὶ μηδαμῇ ἐκβαίνειν τοῦ ἓν εἶναι, ἀλλ' ἀποστῆναι δεῖ καὶ ἐπιστήμης καὶ ἐπιστητῶν καὶ παντὸς ἄλλου καὶ καλοῦ θεάματος. Πᾶν γὰρ καλὸν ὕστερον ἐκείνου καὶ παρ' ἐκείνου, ὥσπερ πᾶν φῶς μεθημερινὸν παρ' ἡλίου. Διὸ οὐδὲ ῥητὸν οὐδὲ γραπτόν, φησιν, ἀλλὰ λέγομεν καὶ γράφομεν πέμποντες εἰς αὐτὸ καὶ ἀνεγείροντες ἐκ τῶν λόγων ἐπὶ τὴν θέαν ὥσπερ ὁδὸν δεικνύντες τῷ τι θεάσασθαι βουλομένῳ. Μέχρι γὰρ τῆς ὁδοῦ καὶ τῆς πορείας ἡ δίδαξις, ἡ δὲ θέα αὐτοῦ ἔργον ἤδη τοῦ ἰδεῖν βεβουλημένου (4, 7-16).

sprechender: Denn die besprochenen Texte haben einen biblischen Sprachgrund, so daß die sprachliche Veränderung umso eher ins Auge springt.

Mose (MThI 3 p. 144): Der Bericht zeigt seine erste Abweichung vom biblischen Text in der Erweiterung, daß Mose auch Lichter sieht. Die Lichter, die "reine und mannigfache Strahlen hervorströmen". "Reine Strahlen" sind die Ursache von Erleuchtungen, und Erleuchtungen lassen uns die einende Kraft Gottes sehen. Plato[27] hat die Lichtmetapher eingeführt, um den Erkenntnisvorgang verständlich zu machen. Obwohl Licht und Sehen zum Bereich sinnlicher Wahrnehmung gehören, werden sie auch für die Aktivität des Geistes benutzt. Die geistige Aktivität und der Vorgang intelligiblen Erkennens beherrschen dann die weitere Beschreibung von des Mose Aufstieg zum Transzendenten. Das Dunkel, in das Mose eintritt, ist das "Dunkel des Nicht-Erkennens". Das ganze Erlebnis besteht darin, das Transzendente zu erreichen, dessen ontologische Position nicht einfach jenseits von aller Wirklichkeit ist, sondern genau jenseits des Erkennens der Vernunft, also jenseits des Intelligiblen. Nichts in dieser Aufstiegsbeschreibung, eingeschlossen die Einung selbst, ist anders als bei dem Neuplatoniker Proclus. Fragen muß man eher, warum Dionysius von Gregor von Nyssa abweicht. Und er weicht fundamental von ihm ab, wenn er dem Mosebericht eine Einung mit dem Transzendenten hinzufügt. Ich denke, daß Dionysius von Proclus etwas gelernt hat. Er hat von Proclus gelernt, daß alle Wirklichkeit ihr intelligibles Sein von einer konstanten Gegenwärtigkeit Gottes in dieser Wirklichkeit hat, wobei aber die göttliche Gegenwärtigkeit nicht mit der Wirklichkeit selbst verwechselt werden darf. Das metaphysische Prinzip, Gott von den Seienden zu unterscheiden, ist mehr als Gottes allumfassende Kausalität (ἡ πάντων αἰτία); das metaphysische Prinzip ist vielmehr die einigende Kraft, die die Wirklichkeit zu einem hierarchisch strukturierten Kosmos macht. Das metaphysische Prinzip bedeutet, daß mehr erkannt ist als die Unerkennbarkeit Gottes; denn es wird als Erkenntnis gewußt, was jenseits von Erkenntnis ist. Die verwirrende Vielfalt sinnlich wahrnehmbarer Eindrücke lichtet sich durch eine metaphysische Vision der Wirklichkeit, die selbst auf der Kenntnis des Wesens der Allursache ruht.

Es ist natürlich nicht zu bezweifeln, daß Dionysius wie auch Proclus die Transzendenz Gottes bewahren wollen, ja auch, daß dieses ihre Intention ist. Beide beharren darauf, daß Gott durch die Vernunft nicht er-

---

[27] Vgl. Resp. 507 d–511 a; 514 a sqq.

kannt werden kann. Gott schafft das Verstehen; die intelligente Erkenntnis tritt ein, wenn die Wirklichkeit aus der Perspektive Gottes erfaßt wird, d.h. in der Einung mit Gott. Die Sprache der religiösen Erfahrung ist also ein noetischer Diskurs, indem die Aktivitäten des Geistes beschrieben werden. Mose, so in den Worten des Dionysius, "ist völlig geeint mit dem gänzlich Unbekannten durch die Unaktivität alles Erkennens" (τῷ παντελῶς δὲ ἀγνώστῳ τῇ πάσης γνώσεως ἀνενεργησίᾳ κατὰ τὸ κρεῖττον ἑνούμενος; p. 144, 13 sq.). Der Abschnitt über Paulus (DN IV 13) fügt hinzu, daß religiöse Erfahrung von Gott verursacht ist; um das deutlich werden zu lassen, wird die Sprache der Liebe oder des Eros verwendet.

Jedoch führt weitere Überlegung zu zwei Problemen. Das erste Problem besteht darin, daß Wissen und Erkennen Gottes als das, was er als Ursache von allem und als darin alles einigend ist, offenbart werden muß. Mose dient Dionysius als Paradigma, weil seine Erfahrung in den göttlichen Worten enthalten ist. Das gleiche gilt für Paulus. Das Problem zeigt sich, wenn man fragt, ob Mose oder Paulus als Paradigmata für einen nachvollziehbaren Weg zu religiöser Erfahrung benutzt werden können. Deren Erfahrung wurde von Gott geschenkt; das ergibt sich schon allein daraus, daß die göttlichen Worte sie bezeugen. Aber die Folge davon ist eine Umkehrung, eine Inversion. Denn die Stufen des Moseauftiegs, insbesondere die vorletzte Stufe einer Wahrnehmung göttlicher Gegenwart "auf den intelligiblen Höhen" (ταῖς νοηταῖς ἀκρότησι; p. 144,8) hängen von der Einung ab. Deswegen ist die Einung nicht eine seltene oder letzte Erfahrung, sei es in diesem oder im jenseitigen Leben, sondern die Einung ist die Voraussetzung aller Wahrnehmung von Gottes Gegenwärtigkeit im Universum. Wenn ich es richtig beschrieben habe, ist also Dionysius mit folgendem Problem konfrontiert: Er kann auf die Tatsache verweisen, daß Erfahrungen der Einung sich ereignet haben und folglich auch uns widerfahren können. Aber Dionysius kann solche Erfahrung nicht herbeiführen, wie ja auch z. B. Paulus nicht herbeiführen konnte, daß die göttliche Liebe ihn ergriff. Natürlich mag es Vorbereitungen für ein solches Widerfahrnis geben; im Fall des Mose werden sie Reinigung genannt. Und es gibt das Gebet um solches Widerfahrnis. Nach dem Gebet wäre es angemessen, auf seine Erfüllung zu warten, es sei denn, daß das Gebet zwar nicht eine automatische Antwort von Gott auslöst, jedoch im Beter einen göttlichen Funken aktiviert; so erklärt es Proclus, indem er voraussetzt, daß etwas

Göttliches im Menschen durchs Gebet auflebe.[28] Dionysius aber appelliert nicht an etwas "Göttliches in uns", so daß es ungeklärt bleibt, was die Gebete, mit denen die Traktate eingeleitet werden, bewirken sollen.[29]

Damit komme ich zu dem zweiten Problem, und das ist noch größer als das erste. Menschen sind intelligente Wesen; folglich ist Gewahren Gottes an Verstehen und Erkennen gebunden. Illumination schafft Erkennen dadurch, daß die "Ursache von allem" mit der Wirklichkeit verbunden wird und so die Wirklichkeit in ihrer metaphysischen Struktur intelligibel macht. Nur wenn die "Ursache von allem" erkannt wird als die einigende Kraft in der Wirklichkeit, gibt es Verstehen und Erkennen; andernfalls herrscht Dunkelheit und Verwirrung. Jedoch ist die "Ursache von allem", der Eins Seiende (ὁ ὢν ἕν), jenseits von Erkenntnis und jenseits der Vernunft, so daß einerseits der Eins Seiende die Intelligibilität der Wirklichkeit durchsichtig macht, aber andererseits alle Intelligibilität von der Einung mit dem Eins Seienden abhängt und Ekstase voraussetzt. Offenbaren und Mitteilen der Ergebnisse von Einung können ganz und gar nicht die Erfahrung der Einung ersetzen. Man muß sich also fragen, was die Darstellungen des Dionysius bewirken sollen. Denn Dionysius kann die Gottesworte nicht einfach wiederholen; das Wiederholen ist totes Nachreden, solange nicht die "Ursache

---

[28] Über das Gebet bei Proclus vgl. den bekannten Abschnitt In Timaeum I (207, 21–214, 12); dazu Beierwaltes, Proklos (wie Anm. 18), 313-320 und Exkurs III, 391-394. οὐδενὸς γὰρ ἀφέστηκε τὸ θεῖον, ἀλλὰ πᾶσιν ἐξ ἴσου πάρεστι. διό, κἂν τὰ ἔσχατα λάβῃς, καὶ τούτοις παρὸν τὸ θεῖον εὑρήσεις· ἔστι γὰρ πανταχοῦ τὸ ἕν, καθὸ τῶν ὄντων ἕκαστον ἐκ θεῶν ὑφέστηκε, προελθόντα δὲ πάντα ἐκ θεῶν οὐκ ἐξελήλυθεν ἀπ' αὐτῶν ἀλλ' ἐνερρίζωται ἐν αὐτοῖς· ποῦ γὰρ ἂν καὶ ἐξέλθοι, πάντα τῶν θεῶν περιειληφότων καὶ προκατειληφότων καὶ ἐν ἑαυτοῖς ἐχόντων; τὸ γὰρ ἐπέκεινα τῶν θεῶν τὸ μηδαμῶς ὄν ἐστι (209, 19-26). τελευταία δὲ ἡ ἕνωσις, αὐτῷ τῷ ἑνὶ τῶν θεῶν τὸ ἓν τῆς ψυχῆς ἐνιδρύουσα καὶ μίαν ἐνέργειαν ἡμῶν τε ποιοῦσα καὶ τῶν θεῶν, καθ' ἣν οὐδὲ ἑαυτῶν ἐσμεν, ἀλλὰ τῶν θεῶν, ἐν τῷ θείῳ φωτὶ μένοντες καὶ ὑπ' αὐτοῦ κύκλῳ περιεχόμενοι. καὶ τοῦτο πέρας ἐστὶ τὸ ἄριστον τῆς ἀληθινῆς εὐχῆς, ἵνα ἐπισυνάψῃ τὴν ἐπιστροφὴν τῇ μονῇ καὶ πᾶν τὸ προελθὸν ἀπὸ τοῦ τῶν θεῶν ἑνὸς αὖθις ἐνιδρύσῃ τῷ ἑνὶ καὶ τὸ ἐν ἡμῖν φῶς τῷ τῶν θεῶν φωτὶ περιλάβῃ (211, 24–212, 1). Ἃ μὲν οὖν περὶ εὐχῆς εἰδέναι δεῖ τὴν πρώτην, τοιαῦτα ἄττα ἐστίν, ὅτι οὐσία μὲν αὐτῆς ἡ συναγωγὸς καὶ συνδετικὴ τῶν ψυχῶν πρὸς τοὺς θεούς, μᾶλλον δὲ ἡ πάντων τῶν δευτέρων ἐνοποιὸς πρὸς τὰ πρότερα (212, 29–213, 2).

[29] Über das Gebet bei Dionysius vgl. besonders DN III 1 (138, 1–139, 16). Nachdem er Gleichnisse (lichtreiche Kette, Tau und Schiff) verwendet hat, faßt er abschließend zusammen: Διὸ καὶ πρὸ παντὸς καὶ μᾶλλον θεολογίας εὐχῆς ἀπάρχεσθαι χρεὼν οὐχ ὡς ἐφελκομένους τὴν ἀπανταχῆ παροῦσαν καὶ οὐδαμῆ δύναμιν, ἀλλ' ὡς ταῖς θείαις μνήμαις καὶ ἐπικλήσεσιν ἡμᾶς αὐτοὺς ἐγχειρίζοντας αὐτῇ καὶ ἑνοῦντας (139, 13-16). Verweis auf das Gebet findet sich in CH I 2 (7, 9 sqq); EH I 2 (65, 20 sq) und, als Gebet formuliert, in MTh I 1 (141, 2–142, 4).

von allem" selbst eben als Verursacher im Reden darüber zum Ausdruck kommt. Dionysius tut das auch, indem er zuerst beteuert, daß die "Ursache von allem" selbst der Grund für die Gottesoffenbarungen an die Gottesmänner ist (DN I 2), und dann, daß er selbst in deren Überlieferung *eingeweiht* wurde (vgl. DN 112, 7; 114,1). Proclus spricht ebenso; die Logik des Gedankens erfordert es. Weiterhin muß man voraussetzen, daß nicht nur die Gottesmänner die Erfahrung der Einung besitzen, sondern daß auch Dionysius selbst sie für sich voraussetzen muß, auch wenn er das nicht ausdrücklich angibt (vgl. DN 108,5; bes. 115,7; auch 116,4). Denn die Logik seiner eigenen Gedanken erfordert, daß die Intelligibilität, aus der heraus er schreibt, selbst wenn er nur sagt, was in den Gottesworten offenbart ist,—daß er diese Intelligibilität besitzen muß, um die in der Realität anwesende Kausalität des Gottesprinzips wahrnehmen zu können. Von Gott her gesehen: Gott zieht hinauf (ἀνατείνει; p. 110, 14); wir als das Wir des Schreibers: wir werden erleuchtet (p. 111, 7).[30]

Bleibt als nächstes zu erklären, wie sich in den Grundgedanken von der Allursache einordnen läßt, was Dionysius an eigenen Gedanken vorträgt. Denn er trägt selbst vor; er begnügt sich nicht damit zu preisen (ὑμνεῖν), was die Gottesmänner preisen, sondern es erläuternd weiterzuführen, z. B. wenn er ausformuliert, was die Gottesmänner an Intelligibilität *vorausgesetzt* haben (vgl. 118, 2!), deutlicher noch, wenn er eine Erklärung mit den Worten einführt: Man muß wagen, auch dieses zu sagen (p. 159, 9; vgl. p. 155, 14). Meist ist es abgesichert, letztlich durch Verweis auf seinen Lehrer (vgl. DN p. 143, 8). Seine eigene Erklärungsfähigkeit—erklären, darstellen, behandeln, entfalten[31]—ist wohl ähnlich zu denken wie die seines Lehrers.

Nun aber das Letzte: Nach seiner eigenen Theorie über die Intelligibilität kann er sich nur denen mitteilen, die die Einung auch erfahren haben, die—in des Dionysius Worten—den Strahl wahrnehmen, der die Allursache in der Wirklichkeit erscheinen läßt.[32] Vom unmittelbaren

---

[30] Vgl. überhaupt 111, 7 sqq.

[31] Wörter, mit denen Dionysius sein eigenes Tun beschreibt, sind beispielhaft folgende: ὑμνεῖν und ἀναπτύσσειν (siehe Register der Ausgabe); ἀνασκέπτεσθαι EH 80, 4; ἐπισκέπειν DN 138,2; CH 58 7; ἀποδεικνύειν DN 116,6; 122, 6; 124, 13; 125, 14; 180, 7; CH 11,7; 56,2; EH 63, 5; 104, 6; 106, 18; ἐκτίθεσθαι DN 116,7; 126, 4; 131, 1; CH 9, 16; 26, 10; EH 79, 4; 104, 4.12; Ep 9, 207, 2; ἐρευνῆσαι CH 25, 2; διαπραγματεύεσθαι DN 116, 5; 139, 20; EH 77,8; κατιδεῖν CH 25, 23; EH 80, 5; 88, 5; ἐπισκοπεῖν DN 218, 17; CH 43, 20; EH 95,5; ἐξετάζειν DN 122, 6; ὁρίζειν DN 206, 2; CH 20, 4; στοχάζεσθαι DN 203, 23; καταστοχάζεσθαι CH 57, 23; ὑφηγεῖσθαι CH 47, 12.

[32] Vgl. MTh I.1 (142, 9-11); z. B. auch DN I.2 (110, 11 sq; ἀκτίς 110, 12).

Adressaten nehme ich an, daß er "vollendet ist"; er wird "Mitpriester" genannt und von den Uneingeweihten unterschieden.[33] Dann aber traut er der Weitergabe, weil sowohl in den Gottesworten wie auch in den Symbolen der *Strahl* der jenseitigen Allursache eingelegt ist. Und zwar so eingelegt, daß der Strahl oder das Licht es sind, die zur Einung hinführen. Hierzu, also zur hinaufführenden Macht der Symbole, muß er auf das zurückgreifen, was Proclus deutlich und prinzipiell herausstellte: es gibt eine der Seele innewohnende Fähigkeit, das Göttliche zu erfassen; es gibt in der Seele etwas dem Göttlichen Gleiches, es gibt eine Anwesenheit des Göttlichen in der Seele. Proclus sagt: "Die Seele wendet sich der ihr eigenen Einheit zu", um "das Eine in uns" als solches zu fassen. Das ist der Weg dialektischer Argumentation zum Geistigen hin; er findet Vollendung, wenn die Seele aus sich heraustritt und in schweigender Ruhe des Einen in seiner Transzendenz gewahr wird.[34]

Daß Dionysius den hinführenden Zweck ausspricht, ist in den beiden Hierarchien am deutlichsten; denn Hierarchie ist ja definiert als Prinzip von Offenbarungsvermittlung.[35] Insbesondere ist aus der "Kirchlichen Hierarchie" Aufschluß über die Hinführung zur Vollkommenheit, zur Einung zu erwarten; denn die Riten der Liturgie haben wenigstens teilweise fortschreitenden Charakter. Entsprechend wird dort, wie auch sonst, betont, daß Erkenntnis jedem entsprechend seinem Fortschritt zu-

---

[33] συμπρεσβύτερος DN 107, 1; CH 7, 1; EH 63, 1. Vgl. die Stellen unter dem Wort ἀμύητος im Register und besonders EH I 5 (68, 4-15).

[34] Vgl. W. Beierwaltes, *Denken des Einen. Studien zur neuplatonischen Philosphie und ihrer Wirkungsgeschichte* (Frankfurt 1985), 254-280. Vgl. Proclus, Theol. plat. I 3: Λείπεται οὖν, εἴπερ ἐστὶ καὶ ὁπωσοῦν τὸ θεῖον γνωστόν, τῇ τῆς ψυχῆς ὑπάρξει καταληπτὸν ὑπάρχειν καὶ διὰ ταύτης γνωρίζεσθαι καθ' ὅσον δυνατόν. τῷ γὰρ ὁμοίῳ πανταχοῦ φαμεν τὰ ὅμοια γινώσκεσθαι· τῇ μὲν αἰσθήσει δηλαδὴ τὸ αἰσθητόν, τῇ δὲ δόξῃ τὸ δοξαστόν, τῇ δὲ διανοίᾳ τὸ διανοητικόν, τῷ δὲ νῷ τὸ νοητόν, ὥστε καὶ τῷ ἑνὶ τὸ ἑνικώτατον καὶ τῷ ἀρρήτῳ τὸ ἄρρητον. Ὀρθῶς γὰρ καὶ ὁ ἐν Ἀλκιβιάδῃ Σωκράτης ἔλεγεν εἰς ἑαυτὴν εἰσιοῦσαν τὴν ψυχὴν τά τε ἄλλα πάντα κατόψεσθαι καὶ τὸν θεόν· συννεύουσα γὰρ εἰς τὴν ἑαυτῆς ἕνωσιν καὶ κέντρον τῆς ἁπάσης ζωῆς καὶ τὸ πλῆθος ἀποσκευαζομένη καὶ τὴν ποικιλίαν τῶν ἐν αὐτῇ παντοδαπῶν δυνάμεων, ἐπ' αὐτὴν ἄνεισι τὴν ἄκραν τῶν ὄντων περιωπήν (15, 15–16, 1 Saffrey-Westerink). Vgl. Ἦ πῶς ἐγγυτέρῳ τοῦ ἑνὸς ἐσόμεθα, μὴ τὸ ἓν τῆς ψυχῆς ἀνεγείραντες, ὅ ἐστιν ἐν ἡμῖν οἷον εἰκὼν τοῦ ἑνός, καθὸ καὶ μάλιστα τὸν ἐνθουσιασμὸν γίνεσθαί φασιν οἱ ἀκριβέστεροι τῶν λόγων; Πῶς δ' ἂν τὸ ἓν αὐτὸ τοῦτο καὶ τὸ ἄνθος τῆς ψυχῆς ἀναλάμψαι ποιήσαιμεν, εἰ μὴ κατὰ νοῦν πρότερον ἐνεργήσαιμεν; Ἡ γὰρ κατὰ νοῦν ἐνέργεια πρὸς τὴν ἤρεμον κατάστασιν καὶ ἐνεργείαν ἄγει τὴν ψυχήν (In Parm. VI 1071, 25-33). Weitere Stellen bei Beierwaltes a.a.O. 274/5 Anm. 87, 88 u. 92.

[35] Dazu sind immer die Untersuchungen von R. Roques, 'L'Univers dionysien', *Théologie* 29 (Paris 1954) zu vergleichen.

geteilt ist.[36] Andeutungen zu der Ordnung des Erhebens zum Geistigen und darüber hinaus zum Übergeistigen lassen erkennen, daß Dionysius Intelligibilität in Stufen annimmt. Es scheint so zu sein, daß es eingeschränkte Intelligibilität und weiter ausgreifende Intelligibilität gibt, insofern im anfänglichen Verstehenshorizont die Einheit nicht in ihrer Totalität ins Spiel kommt, sondern nur als Seinsursache einsichtig zu werden braucht.[37] Eben dabei setzt Dionysius voraus, was er über die religiöse Erfahrung seines Lehrers sagte. "Aus Sympathie mit dem Göttlichen" (DN p. 134,3). Das heißt: Der kirchliche Ritus, die Liturgie, berührt die Seele; sie ist Psychagogie, ist Reinigung der Seele von dem, was ihr geistiges Vermögen verdeckte und behinderte. Die moralische Reinigung, durch die Riten gefördert und gestützt,[38] legt progressiv das geistige Vermögen der Seele frei, und je nach dem Grad dieser Befreiung des der Seele innewohnenden Vermögens wird die Intelligibilität der Betrachtungen zur gradweisen Aktualisierung des Geistes in der Seele. Die Bibel und die kirchliche Liturgie haben also deswegen die Kraft, zur Allursache hinaufzuführen, weil sie zuerst Psychagogie sind und dann gradweise durch die Belehrung in der geistigen Betrachtung das freigelegte geistige Vermögen der Seele aktualisieren, bis sie zur übergeistigen Einung gelangen.

Intelligibilität als solche eignet den Darstellungen des Dionysius nur für den Geeinten, seinem Adressaten, der vom Einen "weiß" und die Erkenntnisse als Erleuchtungen durch das Licht vom Einen erfährt. Die Traktate sind also an solche geschrieben, bei denen Intelligibilität aufgrund ihrer Gotteserfahrung vorausgesetzt werden kann. Allerdings ist die Intelligibilität erweiterbar. Denn so schließt die "Kirchliche Hierarchie": "Auch Dir werden, wie ich glaube, in jedem Fall noch mehr weithin leuchtende und göttliche Schönheiten einleuchten, wenn Du das Gesagte als Sprossen einer Leiter zu höherem Licht benutzt. Gib also, mein Freund, auch Deinerseits mir Anteil an vollkommener Erleuchtung und zeige meinen Augen, was für noch prächtigere und dem Einen mehr verwandte Schönheiten Du etwa schauen kannst. Ich bin nämlich

---

[36] Vgl. EH Θεωρία 6 (85, 3–86, 1), auch VI (118, 19–120, 12).

[37] Vgl. die in Anm. 36 genannte Stelle mit EH II (68, 21–69, 13). Auch in DN I 3 (111, 12–112, 6) gibt es Hinweise auf die Grade der Vervollkomnung.

[38] Vgl. EH II (74, 2 sqq) und III (81, 15 sqq): Δεῦρο δὴ οὖν, ὦ παῖ καλέ, μετὰ τὰς εἰκόνας ἐν τάξει καὶ ἱερῶς ἐπὶ τὴν θεοειδῆ τῶν ἀρχετύπων ἀλήθειαν ἐκεῖνο τοῖς ἔτι τελειουμένοις εἰς ἐναρμόνιον αὐτῶν ψυχαγωγίαν εἰπών ... Ähnlich 83, 11 sqq.

guten Mutes, daß ich durch das Gesagte die in Dir schlummernden Funken des göttlichen Feuers entfachen werde."[39]

Ich füge zwei Bemerkungen an:

Erstens unterscheidet sich der noetische Diskurs eigentlich nicht von Proclus. Jedoch im Unterschied zu Proclus unterdrückt Dionysius den dialektischen Diskurs und das dialektische Argumentieren. Dionysius ist sozusagen eindimensional, es ist die Darstellung eines geschlossenen metaphysischen Systems ohne den Versuch, in das System hineinzuführen, eine Vision, aber kein Argument. Darin ist Dionysius seiner Überzeugung treu, daß "alles Licht von oben gegeben ist", daß alles Offenbarung ist.[40]

Zweitens erweckt Dionysius den Eindruck, daß es eine kataphatische und eine apophatische Theologie gebe, also vom unerkennbaren Seienden herabsteigend und zum unerkennbaren Seienden aufsteigend. Die Stufen, auf denen herab- und aufgestiegen wird und die als theologische Positionen die Gegenwärtigkeit Gottes setzen, ergeben sich aus der Erkenntnis, die durch die Erfahrung der Einung vermittelt ist. Dionysius weiß mehr über den unerkennbar Seienden, als seine Beteuerung: "jenseits der Vernunft" erlaubt. An diesem Punkt ist Gregor von Nyssa dem Grundsatz von Gottes Unerkennbarkeit treuer geblieben.[41]

---

[39] EH VII b. 11 (131, 32–32, 6) Die Übersetzung habe ich von G. Heil übernommen [BGrL 22] (Stuttgart 1986).

[40] Vgl. den Beginn von CH: Πᾶσα δόσις ἀγαθὴ καὶ πᾶν δώρημα τέλειον ἄνωθέν ἐστι καταβαῖνον ἀπὸ τοῦ πατρὸς τῶν φώτων (= *Jakob* 1.17; 7.3 sq). Es ist mir allerdings nirgends eindeutig klargeworden, ob der den Symbolen (Gottesworte und Liturgie) eingelegte Strahl von sich aus zur Einung emporhebt oder ob vielmehr nur der "Vollendete" (Geeinte) die Symbolhaftigkeit durchschaut und damit nur er das emporführende Licht nachträglich als Licht des Einen wahrnimmt.

[41] Wenn dieser Beobachtung die Wertigkeit von Kritik beigemessen wird, dann ergäbe sich, daß sich Dionysius von der Position des Proclus, die Gegenwärtigkeit des Göttlichen in den Seienden setzen zu können, hat blenden lassen.

LITERAL OR METAPHORICAL?
SOME ISSUES OF LANGUAGE IN THE ARIAN CONTROVERSY

CATHERINE OSBORNE

In this article I shall examine some issues concerning the status of language about God that are raised in the course of the Arian controversy. I shall focus particularly on three texts: Athanasius *Contra Arianos* I, Basil *Adversus Eunomium* 2.24, and Gregory of Nyssa *Contra Eunomium* book 2.

Heresy, Refutation and the Vocabulary of Invective

The Arian controversy is one of the more significant disputes in the history of the early Church, and one that initiates a long programme of redefinition and clarification of doctrine. But the fact that Arianism is seen as a threat by a succession of thinkers, who make it their business to challenge the thought and writings of Arius himself and of his disciples, places the controversy in a familiar sequence. Perhaps Arianism poses a more serious problem than earlier heresies. Arguably its challenge is more profound, and certainly more respectable intellectually, than that posed by Valentinus, Basilides, Marcion, the Montanists, or even Manichaeans and Monarchians. But in so far as it provokes a response of hostility in those who hold to the orthodox side of the conflict, and an attempt to defend and justify the traditional teachings on rational grounds, the Arian view belongs in the same sequence as these earlier sources of conflict.

The sense that writers against Arianism locate themselves within a tradition of anti-heretical writings is readily grasped from the style and rhetoric of their writings. Much of the tone and vocabulary of texts such as the *Contra Arianos* of Athanasius is reminiscent of their famous predecessors in Irenaeus, Hippolytus and Epiphanius. In Athanasius we find again the rhetorical appeal to the reader's sense that these thinkers can hardly be viewed as true followers of Christ.[1] And we find the familiar search for some source of corruption, the real origin of the heretical way of thinking. For Arianism, Athanasius suggests, the source cannot even be Greek philosophy; only the devil is sufficiently malign to have invented such a pernicious set of ideas.[2] Nevertheless there is a difference between writing against the Gnostic heresies as Hippolytus and Irenaeus were doing, and the task that faces Athanasius and others in addressing Arian sympathisers. The terms of the refutation have changed in one respect, and that is the possibility of appealing to a common set of scriptural texts.

In the case of the Gnostic heresies the claim to possess secret documents on the part of the heretical sects rendered appeal to a set of authoritative texts unhelpful.[3] Arianism does not pose the same difficulty, given that Arius does not deny the validity of the scriptures recognised by his opponents and the wider Church in general.[4] Nor does he introduce additional texts beyond those standardly used. The status of Arius' *Thalia* is, admittedly, unclear; Athanasius certainly professes to find its genre puzzling, presumably because it appears to belong to a tradition that is neither (pseudo-) sacred scripture nor academic theology. He does at one point imply that Arius wrote the *Thalia* as a substitute for scripture,[5] but its 'effeminate' metre and style place it in the genre of the scurrilous verse of Sotades.[6] Some of Athanasius' comments are plainly rhetorical, but it seems unlikely that the *Thalia* was designed for precisely the same role as the conventional scriptures. It certainly does not seem to provide a source of proof texts; rather it serves as a kind of metrical creed for early Arianism.

Given a basis in some recognised sacred texts, and indeed some recognised turns of phrase,[7] there are now three kinds of option for one

---

[1] E.g. *Contra Arianos* [= *CA*] 1.4.

[2] *CA* 1.10.

[3] In the majority of the Gnostic sects the problem was that they possessed additional books not known to the mainstream Church. With Marcion the difficulty was rather that certain texts recognised by the mainstream Church were not accepted by Marcion.

[4] This is not to say that the extent of the canon was agreed without variation by all (as is evident from Eusebius *H.E.* 3.25 for example) but that there is no defining difference between Arians and their opponents in this respect.

[5] *CA* 1.2, Arius is said to imitate the poet Sotades in place of Moses.

[6] *CA* 1.3; 1.5.

[7] Many of the points Athanasius makes are actually concerned with titles and phrases conventionally used by the Church (we call God 'Father', 'eternal' and so on). Usually he cites support for these phrases from Scriptural passages, but the argument

who would write a refutation of Arian views. One may appeal to the incoherence or unsatisfactory nature of the theological position itself; one may attempt to demonstrate that it derives from sources known to be unreliable or corrupt; or one may argue that it is inconsistent with the traditional language employed by Scripture and the worshipping tradition of the Church.

Refutation with shared scriptures

All three of these approaches figure in the writings against Arius and Arians that we possess. But it is the approach which appeals to shared scriptures and traditional language that is relatively new as an option in the campaign against heretics, and it is this approach that initiates a whole range of issues about the use of language and the reading of texts that refer to God. It is one thing to say that a writer shares with her opponent a body of scriptural texts and a set of conventional phrases acceptable in speaking of God, but it is another thing to establish that those texts are read in the same way or that the phrases mean the same for the two thinkers. As soon as the anti-heretical writer appeals to a text or cites a formula in words she will immediately face the task of establishing how that language functions and what it means. Whereas in the earlier period a writer was likely to meet the response that that text simply does not form part of the authoritative tradition of the opponent in question, now the problem will normally arise in the form of a disagreement as to how the words are to be read.

In this article I shall consider three passages that explicitly raise questions about the language used of God the Father and of God the Son in Scripture and worship, as a result of attempts to show that an opponent has misconstrued the status or meaning of the language in question. The issues raised here will then form the starting point for a consideration of how we should rightly analyse the way in which language about God functions and makes sense.

Two issues of reading: what is it about and what does it say about it?

Using a proof text from scripture or tradition is problematic in two ways. Citing the text will get the writer nowhere unless one can secure agreement on two issues in the reading of the text. One is the question of whether the text is relevant to the matter in hand: is it actually about

is appealing to a shared tradition of language in worship, not merely a written authority.

what we are claiming it is about? What does the text refer to? The other
is the more familiar issue of what it actually says about the matter; supposing that it refers to the subject that we claim it refers to, can we
agree about what it says of that subject?

Both questions may raise issues of the literal or figurative use of language. Particularly in the case of Old Testament texts (though not
exclusively so)[8] an allegorical interpretation will sometimes depend on
locating a reference to a subject not explicitly named in the text. When
Athanasius cites texts from *Deuteronomy*[9] and *Malachi*[10] at CA I.36 he
recognises that he has to justify the claim that they are about (or are to
be taken as spoken by) the Son and not the Father. He allows that someone might say that it was the Father speaking, rather than the Son.
Plainly there is nothing in the biblical context that could establish without question who was speaking in either case. Athanasius' justification
for the claim that in both cases we should read the text as spoken by the
Son amounts to the claim that the utterances make more sense in the
mouth of the Son; only in his case (as opposed to that of the Father) is it
important to specify that he has eternal and unchanging being; that that
is true of the Father is obvious and goes without saying, whereas the
Son needs to say so, as we might otherwise think that due to his incarnation he had become changeable.

There is a problem here, of course, since the argument to establish
that the phrase refers to the Son depends upon the claim that it is an
appropriate thing for scripture to say of the Son. At one level this is precisely what the Arians would deny; in their view it would not be
appropriate for Scripture to say of the Son that he had eternal and
unchanging being, since it would not be true. But Athanasius' argument
does not beg the question to that extent; his point is that it is appropriate
to say it of the Son, not because it is not also true of the Father but
because it is more remarkable in the case of the Son. It is precisely
because one might doubt the unchanging being of the Son (as indeed
some do) that Scripture would need to make itself clear on this point.
Nevertheless there is bound to be a certain circularity to the argument
when in order to establish that 'I' in the text refers to the Son we must
appeal to what it says is true of that 'I', while the point of establishing

---

[8] Cf. *CA* I.11, where Athanasius discusses whether δύναμις in *Romans* 1.20 denotes the Father himself or the Son. The term generally used for what the text refers to
or denotes seems to be σημαίνω (cf. *CA* I.12; 13; 14; 36).

[9] *Deuteronomy* 32.39: ἴδετέ με, ἴδετε ὅτι ἐγώ εἰμι (see me, see that I am).

[10] *Malachi* 3.6: οὐκ ἠλλοίωμαι (I do not change).

that 'I' is the Son was to show that what is there said of 'I' is true of the Son.

We may distinguish in this way between the subject or referent that a text is about, and what it says about that subject. In either case it may simply be unclear what is meant even in a literal sense; it might arguably be difficult to tell on any account who is speaking in *Deuteronomy* 32.39 for example. But what the text is about, and what it says about it, can in some cases both be expressed in terms that we might say are not literal, terms that have a normal usage to refer to or say something else; and in both cases there can be disagreement as to what is the most appropriate way to understand what is said. Thus in many cases the disagreements about the meaning of a text will be about the appropriate interpretation of language that is taken by one or both parties as figurative.

Misconstruing metaphors without taking them literally

In some of these cases it makes sense to say that what is going on is allegory, or allegorical interpretation. This is obviously particularly likely in cases where both the subject and what is said about it are read in a non-literal way; the entire motif is taken as a whole to illustrate a truth that belongs in another context. But where just one of the terms, either the subject or what is said of it, is taken figuratively we are more likely to speak of a metaphor.[11] Metaphor, we are usually told, is where terms familiar from one context are used in an unfamiliar role to say something new.[12] The metaphorical interpretation of the discourse may

---

[11] There has been much written on the subject of metaphor recently by scholars in various fields See for example Max Black, 'Metaphor' in *Models and Metaphors: Studies in Language and Philosophy* (Ithaca New York, 1962), 25-47; Max Black 'How metaphors work: A reply to Donald Davidson' in Sheldon Sacks ed. *On Metaphor* (Chicago 1979),181-92; Max Black, 'More about metaphor' in Andrew Ortony ed. *Metaphor and Thought* (Cambridge 1979), 19-43; Donald Davidson, 'What metaphors mean' in Sheldon Sacks ed. *On Metaphor* (Chicago 1979), 29-45; Jacques Derrida, 'White mythology: metaphor in the text of philosophy', *New Literary History* 6 (1974), 5-74; Paul Ricoeur, *The Rule of Metaphor: Multidisciplinary Studies of the Creation of Meaning in Language.*, trans. R. Czerny, Kathleen McLaughlin and John Costello SJ. (London 1978). I shall not engage in a direct discussion of these works in this context; from the point of view of religious language the most helpful discussion is Janet Martin Soskice, *Metaphor and Religious Language* (Oxford 1985).

[12] 'Speaking of one thing in terms that are seen to be suggestive of another' is Soskice's definition (*op. cit. n. 11*), 15, 49. etc. I have added the terms 'familiar' and 'unfamiliar', and the suggestion that what is said is something 'new'. These elements in the definition serve to exclude metaphors (including so-called 'dead metaphors') that have become so familiar as to seem a normal way of speaking. Arguably the claim that

be obvious to any reader simply from the incongruity of the juxtaposition of ideas if the words were read with their more familiar meaning, or it may be forced upon the reader by her prior assumptions about what is or is not true, and hence what the text might plausibly say. But in either case there may be room for disagreement as to which of the terms in a particular phrase or sentence carry the metaphorical weight.

For example a sentence containing the phrase 'metaphysical baggage' plainly needs to be read as a metaphor; the juxtaposition of ideas in 'metaphysical baggage' is impossible unless one or other term is being used in a metaphorical sense. But given these two terms out of context it is impossible for us to tell (or it is nonsense to ask) which of the two is metaphorical; the meaning can only emerge within a larger text. When we are told that Socrates, in the *Phaedo*, say, imports an array of metaphysical baggage, it is apparent from the context, not only within the sentence itself but doubtless from the wider text and genre of writing or speaking, that we should identify the terms 'imports' and 'baggage' as bearing a non-literal sense. The metaphor as a whole emerges from the fact that Socrates' ontological commitments are spoken of in terms suggestive of physical luggage, but the words that are doing the work in suggesting that other context are the two that are familiar in our discourse concerning physical luggage, and apparently out of place in the context of metaphysics. But we can imagine (though perhaps with some difficulty) another text in which the phrase occurred in a context concerning the ordinary world of porters, luggage and trolleys, a text in which the description 'metaphysical' plainly carried a metaphorical significance.

Given a text in which the language is open to some kind of figurative interpretation, there is plainly room for disagreement on the meaning of the text even among those who share an allegiance to that text as sacred scripture, and as a source of revealed truth. Refutation involving appeal to shared scriptures does not make the task of defence of a particular doctrine easy. In some cases the assumptions that force one side of the dispute to read a text in a figurative way, are precisely the assumptions that the opponent wishes to challenge. Where an incongruity in the literal reading of a text suggests that a figurative reading is essential, they may disagree on whether allegory or metaphor is

---

the other context is more familiar is unnecessary. All that is required is that the metaphor gains its meaning from associations we call to mind from our knowledge of the other context. In the case of a 'dead metaphor' those associations can still be reawakened providing that the other context is still familiar enough to be hinted at.

in play. And even where both sides agree that metaphor is involved they may yet disagree on whether the metaphorical force lies in what the text is about or what it says about it.

Is the opponent literal-minded?

It is sometimes suggested that the difference between the two sides in the Arian controversy comes down to a difference over the understanding of the nature of religious language. In particular it appears at first sight that the reason why Arius, and subsequently Eunomius, are unhappy with the term 'Son', when applied without qualification to the Only-begotten, is because they take the term too literally. If that were the case we should expect to find in the anti-Arian writings that most serious charge, a claim that Arian doctrines depend on an inability to recognise the metaphorical nature of some religious language. But in fact the issues of language that arise are more complicated than that, and the Arians are not accused of taking the terminology at a literal level. Indeed there would be a similar difficulty in reverse, since the Arians are happy to use the term 'creature' of the second person of the Trinity in some extended sense that Athanasius and his followers refuse to recognise.[13] In neither case does a distinction between metaphor and literal language capture the difference in understanding; at one level it might appear that the Arians find the use of the terminology of 'Son' and 'Father' too literal in the writings of their opponents, since their view is that the term 'Son', and indeed the term 'God', can be applied to the only-begotten only in some reduced sense, that is as a kind of analogous use of language, just as we can all be called 'sons of God', or indeed 'gods'.[14] But their objection is not expressed, so far as we can tell, as a disapproval of language taken as literal; it is not clear that they did think the language was used literally. The problem is that it is taken to be true.

The basis of the Arians' rejection of the orthodox interpretation of the title 'Son' is that it maintains in some way that Christ was really a son, not just somewhat like a son, really God, not just comparable with

---

[13] Athanasius objects to the inconsistency of the Arians in understanding begetting in human and physical terms, and not applying the same implications in the case of creating, *CA* 1.23. Note that Athanasius does not suggest that in either case one way is the more literal way of taking the terminology; rather one imports the limitations of the human activity into the context of divine activity. But what do these terms mean literally when applied to the divine? That is the question we shall need to ask.

[14] *CA* 1.6; 1.9, with reference to *Psalm* 81.6 (82.6).

God in some respect. For Arius the language of 'Son', 'God' and so on can be used not because Christ was 'truly' God but because he acquires the title 'by participation in grace, just like the rest'.[15] It appears that we have a distinction between what is true, strictly speaking, and some kind of language that is allowable but does not strictly convey how things really are. But the second does not appear to be less literal, but rather simply less accurate as a description of the nature or essence of what it refers to.[16] It seems to convey a kind of admissible lie or half-truth.

Metaphor: Can We Mean What We Say?

If the distinction between Arians and orthodox is not identified as a simple dispute between metaphorical and literal ways of interpreting traditional language, what was the issue about religious language that arose in the course of the controversy, and does it have anything to do with the metaphorical status of the language? The suggestion is that for the Arians some language was not strictly true; what it nominally appeared to say about the nature of the Son[17] (or in some cases the Father) did not actually correspond to the way things are. To take it seriously as a claim about the essence of God would be to misinterpret the status of the discourse.

Now it might seem that some of these claims about the language of 'Father', 'Son', 'Word' and so on resemble the sort of thing that might be said about metaphorical discourse. In particular it is sometimes said that something is not 'literally true', as though a non-literal statement is saying something that is false in some sense. But clearly the question of

---

[15] *CA* 1.6. Williams doubts whether the language attributed to Arius by Athanasius in these passages accurately represents Arius, but it seems evident that Arius was committed to some use of the conventional terms in a derivative sense. Rowan Williams, *Arius: Heresy and Tradition* (London 1987), 224.

[16] Williams (*op. cit. n. 15*), 224 suggests that Arius held that this conventional use of language was metaphor (apparently using 'metaphor' in the ancient sense of that word). Athanasius says that the terms are applied 'in name only'. It seems impossible to infer that they were given a 'metaphorical' meaning in our sense of the word. Apparently they convey the normal meaning but what they say of the Son is not strictly true. It is just a name.

[17] For want of a suitable term whose status and validity is not disputed I shall be using 'Father' and 'Son' to denote the persons of the Trinity whose proper titles are the subject of the Arian debate.

the truth value of a metaphorical statement is not simply a matter of whether the words taken literally form a true proposition. There will also be a question of truth and falsity (if there is any question of truth and falsity) within the metaphorical reading or readings of the statement.[18] For example, it could be the case that a metaphorical statement was true at one time and not at another, even when understood correctly as a metaphor. There must be room for the notion of a metaphor that is not true, while the literal sense of the statement is likely to be not so much false as nonsense.

What Arius seems to be saying, on the other hand, is that the language of 'Son' or 'Word' is not strictly true in any sense when applied to the Son. It will not help to say that it is to be applied in a metaphorical sense, since we should still need to mean something, and be asserting that as true, in using the term metaphorically of the Son. But in saying that he is Son, Arius apparently claims, we are not saying something *else* that is true of him, but rather we are nominally asserting that he is son, which is strictly speaking not true except insofar as he acquires a right to the title by grace. It does not truly predicate anything of the usual significance of the word 'Son' to the Son.

Clearly this must be different from the way in which metaphor acquires significance and truth. When we say something in metaphor it may well be because there is no ordinary way to say it, but the metaphor has meaning that depends on the conventional significance of the words we use. The reader will understand the metaphor in so far as she picks up what aspects of the usual significance of the words are in play in the metaphorical utterance. That is to understand what we mean, and given that we mean something by a metaphorical utterance we may also expect that we mean it to be true. In a metaphor we mean what we say, though we say it metaphorically, and the metaphor may sometimes be an assertion that something is true.[19] The fact that something is expressed in metaphor does not, as in the Arian use of 'Son', mean that we deny that the apparent significance of the phrase is seriously intended, or claim that mere words are applied without indicating anything about the objects they are applied to.

It may be that Athanasius misrepresents Arius' position on the use of terms that do not apply strictly to the Son, and it may be that I have fur-

---

[18] On the truth and falsity of literal or metaphorical readings of utterances, see Ricoeur (*op. cit. n.11*) and Soskice (*op. cit. n.11*), 84-93.

[19] Metaphors in theological discourse often take this form. Some metaphors obviously occur in fiction, where the nature of the truth claim is more complicated.

ther distorted his view in suggesting that he means the language to be taken as having no significance whatever. Arguably Arius held that language such as 'Son' was used not without significance but in a much reduced sense; that some kind of analogy allowed that the term made sense when applied to the Son as it does when applied to others who are not truly or fully God's sons. Nevertheless it seems plain that his claim is not that we make a true claim expressed in metaphorical language, but that we make a claim that, when properly understood, is not strictly true and must be recognised as misleading.

Shared ground: some religious language uses figurative speech

The dispute between Arius and his opponents does not seem adequately defined as one that hinges on a difference between literal and metaphorical interpretations of the language of 'Son', 'Father' and the rest. It has been suggested that the Platonic or Neoplatonic basis of Arius' philosophical outlook underpins his understanding of language[20] and that the rationalist view of language taken by the Arian thinker Eunomius makes him more confident than his opponents of the ability of language to express truths about God adequately, and leads him to suppose that correct doctrines can be guaranteed by particular forms of words.[21] But although these assumptions about the nature of language may make the Arians more inclined to suppose that there is a single unequivocal reading of some kinds of technical formula, it does not follow that they are committed to a literal interpretation of the conventional phrases of scripture and tradition. Indeed it is not clear what a literal reading of the claim that Christ is the Son of God would be.

It seems clear that both Arians and orthodox were prepared to allow that some religious language had a metaphorical or figurative sense. The question is whether the language, when read in its figurative sense, says something true. The difference over this may, I would suggest, hinge on a different interpretation of the metaphorical significance of a text, but it need not depend on a difference over whether the language is to be taken metaphorically at all.

---

[20] Williams (*op. cit. n. 15*), 215-29.

[21] R.P.C. Hanson, 'Dogma and formula in the Fathers' *Studia Patristica* XIII, II, ed Elizabeth Livingstone, (Berlin 1975); reprinted in R.P.C. Hanson, *Studies in Christian Antiquity* (Edinburgh 1985). Page references are to the latter version, 307-17.

Could All Our Language About God Be Metaphor?

Picking up the pictures from elsewhere.

Given the difficulty of deciding what a literal reading of the formulae in dispute in the Arian controversy would be we might be inclined to suggest that all theological language makes sense only as metaphor. Of course there is a sense in which any language works by invoking the expectations familiar from the use of the terms in previous contexts. What a word means for us derives from the way we and others use it in meaningful ways, and each time we use a term we are alluding to or extending a classification system in some sense. We classify things together by using the same words of them. Metaphor, in a sense, merely extends that process by reclassifying something in the course of using of it the terms that belong in another field of discourse.

But if all our language functions in this way by picking up its implications from contexts in which the words already have meaning for us we cannot make a relevant distinction in this respect between religious language and other forms of discourse. When we use a term for the first time in a theological context it will bring with it the connotations it possesses from other usages already available and known. But equally the same is true of any words used for new purposes in a particular field,[22] which may depend only temporarily on meaning derived from another context before acquiring a distinct and independent sense in the new context. Sometimes, plainly, we shall do the same kind of thing in extending the meaning of a term to a new theological use. But this is nothing peculiar to language about God and certainly will not show that all our theological language still depends upon invoking a non-religious context in which the words have a familiar meaning.

There seems no reason, then, to suppose that all our language of God currently derives its sense from more familiar human contexts. When Athanasius looks at the language of Father and Son in our talk of God he does not suppose that those terms gain meaning first from a human context in which human fathers and sons are the paradigmatic members of the class. He suggests instead that those terms have their proper sense only when applied to God.[23] This point is an important one, because although Athanasius is not saying that the implications of the

---

[22] The most familiar examples in current practice are probably the words used in computer jargon.

[23] *CA* 1.21.

term are precisely the same when applied to human fathers and divine ones, he wants to hold that the latter usage is logically prior. So far from holding that the language means primarily what it means in the more familiar human context, and has then been transferred with some loss of sense to a less appropriate theological context, Athanasius suggests that the proper meaning of the word is that which applies to God.

This reasoning is plainly Platonic in origin. Athanasius' claim that human fathers and sons do not fully represent what it is to be a father or a son depends upon the observation that human fathers are always also sons (and vice versa, though this might seem less inevitable to us).[24] In the case of God on the other hand the Father is simply father and not son, while the Son is simply son and not also father. Just as for Plato the Form that is the primary bearer of a name is also paradigmatically endowed with the qualities signified by that name in no merely relative way and without also displaying contradictory qualities, so in Athanasius the true bearer of the name 'Father' must be one who is not also a son. But while Athanasius justifies his claim on the basis of a Platonic analysis of the relation between words and what they signify, it need not follow that we should reject his conclusion along with the metaphysics of his argument.

The point is this: sometimes a term is used as a name, to refer to an individual. We can use the term 'father' in this way, and when we use it as a name the term signifies that individual no matter what features or qualities she may possess. But when a term is used not as a name but to indicate some feature or quality that belongs to a particular individual, in virtue of which he or she can be said to be a father, the application of the term is open to an analysis not unlike Plato's. The term signifies something other than the object to which it applies. It signifies a feature or description which may or may not be true of the object in question. What is certain is that it will not be the only feature that might belong to that object, nor will it indicate everything that is true of that object. The meaning of the term is not identical to the object it is predicated of, nor will the object possess that feature exclusively and absolutely as a Platonic form did. Thus when we say that someone is a father we have in mind some notion ('fatherhood')

---

[24] *CA* 1.21: 'For this reason there is no one among these (humans and animals) who is properly father or properly son, nor do the term 'father' and the term 'son' hold good of them. For the same individual is son of the one who begat him and father of the one begotten from him.'

that is the feature we speak of, whether or not the candidate adequately exemplifies that feature in practice.

The distinction between the bearer of a name and the meaning of a word is one of the issues that arises in Gregory of Nyssa's treatise against Eunomius. Gregory points out firstly that God is not himself a word, is not essentially a part of language.[25] If that were the case it would indeed be problematic to suggest that language was a human invention and not co-eternal with the divine, as Gregory allows that it is. Eunomius had suggested that this threatened God's own eternity, since he is named by humankind only once humankind exists and uses language. That problem arises, as far as Gregory diagnoses it, because Eunomius has confused the meaning of words with what they signify or stand for. Of course the words had no meaning, or rather since the words did not exist no meaning or significance could attach to them, before humanity gave meaning to language in use. But that is not to say that the things that they would signify could not exist before the words had meaning. God might be unbegotten though there was no language in which that truth might be expressed, and though 'unbegotten' had no meaning. There is a relationship, according to Gregory, between the way things are and the meanings of the words we use to signify those facts. But the relationship does not involve supposing that how things are is simply dependent on our saying so. 'Being is not the same as being spoken of'.[26]

God then is Father, but he is not the meaning of the word 'father', and hence he does not depend on language for his being. But equally no other father, or set of fathers, is the meaning of the word 'father'. Gregory's distinction between the sense and the reference applies equally in the use of language in everyday contexts. And this brings out the point that the significance of our discourse always derives from the context in which the words are used. Eunomius had supposed that there was some simple correspondence between words and things, as names and the things they stand for, where there is no meaning to the name other than the object that it stands for. At CE II. 179 Gregory attributes to Eunomius a theory that denies that language can be meaningfully extended to indicate ideas beyond our immediate experience. Some utterances, according to Eunomius, have no meaning at all, because although they are uttered as if they referred to something, in fact they fail to refer, like

---

[25] Gregory of Nyssa *Contra Eunomium* II [= *CE*]149; 171-2.
[26] *CE* II 160.

names that indicate nothing. Where the language does make reference to something, it will be because the reference is conceived by extension from preconceived ideas: we may imagine, and hence speak meaningfully of, giants, pygmies, multi-headed monsters, centaurs and the like by combining or extending ideas we already have.[27] The point seems to be that the terms have meaning only if they refer to something that we can point to, and names of imaginary things have meaning in virtue of combining or extending references to real things. Gregory takes it that this precludes meaningful discourse in areas of speculative thought such as mathematics and philosophy, where we have to use language to express ideas that are not based on empirical objects. Surely, he suggests, we can discuss theoretical issues where our thoughts are not derived from experience. Eunomius has unduly restricted the possible range of meaningful discourse.[28]

Given that Gregory is inclined to reject a simple theory in which the meaning of a term is identified with the object to which it refers, he along with other anti-Arian writers, must provide some alternative account of how language works. Athanasius had started by suggesting that the language of 'father' and 'son' had its proper significance with reference to God. This depends already on the recognition that it signifies something other than God; indeed it can carry the same significance when applied to God and to human fathers, but what it signifies applies more strictly, perhaps more literally, to God. What then is the account of how the language of 'father' and 'son' acquires significance if it is not, as Eunomius' thought, a name?

Asserting what is true and denying what is false

Two passages offer some contribution to analysing what gives a word significance in a particular text. Firstly we are reminded by Gregory that there is some relationship between asserting one thing of a subject and denying its opposite.[29] We may say that x is f or we may deny that x is *not-f* and these amount to alternative and compatible ways of saying something about x. At this point Gregory suggests that the assertion of the positive and the denial of the negative carry the same implications, though subsequently he observes that, when we speak of God, negations serve only to indicate what God is not like and do not define what

---

[27] *CE* II 179.
[28] *CE* II 180.
[29] *CE* II 130-136.

his nature actually is.[30] Nevertheless his point amounts to the claim that to say something of the divine is implicitly to deny something else; to classify something in one way is implicitly to deny that it falls into some other class.

A similar point is also made by Athanasius.[31] He observes that classification is implicit in language, and that each term predicated of the divine makes sense only with reference to some alternative against which it makes a distinction.

> Just as 'ingenerate' is meant in relation to the things that are generated, so also 'father' is indicative of the son. And in naming God 'maker' and 'creator' and 'ingenerate' one has in one's view and understanding the creatures and generated things. Whereas when one calls God 'Father', one is thinking of and regarding the Son.[32]

We cannot understand what it means to say God is creator unless we recognise the class of creatures in relation to which God stands as creator, and hence understand what kind of claim is being made in saying that God is creator. But Athanasius' analysis suggests only that our use of the term 'Father' makes sense in so far as we see it in relation to the Son. The problem with the Arian understanding was that they took the term 'ingenerate' to be marking a distinction with regard to the Son, whereas it should properly be understood in contrast to created beings. The title 'Father' alludes to a contrast with the Son; the title 'ingenerate' alludes to a contrast with another classification, the things that are created. By taking 'ingenerate' as invoking a contrast with the Son, they are led into the error of supposing that the Son falls into the class of creatures:

> For when they say that God is 'ingenerate' they are saying only that he is maker and creator as distinct from the created works, as I said, but they suppose that they can also mean by this that the Word is a product, in accordance with their own theory.[33]

Basil's two senses of 'Father'

'Father' is a relational predicate, and Athanasius is, of course, right that it implies a correlate son (or as it might be sometimes daughter). But

---

[30] *CE* II 142-7.
[31] *CA* 1.33.
[32] *CA* 1.33.
[33] *CA* 1.33.

this will not be enough to enable us to grasp the meaning of the term in any context. To say that someone is a father is, after all, not necessarily to deny that he is a son. In most cases that would be absurd. Hence it is not clear, as perhaps it is in the case of 'ingenerate', what is being denied or asserted in saying that he is father. What is being said will vary depending on what the implied contrast is.

In *Adversus Eunomium* 2.24 Basil recognises that the term 'father' may mean different things depending on the context. In particular he suggests that Eunomius misunderstands the meaning of texts because he reads the term with the wrong set of connotations. The point is this: 'father' could be used to invoke one of two sets of images, either the implications of relation and affinity,[34] or implications of passion.[35] Of the two sets of images the first is appropriate and the second inappropriate to use of God. Eunomius' difficulty arises from the fact that he assumes that the term 'father' cannot be used without carrying connotations of passion. For Basil we can use the term properly and appropriately of God while invoking only the relationship imagery and implying nothing of the range of connotations of passion.

Basil is happy to say that this use of the language of 'father' is a metaphorical or figurative use,[36] though it is not clear that he needs to do so in order to maintain that only one of a number of different sets of connotations is invoked in the use of a word. It seems clear that even when speaking of human relations we might use the word to convey different points on different occasions, and that the context or field of discourse would indicate what connotations we had in mind[37]. But what Basil's analysis makes clear is that even when the text is taken as a metaphor, there is still room for misinterpretation. We may just as well find the wrong set of connotations in taking a metaphorical utterance as metaphor. If the word carries two or more sets of connotations, how are we to decide which ones are being invoked in a particular text?

Basil's solution to the problem of picking up the right set of implications is to set the metaphor in a much wider context. It is only in the context of the whole range of images used in scripture and tradition that

---

[34] οἰκείωσις, *Adversus Eunomium* [= *AE*] 2.24, PG 29 625B.

[35] πάθος.

[36] δῶμεν δὲ εἶναι τροπικὴν, καὶ ἐκ μεταφορᾶς λέγεσθαι, ὥσπερ καὶ ἄλλας μυρίας καὶ τὴν φωνὴν ταύτην... *AE* 2.24, 625B.

[37] It appears that the motivation for classifying this as a metaphorical use may well be the fact that the other connotations of 'father' language are not merely not intended but actually false.

we recognise the meaning of each. If one read the texts that speak of God in bodily terms in a physical sense one would arrive at doctrines that were not simply false but also in conflict.[38] It is this wider context that alerts the reader to the need to heed not the physical connotations of the terms but some higher meaning. Basil does not explore the point in detail, since his concern is to suggest that perversity on the part of controversialists leads them to press the inappropriate implications of a metaphorical or allegorical text, but it seems clear that one possible approach he might have taken would be to suggest that the possible metaphorical readings of a text are limited by the need for compatibility with the accepted readings of other images; the criterion for reading is an understanding of the coherence of the discourse as a whole. The interpretation comes not from looking merely at the words but at the context and the preconceptions we have to start with.

Relation and creation: the context and meaning of words

I have concentrated on the language of 'father' and 'son' as an issue in the Arian controversy, but these are not the only terms that enter the dispute. In particular it is worth noting that the Arians favour the language of 'creature' and 'product'[39] to describe the relation of the Son to the Father, rather than the language of 'son'. Again the imagery is familiar from a human context and might be supposed to be either a metaphor or to carry some associations from the human context. Why should the Arians be happy with this craft language, and unhappy with the language of 'father' and 'son'?

Basil notes in this context that there seems to be an implicit classification going on in the use of the same term for the Son and the other products of creation. It might seem that Eunomius favours this term because it places the Son in the same category as the creatures. But this is something that Eunomius explicitly denies. He wants to hold that the use of the same word does *not* imply a common nature,[40] a move which Basil considers inconsistent given Eunomius' earlier arguments.[41]

---

[38] *AE* 1.14, PG29 544D.

[39] ποίημα. See for example Basil *AE* 2.24, 628C.

[40] 'No one should be upset at hearing that the son is a product, as if the essence was made the same by the verbal association.' Basil *AE* 2.24, 628C.

[41] Basil recalls that earlier Eunomius had argued that a difference of words entails a difference of essence; here he holds that a common word does not denote a common essence. The two are not obviously inconsistent unless based on a theory of one to one correspondence. But it seems that Eunomius' denial that the use of the same word

Why then does Eunomius favour the description in terms of 'creature' and 'product'? Apparently the preference is not guided by a desire to demote the Son to a common category with ordinary created things. The Son is to be a creature but not like the other creatures, something higher and more honourable. Thus although the anti-Arian objections to the terminology of 'creature' focus on the problems in the nature and classification of the Son, it seems that that was not what motivated the choice of vocabulary on the part of the Arians. Just as the orthodox prefer 'Son' because it guarantees the status of the Son, while the Arians object because it compromises the nature of the Father, so the Arians prefer creature because it guarantees the uniqueness of the Father, and the orthodox object because it compromises the status of the Son. In both cases it seems that the difference lies in two quarters, firstly in the fact that the Arians are more concerned to reserve true divinity for one ingenerate first principle incapable of division of substance, while the orthodox are more concerned to ensure the equal divinity of two divine persons, and secondly in the way that each group focuses on different implications of the imagery used on either side. The second difference clearly arises from the first. It is because the Arians are concerned to preserve the propriety of the Father that they see and reject the unsatisfactory associations of 'father' and 'son' imagery; it is because the orthodox focus on the divinity of the Son that they see and reject the unsatisfactory associations of 'product' imagery.

Why is my reading better than yours?

There are, then, two aspects to the dispute between Arians and orthodox. One is a difference in priorities about which doctrines must at all costs be defended, and the other is an inability on each side to read the language the other uses in the way the other intends it. If that language is conceived as a kind of metaphor, as it is by Basil, we can identify the familiar feature of metaphor that only some of the associations suggested by the motif are appropriate in the new context. The reading of a metaphor depends precisely on being able to recognise which implications of the language apply in the new context. Arius and Eunomius, in so far as they misconstrue the metaphors, do so by pressing asso-

---

implies anything in common between the two objects so described is incoherent unless he holds that the term is simply ambiguous. The alternative is that when he says it does not imply the same 'being' (οὐσία) he does not mean there is nothing whatever in common between them.

ciations that recognisably could not fit the theological context. Both sides agree that those associations cannot apply. They disagree as to whether they are inevitably suggested by the language.[42]

If the disagreement turns on whether a particular kind of language imports unwelcome associations, we may wonder how any theologian on either side of the debate can justify the claim that those associations are or are not present in the language customarily used. How could we establish that when we use an image that has a place in human discourse, the connotations that it brings with it to the theological use are of one kind and not another? The task of refutation becomes a matter of exegesis of the meaning of traditional utterances, and there seems to be no external criterion outside the language of religion itself to which one might appeal. We can only justify our interpretation of the significance of the language and customary practices by appeal to the language and customary practices themselves.

Is there then no way that Athanasius and his followers could demonstrate that the Arian understanding of the traditional language was defective? Clearly there was an appropriate response, and this was, I suggest, the motive behind the extensive discussion of the way language works in the texts I have been discussing. The response lies in the recognition that the Arians' rejection of certain kinds of language depends upon their own understanding of what can truly be said of God. It is because they have a correct grasp of how we can speak of God and what we can appropriately say that they want to reject some kinds of language. But those preconceptions are precisely what is needed in order to grasp what the imagery used in theological discourse is or is not saying. If one understands the conventions of the discourse enough to reject what is misleading one understands it enough to read the conventions of the imagery aright. There is, after all, no danger in potentially misleading imagery for one who correctly grasps the rules of the game.

That would be one way of showing that the Arians were mistaken in supposing that the conventional language was unsuited to its task; and it would suggest that their efforts to change the conventional language, so far from guaranteeing a correct grasp of what can or should be said of God, would undermine that understanding that enables one to read the

---

[42] If the language is conceived as proper to God, as it is by Athanasius, the diagnosis is much the same, only differing in that the Arians press associations that are not part of the literal usage of the terms but acquired in their extended or analogous use in a human context.

text aright. It would be to change the rules of the game; but it is precisely our understanding of the rules of theological discourse that enables us successfully to interpret the significance of the images invoked.

But this is only one side of the picture. Plainly the fact that the Arians raised a question about the language of 'Father' and 'Son' provoked the orthodox writers to define what was the meaning of that language. It was in response to the suggestion that it might import associations of bodily passion that Basil makes clear the distinction between two meanings of father-language, and declares that only one of these is invoked in the conventional language for God. The rules of orthodox interpretation are thus defined and clarified in response to the challenge posed by heresy. Although to reject the conventional language would change the very nature of the game, the orthodox defence of the traditional language changes, or at least defines, the rules of the game in ways that had not been apparent before.

Father: why is this term peculiarly problematic?

Basil's interest focuses on the various meanings of the language of 'father'. He identifies two sets of implications, one of which he thinks is wrongly imported by Eunomius into the interpretation of theological metaphor. But the language of 'father' and 'son' is currently still controversial in a debate not envisaged in Basil's definition of the two meanings of 'father'. What Basil did not mention (and rightly so since it did not figure in the dispute he had in mind) was the connotation of gender imported by the language of 'father'. When we say of some subject that it is a father we may, as Basil noted, be asserting something about the relation between it and another object, or we may be saying something about the process by which it came to bring the other into being. But thirdly, we might be saying that as father, not mother, that subject has a certain gender or bears a particular kind of relation to the other. The term 'father' seems to carry different connotations depending on what classification it invokes, and what implicit contrast it defines it by. If 'father' implies a contrast with 'mother' we get a very different reading of the discourse from that which takes its sense to be 'father, not creator'.

Although Basil and Gregory do not face this challenge, we can see from their discussion of Eunomius' views on language what their response would be. Regardless of whether ultimately we take the discourse as metaphor, we can only ever understand the significance of a term if we grasp what implicit contrast or negation it is making. Perhaps this is peculiarly clear in metaphor, where some connotations of the language are incoherent in the metaphorical context; but arguably it is also true of any ordinary discourse too. I do not know what the term 'father' means until I grasp from the context of your utterance whether your meaning invokes the implications of relation, passion or gender, or some combination of the three.

It might be suggested, then, that to take the language of 'father' and 'son' as carrying connotations of gender is to misconstrue the text. Since the context never invokes a contrast with 'mother', never implies that 'father' entails 'not-female', it would be ridiculous to reject the traditional discourse simply because we could not read it aright. That would be the same mistake as was made by Eunomius. It would be to suppose that if a word is applied to some object, all possible senses of that word are supposed to hold good of that object. Plainly this will not do, and is particularly inappropriate in the case of metaphorical discourse.

On the other hand it seems plain that a metaphor functions not simply by using a separate and distinct, perhaps more limited, sense of a word. If that were so we should be able to identify two independent senses of that word, belonging in two contexts and saying two different though related things, and that would not be metaphor. Metaphor occurs when we are aware of the implications the term would have in another context, when we bring those implications to bear in the new context and when those implications add to the effect of the metaphor. This is precisely what the Arian Eunomius and the twentieth century advocate of inclusive language will be afraid of. If the language of 'father' is serving as a metaphor, we cannot help but call to mind not just the implications that are evidently productive in our new context, the recognition that the Son is fully and closely bound to the Father, but also those which are misleading, the suggestion that physical processes are involved and that God is of the masculine gender. After all, if the language is construed as metaphor, Eunomius is perhaps right that we cannot comfortably get away with it.

Two responses seem to be possible. One is to suggest that our response to religious language should be exactly like our response to other metaphors. We need both to see the implications of the other context suggested by the metaphor and to see that some features of it are absurd. We call to mind the image of the luggage trolley for the metaphysical baggage, and yet we never suppose we shall need to fetch a trolley. It is the presence of those inappropriate features of the image that make the image striking. So also we might suppose that the language we use of God calls to mind the image from another context, but we understand the metaphor precisely in recognising that some of the features of the image are incongruous. In this respect we need not fear to use a metaphor that invokes a masculine image. The incongruity of that image is precisely what alerts us to its status as metaphor. We should have misconstrued the meaning if we then thought we had to refer to God as 'he'.

The other response is to follow Athanasius in concluding that the use of language familiar in a human context to refer to God is not metaphor, but rather the primary sense in a set of related and derivative meanings. The basic image of 'father' does not include anything but what is true of God; it is merely incidental that mortal fathers are generally male and creatures subject to passion, but those associations which we recognise in human fatherhood are no part of what it is to be a father. When we use the term to denote those characteristics we do so by a kind of transferred use, an example of something like metonymy. In this case it would still clearly be a misinterpretation to suppose that when the terms were used of God those human associations were invoked.

What is clear on either view is that there will be severe difficulties if we suppose with Eunomius that any discourse that imports inappropriate associations must be excluded from our language about God. It seems no realistic alternative to allow the vocabulary to remain as a mere name without significance, as Athanasius suggests the Arians would do. Yet to reject all such language will leave us with only one kind of discourse about God, namely language that evokes no associations from any other context. And while Gregory is surely right in his optimism about the ability of language to capture ideas of a speculative and non-empirical nature, it is unclear that it could do so successfully without redeploying words that have meaning in another context, or that it would be better for doing so. It seems rather that such a language would simply be unable to say the sort of thing we wanted to say by using the term 'father'. Clearly the language is the poorer if it can no longer express such truths in words.

Gender

It now becomes clear that there is more work to be done. In the Arian dispute over the language of 'Father' and 'Son', no one sought to raise the difficulty that this language carried implications of gender. That was not at issue, and hence no one sought to clarify the rules in this respect. There is a sense in which their assumption that gender was not at issue was based on a shared implicit understanding of what was or was not being denied in the use of this language, at least in this respect.[43] But until the issue of gender is raised that implicit understanding is not articulated; hence our understanding of what can or cannot be said in the conventional language is clarified in response to a challenge on the issue of gender, just as it was by the challenge of Arianism.

But more than that: the challenge of a potential misreading of the imagery may also change the rules of theological discourse. Once we see how we might read the language wrongly, we can no longer avoid saying that we are not doing so. Basil has to explain what the senses of 'father' might be, in order to declare that he is not using it wrongly. It is not helpful to reject the conventional language altogether, since then we should no longer say what we always sought quite properly to say. That was the Arians' misguided solution to the problem. But we may yet need to say something now that we did not need to say before. We can no longer take for granted the preconceptions that guaranteed the right interpretation on the part of one who understood the rules of theological discourse.

In this respect the recognition that the language of 'father' carries associations of gender demands a response. It will not be sufficient to respond that to object to the language is to have grasped the rules of the discourse and hence to have the basis for the correct reading of the image. We may well find no difficulty in reading the image with its traditional sense as an assertion of the affinity of Father and Son, and there is no reason to suppose that we should be better off not saying that. But we cannot now ignore the issue of gender. If 'Father' language can be used without implications of gender in theological discourse, then so can 'mother' language, and to reject or exclude that language would be to endorse a misleading interpretation of the 'father' language. It would be to imply that the 'father' language was indeed intended to exclude the language of motherhood. The challenge of a potential misreading of the imagery changes what we have to say to get it right.[44]

---

[43] That is to say that Arians and orthodox alike took it as read that the language of 'father' was not serving to deny 'mother'.

[44] I am grateful to Peter Widdicombe who allowed me to see his manuscript *The Fathers on the Fatherhood of God*, and with whom I discussed some of my thoughts before I put pen to paper on this article.

DIE ABSICHT DES CORPUS AREOPAGITICUM

A. M. RITTER

Bevor ich auf mein eigentliches Thema zu sprechen komme, will ich auf die Verfasserfrage eingehen, die lange genug als *die* quaestio Dionysiana schlechthin galt. Mein Grund ist nicht nur der, daß es mindestens einen heute lebenden, sehr verdienstvollen Dionysforscher gibt, der offenbar die Welt nicht mehr versteht, weil sich seit Jahrzehnten in der Verfasserfrage des Corpus Areopagiticum (in Zukunft = CA) nichts mehr bewegt. Leider hat sich diese Verbitterung jüngst auch in einer Besprechung der kommentierten Übersetzungsausgabe der beiden "Hierarchien" durch Günter Heil, meinen Mit-Editor der kritischen Gesamtausgabe (der sich nun nicht mehr selbst wehren kann), einen erschreckenden Ausdruck verschafft.[1] So will ich denn zunächst den Versuch unternehmen, sowohl dem einen als auch dem anderen Genugtuung zu verschaffen.

Dazu muß ich freilich ein wenig weiter ausholen. Zweifel an seiner Echtheit und dogmatischen Korrektheit begleiten das CA bekanntlich fast so lange, wie es überhaupt bekanntgeworden ist.[2] Nachdem erste Zweifel an der Frühdatierung des CA, als Folge der traditionellen Gleichsetzung seines Verfassers mit dem Paulusschüler Dionysios Areopagites,[3] bei Nikolaus von Kues lautgeworden waren,[4] brachte dann der Humanist Lorenzo Valla, dem es zuvor (1440) bereits gelungen war, die berühmt-berüchtigte Donatio Constantini endgültig als eine Fälschung zu erweisen und damit der Kirchenherrschaft eine wesentliche Stütze zu entziehen, jenen Stein ins Rollen, der am Ende einem eher geschichtlichen und damit, wie wir heute überzeugt sind,

---

[1] *Byzantinische Zeitschrift* 81(1988), 64-68.

[2] Erstmals wohl im Zusammenhang einer in Konstantinopel abgehaltenen Konferenz zwischen Gegnern und Anhängern der Zwei-Naturen-Christologie des Konzils von Chalkedon (451) im Jahre 532/33 (Schwartz ACO IV, 2, 172); vgl. dazu noch immer J. Stiglmayr, *Das Aufkommen der Pseudo-Dionysischen Schriften und ihr Eindringen in die christliche Literatur bis zum Laterankonzil 649* (Feldkirch 1895), 3-96.

[3] Diese—vom Autor intendierte—Gleichsetzung hat sich in der Überlieferung des CA von allem Anfang geschlossen durchgesetzt: s.u. S 165 f.

[4] Codex Cus. 44, fol. 1ᵛ; zitiert bei L. Baur, *Cusanus-Texte. III: Marginalien 1. Nicholaus Cusanus und Dionysius Areopagita im Lichte der Zitate und Randbemerkungen des Cusanus* (Heidelberg 1941), 19.

sachgemäßeren Verständnis der rätselhaften Texte des CA den Weg
bahnte. Zwei kurze Bemerkungen aus dem Jahre 1457, Vallas Todes-
jahr, sind es, auf die es in diesem Zusammenhang ankommt: die eine
findet sich in einer (recht merkwürdigen) *Lobrede auf den hl.
Thomas von Aquin*, in der er den Verfasser als einen der "Fürsten der Theologie"
mit Papst Gregor dem Großen auf eine Stufe stellt, allerdings hinzufügt,
bei keinem lateinischen Schriftsteller vor Gregor und bei keinem älteren
Griechen sei er je zitiert worden,[5] die zweite ist in einer ausführlicheren
Note zu *Act* 17.34 innerhalb seiner *Anmerkungen zum Neuen Testament*
enthalten. Valla bezeichnet es hier zum einen als höchst zweifelhaft, ob
der Paulusschüler von *Act* 17.34 überhaupt Schriftliches von sich gegeben habe, da der Begriff "Areopagites" auf einen Richter, nicht auf
einen Philosophen hindeute. Zum andern sei die Behauptung des "Dionys" in einem seiner Briefe (gemeint ist ep 7,2) er habe von außerhalb
Palästinas die Sonnenfinsternis während der Todesstunde Jesu (*Matthäus* 27.45 par) beobachtet, eine eklatante Fiktion. Gewisse zeitgenössische Gelehrte griechischer Zunge, fügt Valla hinzu, hielten zudem
Apollinaris von Laodikeia für den wirklichen Verfasser.[6]

Vallas Kritik ist weiteren Kreisen erst bekannt geworden, als Erasmus von Rotterdam ein Exemplar der Vallaschen *Annotationes* in die
Hand bekam und sich umgehend entschloß, sie im Druck herauszubrin-
gen; das geschah in Paris 1505. 1516 fügte er seiner berühmten Ausgabe des griechischen Neuen Testaments eine Note zu *Act* 17.34 bei, in
der er Vallas Argumente wiederholte, sie um die Erwägung ergänzte,
die vom Autor des CA erwähnten und (allegorisch) gedeuteten kirchlichen Riten paßten kaum in das apostolische Zeitalter, und endlich sich
entschieden gegen die Identifizierung des Autors mit Apollinaris aus-
sprach.[7] Von altgläubiger Seite, besonders von Kartäusermönchen, des-

---

[5] Erstmals veröffentlicht ist diese *Lobrede*, wie es scheint, Ende vergangenen
Jahrhunderts von J. Vahlen innerhalb der Geigerschen *Vierteljahrsschrift für Kultur
und Litteratur der Renaissance* (21[1886]) und danach innerhalb des anast. Nach-
drucks der *Opera Omnia* L. Vallas, besorgt von E. Garin (Turin 1962) II, 346-352;
hier: 351. Gemeint ist bei Gregor die Stelle hom. 34,12 in Ev: PL 76, 1254.

[6] *Opera* (Basel 1540); anast. Nachdruck, besorgt von E. Garin, (Turin 1962) I
852b. Die Identifizierung des Autors mit Apollinaris von Laodikeia geht so gut wie sicher auf das "Religionsgespräch" von 532/33 (s. o. Anm. 2) bzw. auf eine Bemerkung
des Scholiasten ("Maximus") zurück, welcher die Areopagitica bereits gegen den
Vorwurf verteidigen zu müssen glaubte, sie seien συγγράμματα τοῦ Ἀπολλιναρίου
(PG 4,85C).

[7] Novum Instrumentum omne... (Basel 1516), 394f. =*Opera Omnia*, ed. J. Cleri-
cus (Leiden 1706), VI, 503 C-F.

wegen heftig attackiert, hat sich Erasmus dann ausführlich in seiner Antwort auf den 31. Artikel der "Zensur" durch die Pariser theologische Fakultät im Jahre 1531 verteidigt und betont, daß er sich lediglich einem wohlbegründeten wissenschaftlichen Konsens angeschlossen habe.[8]

Seinem Einfluß ist es i.w. zuzuschreiben, wenn am Ende des 16. Jahrhunderts, im protestantischen Lager zumindest, kaum noch ein Zweifel am "pseudepigraphischen" Charakter des CA herrschte, während es den Altgläubigen, zumal westlich des Rheins, sehr viel schwerer fiel, der Dionyslegende den Abschied zu geben. Angesichts seiner angenommenen Identität mit Dionysius von Paris (St. Denis) stand hier sehr viel mehr auf dem Spiel! Aber es gab auch Ausnahmen wie den Dominikaner M. Lequien, auf dessen rasch in Vergessenheit geratenes Werk Ende vorigen Jahrhunderts vor allem J. Stiglmayr und in diesem Jahrhundert U. (R.) Riedinger von neuem aufmerksam gemacht haben.[9] In der zweiten seiner 7 Dissertationes Damascenicae, 1712 unter den Prolegomena seiner Damaszenerausgabe erschienen (und danach bei Migne, PG 94, 261-314 abgedruckt), handelt er über "einige Autoritäten, mit deren Hilfe Eutyches und andere Monophysiten ihre Häresie verteidigten". Daß diesen Autoritäten das CA nicht zuzuzählen ist, steht für Lequien außer Frage. Das geht schon aus dessen Unechtheit hervor, für die er bereits ein mittelalterliches Zeugnis in einem Bericht des Photios[10] anführen zu können glaubt. Die areopagitischen Schriften sind für ihn dem Dionysios nicht etwa zufällig, etwa durch Sorglosigkeit der Kopisten, zugeschrieben, sondern vom Verfasser bewußt gefälscht worden. Die fraglichen Schriften kommen selbst aus monophysitischen Kreisen und werden von Severos von Antiochien zitiert. Der Verfasser des CA neigt der Ansicht der Theopaschiten zu, was darauf schließen läßt, daß er dem monophysitischen Patriarchen von Antiochien, Petros "dem Walker" (Knapheus, Fullo) nahestand, wenn nicht mit ihm identisch war. Für diese Identität sprechen nach Lequien weitere dogmengeschichtliche, liturgiegeschichtliche und stilistische Überlegungen. Vor allem verbindet beide die Rezitation des "Nicaenums" in der Messe und die öffentliche Myronweihe.

---

[8] Declarationes... ad Censuras Lutetiae vulgatas:... (Antwerpen 1532), 180-182 = ebd. IX, 916-17.

[9] Stiglmayr (op. cit. n.2), 34; U. Riedinger, 'Pseudo-Dionysios Areopagites, Pseudo-Kaisarios und die Akoimeten', Byzantinische Zeitschrift 52 (1959), 276-296, bes. 283 ff.

[10] Vgl. dazu bes. I. Hausherr, 'Doutes au sujet du "Divin Denis"', Orientalia Christiana Periodica 2 (1936), 284-290; hier 285 f.

Das sind, wie man zugeben muß, erstaunliche Einsichten, die an revolutionärer Kraft denen des Renaissancephilosophen in nichts nachstehen. Aus Gründen, die ich im Augenblick unerörtert lassen möchte, sind sie jedoch mehr als 200 Jahre lang so gut wie völlig unbeachtet geblieben.

Da es Lequien in seiner genannten Dissertatio lediglich um die Geschichte der monophysitischen Christologie zu tun war, hatte er keinerlei Anlaß, sich mit der geistigen Heimat der areopagitischen Schriften und ihres Autors näher zu befassen. Genau dort setzten Ende des 19. Jahrhunderts die beiden Forscher an, die nach Valla-Erasmus die zweite große Revolution in der Dionysforschung auslösten. Gemeint sind J. Stiglmayr und H. Koch, die 1895 in zwei unabhängig voneinander geführten Untersuchungen,[11] die später durch weitere Arbeiten, eigene und fremde, vertieft wurden, den Nachweis zu führen vermochten: das CA kann überhaupt erst gegen Ende des 5. Jahrhunderts entstanden sein, da es nicht nur aus Plotin (204-270) schöpft, sondern offensichtlich auch die Kenntnis des späteren Neuplatonismus der Athener Schule, Syrians und vor allem seines Schülers Proklos, voraussetzt. Grundlage bildete für beide ein Vergleich zwischen dem areopagitischen Traktat *Über die göttlichen Namen* (= DN) und der Proklosschrift *Über die Subsistenz des Bösen*,[12] der zweifelsfrei ein Abhängigkeitsverhältnis feststellte. Weitere Untersuchungen haben in der Zwischenzeit eine erdrückende Fülle von gedanklichen wie sprachlichbegrifflichen Parallelen zutage gefördert und keinen Zweifel daran gelassen, daß der Autor des CA als der entlehnende Teil, Proklos und andere frühere Philosophen und Theologen als Quelle zu gelten haben. Darüber hinaus sind Syrien bzw. syrische Kreise in der Reichshauptstadt Konstantinopel als Heimat des CA wahrscheinlich gemacht worden. Darauf deutet zum einen hin, daß die Liturgieerklärungen des CA mehrere Besonderheiten des syrisch-antiochenischen Ritus widerspiegeln (Myronweihe, Taufwasserepiklese, Rezitation des nizäno-konstantinopolitanischen Symbols in der Messe, u.W. erstmals 476 für Antiochien bezeugt,[13] u.a.m.), zum andern, daß es unmittelbar nach seiner

---

[11] J. Stiglmayr, 'Der Neuplatoniker Proclus als Vorlage des sogen. Dionysius Areopagita in der Lehre vom Übel', in *Historisches Jahrbuch* 16 (1895), 253/73.721/48; H. Koch, 'Proklus als Quelle des Pseudo-Dionysius Areopagita in der Lehre vom Bösen', *Philologus* 54 (1895), 438-454.

[12] De malorum subsistentia, in *Procli Diadochi tria opuscula*, ed. H. Boese (Berlin 1960).

[13] Theodoros Anagnostes, ed. G.C. Hansen (Berlin 1971) 118, 27/28 [= GCS].

Abfassung ins Syrische übersetzt worden sein muß, und schließlich, daß
es sich inhaltlich (christologisch) am ehesten einem gemäßigt "monophysitischen" Milieu zuordnen läßt, wie es z.b. der bedeutende Syrer
Severos (Patriarch von Antiochien zwischen 512 und 518) in höchst
eindrucksvoller Weise repräsentiert; bei diesem finden sich denn auch
die ersten uns bekannten Zitate aus dem CA.[14]

An dieser ergebnisreichen Debatte mit ihrem bedeutenden Gewinn
nicht zuletzt für die Näherbestimmung der Umwelt des CA ist in signi-
fikanter Weise U. (R.) Riedinger beteiligt gewesen, der darüber hinaus
auf die Frage: Wer war Dionysios Areopagites? seit eh und je eine völlig eindeutige Antwort zu besitzen glaubt: Petros "der Walker". In
einem Aufsatz in der *Byzantinischen Zeitschrift*[15] hat er diese Identifizierung zum ersten Mal eingehend begründet und sich dabei auch auf
Lequien bezogen und dessen Verdienste gebührend herausgestellt. Zwei
Jahre später folgte ein Beitrag im *Salzburger Jahrbuch für Philosophie*[16] mit wichtigen Ergänzungen und Präzisierungen sowie ersten
Reaktionen auf inzwischen publizierte Kritik. 1963 trug er beim 4. In-
ternationalen Patristikerkongreß in Oxford vor, diesmal ohne neue
Aspekte zu eröffnen und neues Material vorzubringen, sondern mehr
bestrebt, die bisherige Argumentation transparenter zu machen, und
veröffentlichte im darauf folgenden Jahr den Text in der *Zeitschrift für
Kirchengeschichte*.[17] Weitere Gelegenheiten zu sachdienlichen Äußerungen boten eine Besprechung, wiederum in der Byzantinische Zeitschrift,[18] ein—glänzend geschriebener, sehr informativer, aber auch
recht spekulativer—Artikel über "Akoimeten" in der *Theologische
Realenzyklopädie*,[19] die schon erwähnte Besprechung von G. Heils
kommentiertem Übersetzungsband[20] und endlich die Einleitung zur
Ausgabe der *Erotapokriseis* des Pseudo-Kaisarios.[21]

---

[14] Vgl. Severus Antioch., Epistula III ad Ioannem Higum.(510?); Adversus apolo-
giam Iuliani (518/28) und dazu Stiglmayr (*op. cit. n. 2*), 47 f.

[15] Riedinger (*op. cit. n. 9*).

[16] U. Riedinger, 'Petros der Walker von Antiocheia als Verfasser der pseudo-dionysischen Schriften', *Salzburger Jahrbuch für Philosophie* 5/6 (Salzburg 1961/62),
135-156.

[17] U. Riedinger, 'Der Verfasser der pseudo-dionysianischen Schriften', *Zeitschrift
für Kirchengeschichte* 75 (1964), 146-152.

[18] *Byzantinische Zeitschrift* 62, (1969), 356-359 (Besprechung von P. Scazzoso,
Ricerche sulla struttura del linguaggio dello Pseudo-Dionigi Areopagita).

[19] *Theologische Realenzyklopädie* 2 (1977), 148-153.

[20] *Byzantinische Zeitschrift* 81 (1988), 64-68.

[21] GCS (1989).

Während der Identifizierungsversuch Riedingers anfangs—sehr verständlicher Weise—großes Interesse fand und einer gründlichen Diskussion empfohlen wurde,[22] ist es um ihn und seinen Autor, jedenfalls in "dionysianischen" Gefilden, immer stiller geworden. Darum ja auch der Verzweiflungsschritt der Veröffentlichung einer ausführlichen Synthese seiner Ansichten über die dionysianische Verfasserfrage in dem "Akoimeten"-Artikel, in dem er, genau genommen, nichts zu suchen hatte. Riedinger kann dahinter offenbar nur das Motiv vermuten, "... daß wir unsere Meinung von dem, was die areopagitischen Schriften sind und was sie wollen, revidieren müßten, wenn wir ihren Autor auch aus anderen Äußerungen kennen würden. Das könnte schließlich ein Grund dafür sein, mit der geheimnisvoll isolierten Stellung des Areopagiten ganz zufrieden zu sein".[23]

Nun ist gar nicht zu leugnen, daß es auch in der Welt der Wissenschaft oft mit merkwürdigen Dingen und sehr ungerecht zugeht. Aber daß Riedinger mit seinem Identifizierungsvorschlag zunehmend in die Isolation gelangt ist, hat er sich nach meiner Überzeugung zum guten Teil selbst zuzuschreiben. Ich übersehe nicht alle Zusammenhänge und maße mir deshalb kein Gesamturteil an. Aber was ich überblicken und beurteilen kann, spricht eindeutig dafür, daß Riedingers Art, mit seinen Kritikern umzuspringen, die Bereitschaft zum Gespräch mit ihm nicht eben befördert hat.[24]

---

[22] L. Abramowski (in *Zeitschrift für Kirchengeschichte* 73 (1962), 417/18).

[23] S. o. (*op. cit. n. 17*), 147. Später wird dieselbe Verdächtigung immer unfreundlicher ausgedrückt.

[24] Ein geradezu abstoßendes Beispiel ist sein Umgang mit J.-M. Hornus, der im 5. Kapitel seines Forschungsberichtes in der *Revue d'Histoire et de Philosophie Religieuses* 41 (1961), 22-81 ('Les recherches dionysiennes de 1955 à 1960') die bislang einzige ausführliche Kritik an Riedingers Verfasserthesen veröffentlicht hat. Riedinger ist dem in seinem Oxforder Vortrag von 1963 noch relativ freundlich-ironisch begegnet; die Auseinandersetzung mit Hornus findet im Vortragstext allenfalls zwischen den Zeilen statt und spielt selbst in den Anmerkungen eine eher marginale Rolle. Jahre später, zum Schluß der Besprechung der Untersuchungen über die sprachliche Struktur des CA aus der Feder P. Scazzosos (Mailand, 1967) in der *Byzantinischen Zeitschrift* 62 (1969), behauptet Riedinger nicht nur, er sei der einzigen 'ausführliche(n) Kritik', die er auf seine Dionysarbeiten erhalten habe, der von Hornus, mit dem *Zeitschrift für Kirchengeschichte*-Aufsatz von 1964 'entgegengetreten', was man naheliegenderweise so versteht, als habe er die Argumente des Kritikers eingehend geprüft und widerlegt, wovon aber schwerlich die Rede sein kann. Viel schlimmer, ja geradezu unverzeihlich ist, daß er dem noch einen wissenschaftlichen Hinrichtungsversuch anfügt, indem er die sachliche und sprachliche Kompetenz seines Kritikers rundweg bestreitet: das eine nicht inhaltlich, sondern formal mit dem Hinweis auf das nicht

Ich bringe dies hier aus dem einzigen Grunde vor, den mir erkennbaren Anteil Riedingers an einer Tragödie kenntlich zu machen, die ich
zutiefst bedauere—und für ganz überflüssig halte. Die andere Seite freilich ist das so gut wie ausnahmslos verweigerte Gespräch! Daß wir
Mitarbeiter an der Göttinger kritischen Dionys-Edition, die nun endlich
geschlossen vorliegt, diesem Gespräch uns bis jetzt nicht gestellt haben,
liegt vor allem daran, daß uns Fragen der Textüberlieferung und des
Textverständnisses ungleich mehr interessierten. Was aber das an-
langte, so war aus den Schriften Riedingers wenig zu lernen. Er konnte
sich immer wieder über das Inhaltliche des CA genauso despektierlich
äußern wie der Neuhumanismus über das *spät*antike Denken, nicht
zuletzt Proklos und seine Schule, überhaupt. Entsprechend wurden
seine Auskünfte über die Absicht des CA immer verstiegener. Hieß es
anfangs noch relativ respektvoll, der Autor der Areopagitica, also für
Riedinger Petros der Walker, habe sie, so "banal es auch klingen mag",
"zu seinem Trost in den langen Jahren seiner Verbannung" verfaßt:
"Hier fand er ein Ventil für seinen Tatendrang, mit dem er in der harten
Gegenwart nicht viel Freude hatte, hier konnte er philosophisch-theolo-
gisch, liturgisch-hierarchisch alles erreichen, was ihm die komplizierte
Reichs- und Kirchenpolitik versagte",[25] so scheute er schließlich vor
einem Vergleich nicht zurück, von dem er allerdings selbst ahnte, daß
er "auch Empörung und Kopfschütteln hervorrufen" werde: "Die Autoren Ps.-Dionysios Areopagites und Karl May... verbinden drei Analo-
gien...:

1. Jeder von ihnen schrieb sich die Enttäuschung über ein Leben vol-
   ler Niederlagen von der Seele,
2. dafür erfanden beide eine literarische Scheinwelt, in der sie alles
   realisieren konnten, was ihnen ihr Leben zu verwirklichen ver-
   wehrt hatte,
3. beide hatten mit ihrer Schriftstellerei einen überwältigenden Er-

---

eben umfangreiche wissenschaftliche Oeuvre, das andere mit einem dicken Über-
setzungsfehler im Vorwort zur deutschen Ausgabe des bekannten Buches 'Évangile et
Labarum', der aber bis zum Beweis des Gegenteils ausschließlich der schlampigen
Redaktion dieser deutschen Ausgabe anzulasten ist. Daß Hornus über die genügende
fachliche und sprachliche Kompetenz verfügte, beweisen seine ausführlichen Litera-
turberichte über die neuere Dionysforschung, beweist insbesondere die im Rahmen eines allgemeinen Literaturberichts ungewöhnlich breite, faire und in der Kritik überaus
zurückhaltende Berichterstattung über Riedingers Identifizierungsversuch (nach der
Erstveröffentlichung in der *Byzantinischen Zeitschrift* 52 (1959)).
[25] Riedinger (*op. cit. n. 16*), 154.

folg,—der Areopagites allerdings erst lange nach seinem Tode..."
Kein Kommentar![26]

Als ich in meinem Beitrag zum Dionys-Artikel des Lexikon des Mittelalters[27]—recht kategorisch—erklärte: "Alle Versuche, den Verfasser
[sc. des CA] mit einem bekannten Theologen des ausgehenden 5.Jhs. zu
identifizieren, haben bisher zu keinem allgemein überzeugenden Resultat geführt—und dürften auch weit weniger belangvoll sein als sorgsame Analysen des Werkes selbst",[28] da setzte das natürlich die gründli-
che Kenntnis des Riedingerschen Identifizierungsversuches, des einzigen fast, über den sich überhaupt noch ernsthaft zu diskutieren lohnt,[29]
voraus. Wie sonst hätte ich mich denn zu einer solchen Erklärung
verstehen können? Auch bestand längst die feste Absicht, in der Ge-
samteinleitung zu dem von mir zu bearbeitenden abschließenden (3.)
Band der kommentierten Übersetzungsausgabe innerhalb der Bibliothek
der Griechischen Literatur ausführlich auch über die jahrhunderte-
langen Identifizierungsversuche des Pseudo-Areopagiten Bericht zu
erstatten. Das war mit dem Herausgeber des patristischen Teils der
Bibliothek der Griechischen Literatur ebenso abgesprochen wie, daß
"die Einleitungen" und entsprechend auch die beigegebenen Literatur-
listen "zu den insgesamt drei Bänden... so aufeinander abgestimmt"
sein werden, daß Wiederholungen unterbleiben.[30] Also bestand nicht

---

[26] Riedinger (*op. cit. n. 20*), 68, A.11.

[27] *Lexikon des Mittelalters* 3 (1986), 1079 f.

[28] *Ibid.*

[29] Vgl. dazu noch immer am ehesten die Übersichten bei R. Roques, 'Denys
l'Aréopagite', *Dictionnaire de Spiritualité* 3 (Paris 1957), 250-257, und R. Hathaway,
Hierarchy and the Definition of Order in the Letters of Pseudo-Dionysius (The Hague
1969), 31-35; zu den beiden anderen m.E. noch nicht ausdiskutierten Identifizier-
ungsversuchen, demjenigen E. Honigmanns, welcher für Petrus den Iberer als Autor
des CA plädierte ('Pierre l'Ibérien et les écrits du pseudo-Denys l'Aréopagite', *Mémoires de l'Académie Royale de Belgique, Classe des Lettres et des Sciences Morales
et Politiques* 47,3 (Brüssel 1952) dazu jetzt vor allem M. van Esbroeck in seinem
noch unveröffentlichten Oxforder Vortrag von 1991 über 'Peter the Iberian and Dionysios the Areopagite: Honigmann's thesis revisited'), und demjenigen des jungen
rumänischen Gelehrten G.I. Dragulin, welcher erstmals in der Forschungsgeschichte,
soviel ich sehe, den Namen des Dionysius Exiguus ins Spiel brachte (*Identitatea lui
Dionisie Pseudo-Areopagitul cu Ieromonahul Dionisie Smeritul [Exiguul]'*, (Craiova
1991), muß ich aus Platzgründen auf meinen Bericht in der *Bibliothek der Griechischen Literatur* (s.o. Text) verweisen.

[30] So das Vorwort des Herausgebers der *Bibliothek der Griechischen Literatur* (W.
Gessel) zu dem 1., von G. Heil bearbeiteten Übersetzungsband; vgl. auch die Vor-
bemerkung zur Literaturauswahl.

der geringste Anlaß anzunehmen, daß etwas nicht mit rechten Dingen zugehen werde oder zugegangen sei, und war der in der erwähnten Besprechung des Heilschen Übersetzungsbandes ausgesprochene Komplottverdacht völlig aus der Luft gegriffen.

Ich will hier jedoch nicht einfach auf diesen Literaturbericht vertrösten, sondern wenigstens in groben Zügen die Leistungsfähigkeit wie die Grenzen des Riedingerschen Identifizierungsversuchs des Pseudo-Areopagiten verdeutlichen, wie sie sich in meinen Augen darstellen. Riedinger hat 1. gelegentlich die Tatsache, daß die Schriften des gesuchten Autors sich uns "in dem Gewande des Paulus-Schülers Dionysios" präsentieren, als den möglichen "Schlüssel" bezeichnen können, "der die Autorenfrage löst".[31] Er hat 2. in seinen Aufsätzen ein beträchtliches Parallelenmaterial—altes und neues—zusammengetragen, genauer gesagt: "Entsprechungen" sichtbar zu machen versucht zwischen dem CA, besonders dem Briefcorpus, und der eigenen Gegenwart des gesuchten Autors, von denen er jedoch selbst einräumt, daß sie vor allem "zum Verständnis der Situation beitragen",[32] aber noch nicht zur Identifizierung des Autors führen. 3. Ein "wirklich schlüssiger Beweis" sei "in der Autorenfrage nur an einer einzigen Stelle gelungen, beim 7. Brief".[33] 4. und letztens sieht Riedinger den "Schlußstein", der das Ganze erst zu einem geschlossenen Beweis werden läßt, in einem Detail der koptischen Version der pseudodionysianischen Autobiographie nämlich, deren Ereignisse hauptsächlich aus dem 7. Brief herausgesponnen wurden.[34]

Ad 1) Daß sich, wie Riedinger meint, der gesuchte Autor selbst unter dem Pseudonym "Dionysios Areopagites" versteckt, gibt für ihn insofern einen Schlüssel zur Lösung der Autorenfrage an die Hand, weil die Wahl dieses Pseudonyms keinen Sinn machte, wenn der Autor "in diesem einzigen Bericht des NT über den Areopagiten nicht ein treffendes Bild seiner eigenen Situation erblickt hätte". Also hieße es "nur" nach allegorischen Entsprechungen zwischen der kurzen Notiz *Act* 17.34 und der Situation in der 2. Hälfte des 5. Jahrhunderts Ausschau zu halten.[35] Ich halte dagegen, daß die Riedingersche Deutung möglich, aber nicht mehr ist. Ebensogut wie auf die Biographie ließen sich aus dem Pseudonym Rückschlüsse auf die Intention des Autors ziehen, z.B.

---

[31] Riedinger (*op. cit. n. 17*), 148.
[32] *Ibid* 149.
[33] *Ibid* 148 f.
[34] *Ibid* 151.
[35] *Ibid* 148.

in der Weise: "der Areopagite Dionysios, der athenische Konvertit, steht an dem Punkt, an dem sich Christus und Plato begegnen. Das Pseudonym drückte des Autors Überzeugung aus, daß die Wahrheiten, die Plato begriff, Christus angehören und nicht preisgegeben werden, indem man den Christusglauben annimmt".[36]

Ad 2) Das Aufgebot an "zeitgeschichtlichen" Anspielungen im bzw. an Entsprechungen zum CA ist eindrucksvoll, wenn auch nur z.T. neu und durchweg von sehr unterschiedlicher Plausibilität. Es führt uns in jedem Falle zur Situation, aber nicht zum Autor des CA. Darin bin ich mir mit Riedinger völlig einig.[37]

Ad 3) Um verständlich zu machen, worum es bei dem einzig "wirklich schlüssigen Beweis... in der Autorenfrage" geht, muß der Inhalt des 7. Briefs kurz in Erinnerung gerufen werden: Der Autor versichert zu Beginn, seines Wissens niemals gegen "Heiden" (Ἕλληνες) oder andere polemisiert zu haben. Gehe er doch davon aus, "rechtschaffenen Leuten genüge es, die Wahrheit selbst so erkennen und aussprechen zu können, wie sie tatsächlich ist" (1). Nun wisse der Adressat zu berichten, ein gewisser Sophist Apollophanes schmähe den Autor und nenne ihn einen "Vatermörder",[38] weil er "von den Errungenschaften der Heiden ("Griechen") unfairen Gebrauch mache, um sie wider die Heiden zu nutzen". Es käme jedoch, hält er dawider, der Wahrheit bedeutend näher, "wenn wir ihm entgegenhielten": es sind Heiden, die sich in unfairer Weise der göttlichen Gabe als Waffen wider das Göttliche bedienen, indem sie nämlich die Weisheit, die doch von Gott kommt, zu dem Versuch benutzen, die Ehrfurcht gegenüber Gott auszutreiben". Die "wahren Philosophen" aber "müßten sich von der Erkenntnis der Dinge, die bei ihm (dem Schmäher Apollophanes nämlich) den schönen Namen 'Philosophie' trägt, während der hl. Paulus von ihr als 'Weisheit Gottes' (*1 Korinther* 1.21-24 u.ö.) spricht, zur Ursache der Dinge sowohl als auch zu ihrer Erkenntnis emporführen lassen". Das wird dann so gewendet, daß die Menschen zwar die Bewegung der Gestirne berechnen können, Gott es aber gewesen sei, der für Josua[39] und Hiskia[40] den Lauf der Gestirne *verändert* habe. Folgt als 3. Beispiel für eine derartige, jeder Berechnung spottende Veränderung der Hinweis darauf, daß er, der Autor, ja mit Apollophanes die Son-

---

[36] A. Louth, *Denys the Areopagite* (London 1989), 11.
[37] S.o.n. 31.
[38] Vgl. Plato, *Sophistes* 241d.
[39] Vgl. *Josua* 10.12-14; *Sirach* 46.5 (4).
[40] Vgl. *2 Könige* 20.8-12; *Jesaja* 38.7 f.

nenfinsternis zur Zeit des heilbringenden Kreuzestodes beobachtet habe. Obwohl an diesem ersten Karfreitag, kurz nach Vollmond, eine Sonnenfinsternis astronomisch unmöglich sei, hätten sie beide bei Heliopolis eben dieses Phänomen beobachtet (2). Und zum Beweis zitiert er ein Wort, das ihm Apollophanes damals gesagt habe (3).

Riedinger nun versteht "diesen Brief als eine Antwort auf die Vorwürfe, die die Neuplatoniker um Proklos nach dessen Tode dem von ihnen abgefallenen und zum Christentum übergelaufenen Petros gemacht hatten"[41]. Ich halte dagegen, daß wir von Petros dem Walker— *sicher* und unabhängig vor allem vom CA—nur wenig und darunter meist nicht besonders Schmeichelhaftes wissen; von philosophischen Ambitionen, gar einer Schülerschaft des Proklos, ist uns gar nichts bekannt. Auch das Zeugnis aus der Isidoros-Vita des Damaskios, das in Riedingers Argumentation seit jeher eine große Rolle spielt,[42] hilft hier nicht weiter. Ganz davon abgesehen, daß es lediglich von einem "Petros" redet, wobei, wenn wir schon mit einem uns (zufällig) noch bekannten prominenten Namensträger dieser Zeit rechnen müssen, ebenso Petros Mongos von Alexandrien gemeint sein könnte (woran auch J.R. Asmus und Cl. Zintzen, die Herausgeber bzw. Übersetzer dieser Vita[43] dachten): Es wird bei Damaskios von diesem "Petros" lediglich ausgesagt, daß er zum herrschenden Klüngel gehöre, sogar Bischof geworden sei, aber als ein unverschämter und grundschlechter Mensch zu gelten habe! Doch dann kommt die stärkste, am meisten Eindruck machende Stelle innerhalb der Riedingerschen Argumentation. Es geht um den Ortsnamen Heliopolis im Zusammenhang der Sonnenfinsternis beim Tode Christi am Kreuz. In Frage kämen sowohl das syrische Baalbek als auch das ägyptische Heliopolis. "Bei dieser Unsicherheit", heißt es bei Riedinger, "ist es so lange geblieben, bis mir der Einfall kam, doch einmal diese Nachricht versuchsweise ernst zu nehmen und die von J.K. Ginzel zusammengestellten Tabellen der antiken Sonnenfinsternisse nachzuschlagen. Und hier fand sich nun etwas äußerst Frappierendes. Denn am 14. Januar 484 fand eine Sonnenfinsternis statt, die kurz nach Sonnenaufgang einsetzte und deren Totalitätszone westlich von Athen beginnt, um über Athen—Milet—Kypros/Baalbek nach Babylon/Susa zu verlaufen. Und nicht genug damit: Der Biograph des Proklos, Marinos, erwähnt (sc. v Procl 37

---

[41] Riedinger (*op. cit. n. 17*), 150.
[42] So bereits Riedinger (*op. cit. n. 9*), 289 f.
[43] Vgl. Riedinger (*op. cit. n. 16*), 140 f; Riedinger (*op. cit. n. 17*), 150 mit n 9.

[p.169]) diese Sonnenfinsternis als Vorzeichen für den Tod seines ge-
feierten Lehrers, mit dem im Jahre 485 die Sonne der Philosophie
erloschen sie"[44] Es gibt aber noch eine dritte Möglichkeit zur Erklärung
dieser Stelle, da sich, wie ich im Kommentar angeben werde, auch für
Ägypten gute Gründe angeben lassen. Nach R. Hathaway wäre nämlich
als Motiv für die Lokalisierung der "Gemeinschaftsvision" des Dionysios und des Apollophanes eher an eine Lesefrucht aus des Damaskios
"Leben des Philosophen Isidoros"[45] zu denken, wonach Damaskios
zusammen mit Isidor nach Heliopolis (in diesem Falle Baalbek) reiste,
um Augenzeuge feuriger Himmelserscheinungen zu sein; möglicher-
weise war in seiner Gesellschaft auch Asklepiades, der nahe bei Heliopolis gelebt zu haben scheint, von Beruf Astronom war und ein Mann,
wohlvertraut mit der ägyptischen Weisheit."[46] Gleichwohl beeindruckt
mich nach wie vor die Riedingersche Erklärung so sehr, daß ich ihr den
Vorzug geben möchte. Aber: beweist das irgend etwas in der Autorenfrage? Paßt es nicht vorzüglich zu unserem generellen Bild von den
engen Beziehungen des CA zu Proklos und seinem Kreis?

Ad 4) Wenn das alles aber so ist, dann hängt auch der "Schlußstein"
des Riedingerschen Beweisganges in der Luft. Denn selbst wenn man
den fraglichen Zusatz innerhalb der koptischen Version der pseudodionysianischen Autobiographie (= lat. *omnis iste terrae motus et astrorum
perturbatio quae acciderunt propter Deum qui crucifixus est*), wie Riedinger, als exakte Entsprechung zum "theopaschitischen" Zusatz zum
Trishagion versteht, was mir jedoch nicht als zwingend erscheint, so
führt uns dieser solchermaßen verstandene Zusatz nach allem doch
nicht weiter als bis zu dem Milieu, in dem ohnehin nach allgemeinem
Konsens das CA angesiedelt ist.

Bleibt es also dabei, daß die Identifizierungsversuche (einschließlich
desjenigen Riedingers) bislang zu keinem allgemein überzeugenden
Resultat geführt haben, dann muß man nach wie vor vor allem die
Schriften des CA selbst befragen, um die verläßlichsten Indizien über
den unbekannten Verfasser zu gewinnen.

---

[44] Riedinger (*op. cit. n. 17*), 150 f.
[45] Damascius, *Vita Isidori* cap.94 (138 Zintzen).
[46] Vgl. Hathaway (*op. cit. n. 29*) 27 f.

***

Zu den Besonderheiten der (ungewöhnlich reichhaltigen) handschrift-
lichen Überlieferung des CA[47]—wir kennen mindestens 157 griechische Handschriften, davon 120 mit dem vollständigen Text—gehört,
wie schon J. Stiglmayr richtig erkannte, ihre Geschlossenheit. Keine der
Einzelschriften hat, soviel wir wissen, je einen anderen Verfassernamen
als den des Dionysios Areopagites getragen; alle sind gleichzeitig
bekannt geworden; und von späteren Bearbeitungen fehlt in der hand-
schriftlichen Überlieferung, auch der (älteren) syrischen, jede Spur. Das
aber heißt auch: andere Areopagitica als die uns überlieferten, und
wären sie auch im CA selbst erwähnt oder gar resümiert (wie z.B. die
Theologischen Skizzen oder die Symbolische Theologie), hat es so gut
wie sicher nie gegeben!

Ich setze den Inhalt dieser Schriften hier voraus und mache nur ein
paar Bemerkungen über die *Mystische Theologie* (in Zukunft = MTh)
und über die Briefe. Die MTh ist—von der Mehrzahl der Briefe abgesehen—die kürzeste Einzelschrift des CA; sie ist nicht annähernd so umfangreich wie das eine Kap. IV von DN und doch—vielleicht—die wir-
kungsvollste von allen. Sie beschreibt in überaus dichter Sprache und
eindringlicher Form die absolute Weltüberlegenheit Gottes, eine Transzendenz, wie sie bereits die (nicht zuletzt an Platon und erst recht Proklos gemahnende) Gebetsanrufung des Anfangs (MTh I, 1:997A.B)
anklingen läßt: "Dreieinigkeit, erhaben über alles Sein, alles Göttliche
und alles Gute, die Du über die Gottesweisheit (θεοσοφία) der Christen
wachst, geleite uns zum Gipfel der geheimnisvollen WORTE (Orakel
[sc. der Hl. Schrift]) empor, über alles Nichtwissen wie über alles
Lichte hinaus. Dort liegen ja der Gotteskunde (θεολογία) Mysterien in
überlichtem Dunkel geheimnisvoll verhüllten Schweigens verborgen:
einfach, absolut und unwandelbar. Inmitten undurchdringlichen Dunkels lassen sie hervorstrahlen, was an Leuchtkraft alles übertrifft;
inmitten des gänzlich Unbegreiflichen und Unsichtbaren machen sie die
(dafür) blinden Geister jenes Glanzes übervoll, welcher an Schönheit
alles übertrifft". Nur indem man den Sinneswahrnehmungen ebenso den
Abschied gibt wie den Verstandesregungen und stattdessen auf nicht-

---

[47] Vgl. dazu B.R. Suchla, *Corpus Dionysiacum I. Pseudo-Dionysius Areopagita,
De divinis nominibus*, [PTS 33] (Berlin 1990),1 ff., (Einleitung in die Gesamtausgabe); ferner B.R. Suchla, *Eine Redaktion des griechischen Corpus Dionysiacum Areopagiticum im Umkreis des Johannes von Skythopolis*, [NGWG, 1985 H.4] (Göttingen
1985), 179 ff.

erkenntnismäßigem Wege, soviel als irgend möglich ist, zur Einung mit demjenigen emporstrebt, "der alles Sein und Erkennen übertrifft", nur indem man sich bedingungslos und uneingeschränkt seiner selbst wie der Dinge "in Reinheit entäußert", besteht die Aussicht, "zum überseienden Strahl des göttlichen Dunkels emporgetragen" zu werden, "alles loslassend und von allem losgelöst" (ebd.: 997B-1000A). Besonderen Eindruck gemacht haben in der Geschichte der christlichen Theologie, wie es scheint, der Gedanke des "Erkennens durch Nichterkennen" (ebd. 1,3;2:1000C-1025B), die Unterscheidung zwischen "kataphatischer" und "apophatischer" Theologie, d.h. bejahenden und verneinenden Gottesprädikaten (ebd.3:1032C-1033D), und endlich die Überzeugung: je weiter unsere Rede von Gott "von unten her zum Transzendenten empor" gelangt, "um so mehr büßt sie an Umfang ein; ist das Ende des Aufstiegs erreicht, wird unsere Rede vollends verstummen und mit dem ganz einswerden, der unaussprechlich ist" (ebd.: 1033C). Dabei störte es kaum, war auch sicher nur den wenigsten bewußt, daß gerade hier der proklische Hintergrund mit Händen zu greifen ist. Es war ja ein christlicher Theologe und dazu ein Zeitgenosse der Apostel, aus dessen Mund man dergleichen vernahm!

Daß man darin lange Zeit so sicher war, lag vor allem an den (10) "verschiedenen Briefen" (Ἐπιστολαὶ διάφοροι, Epistulae [= Epp]), die von Anfang an nahezu konstant als Schlußteil des CA überliefert worden sind (1065A-1120A). Schon die Briefadressaten lassen keinen Zweifel daran, in welcher Zeit wir uns befinden (sollen); handelt es sich dabei doch—mit zwei Ausnahmen (Epp 5 und 8)—um aus dem Neuen Testament bzw. der frühchristlichen Literatur bekannte Namen: So(si)pater, Polykarp, Titus und Johannes, den (wie in der Alten Kirche üblich, mit dem Seher von Patmos identifizierten) Evangelisten. In den Briefen selbst werden dazu noch der Kreter Karpos und der Paulusmitarbeiter Timotheus (Adressat sämtlicher Areopagitica außer den Briefen!) erwähnt, ferner, wie wir schon sahen, die Behauptung gewagt, der Verfasser sei vom (syrischen oder ägyptischen) Heliopolis aus Augenzeuge der "Sonnenfinsternis während der Kreuzigung des Erlösers" (Ep 7,2: 1081A.B) gewesen, und endlich die (aus Clemens Alexandrinus bei Euseb, KG III 23,1 bekannte) Freilassung des Seher-Evangelisten aus dem patmischen Gefängnis und seine Rückkehr zu apostolisch-missionarischem Wirken nach Kleinasien prophezeit (Ep 10:1120A). Überhaupt hat der ganze letzte Brief keine andere Funktion (und im Grunde auch keinen anderen Inhalt), als den Verfasser in die Zeit und den Kreis der Apostel zu versetzen und seine absolute Vertrauenswürdigkeit damit zu unterstreichen. Eine der beiden Ausnahmen von der Regel, daß nur aus dem Neuen Testament oder der "Apostolischen Väter"–Literatur bekannte Namen in den Briefadressen erscheinen, betrifft Brief 8, gerichtet an den (unbekannten) "Therapeuten" (= Mönch) Demophilos. Der Brief fällt auch sonst aus dem Rahmen, nicht nur seines ungewöhnlichen Umfangs wegen, sondern auch deshalb, weil er die kunstvoll eingehaltene aufsteigende Linie hinsichtlich des hierarchischen Rangs der Adressaten jäh unterbricht: Epp 1-4 sind an einen Mönch, 5 an einen Diakon, 6 an einen Presbyter, 7 und 9 an einen Bischof und endlich 10 an einen Apostel gerichtet.[48] Und das paßt auch vortrefflich zu seinem Inhalt: eine gravierende Ordnungswidrigkeit und Kompetenzüberschreitung seitens eines Mönches veranlaßt den Verfasser zu einer ebenso massiven, wortreich vorgetragenen Apotheose der bischöflich-hierarchischen Macht.[49] Ansonsten werden in den Briefen bereits aus den übrigen Areopagitica bekannte Themen wiederaufgegriffen und vertieft, bis auf das des respektvollen Umgangs mit anderen Religionen oder Anschauungen (Ep 6:1077A.B), der Irenik im Verhältnis zwischen Christen und Heiden (Ep 7:1077B-1081C), ein Thema, welches dem Verfasser offenbar besonders am Herzen liegt. "In Sanftmut" soll die Wahrheit der christlichen Religion "in Erfahrung" zu bringen sein, "(jene Wahrheit), die alle Weisheit übertrifft" (ebd. 7,3: 1081C).

***

Es liegt nahe, das letztgenannte Anliegen in Verbindung zu bringen mit der Tatsache, daß unter Justinian I., dem intolerantesten aller spätantiken Kaiser, die Heidenverfolgung[50] seitens des "christlich" gewordenen römischen Staates ihren Höhepunkt erreichte. Die Schließung der traditionsreichen Universität Athen im Jahre 529 war nur eine unter vielen Maßnahmen, die Justinian ergriff, vielleicht aber die mit der größten Symbolkraft. Genauer müßte man (mit Joh. Malalas chron 18,451) vom Verbot des Philosophie- und des Rechtsunterrichtes an jener Hochschule sprechen, die gerade im Jahrhundert zuvor, nicht zuletzt ihrer bedeutenden Philosophen wegen, wieder eine Blütezeit erlebt hatte,

---

[48] Vgl. zu dieser Rangordnung außer der *Kirchlichen Hierarchie* etwa noch *Epistula* 8,4 (PG 3, 1093C = PTS 36, 183).

[49] Vgl. Hathaway (*op. cit. n. 29*), 64 ff.

[50] Vgl. dazu den informativen Artikel von K.L. Noethlichs, 'Heidenverfolgung', *Reallexikon für Antike und Christentum* 13 (1986), 1149-1190.

allerdings auch in dem Rufe befestigt worden war, ein Hort der "heidnischen Reaktion" zu sein. Erst in dieser Perspektive bekommt die areo-
pagitische Irenik wohl ihr volles Profil und Gewicht; allein, führt sie
uns auch zu der *Absicht*, die dem Ganzen zugrundeliegt? Das Gleiche
wird von anderen Indizien (wie den—aufs Ganze gesehen, margina-
len—Anspielungen auf die christologischen Kontroversen der Zeit oder
das bestens in die Situation nach dem Konzil von Chalkedon passende
Postulat der Unterordnung des Mönchtums unter die bischöfliche Gewalt) gelten, über die es teilweise eine lebhafte Forschungsdebatte
gegeben hat: sie erlauben uns wohl, die Umwelt des CA annähernd zu
bestimmen, aber kaum, dessen leitende Intention zu erkennen.

Weiter führt auch hier nur die sorgsame Analyse des Corpus insgesamt, bei der dann auch den Titeln der Werke Aufmerksamkeit zu
schenken ist, die der Autor geschrieben haben will, ohne daß sich die
geringsten Spuren von ihnen erhalten hätten. "Ob er sie nun verfaßt hat
oder ob die Hinweise nur literarische Fiktion sind", es wird aus allem
jedenfalls ein Wille "zur Abrundung einer enzyklopädischen Theologie,
einer Gesamtwissenschaft der christlichen Offenbarung" erkennbar, der
"bei seiner Beurteilung dauernd im Blick bleiben muß".[51] Und zwar ist
es, wenn nicht alles täuscht, der zeitgenössische Platonismus, speziell
die Philosophie des Proklos, von der sich das Glaubensdenken des
(Pseudo-) Areopagiten hat herausfordern lassen. Man wird fragen können, ob die versuchte "Christianisierung", die Synthese von Platonismus und Christentum, ontologischer Seinsdeutung und "Heilsge-
schichte", kosmischer Emanations—bzw. Retroversionslehre und
christlichem Gottesbegriff als gelungen und stimmig zu bezeichnen ist,
ja, ob sie auf den eingeschlagenen Wegen überhaupt erreichbar war.
Aber daß es der unbekannte Verfasser des CA vorzüglich eben darauf
abgesehen hat, das scheint mir gewiß zu sein.

Damit habe ich kurz und bündig zum Ausdruck gebracht, wie ich
über die Absicht des CA denke, und will das nun noch gegenüber einigen anderen neuerdings gemachten Vorschlägen ein wenig abzusichern
und zu verdeutlichen versuchen.

Ich beginne mit P. Rorem, *Biblical and Liturgical Symbols within
the Pseudo-Dionysian Synthesis* (Toronto 1984). Gegenüber der älteren
Arbeit von B. Brons (*Gott und die Seienden*, Göttingen 1976), der ebenfalls einen "neuen Zugang" für notwendig hielt, das Heil aber eher von

---

[51] E.v. Ivánka, Einleitung zu seiner Auswahlübersetzung, *Dionysius Areopagita.
Von den Namen zum Unnennbaren* (Einsiedeln o.J) 16.

einem folgerichtigen methodischen Vorgehen erwartete, erhebt Rorem den Vorwurf, der Autor "himself overlooked the formal starting point of what Dionysius wanted to say. The corpus has a unity of subject matter … Whatever his hidden agenda, this author wished to present his treatises as expositions of the scriptures and of the liturgy. Of his three large works, two treat the biblical names for God and the biblical depictions of the angels [sc. DN + CH], and the third interprets the rituals of the church [EH]. In both realms, Dionysius seeks and interprets the sacred symbols. Yet this announced concern for biblical and liturgical symbolism has been treated as a formality…"(S. 5). Nun, gegen den Entschluß zu einer werkimmanenten Interpretation von Bibel und Liturgie in ihrer Aufnahme im CA ist gar nichts einzuwenden. Wie Rorems Buch zeigt, führt das auch zu ansprechenden, ja äußerst wichtigen Ergebnissen. Wo ich widersprechen würde, da betrifft es die Schein- oder Suggestivalternative, die hier vermittelt wird, namentlich, wenn man in einer Anmerkung zu lesen bekommt: "Brons posed his own questions of Christian orthodoxy to the Dionysian concepts of the Trinity, creation, and the incarnation. The Areopagite fails this examination and is likened to a sincere Sisyphus failing to balance Christian tradition on Neoplatonic foundations" (ebd.,Anm.6). Das ist, wie sich mühelos zeigen ließe, eine völlige Karrikatur. Wichtiger aber ist mir im Augenblick der Hinweis, daß es Interpretationen von biblischen und liturgischen Symbolen vor und nach Dionysios zuhauf gegeben hat, die Besonderheit der dionysianischen Interpretation aber darin liegt, daß sie sich weitgehend eines begrifflichen und sprachlichen Instrumentariums bedient, welches aus Proklos und der Tradition der Athener Philosophie entlehnt ist. Warum hat er das getan? Auf welchen Voraussetzungen basiert das? Zu welchen Ergebnissen führt das? Was wird dabei aus dem biblischen und liturgischen Material, um dessen Interpretation es geht? Das alles sind doch keine Fragen, die in mein Belieben gestellt sind, wenn anders ich verstehen will, was hier vorgeht!

In der jüngsten Dionysmonographie, dem *Denys the Areopagite* von Andrew Louth (London 1989) ist der Dionysius einer ganz bestimmten Wirkungsgeschichte, der Dionys der östlich-byzantinisch-mystischen Tradition mit so viel Kompetenz, Verständnis und Sympathie beschrieben wie wohl niemals zuvor. Die Frage ist nur, ob es der "historische" Dionys sei, der einem aus diesem Buch entgegenblickt! Das Problem mit diesem schönen Buch sind in gewissem Sinne die implizierten Alternativen, Alternativen der Art: Die wirkliche Heimat Dionysius des Areopagiten ist der byzantinische Osten; oder: Dionysius ist kein Neuplatoniker, sondern Christ (S.32). Was die Absicht des Corpus Areopagiticum anlangt, so ist sich Louth unsicher, ob er es als ein "Handbuch für Zelebranten" ansehen solle oder nicht; in jedem Fall beteuert er, die Theologie des Dionys bündele sich in der Liturgie wie in einen Brennpunkt (S. 28). Das Buch steht insofern in deutlicher Affinität zu P. Rorems eben besprochener Untersuchung. Gemeinsam ist beiden Veröffentlichungen nicht zuletzt die Weigerung, sich auf eine Diskussion mit B. Brons einzulassen, der methodisch ganz andere Wege beschreitet und auch zu ganz anderen Ergebnissen gelangt. Louth meint Brons denjenigen zurechnen zu können, "die Dionys für einen Neuplatoniker und überhaupt nicht für einen Christen halten" (S. 32, Anm. 11), was eindeutig auf einem Mißverständnis beruht. Davon abgesehen habe ich in dem Buch einen einzigen (völlig unspezifischen) Hinweis auf Brons (S. 97, Anm. 13), aber keinerlei Diskussion finden können. Der proklische Hintergrund des dionysianischen Denkens wird bei Louth keineswegs ignoriert. Aber welches Bild ist aus seiner Darstellung zu gewinnen? Das Bild Proklos' des Asketen, des Mystikers, des betenden Philosophen (mit einer großen Vorliebe für Theurgie), aber nicht des Mannes, dessen Philosophie für jede christliche Theologie eine massive intellektuelle Herausforderung darstellte!

Allein schon damit, daß er so sprach, wie er sprach, daß er mit fast jedem Satz, mit jedem Gedanken die Assoziation mit Proklos heraufbeschwor, hat der unbekannte Autor des Corpus Areopagiticum seine Absicht bekundet, sich dieser Herausforderung zu stellen; und er war sich allem Anschein nach des Wagnisses durchaus bewußt, auf das er sich damit einließ. Brons hat ihn in diesem Anspruch ernst genommen, und das so gründlich und kundig, daß die künftige Dionysforschung an seinen Analysen nur zu ihrem eigenen Nachteil vorbeigeht. Er hat sich freilich ebenfalls einer Einseitigkeit schuldig gemacht, indem er die Wirkungsgeschichte vollständig vernachlässigte. M.a.W. kann man nach der Lektüre des Bronsschen Dionysbuches kaum verstehen, wieso der unbekannte Autor, der sich hinter dem Pseudonym des "Dionysius vom Areopag" verbirgt,—nicht nur, aber gerade auch im Abendland— eine solch unglaubliche Wirkung hat erzielen können.

Was hieße, die Wirkungsgeschichte hermeneutisch in die Interpretation einzubeziehen? Es hieße: zwischen möglichen und notwendigen Konsequenzen unterscheiden zu lernen; es hieße: zu begreifen, daß gerade Hypotheken, Aporien, unaufgelöste Spannungen einen außerordentlich fruchtbaren Beitrag leisten und viel stärker stimulieren können als alle fertigen, eingängigen Lösungen...

Wenn ich Chistopher Stead in der (von mir mitverantworteten) deutschen Übersetzung seines Werkes über "Philosophie und Theologie" in der Zeit der Alten Kirche[52] recht verstanden habe, dann denken wir in dieser Hinsicht nicht sehr verschieden. In jedem Fall sei ihm das Vorstehende in größtem Respekt vor seiner Lebensarbeit zu seinem 80. Geburtstag dediziert!

---

[52] Ch. Stead, *Philosophie und Theologie I. Die Zeit der Alten Kirche* (Stuttgart 1990); zu Dionysius Areopagita vgl. *ibid* 56.60.

DEUS, PATER ET DOMINUS
BEI AUGUSTINUS VON HIPPO

B. STUDER

Wie bei allen bedeutenden Theologen steht auch bei Augustinus von Hippo die Gottesfrage ganz im Vordergrund.[1] Sein gesamtes Denken kreist um das unergründliche Geheimnis des ewigen Gottes. Mehr als für manchen anderen christlichen Denker war indes für ihn das Suchen nach Gott ein Anliegen des Herzens. Wie der Patriarch Jakob musste er um seinen Gott mit ganzem Einsatz ringen. Nur nach und nach bekehrte er sich zur Einsicht, dass der Glaube seiner Kindheit seinem innersten Sehnen entsprach. In seinem Hunger nach Liebe und Leben entdeckte er nämlich bei Cicero, dass Gott die beseligende Wahrheit ist. Von da an kam er über verschiedene Stufen weiter: er überwand den manichäischen Dualismus, es ging ihm auf, dass Gott nicht ein riesiger Körper sein kann, er erfasste, dass er vielmehr unwandelbar sein muss. So gelangte er zur überwältigenden Offenbarung dessen, der allein im wahren Sinne ist.[2] An dieser Überzeugung hielt er sein ganzes Leben fest. Die späteren Auseinandersetzungen: mit den Manichäern, mit den heidnischen Philosophen und mit den Pelagianern sowie seine Untersuchungen über die vollkommene Gleichheit der drei göttlichen Personen im nizänischen Sinn führten ihn wohl dazu, seine Gotteslehre zu

---

[1] Die vorliegende Untersuchung schliesst sich an drei meiner Studien an, die alle im Zug der Vorbereitung des Artikels 'Deus' für das Augustinus-Lexikon abgefasst worden sind: 'Credo in Deum Patrem Omnipotentem. Zum Gottesbegriff des Heiligen Augustinus', *Studia Ephemeridis "Augustinianum"* 24 (Roma 1987), 163-188; 'Agostino d'Ippona e il Dio dei libri sapienziali', *Studia Ephemeridis "Augustinianum"* 37 (Roma 1992), 115-125; *Deus, Dominus et Pater bei Augustinus von Hippo: FS M. Naldini* (im Druck). In diesen drei Beiträgen finden sich die Angaben von Texten und Studien, welche hier nur zum Teil mitberücksichtigt werden.—Für die Werke des Augustinus werden hier die Abkürzungen des Augustinus-Lexikons benützt.

[2] Vgl. cf 7,14,20. Dazu Studer, 1987 (*op. cit. n. 1*), 166 u. 179, mit anderen Texten aus den Confessiones und den einschlägigen Studien, sowie E.Feldmann, 'Et inde rediens fecerat sibi deus Conf.7,20). Beobachtungen zur Genese des augustinischen Gottesbegriffes und dessen Funktion in den Confessiones' in *Mélanges T.J. Van Bavel* (Leuven 1990), 881-904.

vertiefen. Doch deren Mittelpunkt blieb das *ipsum esse*, wie es nach seiner Auffassung von Gott selbst geoffenbart worden war.[3] Selbst in seinen Predigten vor dem einfachen Volk kam er immer wieder darauf zurück.[4]

Der Bischof von Hippo machte jedoch im Laufe seiner priesterlichen Tätigkeit auch eine andere Erfahrung. Er sah sich fortwährend Leuten gegenüber, für welche Gott ein Ärgernis war.[5] Diese geplagten Menschen widerstanden der Versuchung nicht, gegen ihren Gott zu murren. Sie konnten nicht an seine weise und gütige Vorsehung glauben. Ihnen rief nun Augustinus immer wieder in Erinnerung, dass Gott zugleich Herr und Vater ist: Herr, der alles machtvoll in seinen Händen hält und in gerechter Weise leitet, Vater, der in seiner Güte selbst gegenüber den Seinen hart sein kann, um sie für das ewige Erbe zu erziehen.

In seinem von diesen persönlichen und pastoralen Erfahrungen bestimmten Denken über Gott gelangte Augustinus auch zur grundlegenden Unterscheidung zwischen dem *Deus in se* und dem *Deus ad nos*.. So stellt er in einer Predigt über die Gotteserfahrung des Mose den Gott, der ist, dem Gott der Väter gegenüber; er unterschied das *nomen aeternitatis* und das *nomen misericordiae*, das *illud in se* und das *illud ad nos*, und beschliesst seine Überlegung mit den Worten: *laudemus ergo eius ineffabilemen essentiam et amemus misericordiam*.[6] Damit nimmt Augustinus allerdings nicht die neuzeitliche Unterscheidung zwischen dem Gott der Philosophen und dem Gott der Väter voraus. Seine Gegenüberstellung von *nomen aeternitatis* oder *substantiae* und *nomen misericordiae* steht vielmehr im Zusammenhang mit seiner Auffassung von der religiösen Erkenntnis, in welcher der Glaube und die Erkenntnis der Vernunft immer aufs engste miteinander verbunden sind.[7]

In den Überlegungen, die ich Ihnen hier vorlegen möchte, soll nicht der ganze Komplex der augustinischen Gotteslehre zur Sprache kom-

---

[3] Vgl. cf 7,10,16.

[4] Vgl. ps 38,7; 89,3; 101,2,10; 121,5; 134,4.—Dazu E. Zum Brunn, *L'exégèse augustinienne de 'Ego sum qui sum' et la métaphysique de l'exode: Dieu et l'Etre* (Paris 1978), 141-164.

[5] Vgl. die Angaben diesbezüglicher Texte bei H.U. von Balthasar, *Aurelius Augustinus, Über die Psalmen* (Leipzig 1936), 357: 'Heilssinn des Negativen'.

[6] s 7,7.—Ähnliche Texte: s 13,6; ps 101,2,10; 134,6.

[7] Vgl. A.D.Polmann, *De Theologie van Augustinus. De Leer van God bij Augustinus* (Kampen 1965), 248-255; C.Stead, *Philosophie und Theologie I. Die Zeit der Alten Kirche* (Stuttgart 1990), bes. 151-168.

men. Ich möchte mich vielmehr mit dem *Deus ad nos* benügen, mit
Gott, der zugleich Herr und Vater ist. Trotz dieser vorsätzlichen Be-
schränkung will ich jedoch auf einige mehr methodologische Überlegungen nicht verzichten. Ich mache es mir auch zur Aufgabe darzustel-
len, in welcher Weise Augustinus, wenn er sich an seine Gläubigen mit
ihren Schwierigkeiten und Nöten wandte, auf die Vorstellungen zurück-
griff, die ihnen aus ihrem alltäglichen Leben vertraut waren. Dabei soll
gleichzeitig deutlich werden, in welchem Masse er dabei die in der Heiligen Schrift bezeugten Gotteserfahrungen mit denen seiner römischen
Umwelt zusammenbrachte. Die Bedeutung dieser Fragen eröffnet sich
uns natürlich noch mehr, wenn wir abschliessend die Gotteslehre des
Augustinus auch von der vorausgehenden christlichen Überlieferung
her angehen. Im übrigen besteht kein Zweifel darüber, dass diese ganze
Problematik auch uns heutige Menschen nicht unberührt lässt. Oder
kann es uns gleichgültig sein, ob es heute, da Macht und väterliche Autorität mehr denn je in Frage stehen, noch immer angeht, in Gott unsern
Herrn und Vater zu sehen, wie es die Christen bis in die Neuzeit hinein
taten?

1. *Die wichtigsten Äusserungen des Augustinus*

Was Augustinus unter dem "Gott für uns" versteht, kann man mit den
Begriffen Herr und Vater zusammenfassen. Immer klingt seine Überzeugung an, dass Gott über uns steht und über uns verfügt, zugleich
aber zu uns kommt und uns mit seiner Liebe beglückt.

Augustinus thematisiert allerdings diese Grundauffassung von Gott
als dem Herrn und Vater in seinem umfassenden Werk relativ selten in
ausdrücklicher Weise. Die Formel *Dominus et Pater* ist schon gar nicht
häufig. Dafür lassen sich mehrere Gründe anführen. Im Anschluss an
die Bibel, im besonderen an die Sprache der Psalmen, zieht Augustinus
es vor, von Gott, seinem Herrn, zu sprechen. So redet er in den *Confessiones* seinen Gott oft mit *Domine, Deus meus* an,[8] hingegen relativ
selten mit *Pater* oder *bone Pater*.[9] Es ist jedoch nicht zu übersehen,
dass *Deus* oder *Dominus* zusammen mit *creator, conditor universitatis*
oder *universitatis auctor* stehen und damit die Vateridee miteinschlies-

---

[8] Vgl. zum Einfluss der Psalmen G.N.Knauer, *Psalmenzitate in Augustins Kon-
fessionen* (Göttingen 1955), bes. 84-88.

[9] Vgl. cf 10,31,46; 10,43,69; 13,15,17.

sen;[10] umgekehrt bedeutet *Dominus* auch *Deus*, wie die Formel *Deus potestate, pater bonitate* andeutet.[11] Im Gefolge der bis zum NT zurückreichenden Tradition verwandte Augustinus ferner das Wort *pater* im Zusammenhang mit dem Taufglauben.[12] Vater im Sinne von Ursprung und Erhalter der Geschöpfe musste darum gegenüber Vater mit der Bedeutung von *origo filii* oder *deus qui a nullo est* zurücktreten, wenngleich Augustinus im Vater Jesu Christi auch gerne den Vater der in der Taufe wiedergeborenen Christen sah.[13] Schliesslich bezog er mit den neutestamentlichen und frühchristlichen Christen den Titel *dominus* vorzugsweise auf Jesus Christus[14] und war darum wenig geneigt, von Gott als dem Herrn und Vater zu reden.[15]

Trotzdem fehlen die Texte nicht, in denen Augustinus Gott zugleich mit *dominus* und *pater* betitelt. Es seien wenigstens zwei Zeugnisse im lateinischen Wortlaut angeführt. In der Erklärung zu *Psalm* 62 lesen wir: *Tamen gratias Deo, qui modo in hac eremo non nos deserit....Subtrahit nobis aliquando quae necessaria sunt, et adterit nos, ut sciamus quia Pater et Dominus est, non solum blandiens, sed et flagellans. Praeparat enim nos cuidam hereditati incorruptibili et magnae.*[16] In einer anderen stark apologetisch gefärbten Predigt heisst es: *Gratias Domino Deo nostro...Gratias illi, cui et cordis et oris devotione cantavimus: Deus quis similis tibi? quod eius sanctam caritatem invisceratam sentimus cordibus vestris, quod ipsum tamquam Dominum timetis, tamquam Patrem diligitis...Gratias illi cuius timorem non excutit amor, cuius amorem non impedit timor.*[17]

Häufiger als die wörtliche Antithese *Pater–Dominus* sind die Wendungen und Darlegungen, in welchen die Vaterschaft und Herrschaft

---

[10] Vgl. cf 1,20,31; 11,31,41; sol 1,1,2 (im Kontext auch *pater*); rel 23,26; ci 8,1. In do 1,10,10 hingegen wird nicht der Vater, sondern der dreifaltige Gott Schöpfer genannt.

[11] Vgl. s 213,2.

[12] Vgl. tri 7,4,9; 4,21,30 ff; cf 10,43,69; io 20,6; s 68,2 ps 138,3.

[13] Vgl. C.Eichenseer, *Das Symbolum Apostolicum beim Heiligen Augustinus* (St. Ottilien 1960), 172 f.

[14] Jesus selbst hatte Gott, abgesehen von *Matthäus* 11.25, nicht Herrn genannt, jedoch immer wieder auf die Königsherrschaft seines Vater verwiesen.

[15] Vgl. ps 110,1: Der *dominus* des Evangeliums spricht von der *misericordia* und *severitas* seines Vaters; ep 238,2,10. Dazu Eichenseer (*op, cit. n. 13*), 169 ff.

[16] ps 62,10.

[17] s 24 (a.401),1. Vgl. s 24,4, mit *Matthäus* 11.25.—Andere Texte mit *dominus* und *pater*: s 12,3; fau 3,3 (anti-manichäisch); io 21,3 anti-arianisch); ps 138,3: Gott ist der Vater Christi *secundum formam dei*, der Herr *secundum formam servi*.

Gottes mitgemeint werden, ohne dass sie ausdrücklich genannt sind. Ein für viele andere repräsentatives Beispiel liefert uns eine vor dem Fest des heiligen Cyprian gehaltene Predigt über den *Psalm* 88, der von den göttlichen Verheissungen an David handelt und der Augustinus die Gelegenheit gibt, von der väterlichen Erziehung Gottes zu sprechen. Wir finden darin die göttliche Güte, welche beruft und züchtigt; die väterliche Hand über uns; die Zucht, welche ein guter Sohn nicht zurückweist; die Zucht, welche die Güte nicht aufhebt, sondern das Erbe sicher stellt; das Vertrauen in die Versprechungen des Vaters, welches nicht fürchtet, gezüchtigt, sondern enterbt zu werden; der Herr, der straft, weil er liebt und jeden züchtigt, den er als seinen Sohn annimmt.[18] Augustinus bezeichnet also Gott nicht bloss als Vater und Herrn, sondern umschreibt auch, zum Teil antithetisch, was er darunter versteht.

Diese mehr einschliessliche Art von Gott als dem Herrn und Vater zu reden, charakterisiert im besonderen die Taufkatechese des Bischofs von Hippo. In den Predigten zur *traditio* und *redditio symboli* befasst er sich nach einer Einleitung über den Sinn des *credere* mit dem ersten Glaubensartikel *in Deum Patrem omnipotentem, creatorem caeli et terrae*, wie er im afrikanischen Taufbekenntnis steht.[19] Mit *deus* ist der *dominus deus* des Gesetzes und der Propheten gemeint, der Schöpfer aller Dinge, der Gott Israels, der Gott, den auch Jesus von Nazareth seinen Gott nannte. *Deus* ist gleichsam der Eigenname dessen, zu dem der Christ sich zuerst bekennt. Wenn er auch Vater heisst, dann gewiss speziell, weil er Vater Jesu Christi ist. Doch darüber handelt Augustinus erst bei der Besprechung des zweiten Glaubensartikels.[20] Hier wird Gott vielmehr als Vater aller Geschöpfe und im besonderen aller Gläubigen bekannt. Der Titel Herr hingegen ist im für Augustinus sehr wichtigen Bekenntnis zum allmächtigen Schöpfer miteingeschlossen.[21] Augustinus unterlässt es selbst nicht, dies eigens hervorzuheben. So sagt er einmal: *Credo in Deum Patrem omnipotentem. Vide quam cito dicitur, et*

---

[18] ps 88, 2,2: *Non ergo tantum misericordia vocantis est, sed et verberantis et flagellantis. Sit itaque manus paterna super te, et si filius bonus es, noli repellere disciplinam; quis est enim filius, cui non dat disciplinam pater eius? Det disciplinam, dum non auferat misericordiam; caedat contumacem, dum tamen reddat hereditatem. Tu si promissa patris bene agnovisti, non timeas flagellari, sed exheredari; quem enim diligit Dominus, corripit; flagellat autem omnem filium quem recipit.*

[19] Vgl. zum folgenden Eichenseer (*op. cit. n. 13*),146-189.

[20] Vgl. s 214,5 f; 215,3.

[21] Vgl. s 214,3 ff.

quantum valet. Deus est, et Pater est; Deus potestate, Pater bonitate" und schliesst gleich den Psalmvers an: *benedic anima meo Domino.*[22]

Der Zusammenhang von Gott und Herr und Vater, wie er in den Erklärungen zum Taufsymbol vorausgesetzt wird, erscheint auch in den Ausführungen über das Herrengebet, welche ebenfalls an die *competentes* gerichtet sind.[23] Augustinus geht darin vom Grundsatz aus, dass wir zuerst glauben müssen und erst dann anrufen können. Derjenige, an den wir glauben und den wir anrufen ist der Gott Israels. Der Sohn Gottes aber, den Augustinus in diesem Zusammenhang vorzüglich *dominus* nennt,[24] hat uns gelehrt, dass wir Gott als Vater anrufen dürfen.[25] Sofern Augustinus diesen Gott auch als Schöpfer des Himmels und der Erde bekennt und seinen Willen als entscheidend hinstellt, gibt er zu verstehen, dass er ihn zugleich als Herrn betrachtet, selbst wenn er ihm den Titel *dominus* nicht gibt.[26]

Endlich begegnen wir der gleichen Auffassung auch in den eucharistischen Predigten, welche der Bischof von Hippo an Ostern und in der Osterwoche hielt. Darin kehrt der Hinweis auf die das eucharistische Hochgebet einleitenden Worte *Sursum corda—Habemus ad Dominum—Gratias agamus Domino Deo nostro* mehrmals wieder.[27] Es ist offensichtlich, dass sie sich auf den beziehen, den wir im Taufbekenntis als *Deus Pater omnipotens* bekennen und der in diesen Predigten auch *Pater* genannt wird.[28] Im übrigen begegnen wir einer ähnlichen Gebetsform im berühmten Gebet, mit dem Augustinus viele seiner Predigten beschliesst: *Conversi ad Dominum Deum Patrem omnipotentem... gratias agamus; precantes toto animo singularem mansuetudinem eius, ut preces nostras in beneplacito suo exaudire dignetur...per Iesum Christum Filium eius.* [29] Sie klingt schon in seinen Frühwerken[30] sowie in seinen Bekenntnissen an.[31]

---

[22] s 213,2 (*guelf*[1]).

[23] Vgl. s 56-59.

[24] Vgl. bes. s 58,2,2.

[25] Vgl. bes. s 57,2,2; 58,1,1 f.

[26] Vgl. bes. s 56,2,2; 56,5,7; 57,5,5-6,6.

[27] Vgl. s 227; 229A,3.

[28] Vgl. M.Klöckener, 'Das eucharistische Hochgebet bei Augustinus' in *Festschrift C.P.Mayer* (Würzburg 1989), 461-498.

[29] s 65,5,10; 183; 272, ps 150,8.

[30] Vgl. sol 1,1,5 f; vit 4,36: *gratias ago summo et vero deo patri, domino, liberatori animarum.*

[31] Vgl. cf 11,29,39: *et tu solatium meum, domine, pater meus, aeternus es.* cf 13,15,17.

Die Herrschaft und die Vaterschaft Gottes kommen in einem weiteren Gebiet der augustinischen Verkündigung häufig zur Sprache. Der
Bischof von Hippo hatte es, wie schon angetönt, oft mit Menschen zu
tun, Christen und Heiden, welche mit dem Wirken Gottes in der Welt
nicht fertig wurden. Im besonderen hatte er auf die Einwände zu
antworten, mit denen nach dem Fall von Rom im Jahre 410 der Glauben
an die göttliche Vorsehung bestritten wurde. Vor den damals von Zweifeln zerrissenen Leuten griff er besonders gerne auf die Thematik der
patria disciplina, der göttlichen Erziehung zurück.[32] In der Hauptsache
stützte er sich dabei auf das zwölfte Kapitel des Hebräerbriefes, in dem
Sprichwörter 3.11 f. breit entfaltet werden. So führt er etwa bei der
Erklärung des Verses: *Quoniam ego in flagella paratus sum* (*Psalm*
37.18) aus, dass, wer von Adam abstammt, das ewige Leben, das ihm
bereitet ist, nur erlangen kann, wenn er gezüchtigt wird. Er darf sich
darum nicht beklagen, wenn er der *disciplina Domini* unterworfen wird.
Er soll vielmehr bedenken, dass der Herr, der ihn zurechtweist, ihn liebt
und dass jeder Vater seinen Sohn schlägt. Im dabei angeführten
Bibeltext heisst Gott ausdrücklich Herr; sofern indes gesagt wird, dass
er die Menschen wie Söhne behandelt, wird auch seine Vaterschaft
angesprochen.

Augustinus selbst hebt das im Kontext auch eigens hervor.[33] In
anderen Texten verdeutlicht er diesen Sachverhalt dadurch, dass er
gleichzeitig noch andere Bibeltexte anführt, in denen entweder von
Dominus oder von *Pater* die Rede ist. So zitiert er in seiner Predigt über
den Fall Roms *Ijob* 2.9 und 2.20, *Jesus Sirach* 2.1,4f und *Sprüche* 3.12,
wo von Gott, dem Herrn und dem Sohn des Herrn die Rede ist, und
kann dementsprechend schliessen, dass Gott unser Vater ist, den wir
nicht nur lieben sollen, wenn er uns Gutes tut, sondern den wir auch
annehmen sollen, wenn er uns bestraft.[34] Wie hier, umschreibt er zudem

---

[32] Vgl. zum folgenden S.Poque, *Le langage symbolique dans la prédication
d'Augustin d'Hippone* (Paris 1984), 193-224: 'La loi du Père'.

[33] ps 37,23: *Omnino magnifice, tamquam diceret: Ad hoc natus sum, ut flagella
sufferam. Non enim nasceretur nisi de Adam, cui flagella debentur. Sed aliquando
peccatores in hac vita aut non, aut minus flagellantur, quia iam desperata est intentio
eorum. At vero illi quibus paratur vita sempiterna, necesse est ut hic flagellentur; quia
vera est sententia: Fili, ne deficias in disciplina Domini, neque fatigeris cum ab illo
increparis; quem enim diligit Dominus corripit; flagellat autem omnem filium quem
recipit. Ideo ergo non insultent inimici mei, non magna loquantur; et si flagellat me
Pater meus, in flagella paratus sum, quia mihi hereditas praeparatur.*

[34] s 397,3,3. Vgl. auch ps 31,2,26; ps 118,31,3 f, mit *Hebräer* 12.6, *Sprüche* 24.16
und *1 Petrus* 4.17; s 15,3-6, mit *Hebräer* 12.6, *Psalm* 10.4, *Ijob* 1.21; s 29A,1 f, mit

immer wieder das doppelte Verhalten Gottes mit einer oder mehreren Antithesen.[35] So ist in der Erklärung zu *Psalm* 91 zu lesen: *Cum adest, consolationi Dei gratias agat; cum deest, iustitiae Dei gratias agat. Ubique sit gratus, nusquam ingratus: et Patri consolanti et blandienti gratus sit; et Patri emendanti et flagellanti et disciplinam danti gratus sit; amat enim ille semper, sive blandiatur, sive minetur; et dicat quod audisti in psalmo: Bonum est confiteri Domino et psallere nomini tuo, Altissime.*[36]

Schliesslich sind die Texte in Betracht zu ziehen, in welchen Gott als *pater familias* bezeichnet wird; denn dieses lateinische Wort schliesst bekanntlich sowohl den Begriff *dominus* als auch den Begriff *pater* in sich. Als *pater familias* besitzt Gott die *patria potestas*, steht somit wie ein Herr und Vater über den Menschen und darf von diesen wie von Kindern und Sklaven Gehorsam und Liebe erwarten. Augustinus selbst definiert den *pater familias* als *dominus domus*.[37] Allerdings sind sogleich zwei Dinge zu bedenken. Einmal hat Augustinus in der Mehrzahl der fraglichen Texte den *pater familias* der Gleichnisse Jesu im Auge.[38] Anderseits verwendet er im übertragenen Sinn das Wort nicht nur für Gott, sondern auch für Christus oder für Menschen, welche eine Verantwortung für das Reich Gottes tragen.[39] Immerhin sind die eigentlich theologischen Stellen recht beachtlich. So stellt er den Katechumenen in Aussicht, dass sie nach der Taufe als Söhne der Familie eines grossen Familienvaters leben werden.[40] Dieser grosse Hausherr

---

Psalm 11.1; *Sprüche* 3.16 oder *Hebräer* 12.6; ps. 38.2; fau 22,14, mit *1 Petrus* 4.17 f, *Sprüche* 3.42, *Ijob* 2.10, *Offenbarung* 3.9, 1*Korinther* 11.31 f. Dazu s 108,6, wo es heisst, dass der Vater seine Kinder kommen lässt, um sie die Furcht des Herrn zu lehren.

[35] Vgl. Poque (*op. cit. n. 32*), 197-203; 123*.

[36] ps 91,1. Vgl. s 15A,4; s 24,1; 113A,4; ps 54,2; 31,2,26; 62,10; 134,14; 144,4; s 397, usw.

[37] eu 2,80. Er gibt damit die übliche Übersetzung des ntl. *oikodespotes* wieder. Vgl. auch Locut. Hept.4,80.

[38] Vgl. *Matthäus* 13.36-43: Das Unkraut unter dem Weizen, in manchen anti-donatistischen Texten, wie per 2,23,43; pet 3,4,5, usw.—*Matthäus* 20.1-16: Von den Arbeitern im Weinberg, in s 49,2; 87,3,4; pel 2,7,13.—*Matthäus* 21.33-46: Von den bösen Weingärtnern, in s 87,2,3.—*Matthäus* 24.45-51: Vom guten und bösen Knecht, in s 37,15; vgl.16A,11, ohne *pater familias*.—*Luke* 14.15-24: Von der Einladung zum Gastmahl, ep 93,2,5; ep 208,7; gau 1,37,50.—*Matthäus* 10.25, in sdni 1,22,75; ps 40,8; pet 3,7,8.

[39] Vgl. *Psalm* 40.8, 55.8, spec 25: CSEL 12,163, mit *Matthäus* 10.24; ep 228,2; ep 199,1; ep 18*, 3; s 340A,9; ccre 3,58,64; *Matthäus* 15: CChL 44B,138, mit *Matthäus* 13.51: *doctus in ecclesia*. Dazu ep 173,3: über die Vaterpflichten der Bischöfe.

[40] s 97A,4. Vgl. s 49,2.

wird, wie es anderswo heisst, ganz anders für seine Knechte sorgen, als dies einem irdischen Vater möglich ist, für den die Zukunft immer im Ungewissen bleibt.[41] Gott ist wirklich der mächtige und reiche Familienvater, der uns alles gibt, was wir brauchen.[42] Er kümmert sich selbst dann noch um uns, wenn seine Knechte (die Prediger) ihre Aufgabe vernachlässigen.[43] Die Polemik gegen die Manichäer führte Augustinus überdies dazu, noch anders zwischen Kindern und Knechten zu unterscheiden. Zur Verteidigung des AT hob er nämlich hervor, dass Gott als *pater familias iustissimus* für die Zeit der Knechtschaft etwas anderes angeordnet hatte als für die Zeit der Kindschaft.[44] Ähnlich betonte er gegenüber den Pelagianern anhand des Gleichnisses von den Arbeitern im Weinberg (*Matthäus* 20.1), dass Gott sich immer als gerechter und guter Familienvater erweist.[45]

2. *Die biblische Grundlage*

Ob Augustinus ausdrücklich oder bloss einschliesslich Gott als unsern Herrn und Vater hinstellt, er tut es, wie schon verschiedentlich angedeutet wurde, vorwiegend im Anschluss an die biblischen Bücher.[46] Er zitiert nicht nur die einschlägigen Texte der Weisheitsliteratur,[47] die Gleichnisse der synoptischen Evangelien, in denen vom Hausherr die Rede ist[48] oder andere diesbezügliche Schriftworte, wie *Matthäus*

---

[41] ps 38,11 f.

[42] s 61,4,4. Vgl. s 42,2.

[43] qeua 2,21: zu *Lukas* 11.5.

[44] rel 17,34.

[45] s 87,2,3-3,4. Vgl. pec 2,18,31 f, mit einer Anspielung an *Matthäus* 20.9 f.

[46] Für den biblischen Zusammenhang, vgl. bes. G.Schrenk—G.Quell, 'pater:' *Theologisches Wörterbuch zum Neuen Testament* 5 (1954), 946-1016; L.Derrousseaux, 'La crainte de Dieu' *Lectio Divina* 63, (Paris 1970); H.Ringgren, 'ab' *Theologisches Wörterbuch zum Alten Testament* 1 (1973), 1-19; A.Schenker, 'Gott als Vater–Söhne Gottes. Ein vernachlässigter Aspekt einer biblischen Metapher' *Freiburger Zeitschrift für Philosophie und Theologie* 25 (1978), 3-55.

[47] Es werden zitiert, zum Teil nur in De scriptura sacra speculum, *Sprüche* 3.11 f; 13.24; 15.5; *Ijob* 1.12; 36.5; *Sirach* 23.1,4; *Weisheit* 14.3; *Psalm* 102.13, usw. Vgl. B. Studer, *Libri sapienziali* (*op. cit. n. 1*). Unter den dort verzeichneten Studien, vgl. bes. A.-M. La Bonnardière, *Biblia Augustiniana, AT. Le livre de la Sagesse* (Paris 1970); A.-M. La Bonnardière, *Biblia Augustiniana. Le livre des Proverbes* (Paris 1975).

[48] Vgl. n. 32.

11.25[49] oder *l Petrus* 4.17.[50] Er hält sich auch und vor allem an die Heilige Schrift insgesamt, in welcher die Autorität und Liebe Gottes als Grundidee erscheinen.[51]

Es ist jedoch ohne weiteres zuzugeben, dass Augustinus nicht einfach von der Bibel herkommt. Er befasst sich im allgemeinen mit den einschlägigen Stellen nicht in Kommentaren der Bücher, denen sie entnommen sind. Von *Psalm* 102.13 sowie den in *De scriptura sacra speculum* und in den *Adnotationes in Iob* kommentierten Texten abgesehen,[52] verwendet er die biblischen Worte vielmehr ausserhalb ihres Kontextes. Er greift in der Taufkatechese auf die Heiligen Schriften zurück, um den Taufglauben, das Vater Unser und den Sinn der eucharistischen Feier zu erklären. Er verteidigt gegenüber den Manichäern und Pelagianer den gerechten und gütigen Gott.[53] Vor allem benutzt er die Bibel, um allen Zweiflern und Geplagten zu helfen, die göttliche Erziehung zu verstehen. Allerdings stehen diese eigenen Anliegen immer im Horizont der Bibel oder werden sogar in den Kommentaren zu anderen biblischen Büchern, vor allem in den *Enarrationes in Psalmos* behandelt.[54]

Wie die ganze Alte Kirche betrachtet Augustinus dabei die Heilige Schrift als ein Buch, als eine einzige Rede Gottes. Er unterscheidet wohl zwischen der salomonischen und nicht-salomonischen Weisheitsliteratur.[55] Aber er erläutert dennoch die früheren mit den späteren Büchern und gibt damit auch den Aussagen über die väterliche Erziehung Gottes im Buch der *Sprüche* und bei *Ijob* den eschatologischen Sinn des Buches der *Weisheit*. Wenn in den früheren Schriften das Walten Gottes als Erziehung zur Weisheit verstanden wird, zielen dar-

---

[49] Vgl. s 24,4; s 67,4,7; 68,2; s 138,4; ps 144,13, usw.

[50] Vgl. ps 9,1; 59,6; 93,23, usw. Dazu La Bonnardière, 1975 (*op. cit. n. 47*), 110-114.

[51] Vgl.Derrousseau (*op. cit. n. 46*), 364.—Diese Idee, wie sie vor allem in der Gegenüberstellung von Vater und Herr zum Ausdruck kommt, wird im Artikel 'pater' im *Theologisches Wörterbuch zum Neuen Testament* immer wieder hervorgehoben; vgl. 970; 975 (Philo); 979: Vater und Herr (Judentum); 984 f (Jesus); 992; 995; 1005 (Hbr 12); 1010 f. Vgl. auch W.Eichrodt, *Theologie des AT.*, 2 vols.(Göttingen 1962-64), I, 330, u. II, 152 f.

[52] Vgl. ps 102,20; spec: PL 34,913 f u. 961 f; ib: PL 34,861-880.

[53] Vgl. rel 17,34; fau 3,3; 22,14. Dazu La Bonnardière, 1970 (*op. cit. n. 47*), 103-107.

[54] Vgl. z.B. ps 58,2,6; 70,2,10. Dazu La Bonnardière, 1975 (*op. cit. n. 47*) 83-96.

[55] Vgl. Studer, 1992 (*op. cit. n.1*) 116, mit ci 17,20,1; spec: PL 34,912 f; 924 f; 946 ff.

um ihre Ermahnungen und Empfehlungen in der Reinterpretation des Augustinus wie jene des jüngsten Weisheitsbuches ebenfalls auf den ewigen Besitz Gottes ab.[56] Vor allem stellt Augustinus die atl. Texte in das Licht des Evangeliums. Damit verstärkt er nicht bloss ihren eschatologischen Sinn,[57] sondern gibt dem Glauben der jüdischen Weisen an die Liebe des gestrengen Gottes eine neue Tiefe: Gott hat seinen eigenen Sohn nicht verschont und damit bewiesen, dass nur jene zu ihm als Herrn und Vater aufblicken können, welche von ihm in Zucht genommen werden.[58]

Weil Augustinus von der Bibel als der einen Rede Gottes ausgeht, deutet er die fraglichen Texte zudem in einer heilsgeschichtlichen Perspektive. Die göttliche Erziehung, von der sie sprechen, erscheint darum als Prozess, der von der Knechtschaft zur Kindschaft führt.[59] Das trifft nicht bloss auf den Übergang vom Alten zum Neuen Bund zu. Es gilt auch vom Leben des einzelnen Menschen. Jeder Christ soll vom *timor servilis* gegenüber seinem Herrgott zum *timor castus* gegenüber seinem himmlischen Vater, von der Angst vor ewiger Strafe zur Liebe, zur Gerechtigkeit gelangen.[60]

Es unterliegt also keinem Zweifel, dass der Bischof von Hippo sich in seiner Lehre von Gott, dem Herrn und Vater, innerhalb des Horizontes der Bibel bewegt. Nicht weniger offensichtlich ist jedoch, dass er die biblischen Gegebenheiten in den Dienst seiner pastoralen und theologischen Anliegen stellt und sie damit fortwährend neu interpretiert. Dass er dabei ganz von seiner gesellschaftlichen Umwelt bestimmt wird, ist ebenfalls zu erwarten. Doch das ist noch genauer aufzuzeigen.

3. *Der römische Hintergrund*

Zum vollen Verständnis der Rezeption der biblischen Gedanken und Ausdrucksformen genügt es tatsächlich nicht, sich gegenwärtig zu halten, was Augustinus als Seelsorger und Theologe bewegte. Man

---

[56] *Ibid* 4 ff.
[57] *Ibid* 8.
[58] *Ibid* 10.
[59] Vgl. ps 134,1.
[60] Vgl. rel 17,33s; ps 118,25,7. Dazu W.Mundle, 'Furcht Gottes, "C.Christlich"': *Reallexikon für Antike und Christentum* 8 (1972) 676-698, bes. 695 ff, u. A.Zumkeller, 'Augustinus Verständnis des Wortpaares castitas/castus im religiösen Bereich' in *Mélanges T.J. van Bavel* (Leuven 1990), 829-846.

muss auch bedenken, von welcher kulturellen Umwelt seine Hörer und Leser und er selbst geprägt waren. Es mag banal sein, es eigens zu sagen, aber er konnte wirklich nur in jenen Tönen vor ihnen die Herrschaft und Vaterschaft Gottes preisen, für welche ihre Ohren offen waren, und um sie erklingen zu lassen, musste er selbst über das nötige Instrumentar verfügen.

Diese ohne weiteres einleuchtende allgemeine Feststellung gilt vorerst einmal vom lateinischen Bibeltext, den Augustinus in seiner Verkündigung und in seiner theologischen Arbeit benützte. Konkret bedeutet das unter anderem,[61] dass in der lateinischen Bibel das Wort *pater familias* gebraucht wird, das im Griechischen kein volles Äquivalent besitzt. In dem dafür stehenden Wort *oikodespotes* fehlt der ausdrückliche Hinweis auf den Vater und die damit verbundenen Nebentöne von Herzengüte und sorgender Liebe.

Nicht weniger beachtenswert ist im Lateinischen der Zusammenhang von *patria potestas* und *disciplina* oder *eruditio*. Als gewiegter Rhetor gibt sich Augustinus denn auch Rechenschaft darüber, dass mit den zuletzt genannten Wörtern das griechische Wort *paideia* wiedergegeben wird.[62] Ob er sich auch bewusst war, dass dessen Bedeutung in der griechischen Bibel unter dem Einfluss der hebräischen Originalsprache den Sinn von Strafe und Züchtigung erhielt, ist mehr als fraglich.[63] Immerhin bestimmt er im Sinn der hebräischen Bibel die *paideia/disciplina* als *eruditio per molestias* und braucht im Zusammenhang damit entsprechend dem biblischen Urtext die Begriffe *castigatio, correptio, emendatio*.[64] Dazu scheint er sich im klaren gewesen zu sein, dass die Wörter *eruditio* und *disciplina*, welche sich von *erudire* und *discere* herleiten, andere Wurzeln haben als das griechische Wort *paideia*.[65]

---

[61] Die grosse Bedeutung des Gottesnamen dominus bei Augustinus ist nicht typisch lateinisch. Sie hängt vielmehr mit der Ersetzung von Jahwe durch adon und dessen griechische übersetzung durch kyrios zusammen.

[62] Vgl. ps 118,17,2: *Addidit autem eruditionem* (Psalm 118,66); *vel sicut plures codices habent, disciplinam. Sed disciplinam, quam graeci appellant paideian, ibi scripturae nostrae ponere consueverunt, ubi intelligenda est per molestias eruditio; secundum illum: Quem diligit Dominus corripit, flagellat autem omnem filium quem recipit Sprüche* 3.12; *Hebräer* 12.6). *Haec apud ecclesiasticas litteras dici assolet disciplina, interpretata de graeco ubi legitur paideia*.

[63] Zum hebräischen Hintergrund der biblischen Verwendung von *paideia* vgl. G.Bertram, 'paideia' *Theologisches Wörterbuch zum Neuen Testament* 5, 607-611; C.Spicq, *L'Épître aux Hébreux* (Paris 1977), 202-205.

[64] Vgl. ps 118,17,2. Dazu Poque (*op. cit. n. 32*), 199 ff.

[65] Vgl. die Definition von *disciplina* als Ableitung von *discere* in disc 1,3: *discipli-*

Die Anpassung der biblischen Daten an die eigenen Vorausetzungen
bestand indes vor allem darin, dass Augustinus die Aussagen über Gott,
den Herrn und Vater im Licht des *pater familias* der Römer rezipierte.[66]
Seine schon erwähnte Definition des *pater familias* als *dominus domus*
verrät tatsächlich grosse Ähnlichkeit mit der Definition der Juristen.[67]
Entscheidender ist jedoch, dass sein Gottesbild die Züge des römischen
Familienvaters trägt. Er spricht von Gott als dem Herrn, der zurecht-
weist und züchtigt und zugleich vom Vater, der tröstet und bestärkt, von
Gott, dem die Menschen sowohl Ehrfurcht als auch Liebe schulden, von
Gott, der sich für die Ordnung in seinem Haus einsetzt, um damit den
Seinen das ewige Erbe zu sichern.[68]

Wie berechtigt es ist, in diesem Gottesbild römische Züge zu
unterscheiden, geht vor allem aus der Art hervor, mit der Augustinus
selbst in seiner Apologie *De Civitate Dei* in den von Varro übernomme-
nen Ausführungen über den Frieden die *pax domestica* umschreibt.[69]

---

na a discenda dicta est; disciplinae domus ecclesia est. Dazu Poque (*op. cit. n. 32*),
198 f.

[66] Vgl. zu dieser Thematik J.Marquardt, *Das Privatleben der Römer* I (Neudruck
der 2.Aufl. von 1886, Darmstadt 1964), 1-6; E.Sachers, 'Pater familias' *Paulys Real-
Encyclopädie der classischen Alterthumswissenschaft*, 18/2 (1949), 2121-2157;
J.Gaudemet, 'Familie': *Reallexikon für Antike und Christentum* 7 (1969), 286-358;
J.Gaudemet, *Le droit romain dans la littérature chrétienne occidentale du IIIe au Ve
siècle* (Milano 1978), 152-162.—Weitere Literatur zur Frage bei A. Wlosok, 'Die
Gottesprädikation Pater et Dominus bei Laktanz. Gott in Analogie zum römischen
pater familias' *Laktanz und die philosophische Gnosis* (Heidelberg 1960), 233-246;
Der *Kleine Pauly* 4, 545 ff, mit dem Hinweis auf M.Kaser, *Das römische Privatrecht*,
2 vols. (München 1955-59), sowie bei Poque (*op. cit. n. 32*), 205-208.

[67] Vgl. H.Heumann–E.Seckel, *Handlexikon zu den Quellen des römischen Rechts*
(Graz 1971), 408 f: *Pater*, mit 1.195 §2 D.50,16: *Pater familias appellatur, qui in
domo dominium habet...quamvis filium non habet...*

[68] Zur doppelten Funktion des Familienvaters und der doppelten Ehrenbezeugung
von Seiten der Untergebenen, vgl. Wlosok *(op. cit. n. 66)*, 242 f, mit den Texten aus
Laktanz und Ulpian. Dazu Heumann–Seckel *(op. cit. n. 67)*, 408 f, mit 1.4 D 50,17:
velle non creditur, qui obsequitur imperio patris vel domino.—In diesem Zusammenhang müsste man im besonderen auf die typisch römischen Begriffe *pietas* und *obsequium*, *potestas* und *diligentia* näher eingehen. Vgl. W.Dürig, *Pietas Liturgica*
(Regensburg 1958), bes. 136; 154 ff; 182 ff.

[69] ci 19,16. Vgl. H.Fuchs, *Augustin und der antike Friedensgedanke* (Berlin 1926),
bes. 92 f; 139-154; W.Dürig, 'Disciplina. Eine Studie zum Bedeutungsumfang des
Wortes in der Sprache der Liturgie und der Väter': *Sacris Erudiri* 4 (1952), 245-279,
bes. 254-262: 'Domestica disciplina'; V.Morel, 'Disciplina': *Reallexikon für Antike
und Christentum* 3 (1957), 1218: *disciplina domestica*; M.Schrama, 'Praeposito tamquam patri oboediatur. Augustinus über Frieden und Gehorsam' in *Mélanges T.J. van
Bavel* (Leuven 1990), 846-876, bes.848-860.

Danach kommt es dem Familienvater zu, die Herrschaft auszuüben
(*dominari*), zu befehlen (*imperare*), in Liebe zu sorgen (*consulere
dilectione*) und, wenn nötig, mit Worten oder Schlägen oder anderen
rechtmässigen Zuchtmitteln zurechtzuweisen (*corripere seu verbo seu
verbere seu alio genere poenae*). Umgekehrt kommt es den Kindern
und Sklaven zu, zu gehorchen und sich dem häuslichen Frieden
einzufügen (*paci coaptetur*). Damit wird die gegenseitige Verantwortung (*officium imperandi et oboediendi*) verwirklicht und durch Befehlen und Gehorchen die Eintracht der Hausgenossen erreicht (*concordia
cohabitantium*). Eine ähnliche Beschreibung der Stellung des *pater
familias* findet sich in einem Briefe wieder, in dem Augustinus zeigen
will, wie falsch es ist, seine eigenen Fehler dem Schicksal zuzuschreiben. Eine solche Auffassung wird nämlich durch den Familienvater
Lügen gestraft, der, kraft seines Rechtes und seiner Sorgfalt, die Leute,
welche ihm für eine Zeit unterstellt sind, zum Guten mahnt und vom
Bösen abhält, von ihnen Gehorsam fordert, die Gehorsamen ehrt und
die Ungehorsamen bestraft, den Guten seine Gunst erweist und die
Undankbaren hasst.[70]

Die Hinweise auf die Verantwortung des römischen Hausvaters für
den häuslichen Frieden bekommen noch mehr Gewicht, wenn wir uns
gegenwärtig halten, dass Augustinus in seinen Darlegungen über den
Frieden mit der römischen Tradition die Ordnung des Hauses im
Zusammenhang mit der staatlichen und der kosmischen Ordnung sieht.
Wenn er nämlich immer wieder Gott als *imperator* oder als *rector
mundi* bezeichnet,[71] fügt sich das ganz in jene Schau ein, nach welcher
der Kaiser und die Gottheit die Rolle des Familienvaters im Grossen

---

[70] ep 246,3: *Si autem iure proprio et patrisfamilias diligentia. quorum homines pro
tempore in potestate habet, hortatur ad bonum, deterret a malo, imperat suae volun-
tati ut obtemperent, honorat eos qui sibi ad nutum oboediunt, vindicat in eos qui se
contemnunt, rependit gratiam beneficis, odit ingratos..,*—Zum technischen Ausdruck
diligentia, vgl. Sachers, 'Der Typus des diligens p.f. *Paulys Real-Encyclopädie der
classischen Alterthumswissenschaft*, 18/2 (1949), 2155 ff: Vgl. auch ep 105,5,16, wo
die Rede von *diligentia caritatis* die Rede ist; ps 118,31,3: *patres a filiis piis et timen-
tur et amantur* sowie ep 243, wo Augustinus *Lukas* 14.26-33 erklärt und dabei auch
von den Familienpflichten spricht, aber wie der biblische Text nicht vom Familienvater, sondern von der Mutter spricht, jedoch nicht ohne Gott Vater zu nennen.

[71] Vgl. trin 3,4,9; ps 49,15: *Deus noster, imperator et rex noster, quod vectigal nobis indicit, quoniam voluit esse rex noster, et voluit nos esse provinciam suam?* mit ps
36,3,4, wo *Christus imperator* genannt wird; 70,2,2; 103,1,15: die Engel sind in einer
republica magna imperatoris Dei; 138,14.—Vgl. ps 30/2,3,2: *Huius mundi rector non
est nisi creator* weiter cf 3,8: *fons vitae, qui es unus et verus creator et rector universitatis*; rel 23,26; ci 7,12; trin 12,9.

erfüllen und damit auch auf das *obsequium* und die *pietas* ihrer Untergebenen zählen dürfen.[72] Von da aus gesehen, versteht man auch besser, warum Augustinus im ersten, einleitenden Buch von *De Civitate
Dei* im Zusammenhang mit der göttlichen Erziehung von der *familia
dei* spricht.[73] Der Herr des himmlischen Staates erscheint so von Anfang an als ihr Erzieher und Vater.

Drei Einzelheiten mögen das Gesagte noch ergänzen. Vorerst ist
daran zu erinnern, dass nach Augustinus der Ausdruck *Deus Pater* auch
Porphyrius geläufig ist.[74] Man muss darum mindestens in *De Civitate
Dei* mit Interferenzen zwischen dem alltäglichen Vaterbild und dem philosophischen Gottesbegriff rechnen, wie er vor allem der platonischen
Tradition eigen ist.[75] —Weiter wird der römische Charakter der *patria
potestas*, wie sie Augustinus voraussetzt, noch verständlicher, wenn man
sich gegenwärtig hält, wie er auch sonst die *potestas* ganz nach römischer Art umschreibt. So heisst es etwa bei der Erklärung des Schöp-
fungsberichtes, dass Gott unser Herr unseren Dienst nicht braucht, wir
aber seine Herrschaft nötig haben, damit er uns behüte, und dass wir ihm
nicht für ihn dienen, sondern zu unserem Nutzen und unserem Heil.[76] —
Schliesslich und vor allem ist festzuhalten, wie Augustinus ganz auf den
Spuren der römischen Überlieferung die Vaterschaft mit dem *patrimo-
nium*, dem Familienbesitz, in Verbindung bringt.[77] Viel mehr als die von
ihm rezipierten biblischen Texte stellt er immer wieder die Sicherstel-

---

[72] Vgl. Cicero, *nat.deor.* 3,85, wo die Dreiteilung *domus, respublica, moderatio
divina mundi* mit der *disciplina* verbunden wird. Dazu Dürig (*op. cit. n. 69*), 255.

[73] Vgl. ci 1,8,1: über die Erziehung der Guten und der Bösen, mit ci 1,29: *Habet
itaque omnis familia summi et veri Dei consolationem suam, non fallacem nec in spe
rerum nutantium vel labentium constitutam, vitamque etiam ipsa temporalem minime
paenitendam, in qua eruditur ad aeternam, bonisque terrenis quamquam peregrina
utitur nec capitur, malis autem probatur aut emendatur.* Man beachte die Wörter *con-
solatio, erudire, probare, emendare* mit denen anderswo die Pflichten des Familienvaters umschrieben werden.—Von *familia Dei* ist auch anderswo die Rede, z.B. ps
78,9, zusammen mit *pater familias, dominus, domus, servi*; 108,15; ep 43,9,25, zusammen mit *hereditas*; 248,2: im Sinne von Gemeinde.

[74] Vgl. ci 19,23,4: CChL 48,693.

[75] Vgl. unten.

[76] Gnl 8,11,24: *Ille quippe nostra servitute non indiget, nos vero dominatione illius
indigemus, ut operetur et custodiat nos; et ideo verus solus est Dominus, quia non illi
ad suam, sed ad nostram utilitatem salutemque servimus.*

[77] Vgl. für das folgende, J. Fellermayr, *Tradition und Sukzession im Licht des rö-
misch-antiken Erbdenkens* (München 1973), bes. 21-43; La Bonnardière, 1975 (*op.
cit. n. 47*), 119-123; Poque (*op. cit. n. 32)*, 209 ff; 217 ff, wo jedoch m.E. der biblische
Einfluss überschätzt wird.

lung des Erbes als Ziel der göttlichen Erziehung hin. Er kann selbst die Warnung aussprechen, Gott kümmere sich nur um jene Kinder, welche sich erziehen lassen und damit berechtigte Hoffnung auf die Wahrung des Familienerbes geben.[78] Gerade diese Hoffnung war für die Römer entscheidend; denn durch die Weitergabe des Familienbesitzes wollten sie die fortwährende Verehrung ihrer Ahnen sichern.[79]

Noch etwas: wenn Augustinus in seinem Reden über Gott sich in die römische Sicht der *potestas patria* stellte, bewegte er sich ohne Zweifel auf der Ebene des Vergleiches.[80] Den metaphorischen Charakter dieser Ausdrucksweise bestätigen zwei Tatsachen. Einmal konnte Augustinus in ähnlicher Weise, wie er Gott mit einem väterlichen Erzieher verglich, auch vom göttlichen Lehrer sprechen.[81] Zudem betrachtete er mit der Antike die Erziehungsarbeit auch als Therapie; für ihn war also der göttliche Erzieher zugleich ein Arzt.[82] Dennoch bleibt Augustinus, wenn er als Römer von Gott als dem Herrn und Vater spricht und ihn auch als solchen anredet, nicht beim einfachen Vergleich zwischen Gott und dem römischen *pater familias* stehen. Er schreibt vielmehr Gott, wenn auch auf analoge Weise, etwas zu, was ihm wirklich zukommt, die schöpferische Kraft und die fürsorgende Liebe.

4. Auf den Spuren der frühchristlichen Überlieferung

Augustinus war mit seiner römisch geprägten Auffassung von Gott als dem Herrn und Vater und der damit verbundenen "Relecture" der bibli-

---

[78] Vgl. *ps 70,2,10: disciplina–hereditas*. Vgl. weiter, 62,10 u. s 55,5,5, mit dem ausdrücklichen Vergleich zwischen dem irdischen Vater und dem Vatergott, sowie ps 91,8; 93,17.

[79] Wenn einer sein Vermögen testamentarisch einer Person vermachte, welche nicht zu seinen Nachkommen zählte, musste diese sich dennoch verpflichten, für den Kult der Ahnen jener Familie zu sorgen. Vgl. Marquardt (*op. cit. n. 66*), 385.

[80] Vgl. Poque (*op. cit. n. 32*) bes. 217 ff.

[81] Vgl. s 15A,3.

[82] Vgl. q 82,3, mit *Hebräer* 12.6; ps 114,5; s 114A,9; ps 37,4; 40,6.—Dazu La Bonnardière, 1975 (*op. cit. n. 47*) 118f; Bertram (*op. cit. n. 63*), 5,602, sowie P. Nemeshegy, *La paternité de Dieu chez Origène* (Tournai 1960), 155, Origenes, *Hom.Jer.* 15,5; 20,3. Vgl. weiter Tertullian, *Adv.Marc.* 2,16,1f; Ambrosius, *Exp.Ps.* 118,9,16, im Zusammenhang mit der *disciplina* des gestrengen und gütigen Gottes; Chrysologus, *serm.* 108,3, mit *disciplina, pater, medicus*. Man beachte zudem, dass auch der für Augustinus fundamentale Text von *Hebräer* 12.4-13 einen Zusammenhang zwischen dem züchtigenden Vater und dem unangenehme Mittel anwendenden Arzt herstellt.

schen Texte natürlich nicht der erste. Die schon erwähnte Tatsache, dass er sich an die lateinische, auf der griechischen Übersetzung der LXX beruhenden Bibel hielt, ist allein schon bezeichnend genug. *Pater familias, eruditio, disciplina* und andere von den lateinischen Bibelübersetzern aus der römischen Tradition übernommene Ausdrücke hatten längst vor ihm die westliche Theologie bestimmt.[83]

Vor allem hatten die grossen lateinischen Apologeten schon lange vor Augustinus Gott als Herrn und Vater bezeichnet. Unter ihnen nimmt Laktanz, der christliche Cicero, ohne Zweifel die erste Stelle ein. Was damit gemeint ist, hat A.Wlosok in einer gut fundierten Untersuchung unlängst aufgezeigt.[84] Danach kommt bei Laktanz das doppelte Gottesprädikat *Dominus et Pater* nicht nur häufig vor, sondern stellt im Grunde genommen die einzige Bezeichnung für Gott dar. Dieses Gottesbild ist zunächst auf den Hintergrund der *patria potestas* der Römer zu sehen, dank welcher der *pater familias* eine rechtliche Vollmacht über das Hauswesen (*familia*) besitzt wie der *imperator* über den Staat. Die väterliche Amtsgewalt umfasst gegenüber Kindern und Sklaven auf der einen Seite die Herrschaft- und Strafgewalt, auf der anderen Seite die Schutz- und Fürsorgepflicht. Die beiden Funktionen erscheinen manchmal auf den *dominus* und den *pater* aufgeteilt oder sind im *pater familias* zusammengefasst. Von einiger Bedeutung ist jedoch für die römische Überlieferung auch der kultische Zusammenhang. Er ist umso mehr zu beachten, als bei Laktanz die Weisheit und die Religion zusammengehören.[85] Wenn also die Römer Zeus, die oberste Gottheit, *Optimus Maximus* nannten, verehrten sie in ihm den Herrn und Vater.[86] Allerdings wurde in der späteren römischen Tradition, wie etwa bei Seneca, der Akzent auf die Güte gesetzt. Man anerkannte zwar die Strenge weiterhin, aber man sprach nicht vom strafenden Gott. Die Christen hingegen, Laktanz voran, vereinigten das Herrscherliche und das Väterliche erneut zu einer ausgewogenen Synthese. Von seinen

---

[83] Für *disciplina* vgl. O. Mauch, *Der lateinische Begriff* disciplina, (Freiburg 1941); Dürig (*op. cit. n. 72*), 245-279, bes. 278, mit Beispielen von lateinischen Übersetzungen von *musar* bzw. *paideia*; Morel (*op. cit. n. 69*), 1213-1229, bes. 1222-1229. Für *eruditio* vgl. P.Blomenkamp, 'Erziehung': *Reallexikon für Antike und Christentum* 6 (1966), 502-559, bes. 520 über den Wortgebrauch.—Für *pater familias* vgl. unten.

[84] Wlosok (*op. cit. n. 66*), 232-246.

[85] Vgl. Wlosok (*op. cit. n. 66*), 244.

[86] Vgl. Wlosok (*op. cit. n. 66*), 237, mit den Hinweisen auf Cicero, *nat.deor.* 2,64; Horaz, *carm.*I,12,13 ff. Dazu ist weiter zu vergleichen Augustinus, cf 1,20,31, mit der Anspielung auf den *Optimus Maximus*.

sozialen und religiösen Vorstellungen her kam dieser grosse lateinische Apologet tatsächlich dazu, Gott die *summa potestas* zuschreiben, in welcher die Herrschaft und die Vaterschaft vereint sind. Die menschlichen Auffassungen von *pater* und *dominus* sind damit zur Idee vom einen Erschaffer und Herrscher der Welten gesteigert, dem der Mensch allein *pietas* und *obsequium* schuldet. Somit fliessen in der alles umfassenden Macht Gottes auch die beiden menschlichen Institutionen des *pater familias* und des *imperator* zusammen.[87]

Diese beachtliche theologische Zusammenschau des Laktanz war selbst eine Weiterentfaltung früherer Ansätze. Schon Tertullian, der erste lateinische Theologe, vertrat in seiner Vater-Unser-Erklärung mit der Unterscheidung von *potestas* und *pietas* ein römisch gefärbtes Gottesbild.[88] In der Widerlegung des Marcion stellte er gar ausdrücklich den *pater*, dem wir Liebe und Ehrfurcht schulden, dem *dominus legitimus* gegenüber, den wir wegen seiner Güte lieben, wegen seiner Zucht fürchten sollen.[89] In der gleichen Schrift dient ihm der ganz römisch verstandene Doppelbegriff *dominus—pater* dazu, die Einheit der Gerechtigkeit und Güte in Gott zu beweisen. Danach verwirklicht Gott als Vater seine Güte, als Herr hingegen seine Strenge. Wenn er dabei die römische Antithese von *timere* und *diligere* rezipiert, tut Tertullian es dennoch nicht, ohne sie mit den biblischen Gegensatzpaaren *misericordia—sacrificium, peccatum—paenitentia* zu ergänzen und ohne damit zur biblischen Forderung zu gelangen: du sollst deinen Gott lieben und fürchten.[90] So charakterisiert die römische Denkform des *pater familias* auch seine Gotteslehre, selbst wenn er die Analogie zwischen dem Familienvater und Gott nicht so konsequent durchgeführt hat wie später Laktanz.[91]

Vor diesem begegnet man den römischen Familienvorstellungen auch im Gottesbild des Minucius Felix, obwohl natürlich nicht im glei-

---

[87] Wlosok (*op. cit. n. 66*), 245 f.

[88] Tertullian, *orat.* 2,4. Vgl. *bapt.* 20,5.

[89] Tertullian, *Adv. Marc.* 1,27,3: *plane nec pater tuus est, in quem competat et amor propter pietatem et timor propter potestatem nec legitimus dominus, ut diligas propter humanitatem et timeas propter disciplinam* Vgl. *Prax.*11: *dominus potestate.*

[90] Vgl. Wlosok (*op. cit. n. 66*), 240, mit *Adv.Marc.* 2,13,1-5, bes. *Usque adeo iustitia etiam plenitudo est divinitatis ipsius, exhibens deum perfectum, et patrem et dominum, patrem clementia, dominum disciplina, patrem potestate blanda, dominum severa, patrem diligendum pie, dominum timendum necessarie... Ideo lex utrumque definiti: diliges deum et timebis deum.*

[91] Vgl. Wlosok (*op. cit. n. 66*), 241. Ausserdem J.Moingt, *Théologie trinitaire de Tertullien IV* (Paris 1969),140 f, mit verschiedenen Texten.

chen Masse wie bei Tertullian.[92] Bemerkenswert ist ebenso, wie ein anderer Apologet, Arnobius von Sica, den Gott der Christen dem höchsten Gott der Heiden gegenüberstellt und dabei vom *deus primus solus, pater rerum ac dominus, constitutor moderatorque cunctorum* redet.[93] Weniger aus apologetischen Gründen als in Rücksicht auf das Fassungsvermögen seiner Gäubigen hatte schon zuvor Cyprian von Karthago ganz nach römischer Art von Gott, dem Herrn und Vater, gesprochen.[94] Das gleiche gilt für die lateinischen Autoren des vierten und fünften Jahrhunderts. Es ist nicht möglich, dies hier im einzelnen zu entfalten. Es sei jedoch wenigstens darauf verwiesen, dass solche Zeugnisse bei Hilarius, Ambrosius, Hieronymus, Chromatius und Petrus Chrysologus zu finden sind.[95]

Der Zusammenhang der Antithese von Herr und Vater und jener von Gerechtigkeit und Güte, welchen wir in der anti-marcionitischen Polemik des Tertullian vorfanden, durchlief im übrigen allein schon eine beachtliche geschichtliche Entwicklung, und das umso mehr, als er in der Bibel selbst verwurzelt ist.[96] Auch hier können wir nicht auf die

---

[92] Minucius Felix, *Octav.* 18,4: *Ita in hac mundi domo cum caelum terramque ... perspicias providentiam ... crede esse universitatis dominum parentemque ... totius mundi partibus pulchriorem*—Vgl. 18,7.10; 35,4.

[93] Arnobius, *Adv.nat.* 3,2: CSEL 4,112 f. Vgl. 2,74: CSEL 4,108 f.

[94] Cyprian, *Patient.* 3: CSEL 3,398 f: *Si dominus nobis et pater deus est, sectemur patientiam domini pariter et patris, quia et servos esse oportet obsequentes et filios non decet esse degeneres.*

[95] Hilarius, *Trin.* I,4 (apologetisch): *universitatis dominus atque infinitatis parens,* sonst nicht am Thema interessiert.—Ambrosius, *Exp. Ps* 118.9,7-15, mit *Römer* 11.22, *Hebräer* 12.6, *Matthäus* 7.11; *En.Ps.* 43,3, mit *Sprüche* 3.11 f; *Bened.Patr.* 4,17; *Abraham.* 2,10,69, mit *Matthäus* 22.37 u. *parens omnium*; ep. 74,10:*Deus diligi maluit quam timeri*— Hieronymus, *In Hiezechielem,* 6,20,15-17: CChL 75,263: *Ut autem sententiam Domini in filios et famulos non perditionem esse, sed emendationem, audiamus testimonia scripturarum,* es folgen *Sprüche* 3.11 f, *Hebräer* 12.5 f, *Psalm* 77.34, *Deuteronomium* 32.39); *In Sophoniam* 1,12: CChL 76A,670: Gott wird verglichen mit einem Arzt, einem Vater und einem Lehrer, dazu *Hebräer* 12.11; *In Malachiam* 1.6 f: CChL 76A,906: der Vater verdient *honor* und *pietas,* der Herr *timor*; *In Esaiam* 17,63,17 ff: CChL 73A,731 f.—Chromatius, *serm.* 2,1 zu *Matthäus* 13.24 f): *pater familias,* wird im biblischen *Malachi* 1.6) und zugleich römischen Sinn erklärt, aber auf Christus angewandt.—Petrus Chrysologus, *serm.* 108,3:*Rogat deus, quia non tam dominus vult esse quam pater. Rogat deus per misericordiam, ne vindicet per rigorem.* Das wird von Christus gesagt, während zuvor, *serm.* 108,1 es von Paulus gesagt worden war.

[96] Die Theologie des gerechten und guten Gottes müsste eingehender studiert werden. Vgl. wenigstens die Hinweise auf Irenäus, Tertullian, Ambrosius und Augustinus bei H.Merkel, 'Gerechtigkeit IV. Alte Kirche': *Theologische Realenzyklopädie,* 12 (1984), 420-424.

Einzelheiten eingehen. Es sei bloss vermerkt, dass auch von dieser sehr komplexen Thematik einiges Licht auf die augustinische Auffassung von Gott als Herrn und Vater fällt.[97] So heisst es etwa, dass Gott der Herr seinen Knechten in dieser Zeit der Bekehrung und Bewährung als *pater corrigens*, nicht als *iudex damnans* zürnt.[98] Oder es ist von der Güte und der Wahrheit des Herrn und Gottes die Rede, welche offen an den Tag treten werden, wenn Christus die Gesegneten des Vaters von den Verdammten scheiden wird.[99] In einer eingehenden Erklärung zu *Psalm* 88.31-35 führt Augustinus schliesslich aus, dass Gott die Christen, welche seine Kinder sind, selbst wenn sie sündigen, nicht dem Verderben überlässt; er wird von seiner Barmherzigkeit gegenüber ihnen nicht ablassen, sondern sie als gütiger Vater vielmehr züchtigen, damit seine richterliche Wahrhaftigkeit (*veritas vindicantis*) ihnen keinen Schaden zuzufügen braucht.[100]

Nicht weniger beachtlich ist der traditionelle, in der arianischen Kontroverse noch verschärfte Zusammenhang zwischen der Gottes- und Schöpfungslehre.[101] Wenn nämlich Augustinus unter dem allmächtigen Vater den Schöpfer und Herrn versteht, setzt er den radikalen Unterschied von Gott und Welt voraus, der in der schon von den griechischen Apologeten und dann vor allem von den nizänischen Theologen vertretenen Lehre von der *creatio ex nihilo* enthalten ist.[102] Damit ist der christliche Glaube an den Herrn und Vater, wie ihn auch Augustinus vertritt, klar von der antiken Tradition abgehoben, in welcher der *parens omnium* zum Kosmos selbst gehört.[103]

Ähnliches gilt von der anderen antiarianischen Unterscheidung von *per naturam* und *per voluntatem*.[104] Der Natur nach ist nämlich Gott nur der Vater seines einzigen Sohnes Jesus Christus, dem Willen nach hingegen ist er der Vater aller Menschen, besonders jener, in denen er

---

[97] Dabei ist zu beachten, dass nach Augustinus, quhept 1,66 u. 1,161, die in der Bibel häufig sich findenden Doppelausdrücke *misericordia–iustitia, misericordia–iudicium, misericordia–veritas* gleichwertig sind und der Herr und Vater auch richterliche Gewalt hat.

[98] ps 79,5, mit *Sirach* 2.1 u. *Hebräer* 12.6.

[99] ps 39,19, mit *Psalm* 79.11 u. *Matthäus* 25.32.

[100] ps 88,2,2-4.

[101] Vgl. Studer (*op. cit. n. 9*), 183 f; M.-A. Vannier, 'S. Augustin et la création' in *Mélanges T.J. van Bavel* (Leuven 1990), 522-544.

[102] Vgl. etwa cf 12,7,7; ench 3,9. Dazu Studer, 1987 (*op. cit. n. 1*), 174.

[103] Vgl. dazu auch ep 138,1,6:*Ideo verus est Dominus, qui servo non indiget, et quo servus indiget* ebenso ps 69,5.

[104] Vgl. Studer, 1987 (*op. cit. n. 1*), 174 f; 184 f.

Wohnung genommen hat.[105] Seine ewige Vaterschaft ist darum von seiner gnadenhaften Vaterschaft in der Zeit verschieden. Trotzdem ist anzunehmen, dass sein ewiger Wille auch in der Bewegung der Zeit unveränderlich geblieben ist.[106] Mit anderen Worten, Gott ist in der Geschichte Herr und Vater geworden, ohne sich damit selbst zu verändern.[107]

Endlich verbindet Augustinus wie die vorausgehende christliche Überlieferung mit der Schöpfung die fortwährende Erhaltung der Welt.[108] Wie Gott durch seinen Willen alles erschaffen hat, so erhält er die Dinge nach seinem Willen.[109] Seine *patria potestas*, welche sich in der Erschaffung und in der Erhaltung aller Dinge verwirklicht, muss in bezug auf die freien Geschöpfe selbst als ewige Vorherbestimmung begriffen werden. Gewiss hat Augustinus diese Prädestination bei der Verteidigung der Notwendigkeit der Gnade Christi recht einseitig formuliert und damit zugleich das Ordnungsdenken seiner Frühschriften in Frage gestellt.[110] Man muss jedoch auch bedenken, dass seine Gnadenlehre in der Vorauswahl Christi gipfelt.[111] Im Geheimnis der Inkarnation des Wortes erwies sich nämlich nicht bloss in aller Klarheit, dass die Menschen Geschöpfe sind, denen der Herr und Vater rein nichts schuldet.[112] Es wurde darin auch die Liebe des demütigen Gottes offenbar, der sich selbst nichts schuldig bleibt.[113] Damit erschloss sich der

---

[105] Besonders bezeichnend ist, wie Augustinus in fau 3,3 gegenüber dem manichäischen Einwand gegenüber einer Vaterschaft Gottes mit Hilfe des nizänischen Glaubens und seiner Terminologie die göttliche Vaterschaft in bezug auf den Sohn, die Geschöpfe und die Getauften bestimmt und seine Antwort demgemäss beschliesst: *Ipsum quippe habemus et Deum et Dominum et Patrem; Deum quod ab ipso... conditi sumus; Dominum quod ei subditi sumus,Patrem quod eius adoptione renati sumus* Vgl. weiter ps 134,6; trin 1,10,21; prae 10,19; 17,34. Vgl. auch fau 3,3, wo *deus* auf die Schöpfung, *dominus* auf die Unterwerfung, *pater* auf die Wiedergeburt des Menschen bezogen sind, sowie ps 138,3, wo es heisst, dass Christus, sofern er Mensch ist, den Vater als Herrn anredet, während Gott für ihn in der forma dei Vater ist.

[106] Vgl. vor allem gnl 8,18,37-27,50, bes.8,23,44. Weiter cf 12,15,18; s 261,4,4.

[107] Vgl. vor allem die Texte, in denen Augustinus, zum Teil sehr vorsichtig, die Frage diskutiert, ob Gott schon vor der Schöpfung Herr gewesen sei: tri 5,16,17; gnl 8.11,24; ci 12,15,1.3.

[108] Vgl. die Unterscheidung von *conditio* und *administratio* in gnl 5,11,27; 5,17,35.

[109] Vgl. gnl 8,24,45.

[110] Vgl. Studer,1987 (*op. cit. n. 1*), 180 f, sowie E.Przywara, *Augustinus. Die Gestalt als Gefüge* (Leipzig 1934), 439f, mit den Texten auf S.450-453..

[111] Vgl. prae 15,30; pers 24,67.

[112] Vgl. s 67,4,7; ci 10,29,1; tri 13,17,22. Dazu Studer, 1987 (*op. cit. n. 1*), 181.

[113] B.Studer, 'Zur Soteriologie der Kirchenväter', *Handbuch der Dogmengeschichte* III/2a (Freiburg Br. 1978), 163 f.

tiefste Sinn der *disciplina paterna*. Gott machte klar, dass er allein aus väterlicher Liebe Herr der Menschen sein will. Wie Jesus können darum auch wir uns nur in die Hände des gerechten Vaters empfehlen, wenn wir die manchmal hart anfassenden Hände des gütigen Herrn zu spüren bekommen.

Vor mehr als hundertfünfzig Jahren hielt John Henry Newman in Oxford eine Predigt über den "Frieden und die Freude inmitten der Züchtigung".[114] Er liebte es auch sonst, von der Gerechtigkeit und Liebe Gottes zu sprechen und seine Zuhörer zur Ehrfurcht und Liebe gegenüber Gott zu ermahnen. Ich bin nicht sicher, ob seine recht ernsten Worte heute mit der Unbefangenheit der Gläubigen von damals angenommen würden. Doch selbst wer der modernen Kritik gegenüber einem übermächtig väterlichen, so wenig mütterlichen Gott viel Raum gewährt, vermag der traditionellen Verbindung der biblischen Auffassung von der *disciplina paterna* und der römischen *potestas patria* manches abzugewinnen. S.Poque leistet dafür in dem mit "La loi du Père" betitelten Kapitel ihrer bemerkenswerten Untersuchung der Symbolsprache des Augustinus einen recht eindrücklichen Beweis.[115] Sie gibt darin nicht bloss eine ausgezeichnete Übersicht über das Zusammenspiel der biblischen und römischen Züge im augustinischen Gottesbild. Es ist ihr auch gelungen, so meine ich, mit einer Feinheit, wie sie nur einer Frau möglich ist, von der modernen Anthropologie her, wie sie etwa Ricoeur vertritt, aufzuzeigen, dass der Mensch letztlich im Leiden zur vollen Reife gelangt. Selbst wenn der heutige Mensch die *disciplina paterna* noch weniger versteht als die Leute von Hippo und Karthago, kann er also dennoch erahnen, dass Gott seine alles überragende Grösse mit seiner noch grösseren Liebe durchsetzen will.

Eines scheint mir jedenfalls sicher: es lohnt sich wirklich, sich mit dem *Deus ad nos*, dem *Dominus et Pater* des Augustinus zu beschäftigen. Wir lernen dabei, wie notwendig es ist, die biblische Botschaft in unsere Sprache zu übertragen, und wie bedingt und zerbrechlich gerade darum unser Reden von Gott bleibt. Dabei drängt sich uns die Frage auf, wie weit die Menschen ausserhalb der biblischen Erzählung der Grosstaten Gottes schon das Heilige erfahren, das erschreckt und anzieht. Gerade die Art, wie Augustinus von seinem Herrn und Vater denkt und predigt, zwingt uns schliesslich, seine Auffassungen von der religiösen Erkenntnis zu überdenken. Ist die Verkündigung des *Deus ad*

---

[114] J.H.Newman, *Predigten: dt.Gesamtausgabe* 4 (Stuttgart 1952), 136-153.
[115] Poque (*op. cit. n. 32*),193-224.

nos nur Weg zur Auffindung des *Deus in se*? Geschieht im Glauben an den Gott der Väter nur die Reinigung des Herzens, welche es braucht, um den zu erkennen, DER IST? Müssen wir nicht vielmehr annehmen, dass die *disciplina paterna*, wie sie uns im vollen Sinn nur im Evangelium Jesu Christi zugänglich geworden ist, uns göttliche Tiefen erschliesst, welche selbst einem durch die glaubende Unterwerfung von allem Stolz gereinigten Herzen verborgen bleiben müssen? Auf jeden Fall hat Augustinus selbst nicht zum *ens immutabile* gebetet.[116] Er redete von Anfang an seinen Gott voll Vertrauen mit *bone pater* an und erhob später zusammen mit seinen Gläubigen sein Herz immer wieder in Dankbarkeit zu seinem Herrn.

---

[116] Vgl. Solignac, in *Bibliothèque Augustinienne* 3,12 f, zu cf 1,1,1.

THE IGNORANCE OF CHRIST:
A PROBLEM FOR THE ANCIENT THEOLOGY

LIONEL WICKHAM

I

Well, shall I be permitted to speak of 'the ancient theology' in an essay for a friend and mentor who notes carefully one's more pretentious utterances? Did it ever exist? After all, we meet in the written memorials of the patristic period (and let us say that the period runs from the Apostolic Fathers to John of Damascus) not so much a 'one' as a 'many'. The voices we hear, speak of God, Christ and the human condition (and that makes their utterances 'theology'), in many different ways: through varying media which determine what is to be said (for no one will say in a sermon precisely what he would say in a combative treatise against a heretic); in different circumstances (for a letter of consolation to the bereaved, say, will attempt an encounter with the grieving heart and leave behind those considerations of evil's nullity which may suit less anguished moments). The writers we call 'patristic' and recognize as classic, do not speak with one harmonious accord, however much grand talk there may be, amongst those who have little direct acquaintance with it, of 'the mind of the fathers'.

Yes, that, and much else along the same lines is all true. And yet it remains the case that there *is* a unity in the patristic, the ancient, theology. Let us take a very large view from a dangerous (I grant you) height. Do you not see common themes and presuppositions, a shared approach, which you would have to be an incorrigible nominalist to discredit and locate only in the viewer's eye? For one thing, the public declarations of the Church in conciliar decisions and creeds mark them out. We perceive a common 'world' of ideas, out of which, and to which, these decisions are uttered. The ancient theology is not simply these decisions and creeds, not simply the 'doctrines' alluded to or taught there in the catchwords and formulae ('consubstantial', 'three persons in one substance', 'hypostatic union' and the like) to which the historian of doctrine is apt to reduce it all, imposing certainly thereby more uniformity than is natural. Yet they do convey the distinctive approach and tone. The formulae are the product of long debates which occupied the anguished consciences and fertile brains of ministers of religion and servants of the state who might (to the philistine mind) have been engaged in occupations more productive of human happiness. Yes, and I will not pretend that the very religiousness of the milieu which created the ancient theology is free from moral ambiguity: there can be a surfeit of debate and too much interest of a trivializing kind in religion, too much mere *phlyaria*, as more than one distinguished theologian pointed out at the time. The construction of theology was irresistibly entertaining to those who engaged in it and served many other purposes (some of these to do with politics and power) besides the advancement of the knowledge of God. But entertainment is not so opposed to seriousness of intention that it nullifies the enterprise, and games are only worth playing if there is something at stake. The ancient theologian who lost the argument might lose much else besides; and that sharpened his wits and put a brake, too, upon the merely teasing. 'Radical' theology has always been something of a commercial venture, but in ancient times its practice did not encourage insouciance. Marcellus of Ancyra, Eunomius and Nestorius did not make the ancient equivalent of the walk from the television studio to the bank.

Formulae, then, of a 'technical' character; their roots in a proneness to debate and in the asking of questions (characteristically about the being and nature of alleged agencies and things) to which it is presumed that there are correct answers: this we recognize (I suggest) in the ancient theology as typical of its style. It is the style, as it is also an echoing of the vocabulary, of philosophers, who ask questions, argue and 'dogmatize'. We perceive the ancient theology as the peculiar construction it is, because in it a narrative of faith was linked to philosophy: not so much to a defined school as to the philosophical enterprise itself. The ancient Church came to present a religion about which questions could be asked. From the Apologists onwards, it made what was to be believed open and vulnerable to public discussion of a kind we recognize as rational. It could, one might imagine, all have evolved differently. You can think into possible existence a succession of figures like St. Paul or St. John, intuitive, inspired minds which do not descend so far from the mountain of vision as to explain how all that they have to tell us could be true at once or relate to what the crowd sees on level ground. Yes, and we might admit that the Christian Gnostics could quite legitimately claim to be diadochi in such a transmission of divine mysteries; and if they had had their way, the Christian faith would have been conceived of as a series of episodes in a drama ungrounded save in free-floating fantasy and the intuitive sympathy of the audience. The Valentinian myth of Sophia and the drama of the world's making, unmaking and re-making is beautiful and touching; it would make a splendid church ballet, and send the audience home moved and stimulated. It is theology of a sort, a possible continuation of the New Testament: not on the same level (no one, not even its author, would have ventured quite to think that) but after the same manner, picking up a style and themes in the same way that apocryphal gospels and acts (though I will not call them 'theology') also pick up style and themes to fill out the narrative gaps. But you cannot argue with a guru. You have to take on trust what he says. A common-sensical mind, the vulgar mind, the mind which is crudely 'philosophical' and questions, could never trust Valentinus far. Who could take *au plein sérieux,* or risk life for, a tale with so implausible a starting-point: why was Sophia so silly as to attempt to know Bythus? And what would have happened, if she had not tried to? The thing becomes absurd, as ultimate narrative 'explanations' necessarily become absurd. And more than that is wrong with it, of course. To set the explanation of all things in the quest for explanation is like making cartography the cause of the disposition of the continents. The interior life of faith, with all its frustrations and contradictions is not to be identified with the external actualities which produce them, the conditions of knowledge with its existence. We owe a debt of gratitude to Valentinus for being so desperately wrong and made us all so clear on the matter that we need never be troubled by Feuerbach. The Gnostics were rejected. The ancient theology came about, which limited narrative and invoked divine reason, the rational purpose such as operates where problems are raised and solved, as the subject of the narrative and its principle of interpretation. It became possible to think of the Christian faith as in tune with, and analogous to, the knowledge with which we know the world around us. Not 'why is there Godhead and a world?' but 'who and what are Godhead and the world?' becomes the question; and that because, it is alleged, an answer is in principle discernible in a true account of Christ. The movement from 'myth' to 'philosophy' is also a shifting of Christ to (as it were) centre-stage. The ancient theology very nearly became a philosophy, but a philosophy cannot cope with the arbitrarily given particularities of the life of Christ in the setting of Israelite religion. The ancient theology

is, rather, faith turned philosophical, not faith swallowed up in philosophy; its theology was a philosophical theology.

The effect was remarkably successful. You can criticize Christianity
for being so loquacious and so argumentative; and I grant that the union
with philosophy is partly responsible for that. But if I try to think away
the notions of God in Trinity, as source and goal of all goodness
because source of all being, or of divine Incarnation I do not recognize
the Christian religion. And I do not think I am unusual in that. The
accounts of God and of human nature (the markedly 'philosophical' elements, because abstractions from particularities) cohere well (or so I
should suggest) with the story of Christ to convey grounds for optimism
about the sovereignty of the good and the ultimate security of the soul.
One may cavil at many things, but the ancient theology remains, in
many respects, Christian theology per se: there is no other.

But the ancient theology is unevenly developed and often embar-
rassingly crude. Who does not wince at every recurrence of that pitiful
Stoic borrowing: the illustration of divinizing grace from heat trans-
ference (the 'iron in the fire' analogy)? It is poor on the individual and
personal. It is weak on the sacraments; faith as an attitude of mind, distinct from the assent to revealed truths, was never properly discussed;
and it has often been felt to leave us with a dubiously human Christ.
Too interested in juggling with 'natures' and 'hypostases', it neglected
the actual historical person; too quick to bring God down from heaven,
it deprived the human Jesus of his endearing humanity. The 'philosophy' is so heavily pasted over the actual figure as to render him invisible; he becomes a cipher. Superb (it might be allowed) at affirming
the divine stranger in our midst who is God-with-us, bearing our sufferings, the ancient theology effaced the particular man who had,
simply by being particular and human, this and this (shall we call them
'intellectual') limitations. There is something, I think, in that charge;
but not so much that it should make for an immediate conviction on
grounds of negligence.

The ancient theology was well aware of the problem; and it surfaced
in a discussion that turns up in different forms at different periods, in
relation to the biblical texts which ascribe, or appear to ascribe the
limitation of ignorance to Christ, especially *Matthew* 24.36 and *Mark*
13.32. Was he, or was he not, ignorant of the End? Now although, so far
as I can see, there is only one text in the Bible which unequivocally
ascribes knowledge of all future events to God (*History of Susanna* 42),
the assumption is general for the ancient theology that absolute God-

head knows all. But if Christ knows all, and human beings do not, then human is not an adjective which can be used of him without considerable qualification, if at all. I approach this dilemma from a brief study of a text dealing with it.

II

The text [= CPG 7005], whose translation I set down, is a fragment found in the Florentine Codex Laurentianus VII, 26, of an essay by Stephen of Hierapolis. It occupies, in its fragmentary form four folios of the manuscript. Four folios are lost, so we have about half of the original. F. Diekamp edited the text which was printed in *Analecta Patristica* 154 ff. [= *Orientalia Christiana Analecta* 117] (Rome 1938). Almost certainly the author is the Stephen we read about in Evagrius' *Church History* 6,20 as having composed an account of the life and sufferings of Golindouch (died 31 July 591), the Persian convert from Zoroastrianism, a prophetess and confessor [= CPG 7006]. That work survives in Georgian, and a Latin translation, with introduction, by G. Garitte was published in *Analecta Bollandiana* 74 (1956) 405-440. Stephen was bishop of Hierapolis (Hierapolis Euphratensis, present-day Membij) sometime in the late sixth century. Apart from his see and approximate date we know nothing about Stephen beyond what can be deduced from the present text, which at least lets us see that Stephen is a Chalcedonian. The piece is as follows:

> *Essay by the most holy and blessed Stephen, archbishop of Hierapolis:* that it was on account of a beneficial and necessary mystery, and not because he was ignorant of the day of the End, that the Lord is represented by Matthew as saying, 'But of that day and hour no one knows, not even the angels of heaven, but only my Father' (*Matthew* 24.36), and by Mark as saying, 'But of that day and hour no one knows, not even the angels of heaven, not even the Son, but the Father' (*Mark* 13.32).
>
> 1. Many people frequently, under pressure from the passions which vex and disturb [our] nature, interpret the real facts otherwise than they are and have published their own error as law. Their nonsense, gaining strength with the progress of time, is maintained as an object of veneration; and the disreputable comes to be considered a reputable opinion. Indeed, just as an oar moving in the water seems to be different in shape because the eye is deceived, so not paying due and

careful attention to the divine utterances breeds very great error and produces a lapse from truth. For superficial inspection and length of time can get the better of the truth.

2. It stands, then, as one of the best and greatest things to blend knowledge and eagerness in divine matters with caution, and not to remove the ancient landmarks (cf. *Proverbs* 22.28) which the divine legislation and our sacred and glorious fathers who thereafter appeared at various times, have handed down. For he who spoke in his own Gospel word, 'Ask and it will be given, seek and you shall find, knock and it' (i.e. the door of knowledge) 'will be opened to you' (*Matthew* 7.7) is the same who says, using the prophet as his vehicle, 'If you seek, seek and dwell with me' (*Isaiah* 21.12), thereby instructing us very clearly never to veer to right or left but to make our way within the bounds of true religion (cf. *Numbers* 20.17) and to tread the paths of truth. For idle speculation can render a mind distraught and leads it to wrong.

3. This, then, is the fate which those who have erupted from the party of Apolinarius and Eutyches and those who hold very similar views to them, have suffered. They have abandoned Christ's rock (I mean the Catholic and Apostolic Church); have built upon sand, like Simon Magus; and have made Christ out to be one nature, in negation, that is, of one of the pair from which and in which he exists. They do not tremble to say in their delirium that he is ignorant, or their alleged one nature is ignorant, of the day and hour of the End of the present world he created in the beginning. And this despite his exclaiming, at one point, 'As the Father knows me, I too know the Father' (*John* 10.15); and at another, 'No one knows the Son save the Father but no one knows the Father save the Son and he to whom the Son wills to give revelation' (*Matthew* 11.27): meaning that he wanted to reveal the knowledge of his Father to the first-fruits of his new covenant (his leading disciples). To them he said in these very words: 'if you knew me, you would know my Father too, and from now on you know him and have seen him'. Philip says to him, 'Lord, show us the Father and we are satisfied'. Jesus says to him: "Have I been with you so long and you do not know me, Philip? He who has seen me has seen the Father. How can you say, "Show us the Father"? Do you not believe that I am in the Father and the Father is in me? The words which I speak to you, I do not speak from myself. But the Father, abiding in me, himself does the works (*John* 14.7-10)'. From which we plainly learn that those whose substance and nature are one, though they differ in their hypostases, clearly exist in one another, and their prosopa are such as to be mutually marked out. And so, quite conformably, the Son is elsewhere called the 'stamp of the Father's hypostasis' (*Hebrews* 1.3), his 'image' (*Colos-*

sians 1.15), 'light of light', 'beam from spiritual Sun', 'Word from mind inconceivable:', 'Son of Father immaculate'. Their properties in no way whatever eliminate their sameness in nature.

4. Therefore, then, the All-holy Spirit, connatural with him and with his immaculate Father, having as the Spirit does, the same essential knowledge as they, needed no revelation. Which is why the 'No one' is not used here in contrast with the All-holy Spirit, but with creatures, and especially, because what are very similar to the ...

5. ... and the knowledge of the Father and Holy Ghost. But, as I said to you before my passion and resurrection, "the Gospel will be preached in the whole world, and then will come the End" (*Matthew* 24.14). And now I say the same thing in other words: "You will be my witnesses in Jerusalem, Judaea, Samaria and to the ends of the Earth" (*Acts* 1.8) Which is the same as saying, 'The Gospel will be preached to the whole world and then will come the End'. David too once said: 'And all the Earth shall be filled with his glory. So be it, so be it'.

6. So, no one is to arianize by attaching ignorance to Christ's Godhead or paulianize or nestorianize by attaching it to his manhood. For being one and the same in prosopon and hypostasis he clearly has acquaintance with the day and hour, and with his holy Father and the life-giving Spirit, with whom he blesses, hallows and enlightens every human being come and to come into the world, along with all the fullness of the Church, now and ever and world without end, Amen.

III

I pass to some annotations.

(i) *The title and setting*

The title is not by Stephen, at least not as it now stands; for nobody calls himself 'most holy and blessed'. It is simply called a 'logos', which I have rendered 'essay'. What sort of a piece is it? A fragment, of course, because a good portion of the essay is missing; but a fragment of what: a sermon, a treatise or a letter? Pretty certainly not a letter, or we should have expected a correspondent or addressee to be named. It is much more likely (I should suggest) to have seen the light of day as a doctrinal address by the archbishop at an occasion when the clergy were assembled round him and were expecting of him some statement of the Church's teaching in the face of a current doctrinal deviation. The doxology at the end, and the firm note of authority in the last paragraph ('no one is to ...') seem to give that away.[1]

The form of the quotation from Mark is identical with that printed in Nestle-Aland, save for the omission of the definite article before 'hour' (a scribal error?); the form of the quotation from Matthew is listed among the variants. If any point turned, for Stephen, upon the different versions of the saying in Matthew and Mark, we do not know what it was. I suspect it did not.[2]

(ii) *The argument*

The first two paragraphs introduce the theme. We are faced with a paradox in the words of Christ, similar to the paradoxes of sense-perception. To resolve it, we need to look closely at the sense of the words and interpret them conformably to the tradition of the Church, without indulging in wanton speculation. Paragraph three identifies those who have fallen into error. They do not belong to Stephen's own communion but are amongst the non-conforming opponents of the council of Chalcedon. The references to Apolinarius, Eutyches and Simon Magus are purely 'functional': that is to say, they define the opposition by ascribing to it a genesis which has only tenuous relation to actuality. The 'monophysites', including those who said that Christ was ignorant of the date and time of the End, vigorously repudiated Apolinarius and Eutyches as heretics. Indeed, it is not a question of mainstream monophysitism; for we can read in Stephen's words a reference to the 'Themistians' or 'Agnoetes', followers of Themistius[3], a deacon of Alexandria, who, in the earlier part of the century, had claimed that Christ's ignorance was real. A few fragments only of Themistius survive (listed under 7285-7292 in CPG) mostly as what one might call 'negative'

---

[1] Diekamp headed the text 'Aus einem Traktate gegen die Agnoeten' and remarks (p. 156) that it is a very rare example of a special treatise devoted to the rebuttal of Agnoetism (the only other known to him being the work of Eulogius, to which I refer below). I would think 'treatise' a fair description, provided an initial oral delivery be allowed for. As for the rarity of the *genre*, there were, as that most distinguished scholar knew, other works written against the 'heresy', the most notable being Theodosius' *Tome*. What Diekamp meant, I think, is that this is a very rare survivor from the Chalcedonian side in Greek. That remains correct.

[2] There are several variants from the Nestle-Aland text in the quotations from *John* 14 and *Acts*, but all are attested elsewhere.

[3] The literature on Themistius is listed by S. Stiernon in *Encyclopedia of the Early Church* (Eng. tr. London, 1992) s.v. The article by E. Amann in *Dictionnaire de Théologie Catholique* 15, s.v. remains valuable.

proof-texts, produced at the third council of Constantinople (687) to indicate what was to be rejected. He was clearly a theologian of distinction: John Philoponus was in controversy with him; his arguments elicited (as we are told by 'Leontius' *De Sectis*–CPG 6823–PG 86a, 1232, and as the lemmata to certain of the fragments bear out) a refutation from Theodosius, pope of Alexandria (died 566) and leader of the union of nonconforming churches of Egypt and Syria. Theodosius' rebuttal[4] was presented to the Empress Theodora, who had a special concern for the nonconformists and the pope's cause. Themistius was not to be silenced and he responded at length in more than one book to his pope. The surviving fragments make clear that for Themistius the starting-point of discussion is the one knowledge, will and activity which Christ has. A fragment from his book *Against Theodosius' Tome* (= CPG 7285) will make the general scheme clear: 'But we do not speak, my good sir, of two knowings (*gnoseis*) of his or two actings (*energeias*). For the acting is one and the knowing is one, of the truly incarnate Word; and we know that all are of the one Christ, even though he knows some things divinely and effects them through his own flesh, and others humanly. For not because sacred Athanasius said that Christ displayed two volitions (*thelemata*) at the time of his passion are we to assign to him two wills (*theleseis*), and these mutually repugnant, in accordance with your syllogisms; but we shall acknowledge with true religion the one will of Emmanuel moved sometimes humanly sometime divinely'. Another fragment, this time from a letter to Marcellinus and Stephen (= CPG 7287) is worth reproducing since it shows that Themistius had taken to heart the formula of Ps-Dionysius: 'For Christ's acting (*energeia*), involved in all things human and divine, is not one and another but one and the same, since all the things are of one and the same. Which is why Dionysius the Areopagite called it "theandric"'. Liberatus, the African church historian, who tells us a little about Themistius (*Breviarium* XIX, ACO 2,5,134), and 'Leontius' both agree that Themistius argued from the unity of Christ's nature and the completeness of his assumed manhood to his genuine ignorance. Stephen says the same about the heretics he is opposing here, though he puts it in a polemical manner: [the Agnoetes] reach their conclusion because they make Christ out to be a single nature and deny one of the two natures 'from which and in which he exists'. Monophysites freely

---

[4] A. Van Roey has prepared an edition of the extensive fragments of Theodosius *Tome,* together with other anti-Agnoete texts, surviving in Syriac.

granted that Christ was 'from two natures' (for that is one way to determine the meaning of 'incarnation'); but they repudiated the expression enshrined in the Chalcedonian formula, 'in two natures'. The reason behind their objection may be expressed, with a large degree of simplification, as a refusal of all talk of Christ which analyses his actions and words into the 'human' and the 'divine': 'out of' is to be read as precluding such an analysis; 'in' allows its possibility. We are not told in these fragments how Themistius argued to Christ's real ignorance, but it must have been along the lines that ignorance of some matters is an essential attribute of humanity; therefore as fully human, Christ was ignorant of such matters as human beings are by necessity ignorant of. But what does that mean? For Christ, according to Themistius, has human limitations but he also has the Father's mind. 'Knowing', for Themistius, is a special case of 'doing'; there is a single 'theandric' *energeia,* whereby Christ does some things humanly, some divinely; Christ knows (actively), and some things he knows divinely some humanly. When Christ says he did not know the date of the end, he is knowing humanly viz. *not* knowing. I will not linger on trying to explain or justify this, for I do not think I can: it seems to me formula without content. It looks as though Themistius was better at pointing to the difficulties than at resolving them.

Stephen's christology is more 'dualist' in formula than the Monophysites'. He is 'neo-Chalcedonian' in using both 'out of' and 'in': according to this standpoint, the prepositions are not exclusive, for the one qualifies the other, and 'in' underlines the continuity of the indivisible union. He is not likely to have been a monenergist or monothelete, but talk of 'theandric' *energeia* would no doubt have seemed to him fully orthodox and the formula of a single will did not overstep the verbal boundaries of the Chalcedonian definition. At any rate, he rejects any solution which proceeds from an analysis into two natures, such that the ignorance could have been real in one of the natures: it is 'Arianism' to ascribe it to Christ's Godhead; 'Paulianism' (i.e. the teaching of Paul of Samosata) or 'Nestorianism' to credit it to the human being on his own; he actually knows because he is one and the same in prosopon and hypostasis. If Stephen is making any distinction between 'prosopon' and 'hypostasis' (for the terms are almost synonymous) he can be glossed as saying: 'one and the same subject' (hypostasis) 'with the distinguishing name, "Jesus"'. Most of Stephen's argument towards this conclusion (viz. that Christ knew the End) is lost. But we have two points that he made: first, that Christ must have known when the End would come because of the saying in *Acts* 1.8; secondly, that if it is literally true that only the Father knows it, then the Holy Ghost does not know it either (sc. which is absurd).

How, then, may we guess, did Stephen reach his conclusion that Christ's ignorance here is only a paradox to the untrained or wilfully obtuse mind? Let us look at some solutions he might well have known about.

(iii) *Some discussions of the passage*

I start from the 'Arians', who are not to be thought of as having more than a loose connection with Arius himself, but rather as theologians of the fourth century who resented any suggestion that the Only-begotten Son and Word of God could be a co-eternal first principle, co-absolute with the 'Sole true God' (*John* 17.3) whom Christ addressed as 'Father'. For some of them it was a decisive objection that Christ was ignorant of the End which only the Father knew. Athanasius produces in *Contra Arianos* III, 42 ff an exegesis designed to assuage the objection. I find the passage difficult to understand, but the implication is that Christ's self-ascription of ignorance is by way of condescension to our human condition. What Christ means is, '*I* know but *you* cannot: human nature is incapable of knowing such a thing'. Cyril of Alexandria adapted Athanasius' exegesis with slight modifications in his *Thesaurus* c.22, and repeated it elsewhere (*Dialogues on the Trinity* 6 and *Answers to Tiberius* 4)[5]. I do not think he wanted to say (as Athanasius probably did) that the ignorance was ironic or pretended; rather, that Christ shares to the full all that belongs to the weakness of the human nature he has taken on, including its limitations of knowledge. Certainly he has knowledge, for he is God, of the future, but as incarnate he cannot disclose it. In effect, Christ is telling his disciples not to feel rebuffed because knowledge, hidden even from the angels, is not granted them. 'Even I will not tell you that, for you could not understand it'. Cyril rejects any solution which suggests that the ignorance is real in the manhood ('the form of the servant') as distinct from his Godhead. When Theodoret propounded it (*Rebuttal of Cyril's Fourth Ana-thematism* ACO 1,1,6 pp. 121 ff) he accused him (predictably) of using

---

[5] PG 75, 368 ff; *ibid.*—Aubert's pagination—623; my edition (*Oxford Early Christian Texts* 1983) 150 ff.

the passage to support a duality of 'sons'. Cyril meant to preserve a unity of consciousness in Christ at the same time as he gives due weight to human limitations of comprehension.

The 'Alexandrine' solution is different from that of the Cappadocians, Basil (*Ep.* 236) and Gregory Nazianzen (*Or.* 30,15). Basil interprets the words as relating to the economy, the divine scheme of salvation. 'All that the Father has is mine' (*John* 16.15) implies that Christ has all knowledge including that of the End. The text of Mark is to be explained as meaning that not even the Son would have known, if the Father had not known. Characteristically for Basil there is a 'priority' of the Father to which the Son defers (though this is not meant to imply an ontological inferiority). Gregory offers a more complex treatment which can be paraphrased as saying that as God Christ knows, but as man he does not know (the Athanasian solution); furthermore, the Son knows because the Father knows what can be known only by ultimate reality.

The passage was a bone of contention for the Anomeans, after Eunomius had ceased active leadership of the heresy. His followers divided over the question, but Eunomius himself held (so Sozomen *Church History* 7,17 tells us) that the Son does know the date and hour of the End. Indeed that seems consistent: must not the immediate expression of ultimate creative will, who has received all things from the Father (*Luke* 10.22), know all that pertains to creation? It will, I think, have been along lines like these that Eunomius maintained the Son's knowledge. How he will have related this to the passage in Mark we do not know. It will not have been interpreted in terms of 'knowledge as man, ignorance as God', since the notions of a duality of natures or a sharp distinction between the conditions of the economy and the pre-incarnate state are foreign to the Anomean approach. I guess that it may well have sounded very much the same solution as Basil's.

Last I mention a discussion which may be nearly contemporary with Stephen's, though I do not suggest he knew it: a treatise *Against Agnoetes* by Eulogius (Chalcedonian) Patriarch of Alexandria from 580-607, summarized by Photius (*Bibliotheca* cod. 230). Eulogius suggested three lines of argument, apparently. First, he points to Christ's asking of questions ('where is Lazarus?') and compares this with the declaration of ignorance. It is ignorance in a transferred, as distinct from a genuine, sense. Christ was really thirsty (*John* 19.28) but only 'sin' (2 *Corinthians* 5.21) in a modified, non-literal sense by a figure of speech. Secondly, the ignorance is an adaptation to human conditions, intended (so to say) to keep the disciples on their toes with surprises to look forward to. Thirdly, the ignorance may be viewed as a mark of the humanity of Christ, divided at the level of theoretical, quasi-scientific, inspection, from the Godhead. The first line of argument Eulogius regards as the most religious. Eulogius sent a copy of the treatise to Pope Gregory who replied in a letter of August 600 (*Reg.* X,21–CCSL 140A pp. 852 ff.) congratulating the author of the work and affirming its consonance with the Latin fathers. He refers to Augustine's several times repeated interpretation of the passage as a figure of speech,[6] which he now adopts himself: 'Just as we call a day "happy" not because the day is itself happy but because it makes us happy, so the omnipotent Son says he does not know the day which he makes to be unknown, not because the Son himself does not know but because he by no means allows the day to be known. Accordingly, the Father alone is said to know, because his consubstantial Son has, from (*ex*) his superangelic nature, the capacity to know what angels are ignorant of. Moreover, thence too, an even more refined interpretation is possible: the Only-begotten when incarnate and made perfect man for our sake, knew the day and hour *in* the nature of the humanity but yet did not know it *from* the nature of the humanity'. The refinement harks back, with its 'in', to Leo's *Tome* and the definition of Chalcedon. I should like to be able to explain, or at least gloss or paraphrase, Gregory here. It is a clever phrase, and sometimes I seem to understand what it means; and then I realise I do not. Fortunately it has, I would think, no special bearing upon Stephen's understanding of the matter, which I would guess must have had a less dualist ring to it.

In the light of these discussions can we surmise how Stephen's argument ran? It would have cohered neatly with the opening of the essay (one can say at least that, but not more) if it picked up the idea of 'paradox' by explaining Christ's words as involving a figure of speech. As for the rest (this is the best I can do) it must be very likely that the solution made reference to the 'economy' and to an educative phase in the preparation of the disciples.

---

[6] See *de Gen. c. Man.* I, xxii.34; *de div. qq. LXXXIII*, 60; *En. in ps.VI* init.; *de Trin.* I, 12, 23 *ad fin.*

IV

Selective quotation from patristic writings can often ferret out some doctrine or idea that seems to deserve promotion. However, I doubt whether the ancient theology offers comfort and support for notions of a 'human' Christ, tolerable with a few frailties, friendly and undemanding, essentially our intellectual inferior. It is exceptional and isolated groups which took Christ's profession of ignorance seriously enough to make it a point of principle. No one, perhaps, would wish to defend them. No more would one wish to defend the ancient orthodoxy which proffered these (one must surely admit) feeble solutions to the paradox of his 'ignorance'. They limp so desperately and become so very difficult to understand.

I would only say this on their behalf: they do not present a Christ who is a mere cipher or deprive the historical figure of his actuality. It would not be fair to say that the ancient theology only yields a sort of 'docetic' Christ. This is quite evident from the way the 'problem' of Christ's ignorance is set up by Stephen and the others: a real, historical person is said to have uttered a paradox, by declaring he does not know something which he clearly (from the rest of the story and considerations of reason) must know. The human sympathy of Christ is given a special warmth by those 'solutions' to the paradox, which emphasize the concern he has for his disciples. The human engagement of God is given a fresh and vivid illustration. The Christian intuition of the ultimate in our midst is expressed in terms which owe something, but not much, to talk of 'natures'. I must not argue from the particular to the general, but I may be allowed to affirm as a point of belief that the ancient theology did not lose sight of the adjectival qualification 'in out midst'; and I think I have shown that the discussions I have drawn attention to, whatever their merits on other grounds, do not present a Christ whose actuality has been obscured by technical philosophy.

MACRINA'S DEATHBED REVISITED:
GREGORY OF NYSSA ON MIND AND PASSION

ROWAN WILLIAMS

It is surprising—and very regrettable—that we still lack a full modern treatment of Gregory of Nyssa's anthropology. There are plenty of studies that cover significant areas of the territory,[1] but little of value attempting to synthesise what is, all in all, one of the more substantially original clusters of ideas in patristic theology. We know something about Gregory's acquaintance with the medical ideas of his day, and his physiological assumptions have been (sketchily) discussed.[2] We know a fair bit about his understanding of the divine image in human beings,[3]

---

[1] H. Cherniss, *The Platonism of Gregory of Nyssa* [UCPCP XI.1] (Berkeley 1930), 12-25, has exerted a significant and not always benign influence on studies in the field. See also A.H. Armstrong, 'Platonic Elements in St Gregory of Nyssa's Doctrine of Man', *Dominican Studies* 1 (1948), 113-126 (especially 120-6), S. de Boer, *De anthropologie van Gregorius van Nyssa* (1968), for a thorough but rather mechanical account, and J. Cavarnos, 'The Relation of the Body and Soul in the Thought of Gregory of Nyssa'; in *Gregor von Nyssa und die Philosophie; Zweites Internationales Kolloquium über Gregor von Nyssa*, ed. H. Dörrie, M. Altenburger and U. Schramm (Leiden 1976), 61-78, which is good on the different sorts of conceptual division used by Gregory in discussing the soul. Perhaps the best and most judicious study is still G. Ladner, 'The Philosophical Anthropology of St Gregory of Nyssa', *Dumbarton Oaks Papers* 12 (1958), 59-74. The recent dissertation of Charalambos Apostoloulos, *Phaedo Christianus: Studien zur Verbindung und Abwägung des Verhältnisses zwischen den platonischen "Phaidon" und dem Dialog Gregors von Nyssa "Ueber die Seele und die Auferstehung"*, Diss. Frankfurt am Main 1986, should also be mentioned.

[2] Cavarnos (*op. cit. n.1*), 71-3; see also Cuesta J. Janini, *La antropologia y medicina pastoral de s. Gregorio de Nyssa* (Madrid 1946). In addition to the use of medical information in *de anima et resurrectione* and *de hominis opificio*, the *epistula canonica* (PG 45, 224A-225B) also speaks in medical language about the taming of the passions. The general notions here of 'therapy' for the soul by the training of the passions can be found particularly in Galen's *de cognoscendis curandisque animi morbis* (translated as *Galen on the Passions and Errors of the Soul* by P.W. Harkin (Ohio State University Press 1963)).

[3] The standard work remains R. Leys, *L'image de Dieu chez Grégoire de Nysse* (Brussels 1951), though the reader should be aware of how its presentation is shaped by the contemporary controversies over the *nouvelle théologie*—in particular, the

and his spiritual teaching, with its carefully nuanced ambivalence about
the glory and the finitude of the created *nous*, has been explored with
exemplary care and sympathetic imagination in some of the finest
works of patristic interpretation in this century.[4] But is there a coherent
understanding of the human constitution in which all these elements
find their place? This paper does not set out to offer a grand synthesis of
Gregory's thought on human nature, but simply to examine one particular area in which his consistency and intelligibility has been challenged. Debate about the 'divisions' of the soul in Gregory go back to
the first decades of this century,[5] and a good deal of more recent discussion has, I think, been hampered by assumptions made in earlier
writing. I propose to suggest some readings of Gregory which might
help to minimise more obvious tensions, while granting that many remain, and to advance our grasp of the themes that unify Gregory's
anthropology and render it such a distinctive, even if unsystematic, contribution to Christian theology.

In an article of 1982, very typical in its breadth of reference and clarity of exposition,[6] Christopher Stead intimates that one of Gregory's
most extended treatments of the nature of the human subject, the *de
anima et resurrectione* (henceforth DAR),[7] is pervaded by some old and

---

question of the gratuity of grace and the possibility of human life lived entirely in a
'natural' mode. See also H. Merki, *Homoiosis theo(i). Von der platonischen Anglei-
chung an Gott zur Gottähnlichkeit bei Gregor von Nyssa* (Freiburg 1952).

[4] Above all the works of H.U.von Balthasar, *Présence et pensée. La philosophie
religieuse de Grègoire de Nysse* (Paris 1942). Also J. Daniélou, *Platonisme et théologie mystique: doctrine spirituelle de s. Grègoire de Nysse* (Paris 1953) and E.
Mühlenberg, *Die Unendlichkeit Gottes bei Gregor von Nyssa* (Göttingen 1966).

[5] Gregory was claimed as teaching a Posidonian view in the celebrated work of K.
Gronau, *Poseidonios und die Jüdisch-Christliche Genesisexegese* (Berlin 1914). This
was sharply criticised in a review by R.Jones in *Classical Philology* 12 (1917), though
even he grants some points of contact between Gregory and Posidonius (see below,
n.30). Cherniss' work represents the high watermark of reaction against pan-Posido-
nianism, in favour of seeing Gregory as an exponent of Plato's teaching about the soul
as essentially indivisible and immutable, though attended by passionate and changeable elements. I am much indebted in the consideration of these questions to the re-
search of Michel Barnes of the University of St Michael's College, Toronto, whose
doctoral dissertation contains a full discussion of the points at issue between Gronau
and his American critics.

[6] G. C. Stead, 'The Concept of Mind and the Concept of God in the Christian
Fathers', in *The Philosophical Frontiers of Christian Theology. Essays Presented to
Donald MacKinnon*, ed. B. Hebblethwaite and S. Sutherland (Cambridge 1982), 39-54.

[7] Sadly, no modern critical edition yet exists; all references are to the text in PG
46.

obstinate misunderstandings of what can intelligibly be said about human psychology, misunderstandings whose pedigree is traceable to both Plato and Aristotle. Despite a 'disavowal of Gnostic pessimism', the work leaves us with a doctrine that alienates what is 'essentially' human, the rational power in which is the image of God, from the 'accretions' represented by animal impulse, neutral in itself, but transformed into corrupting passion when it escapes from rational control. The picture of the human subject as a core of rationality with impulse added on by extraneous circumstance has the effect of repeating 'Aristotle's mistake of regarding man simply as an animal with reason added on as an extra capacity'.[8] That is to say, it perpetuates the myth that the human subject is a hybrid, with no single or integrated *good*: the goods sought by one element are inimical to the goods of the other(s). In this, Aristotle and Plato stand together.[9] The further implication, Stead suggests, is that the rational faculty itself is thus 'exempted from moral evaluation'[10]: there is no way of discriminating morally between intelligence collaborating with and furthering the ends of selfish impulse and intelligence harnessed to love or generosity, since reason, the *logikē dunamis*, is good in and of itself. The disjunction of reason from passion ignores the fact that concrete moral life is always a matter of intelligence interacting with impulse. Gregory's account of human subjectivity and intentionality, as presented in the dialogue through the mouth of his sister Macrina, is thus highly problematic; the Platonic tradition from which it stems is internally inconsistent and unsustainable,[11] and also irreconcilable with the Christian commitment to loving engagement, which has a necessarily affective component. DAR exemplifies the final unsatisfactoriness of Platonised Christianity.

The question of what Plato is really doing with his divisions of the soul is a complicated one, already a subject of discussion in antiquity.[12]

---

[8] Stead (*op. cit. n. 6*), 48.

[9] *Ibid*; both, according to Stead, fail to consider the dangers of treating intelligence as an *adjunct* to impulse. When so regarded, intelligence is understood as standing alongside impulse with a set of rival goals—goals which, in the case of intelligence, are treated as necessarily good, while other goals are indifferent or bad. Such a picture neglects the inevitable interaction of intelligence and impulse, and the possibility of corrupt intelligence. As I hope to show, the position Gregory takes, not at all untypical of his age, is by no means as *simpliste* as this suggests.

[10] *Ibid.*

[11] *Ibid* 43-5, 46.

[12] For Galen's treatment of the divided soul in the Republic, see his *de placitis Hippocratis and Platonis* VI/1 (p 512-3 in the Leipzig edition of 1823); *ibid* VI/.2 on

I shall not engage in length with this here, though I hope to do so at more suitable length elsewhere.[13] Enough for now to observe that both the *Symposium* and the *Phaedrus* are attempts to salvage the idea of a unitary good for the soul, as against the more fragmented images offered in the *Phaedo* or the *Republic*. This is particularly acute in the latter, where elements of the soul with incompatible goods are brought into line by the skilful management of a 'highest' part which can unite rhetoric and coercion. That Gregory is the inheritor, albeit remotely, of the tensions thus set up is past question, whatever our judgment on the very vexed issue of his immediate philosophical sources.[14] But I shall argue that a closer reading of DAR, in tandem with the roughly contemporary *de hominis opificio* (henceforth DHO),[15] reveals a good deal more nuance than Stead's summary might suggest, and offers some illuminating sidelights on other areas of Gregory's thought. More can be said, I believe, about Gregory's self-consistency and about his consistency with the fundamental orientations of the Christian tradition; and this may perhaps serve as an incentive for some further examination of what is undoubtedly an elusive and many-sided anthropological vision.

I

In a well-known section of DAR (49C-52A), Macrina briskly dismisses 'Plato's chariot' as a suitable vehicle (so to speak) for thinking about the soul, and declares that she will base her own analysis on scripture rather than philosophy. Since the triad of reason, *thumos* and *epithumia* is taken pretty consistently for granted in DAR (it has just been set out

---

differences between the anthropology of the *Phaedrus* and that of Aristotle, and on the distinction between the Posidonian language of the soul's faculties or powers and Plato's alleged doctrine of the soul's *parts (merē)*.

[13] The present essay arises out of a more extended study of the history of classical and early Christian attitudes to passion and its role in the life of the mind, from Plato to Augustine.

[14] It is now generally agreed to be a mistake to look for a single dominant philosophical influence in Gregory, whether Plato or Posidonius or even Aristotle. If the present paper leans towards an emphasis on Stoic affinities, this is partly because these are still under-explored in a great deal of the literature.

[15] Again, we lack a full critical text, and I have used PG 44; in references, I have employed the division of the text into chapter and subsections followed in the Nicene and Post-Nicene Fathers translation. The French version in *Sources Chrétiennes* (Paris 1943), with the introduction and translation by J. Laplace and J. Daniélou, is helpful.

in 48C-49A), this remark is often read as rather disingenuous—the more so since there are other clear allusions to the *Phaedrus* analogy at 12A and 61BC. In fact, as we shall see, such a reading is not so obvious; and Macrina's (and Gregory's) relation to the *Phaedrus* is more critically differentiated than might at first appear. Take the allusion at the very beginning of the dialogue (12A): Gregory arrives at Macrina's deathbed and is at once overcome by grief; 'but she indulged me for a while, as expert drivers of horses do, letting me yield to the force of passion', before bringing Gregory back to a reasoned perception. Two things are worth noting here. First the oblique reference, as it surely must be, to the Platonic image should remind us that giving rein to passion is itself, for Plato, instrumental to bringing reason closer to its goal: it is a fusion of 'ordinary' desire with the mind's yearning for truth and beauty, the former energising the latter. The passion in question here, however, is not simply the *epithumia* of the Platonic structure: it is grief over impending bereavement, a standard problem in Stoic and sub-Stoic discussions:[16] grief, notoriously, was the one of the four basic affects in Stoic thought hardest to understand in a morally constructive sense.[17] Macrina thus brings the pain of human loss within the pedagogy of the spirit. In what sense? As the discussion immediately goes on to show, it is by making clear to us our fundamental uncertainties or confusions about the nature of the soul, its independence and immortality. The remedy for this disproportionate grief is to learn what the soul is; but we should not know how little we understand the soul if we did not give way to the full instinctive weight of grief. The second point is that, in contrast to the *Phaedrus*, what is at issue is the indulging or yielding to the grief of *someone else*. Letting another person experience their pain without immediate rebuke is the necessary preliminary to educating them in a true perception of the soul's nature.

The dialogue allows Gregory plenty of space (13A-17A) to explain why grief is 'natural', connecting it with our own natural instinct of self-preservation (13Bff); and while Macrina eventually replies with some severity, the dialogue form not only enacts what it discusses (the protracted exploration of an emotion) but, later on, allows Macrina to

---

[16] A very lucid survey is provided by R.C. Gregg, *Consolation Philosophy Greek and Christian Paideia in Basil and the Two Gregories* (Cambridge Mass. 1975), chs. 1 and 2.

[17] *Ibid* ch.3; see also J.M. Dillon, '*Metriopatheia* and *Apatheia*: Some Reflections on a Controversy in Later Greek Ethics', in *Essays in Ancient Philosophy* II, ed. J.P. Anton and A. Preu (Albany 1983), 508-17, especially 509-10.

modify her initial rigorism in response to Gregory's objections on behalf of the emotions. In short, we are treated, at the outset of the dialogue, to a skilful rhetorical fusion of form and content; and the *Phaedrus* analogy is evoked at this early stage to pre-empt any undialectical reading of Macrina's apparent critique of the passions wholesale. We know already that she has used a Platonic pedagogy of passion. So, when we come to her later dismissal of the chariot analogy (after a full discussion of the soul's integrity that reflects themes from the *Phaedo*),[18] we should be alert to its implications. What she rejects is the notion of a yoking together of 'colts' that are 'unlike one another in their impulses' (*hormai*—not Plato's word in the *Phaedrus*, though it can be found elsewhere in his work; here it seems like a deliberate Stoicising of the vocabulary);[19] that is to say, she is wary of the so-called *homunculus* problem in writing about the passions, the tendency to treat parts or powers of the soul as quasi-subjects.[20] What follows in Macrina's exposition is in fact a careful ruling-out of any 'independence' for the affective life, while at the same time denying that it is 'intrinsic' to the soul. This is a difficult notion to carry through, and its difficulty has much to do with some of the more flawed readings of DAR common in the literature; though Macrina (or Gregory) certainly cannot be acquitted of some confusion.

The *psuchē* is in God's image, says Macrina, and God is agreed to be without passion (52AB); thus passion cannot be associated with the *ousia* of the soul (*Oude tē(i) psuchē(i) sunousiasthai*). Hence too we cannot say that passion represents what is essential in human nature: passion is what we have in common with the animals (53AB). In looking for the definition of something, we ought to identify what is *unique* to it; what does not belong to this unique character has no power to modify the definition of the nature. Thus the two passionate forces, the *epithumia* and the *thumoeides*, are alien to essential humanity, and, a little later on, are said to be added to it from outside (*exōthen*, 57C).

---

[18] Notably in its discussion of whether the soul is a harmony of the (material) components of the person, not a subject in its own right. On the whole question of DAR's relation to the *Phaedo*, see Apostolopoulos, *(op. cit. n.1)* which, if at times fanciful, identifies some important themes.

[19] The term appears in the *Philebus*, but, as connected to the divisions of the soul, is a predominantly and characteristically Stoic word. *Hormai* are predicated of a reasoning subject; thus their use of the two horses in the *Phaedrus* indicates here that the animals are being taken as quasi-subjects.

[20] On the *homunculus* problem, see, for example, J. Annas, *An Introduction to Plato's Republic* (Oxford 1981), 142 ff., 150-1.

Here, surely, we have an internal plurality of the most crude kind, justifying all the strictures of Stead and others. Yet it stands alongside a notably different model of the relation between rational and animal, developed in 60Aff: here the language is to do with the *inclusion* of the latter in the former, the animal as the basis on which the rational grows. The 'power of animation' (*zōtikē dunamis*) advances slowly through the different levels of material life, from vegetable to animal to rational; and in rational life it is most fully active precisely *as* reason. Yet even at this stage its actual working cannot be divorced from matter and sense experience. Our own *logikē dunamis* requires sense experience for it to operate at all, and we are certainly not exempt, as rational, from the animal instinct for self-preservation (60A-61A9). As 57C has already insisted, the passions may come *exōthen*, but human nature (*phusis*) cannot be examined or understood apart from these motions in the soul.

Is Macrina (or Gregory) simply muddled? How are we to hold together the affirmation that human *phusis* qua rational includes animality—i.e. the vulnerability of the soul to being moved—and the equally clear conviction that human *ousia* is, in effect, impassibly reasonable? To sort this out, we need to go back to an earlier point in the discussion, and also to relate the whole treatment to Gregory's parallel account in DHO. 29Bff of DAR attempts to define *psuchē* in itself (the notion of soul as a harmony of material parts having been discarded in good *Phaedo* style), and concludes that the most satisfactory definition is in terms of *motive power*: soul is what effects motion, and thus is an analogical term, applicable to whatever it is that, at a particular level of existence, produces and sustains the motion appropriate to that level. Hence the expression we have already met, *zōtikē dunamis*, 'animating power', as a characterisation of soul. In human beings, then, soul is a complex concept because the motion appropriate to humans is complex: human *psuchē* is 'created, living, intelligent', but it is also an animating power that works in conjunction with sensible life (29C). Concretely speaking, human intelligence is both an initiator of projects and responsive or susceptible (*antilēptikē*) to a material environment. We might conclude from this that the *distinctive* motive force in human beings is active intelligence, which by its very nature cannot be defined down to the level of stimulus and response; but also that this is not the whole story about human motion, and that active intelligence has no reality apart from the materiality which it animates and with which it interacts. It would be rash to ascribe to Gregory a wholly precise and consistent terminology, but it is noteworthy that he will generally use

ousia for the soul as distinctively active and intelligent, and *phusis* for
the more complex lived reality of soul as animating a body—a point
which should recall the element of fluidity in Aristotle's account of
phusis,[21] and which helps explain the Christological confusions over the
word. Gregory's vocabulary overall certainly does not support a simple
identity of reference between *ousia* and *phusis*:[22] the closest he comes
to this is at DAR 53C, but this is a passage with other difficulties to
which I shall return later.

It is just this distinction which operates in DHO, where the concrete
unity of soul and body is given striking expression. The idea of rational
soul as 'including' lower or more rudimentary forms of soul (vegetative
or 'nutritive' and sensible) is introduced early in the discussion
(VIII.4ff), as is the notion, recurring at the end of the work, of the body
as *showing* the nature of the higher soul. IX.1-3 speaks of the 'music' of
the body, its harmony of behaviour, communicating the soul's reality,
and XXIX.9 tells us to 'read the history of the soul' in the life of the
body (a startling anticipation of Wittgenstein's famous dictum[23] that the
human body is the best picture of the human soul!). Gregory is also
careful to deny the possible implication that there really are a lot of
quasi-agents around, or that the human soul includes subsidiary agencies (*homunculi*):[24] if *psuchē* is an analogical term, its primary and
univocal referent is the reasoning power in us, that which simply and
directly animates by an agency intrinsic to it (XV). But how does this
self-moving power become the motive force in a complex material life
subject to non-rational motivation? There is no human *phusis* free from
passion (XVI.4); why should passion, passivity, be admitted into a life
that should be purely active and self-motivated—for the vulnerable and
passive body certainly does affect, even though it does not determine,
the soul's existence (XII.3ff)? Gregory's answer is a bold demytho-

---

[21] See especially *Physics* II. 1 and 2, and the excellent discussion of J. Lear, *Aristotle. The Desire to Understand* (Cambridge 1988), ch. 2. *Phusis* is the principle by
which any subsistent attains its full or optimal state, a power of intelligible change, the
structure of a process. Cf. P. Ricoeur, *The Rule of Metaphor. Multi-disciplinary Studies of the Creation of Meaning in Language* (Toronto 1977), 42-3: 'Greek man was
far less quick than we are to identify *phusis* with some inert "given"' (42).

[22] Occasionally he can use the terms as functionally equivalent in speaking of the
Trinity, or , in the most general terms, of the character of something; see the entry on
phusis in PGL for examples.

[23] *Philosophical Investigations* 178; cf. *Remarks on the Philosophy of Psychology*
I.281.

[24] See above, n. 20.

logising of Origen. God foresees the instability and infidelity of our created intellects: they will fall from pure contemplation and become incapable of sustaining and transmitting their life as they should (by 'angelic' forms of reproduction inscrutable to us).[25] God thus unites them to animal bodies because these bodies have an unproblematic structure of self-preservation and reproduction: they possess instincts, *hormai*, proper to the maintenance of their kind. The soul or intellect bound to the body is thus enabled to conserve and propagate its life in tandem with the propagation of bodily or animal existence. Sexual division is part of this providential dispensation; and since rational humanity now propagates itself by animal means, animal instinct is passed on alongside the reasoning power (XVI. 7-XVII).

It would be a mistake to think that 'animality' was here being used in an evaluative way. Gregory is quite clear that instinct, including sexuality, is neutral in the animal context and acquires moral colouring only in relation to the goals and activity of mind. Uncontrolled instinct —instinct divorced from any question of specifically human meanings—is what we call *passion* in the human agent: when thought allows itself to be dominated by this non-specifically-human level of motivation, we can rightly call the motion in question evil (XVIII.1);[26] and when thought moulds or controls the instinctive, affects are the raw material of virtue (XVIII.5).[27] Animality is thus capable of *moral* inclusion in the life of mind: it is part of how mind realises itself, its natural finality. This is why it is fatuous to suppose either that body pre-exists soul or that soul pre-exists body (XXVIII): the life of both begins together, and the reasoning power comes to maturity as the body grows (XXIX)—hence the 'Wittgensteinian' observation quoted above about the soul's history. What Gregory effectively says is that human spirituality or intellectuality is not capable of being itself in a 'pure' form:

---

[25] DHO XVII; on the question of postlapsarian sexual differentiation, see F. Floeri, 'Le sens de la "division des sexes" chez Grégoire de Nysse', *Revue des Sciences Religieuses* 27 (1953), 105-11, which sets out the material pretty fully, although its final assessment seems to me to overlook some significant implications.

[26] This passage tells strongly against Stead's interpretation of Gregory/Macrina's view of the passion-intelligence relation in Stead (*op. cit. n. 6*), 48. The possibility of corrupt intelligence is clearly envisaged.

[27] Such a position eventually becomes canonical for Christian moral theology; see Aquinas' treatise on the passions (*Summa Theologiae* Ia IIae, 49-70) for the developed idea that virtue is passion directed to proper ends rather than something proper to intellect in a void.

paradoxically, it can do what it is meant to do only in the hybrid *phusis* which is humanity as we actually know it.

All this strongly confirms a reading of DAR which puts in the forefront the importance of passion and the articulated and differentiated unity of the human agent in history. Whatever Gregory believed, it was *not* that the human subject consisted of a rational core with some embarrassing additions. The language about passion being extrinsic to the definition of human spirituality is partly a self-evident consequence of treating intellectual or spiritual life as intrinsically active and initiatory, partly the result of an unhappy and rather confused assumption that 'essential' definition has to do with some sort of unique substrate only. I am not by any means seeking to acquit Gregory of philosophical muddle. It is true that Macrina's first essay in sorting out the relation of mind to passion makes some very drastic moves—though even here we have to read carefully. Macrina follows Philo[28] in taking Moses as the example of passionless life, when Gregory has objected to the idea that passion is alien to our nature (53BC). How can we properly repudiate what is unmistakably real within us? Macrina's reply seems to oscillate between two different models: she can say that Moses rose above (literally 'was superior to') anger and desire, that he had no resentment and did not desire what *epithumia* usually goes after; and she goes on to say that the *allotriōsis* (alienation) of these passions is not only possible but beneficial for our *ousia*. In fact, *aphanismos* (extermination or obliteration) of passion is a proper goal. In what immediately follows (56A-57A), Macrina uses the argument that, if the soul can be involved in contradictory attitudes because of passion (cowardice and bravery, and so on), these attitudes, which can all be reduced to aggression and desire, cannot be part of the soul's essence, which is simply and immutably 'what it is' (56A).

Gregory is still unhappy (56C-57A), and with some cause. Macrina had left the door open, in her earlier remarks, to the notion that Moses' virtue might consist in not being dominated by passions, or even in having instincts like desire directed to good and unusual ends; but her argument has apparently landed up with the conclusion that *all* affects are bad and should be suppressed. Gregory objects that there are figures in Scripture commended for desire and anger,[29] and that a range of affects

---

[28] See especially *de legum allegoriis* III. 132-4.

[29] Phineas and Daniel: in the case of the latter, the interpretation rests on a Septuagintal mistranslation of *Daniel* 10.19, where 'man greatly loved' is rendered as 'man of desires', *anēr epithumiōn*.

can be found associated with virtue and holiness in assorted biblical texts. Doesn't Macrina's presentation of the case suggest that this ought to be impossible?

Macrina admits (57B) that she has been unclear and concedes the point we have already discussed: *concrete* humanity cannot be thought about without reference to passion. The reasonable soul is the crown of an evolving history of animality, gradually blended with increasing degrees of self-moving capacity. In our present condition, the neutral instincts of animality are liable to turn into self-serving; but we still have the possibility of using the affective life as an *instrument* (60C-61B). Our animality can itself be turned to virtue when reason directs desire and aggression, which are *not* bad in themselves (61A). Aggression can be turned against itself; desire and the 'drive for pleasure' (*hedones energeia*) can be educated towards the soul's good (61C). Macrina rounds off her case with a rather convoluted exegesis of the parable of the wheat and the tares: *hormai* are the good seed sown in the field of our nature; but error, bad judgement about our human ends, is sown among the young shoots of impulse, and so our affective energies settle on distorted goals—anger against others replacing courage and endurance in our inner struggles, desire for material gratification replacing love (*agapē*) for what the mind sees (64B-65B). What cannot be done is to uproot the whole field—since the passions are not different *things* from animal impulse. Thus, the scriptural heroes commended for *epithumia* or *thumos* are those in whom affective impulse moves towards what is higher (*to kreitton*); otherwise these impulses 'become passions and are so designated' (65C-68A).

Thus we have a terminological point rather like the distinction of *ousia* from *phusis*: 'passion' is impulse or affect (i.e. and kind of 'motion' other than the self-movement of the mind) divorced from the proper ends of a reasoning being, impulse as leader (the horse controlling the driver and pulling him along—61B, another *Phaedrus* echo) not as instrument. Presumably then, Moses is not meant to be an example of a life literally without desire and aggression, and what is 'exterminated' in him is passion in the strict sense, impulse being treated by reason as authoritative with reference to nothing but the immediate goals of self-preservation and gratification of material needs. Passion is an internal 'trahison des clercs', reason betraying itself; but it is also therefore something that makes it impossible for impulse itself to do the job it is made to do, which is to sustain the life of a distinctively *reasonable* subject. Self-preservation and self-propagation allied to debased reason become organised and sophisticated refinements of self-seeking, instead of being the support system for a life of contemplating and realising the good. It has to be said that the account given of Moses comes disturbingly near, as it stands, to denying even impulse in his soul; but Macrina, as we noted, has left the door open for her later clarification by speaking of Moses being 'above' the two basic *hormai*. Given this, and the ambiguous phrase about Moses not desiring what others desire, it is still possible to read what is said about Moses as broadly compatible with a doctrine of the potential unity of soul and *hormai*. What has to be obliterated is the corruption of the impulses into 'passions'—conscious abdications by the mind of its vocation in the face of motions outside itself. Macrina does indeed apologise (57B) for not being systematic in her exposition: presumably a more consequent account would have had to begin with the restrictive definition of passion at which she eventually arrives, so as to allow the conclusion that the motions (*kinēmata*) of the soul are in themselves neither virtuous nor vicious—which is, of course, precisely the conclusion of DHO.

II

Locating this scheme against the background of ancient philosophy is harder than it looks. Gregory's final perspective is in many respects far closer to Posidonius than to Plato[30]—the mind governing impulses which are in some sense included in its life, the mind unable to realise its own goals without deploying impulse and affect.[31] Yet the insistence upon the mind's 'essential' integrity, with the *hormai* as extrinsic, though inseparable, elements, and his resolute anti-materialism are very un-Posidonian. In fact, like a good many early Christian moralists,

---

[30] Granting all the notorious difficulties about determining what any of Posidonius' doctrines were, it is still reasonably certain that he taught the presence of different kinds of *attrait* in a single soul, and that 'irrational' motivation had a part to play in the learning of virtue. Jones, in his review of Gronau (*op cit. n.5*) observes that 'Gregory's theory of the relation of the *hormai* to the *logikon* bears a certain resemblance to Posidonius'—though he adds that it is 'too indefinite to allow us to draw any definite conclusions concerning the source' (109). As far as Gregory's immediate sources are concerned, this is true; but it is an observation which ought to have warned us off too facile a Platonic genealogy for the saint.

[31] Posidonius remains enough of a Stoic to understand the soul as organically connected with the life and affects of the animal body, though he does allow a far more radical differentiation of possible human goods than does the Old Stoa.

Gregory unites a predominantly Stoic ethic with the residue of Platonic metaphysical pluralism about the soul, so as to uphold two insights regarded as essential to Christian anthropology: the unity of the soul and the reality of its temptations. A soul that is divisible cannot be immortal; and if the 'divided soul' is really three distinct subjects, not one of them can *really* be a soul in the sense, presumably, of a complex moral agent capable of being judged for good and bad actions (DAR 49A). But the soul is a *complex* agent: its concrete existence is manifestly one in which actions are affected by varying circumstances, internal and external, for good and ill; and a doctrine of the soul's unity which does not account for what a Christian would see as constructive or meritorious struggle is not sustainable. Of course, this is not an exclusively Christian problematic: plenty of other writers arrive at a similar picture. But the issues are sharpened considerably for Christians by the two non-negotiable theological commitments which mark the boundaries of anthropology—a wholly good (intelligible, purposeful) creation and a wholly just judgment.

Does Gregory contribute anything new to reflection on all this? I believe that there are two, related, ways in which he moves the discussion on. The first is his account of a *progressive* integration of 'animating power' with the material world in DAR 60Aff. and DHO VIII, XVI-XVIII and XXIX. The passage from lower to higher stages in creation is not a movement simply from the anarchic to the ordered, the irrational to the rational, in the usual sense of those words. At every level, there is to be found an activating and structuring principle that preserves a kind of balance in things, a conserving and sustaining force. The balance can be upset; excesses of appetite do occur in the animal realm (DAR 61C). But the sub-human creation, in which structuring life battles with the recalcitrance and chanciness of matter, is on the way towards that level of existence in which the structuring force is 'aware of itself', capable of conscious and discriminating action upon its raw material—which now includes not only matter, but those earlier stages of intelligence represented by impulse or appetite. There is no absolute gulf between the animal and the human: the difference is that the *zōtike dunamis* at last comes to full awareness, to the capacity for freely shaping its animality and its environment. Considered *as* free and active in this context, it is by 'essence' distinct from what precedes it— hence the awkwardness of Gregory's exposition, since this does indeed set up what looks like a serious rift in the middle of our psyches. But considered as the formative agency within an animal, instinctual body, it is unintelligible without what it forms and animates,[32] and, as Gregory is at pains to clarify in DHO XXVIII-XXIX, it is entirely contemporary with the body. Neither soul nor body pre-exists the other, as we have noted above. The soul's growth in tandem with the body's thus recapitulates the history of the material-animal creation as a whole—life-giving energy gradually coming to free consciousness.

Gregory is hardly a nineteenth-century evolutionist;[33] 'the history of the material-animal creation' is simply, for him, the history of the six days of creation. But his emphasis on a *single* story of animating intelligence provides him with a distinctive tool for dealing with the problem of uniting psychic unity with psychic conflict. Despite the persistence of the idea of a pure, separable, authentic *psychē,* untouched by 'motions' from outside, the one moral agent to which our theological attention is directed is consistently engaged with the history it inherits, with the body from which it is in practice inseparable and the inchoate rational structure of that body as impulse or *kinēma.* Because the soul is the active rationality of a body that has come into being because of impulse (sexual desire), its agenda, as one might say, is set by that legacy (DHO XVIII.1). What must be grasped is the kinship or continuity of 'animating power' at all its levels. Overlook this, and mind itself is weakened in realising its goals, since it seems that, in the world as it is, the force of 'pure' mind to move towards what it wants is inadequate—or even void (DAR 61B and—even more strongly—65AB: how could we really long for God or battle against evil if desire and aggression were taken away?). The conflict of mind and passion arises only when we are forgetful of their continuity—passion (in the wider sense) sustaining a body which is charged with making sense of itself, coming to 'mean' something, to bear the task of an intelligible communication in the world of what God's life is like; and reason being incapable of so moulding bodily life into meaning without harmony with those impulses which are its own foundation or inchoate forms.

Gregory's second contribution arises out of this. Later in DAR we are taken back yet again to the role of *thumos* and *epithumia* in the spirit's life (88Cff.), and hear again from Gregory an objection to the idea that there will come a point at which desire disappears: even when passion qua irrational or corrupt is purged away, do we not still feel

---

[32] A good Aristotelian point, well taken in Plotinus' recognition that 'matter' of a sort—i.e. passivity of a sort—must be allowed even in the intelligible world, since form must have something to *in*form. See Enneads 2.4 on this question.

[33] There are some useful observations on this in Ladner (*op. cit. n. 1*), 75, n. 66.

longing for the Good (89A)? Macrina's reply is long and quite complex. When the soul simply and directly perceives its own nature as God's image, it cannot be conscious of any lack that has to be made good; but desire presupposes that there are impediments to our being where we want or what we want. When we have what we want, 'enjoyment takes over from desire' (89C). Our created human nature is always 'in movement' (92A)[34]—led by hope, sobered by memory, animated by longing for what is ahead, spurred to new efforts by shame or remorse. God's nature is utterly other: it 'wants' what it is and it is eternally itself. So when the soul is conformed to the divine nature, purified and simplified, it can have no restless searching for what it does not possess (93BC). The only 'motion' left is love for 'the one thing worth loving and longing for (*agapēton kai erasmion*), which it is for ever laying hold on and discovering' (93C). This is love without faith or hope (the reference is to 1 Cor. 13.13), but also love without limit: there is no *koros* for this love, no possibility of having had enough or too much. The action of love has no boundary because the beautiful or good itself has no boundary:[35] it is its nature to be loved and so it cannot ever be loved enough (94C-95A). Thus the purged soul moves Godwards, without impediment, eternally (97B).

That God is described as *erasmion*, an object of *erōs*, is significant. The passionless love of the perfected saint continues to be a search, a movement into new discoveries, not a purely static contemplation. Gregory's belief that the soul's eternal life is eternal growth is one of the best-known and most distinctive of his contributions to the evolution of Christian spirituality: our goal is not timeless repletion but a steady expansion of loving awareness—we might even say, a renewal of wonder. In other works,[36] it is made clear that this is, metaphysically considered, the consequence of an absolute incommensurability between God the creator and the human mind even when fully restored in God's image. But what is suggested by the shape of the argument in DAR is that passion in general and *epithumia* in particular are a kind of lower level image of the soul's natural motion, its endless expansion into the awareness of God. Just as an instinct is an inchoate kind of

---

[34] Cf. the well-known articulations of similar ideas in Gregory's *de vita Moysis*, especially 301B, 377C, 401B.

[35] Cf. again the *de vita Moysis* 300D. For other uses of the language of *erōs* in connection with spirituality, see particularly *de vita Macrinae* 22, 984A.

[36] E.g. *de beatitudinibus* 1, PG44, 1197B, and 6, PG44, 1268ff. See Mühlenberg's work, (*op. cit. n. 4*) for a classic account of this theme.

reasoning, so also it is an inchoate version of that yearning for God which is the soul's 'essential' destiny. Instinct sustains and perpetuates animal life; instinct in harmony with mind sustains the historical life of reasoning animals; mind set free from instinct sustains simply its own existence in pilgrimage towards God's eternally elusive fullness. But this freedom from instinct is—again, concretely and historically—un-realisable without the force of desire in our present empirical humanity to 'launch' it. Desire, bound up with hope and memory in the way Gregory/Macrina describes, looks to satisfactions, goals met or not met, achievements won or lost; it is about lack, want, and so it is, even at its highest, bound to imagined objects and states. Released from this bind-ing through the mind's pedagogy, through being consistently 'moved on' from attachment to specific things and situations, it, and the whole of our psychic constitution, enter into a kind of naked openness to reality beyond specific things and situations—*to kalon*, God: in very un-Gregorian and unclassical language, a passionate receptivity, not tied to gratification (not liable to the *koros* of 94C).

If this is a correct reading of DAR, Gregory has at least outlined a coherent trajectory for a unitary but complex soul. The soul as it actually exists in us is a hierarchy of intentional activities, from the instinctually self-preservative to the reflective and self-directive. Using the latter simply as tools to reinforce and develop the former is a moral and meta-physical nonsense, as well as a recipe for destructive conflict between agents, comparable to the occasional mutually lethal combats of aggressive animals in the subhuman world. Using the former to rein-force or energise the latter is the essence of virtue: in a material and temporal world, reflection moves towards its goals only by deploying the instinctual life of the body, sensitive to concrete incentives and dis-suasives. But—while there is no short cut that allows us to skirt this complex management of the passionate life—this is not the final stage for the reasoning agent. The conviction of our dependence on an un-changeably loving God draws us into a state of strictly objectless atten-tion, love without projection or condition, moving and expanding but not restless, a kind of *erōs*, yet only capable of being called 'desire' in a rather eccentric sense, because of its distance from the processes of wanting and getting, lack and satisfaction. We are challenged to ima-gine a radical lack, accepted without anxiety, hunger, fantasy. *That* is the final form or structure of spirit, the structure within which the whole of our intentionality fits, the prime analogate for the movements of instinct and mind.

III

Three brief observations by way of conclusion:

(i)   There is no opposition in Gregory's thought between the claims of contemplation and the command to love the neighbour as well as God. Neither DAR nor DHO, of course, directly addresses the issues of interpersonal ethics, but there are clues to be followed up; and Gregory's other works—notably his exegeses of the Beatitudes and the Lord's prayer[37]—spell out in plain terms that conformation to the divine life is conformation to the divine act of love for the world. DAR supports this at least negatively: references to the evil use of *thumos* (as at 56AB, 61BC and 65A) underline the destructiveness of resentment or vengefulness against fellow human beings. And it could also be said that the whole text takes ordinary human grief over bereavement, understandable and permissible, as a paradigm of *desire*—i.e. of fixation on an object: grief that is moulded by or attuned to mind ought, presumably, to be able to see the other as more than merely the object of my attachment. This is to read Gregory as faintly anticipating Augustine's remarkable treatment of this matter in Conf. IV, and is admittedly an extrapolation from the text of DAR—but not, I think, an unnatural or indefensible one. Other texts[38] in which Gregory seems to allow full and lasting value to personal diversity in the eyes of God support this general understanding; we should not assume that the focus in DAR on entering into God's self-contemplation implies a closing off of relation or mutual human charity.

(ii)   Gregory clearly sees the soul as essentially without gender, acquiring sexual differentiation only because of God's pre-vision of the Fall. As an excellent recent discussion stresses,[39] this associates sexuality with the whole complex of contingency and materiality, and gives little houseroom to any doctrines of mysterious polarities between male and female in the very depths of psychic life. It allows Gregory to take for granted a fundamental spiritual equality between male and female,[40] a point ironically reinforced by the dramatic setting and even the voca-

---

[37] E.g. *de beatitudinibus* 1, 1208AB, *de oratione dominica*, PG 44, 1180A-Detc.

[38] See, e.g. the text from *de mortuis* quoted by V.E.F. Harrison, 'Male and Female in Cappadocian Theology', *Journal of Theological Studies* (NS) 41 (1990), 441-71, 470.

[39] Harrison (*op. cit. n. 38*).

[40] As in DHO XVI-XVII; cf. the reference to *de triduo spatio* in Harrison (*op. cit. n. 38*), 466, and the whole of her discussion in 465-8.

bulary of DAR. As in the *Symposium*, the sage is being instructed by a holy woman, whose sexual indeterminacy qua spiritual guide is here signalled by her repeated designation as *hē didaskalos*—female article with male noun. Some recent theoretical studies have, of course, argued that the de-gendering of the soul is effectively a masculine strategy to erase the reality of an 'otherness' in human discourse, the otherness always signified in gender difference and sexual polarity overall. In the hands of a male ideologue, this eroding of difference is a plainly political move to neutralise the language of what that discourse cannot contain or control. No doubt this is an element in the language of Gregory and other patristic writers, but I think there may be more to be said. For Gregory, there is, we could say, no such *thing* as the soul in itself: it is always implicated in contingent matter, and even its final liberation for pilgrimage into God depends, as we have seen, upon the deployment and integration of bodiliniess and animality. That is to say, the ungenderedness of the soul is never the actual state of a real subject. But the idea serves a number of purposes: it establishes, as we have noted, an area in which male and female are not determined simply by their opposition/complementarity; they are equal precisely as *embodied mind*, struggling equally with the task of making animal existence into a life that is meaningful or communicative. Among those factors concretely setting the agenda for this task, sexuality has a place, but not a uniquely determinative place. Sexual desire, *erōs* in the usual sense, is, like other features of our instinctual life, capable of carrying reasonable meaning, and is analogous to that fundamental *erōs* for the endless God that binds the polyphony of our intentionality into some sort of unity. Beyond the otherness of gender, or even of embodiedness itself, is the wholly inexhaustible otherness of God, never to be fully assimilated or resolved into identity. If gendered otherness were final or unique, what we could call the civic or civil collaboration of men and women would be constantly shadowed by a difference never to be negotiated—a conclusion menacing to any doctrine of a common human good.[41] This question takes us far from Gregory's actual text, but, again, not impossibly far: there are matters here of considerable import for politics, sexual politics, and the often bizarre appropriation of the latter in contemporary ecclesiastical politics.[42]

---

[41] For a massively subtle and suggestive treatment of this, see Gillian Rose, *The Broken Middle. Out of Our Ancient Society* (Oxford 1992), especially chs. 2 and 5.

[42] In particular the debate over women's ordination and the common claim that tra-

(iii)   Much has been made in modern Gregorian scholarship[43] of the way in which Gregory ties the human enterprise to *temporality* in a way hard to parallel in earlier philosophy. DAR and DHO clearly bear this out: there is no evading the life of animality, which is a life extended in time and propagating itself in time. What these works bring into the foreground is that this entails a serious treatment of how contingency, the particularities of biography, shape spiritual identify. Even when the rhetoric veers closest to speaking of a pure and separable soul, the weight of the argument as a whole returns us to this valuation of human particularity as bound up with the valuation of temporality. It would be interesting—though matter for another paper—to explore how this relates to Gregory's understanding of the resurrection of the body in terms of the conservation of the specific matter of our bodies as well as the individual *eidos*.[44] Obviously, there are large questions here which Gregory does not tackle directly, and which we should hardly expect a theologian of his age and culture to tackle directly. But it is not difficult to see here some anticipation of the Augustinian problematic, paralleled to some extent in the Christian East by Maximus the Confessor, in which strong emphasis is laid upon the uniqueness of the person as interwoven with his or her realising of the divine image. That is to say, we see in Gregory early signs of the direction in which distinctly Christian concerns are beginning to mould philosophical anthropology, in the widest sense.

That the interlocking frames of history, gender and passion form the concrete structure for the soul's journey towards a God who is free from all of them is a paradox, perhaps, but a paradox appropriate to incarnational Christianity. However, lest we should give way to a Christian intellectual triumphalism, it is worth remembering that such a project is not so very far away from what—in a very different register—underlies and informs the *Phaedrus* itself.[45] Macrina's sense of the risks of that

---

ditional Christianity presupposes the kind of ontological difference between male and female that precludes women from exercising priestly functions. As Harrison (*op. cit. n. 38*) points out (469, n.93), nothing in Gregory of Nyssa and little in the other Cappadocians would support this.

[43] Especially in Daniélou (*op. cit. n. 4*) and *L'être et le temps chez Grégoire de Nysse* (Leiden 1970).

[44] This has been well discussed by G.C. Stead, 'Individual Personality in Origen and the Cappadocian Fathers' in *Arché e Telos. L'antropologia di Origene e di Gregorio di Nissa* ed. U. Bianchi (Milan 1981), 170-191.

[45] See especially, the discussion in M. Nussbaum, *The Fragility of Goodness. Luck and Ethics in Greek Tragedy and Philosophy* (Cambridge 1986), ch.7.

dialogue's mythology is real enough; but she is no less haunted, on this her literary deathbed in DAR, by the same challenge, the challenge to reconceive mind itself as the ultimate—and never sated or exhausted—case of *erōs*.

THE PUBLICATIONS OF CHRISTOPHER STEAD

GRAHAM GOULD

Books

1977   *Divine Substance* (Oxford)

1985   *Substance and Illusion in the Christian Fathers, Collected Studies* 224 (London)

1990   *Theologie und Philosophie I: Die Zeit der Alten Kirche, Theologische Wissenschaft* 14.4, trans. Christian Wildberg, ed. A. M. Ritter (Stuttgart, Berlin, Köln)

Translations

1965   E. Hennecke (ed. W. Schneemelcher, English translation ed. R. McL. Wilson), *New Testament Apocrypha* (London), vol. 2, 167-390 [*The Acts of John, The Acts of Peter, The Acts of Paul*]

1972   Werner Foerster (English translation ed. R. McL. Wilson), *Gnosis: A Selection of Gnostic Texts. I: Patristic Evidence* (Oxford), 244-325

Articles in Periodicals, Festschriften *and Collections*

(an asterisk marks an item reprinted in *Substance and Illusion in the Christian Fathers*)

1957   "How Theologians Reason", *Faith and Logic: Oxford Essays in Philosophical Theology*, ed. Basil Mitchell (London), 108-31 [reprinted 1958]

1959   "New Gospel Discoveries", *Theology* 62, 321-7

1961   * "The Significance of the *Homousios*", *Studia Patristica* 3, ed. F.L. Cross, *Texte und Untersuchungen zur Geschichte der altchristlichen Literatur* 78 (Berlin), 397-412

1963   * "Divine Substance in Tertullian", *Journal of Theological Studies*
         14, 46-66

         "Revised Reviews: XX—Essays Catholic and Critical", *Theology*
         66, 15-19

1964   "Some Reflections on the Gospel of Thomas", *Studia Evangelica* 3,
         ed. F.L. Cross, *Texte und Untersuchungen zur Geschichte der alt-
         christlichen Literatur* 88 (Berlin), 390-402

         * "The Platonism of Arius", *Journal of Theological Studies* 15, 16-
         31

1969   * "The Valentinian Myth of Sophia", *Journal of Theological Studies*
         20, 75-104

1973   * "'Eusebius' and the Council of Nicaea", *Journal of Theological
         Studies* 24, 85-100

1974   * "The Origins of the Doctrine of the Trinity", *Theology* 77, 508-17,
         582-88

         "'Homoousios' dans la Pensée de saint Athanase", *Politique et
         Théologie chez Athanase d'Alexandrie: Actes du Colloque de Chan-
         tilly de 23-25 Septembre 1973*, ed. C. Kannengiesser, *Théologie His-
         torique* 27 (Paris), 231-53

1975   * "The Concept of Divine Substance", *Vigiliae Christianae* 29, 1-14

1976   * "Rhetorical Method in Athanasius", *Vigiliae Christianae* 30, 121-
         37

         * "Ontology and Terminology in Gregory of Nyssa", *Gregor von
         Nyssa und die Philosophie. Zweites internationales Kolloquium
         über Gregor von Nyssa, Freckenhorst bei Münster, 18-23 Septem-
         ber 1972*, ed. H. Dörrie, M. Altenberger and U. Schramm (Leiden),
         107-27

         "Interpretation of 'De Infantibus' 11, 16-14, 22", *Colloquii Grego-
         riani III Leidensis 18/23-IX-1974 Acta*, ed. J.C.M. van Winden and
         A. van Heck (Leiden), 34-41

1978   * "The *Thalia* of Arius and the Testimony of Athanasius", *Journal
         of Theological Studies* 29, 20-52

1979   "Foundation Documents of the Faith I: The Apostles' Creed",
         Expository Times 91, 4-8

1980   * "Athanasius' *De Incarnatione*: an Edition Reviewed", *Journal of Theological Studies* 31, 378-90

* "In Search of Valentinus", *The Rediscovery of Gnosticism I: The School of Valentinus. Proceedings of the International Conference at Yale, New Haven, Ct., March 28-31 1978*, ed. Bentley Layton, *Studies in the History of Religions* 12 (Leiden), 75-95

1981   * "Individual Personality in Origen and the Cappadocian Fathers", *Arché e Telos. L'antropologia di Origene e di Gregorio di Nissa. Analisi storico-religiosa (Atti del Colloquio, Milano, 17-19 maggio 1979*, ed. U. Bianchi with H. Crouzel *Studia Patristica Mediolanensia* 12 (Milan), 170-91

"Conjectures on the *Acts of John*", *Journal of Theological Studies* 32, 152-3

"Introduction", *The Easter Sermons of Gregory of Nyssa. Translation and Commentary. Proceedings of the Fourth International Colloquium on Gregory of Nyssa. Cambridge, England, 11-15 September 1978*, ed. Andreas Spira and Christoph Klock, *Patristic Monograph Series* 9 (Cambridge, Ma.), vii-viii

1982   * "The Concept of Mind and the Concept of God in the Christian Fathers", *The Philosophical Frontiers of Christian Theology: Essays Presented to D.M. MacKinnon*, ed. B. Hebblethwaite and S.R. Sutherland (Cambridge), 39-54

* "The Motives of Christian Confession in the Ancient Church", *Confessio Fidei (International Ecumenical Colloquium, Rome, 3-8 November 1980)*, *Studia Anselmiana* 81 (Rome), 37-53

"The Scriptures and the Soul of Christ in Athanasius", *Vigiliae Christianae* 36, 233-50

"Reflections on the Arian Crisis", response to C. Kannengiesser, *Holy Scripture and Hellenistic Hermeneutics in Alexandrian Christology: The Arian Crisis, Center for Hermeneutical Studies in Hellenistic and Modern Culture, Colloquy 41* (Berkeley), 73-6

1983   "Atanasio", *Dizionario patristico e di antichità cristiane*, ed. Angelo di Berardino (Rome), vol. 1, cols. 423-32

* "The Freedom of the Will and the Arian Controversy", *Platonismus und Christentum: Festschrift für Heinrich Dörrie*, ed. H.-D. Blume and F. Mann, *Jahrbuch für Antike und Christentum, Ergänzungsband* 10 (Münster Westfalen), 245-57

1984   "Gott V: Alte Kirche", *Theologische Realenzyklopädie*, ed. G. Müller (Berlin), vol. 13, 652-7

1985   "St. Athanasius on the Psalms", *Vigiliae Christianae* 39, 65-78

"Arius on God's 'Many Words'", *Journal of Theological Studies* 36, 153-7

1986   "Accidens", *Augustinus-Lexicon*, ed. Cornelius Mayer *et. al.* (Basel), vol. 1, fasc. 1-2, cols. 51-3

1987   "The Apostles' Creed", *Foundation Documents of the Faith*, ed. C.S. Rodd (Edinburgh), 1-11 [reprinted from 1979]

1988   "Athanasius' Earliest Written Work", *Journal of Theological Studies* 39, 76-91

"Logic and the Application of Names to God", *El Contra Eunomium I en la Produccion Literaria de Gregorio de Nisa*, ed. L.F. Mateo-Seco and J.L. Bastero (Pamplona), 303-20

"Aristoteles", *Augustinus-Lexicon*, ed. Cornelius Mayer *et. al.* (Basel), vol. 1, fasc. 3, cols. 445-8

1989   "The Knowledge of God in Eusebius and Athanasius", *The Knowledge of God in the Graeco-Roman World*, ed. J. Mansfield *et. al.* (Leiden), 229-42

"Divine Simplicity as a Problem for Orthodoxy', *The Making of Orthodoxy: Essays in Honour of Henry Chadwick*, ed. Rowan Williams (Cambridge), 255-69

"Augustine's Philosophy of Being", *The Philosophy in Christianity*, ed. Godfrey Vesey (Cambridge), 71-84

"Augustine's 'De Magistro': a Philosopher's View", *Signum Pietatis: Festgabe für Cornelius Mayer OSA zum 60. Geburtstag,* ed. Adolar Zumkeller OSA (Wurzburg), 63-73

1990   "The Arian Controversy: A New Perspective", Ἑρμηνεύματα: *Festschrift für Hadwig Hörner zum sechzigsten Geburtstag*, ed. Herbert Eisenberger (Heidelberg), 51-9

"Why Not Three Gods? The Logic of Gregory of Nyssa's Trinitarian Doctrine", *Studien zu Gregor von Nyssa und der Christlichen Spätantike*, ed. Hubertus R. Drobner and Christoph Klock, *Supplements to Vigiliae Christianae* 12 (Leiden), 149-63

1991   "Greek Influence on Christian Thought", *Early Christianity: Origins and Evolution to A.D. 600. In Honour of W.H.C. Frend*, ed. Ian Hazlett (London), 175-85

"Logos", *Theologische Realenzyklopädie*, ed. G. Müller (Berlin), vol. 21, 432-44

"Athanasius", *Encyclopedia of the Early Church*, ed. Angelo di Berardino, trans. Adrian Walford (Cambridge), 93-5 [see 1983 for original publication]

Reviews

1951   Gavin Ardley, *Aquinas and Kant* (London, 1950), *Journal of Theological Studies* 2, 126-7

1952   H.D. Lewis, *Morals and Revelation* (London, 1951); W.H.V. Reade, *The Christian Challenge to Philosophy* (London 1951), *Journal of Theological Studies* 3, 152-4

1953   Fulton J. Sheen, *Philosophy of Religion* (Dublin and London 1952), *Journal of Theological Studies* 4, 139

C.H. Dodd, *Gospel and Law* (Cambridge 1951); *Journal of Theological Studies* 4, 139-41

F.H. Heinemann, *Existentialism and the Modern Predicament* (London 1953), *Theology* 56, 433-4

1957   E.L. Mascall, *Via Media, an Essay in Theological Synthesis* (London 1956), *Journal of Theological Studies* 8, 382-5

1959   G.F. Woods, *Theological Explanation* (London 1959), *Theology*, 432-3

1960   R. McL. Wilson, *The Gnostic Problem* (London 1958), *Journal of Theological Studies* 11, 156-8

J. Daniélou, *The Lord of History: Reflections on the Inner Meaning of History* tr. N. Abercrombie (London and Chicago 1958), *Journal of Theological Studies* 11, 235

1961   R. McL. Wilson, *Studies in the Gospel of Thomas* (London, 1960); Bertil Gärtner, *The Theology of the Gospel of Thomas* (London 1960); *The Gospels Reconsidered* by various authors (Oxford 1960);

J.N. Birdsall, *The Bodmer Papyrus of the Gospel of John* (Leicester 1960), *Theology* 64, 429-31

1963   A.R. Vidler (ed.), *Soundings: Essays Concerning Christian Understanding* (Cambridge 1962), *Journal of Theological Studies* 14, 559-64

Ernst Haenchen, *Die Botschaft des Thomas-Evangeliums, Theologische Bibliothek Töpelmann* 6 (Berlin 1961), *New Testament Studies* 9, 300-01

1964   Paul L. Lehmann, *Ethics in a Christian Context* (London 1963), *Journal of Theological Studies* 15, 490-3

Hugo Rahner, *Greek Myths and Christian Mystery* (London 1963), *Classical Review* 78, 184-5

1965   E. Hennecke, *Neutestamentliches Apocryphen in deutscher Übersetzung*, 3rd ed. rev. W. Schneemelcher, vol. 2 (Tübingen 1964), *Journal of Theological Studies* 16, 171-5

1966   Manfred Hornschuh, *Studien zur Epistula Apostolorum, Patristische Texte und Studien* 5 (Berlin 1965), *Journal of Theological Studies* 17, 171-3

Peter Gerlitz, *Ausserchristlichen Einflüsse auf die Entwicklung des christlichen Trinitätsdogmas* (Leiden 1963), *Journal of Theological Studies* 17, 173-4

Joachim Jeremias, *Unknown Sayings of Jesus*, tr. R.H. Fuller (London 1964), *Journal of Theological Studies* 17, 432-3

1968   Richard A. Norris, *God and the World in Early Christian Theology: A Study in Justin Martyr, Irenaeus, Tertullian and Origen* (London 1966), *Journal of Theological Studies* 19, 443

1969   R. McL. Wilson, *Gnosis and the New Testament* (Oxford 1968), *Journal of Theological Studies* 20, 626-7

1970   Jacques Liébart, *Deux Homélies Anoméennes pour l'Octave de Pâques, Sources Chrétiennes* 146 (Paris 1969), *Journal of Theological Studies* 21, 191-5

Michel Malinine, Henri-Charles Puech, Gilles Quispel, Walter Till, Rodolphe Kasser, R. McL. Wilson, Jan Zandee, *Epistula Jacobi Apocrypha, Codex Jung F. I^r-F. VIII^v (pp. 1-16)* (Zürich and Stuttgart 1968), *Journal of Theological Studies* 21, 483-5

1971   T.E. Pollard, *Johannine Christology and the Early Church*, Society for New Testament Studies Monograph Series 13 (Cambridge 1970), *Journal of Theological Studies* 22, 610-12

1972   W.E.G. Floyd, *Clement of Alexandria's Treatment of the Problem of Evil* (Oxford 1971), *Journal of Theological Studies* 23, 495

1973   Walter Bauer, *Orthodoxy and Heresy in Earliest Christianity*, edited by R.A. Kraft and G. Krodel (London 1972), *Theology* 76, 433-4

1974   Salvatore R.C. Lilla, *Clement of Alexandria: A Study in Christian Platonism and Gnosticism* (Oxford 1971), *Journal of Theological Studies* 25, 189-90

        Éphrem Boularand, *L'Hérésie d'Arius et la 'Foi' de Nicée. Première partie: L'Hérésie d'Arius* (Paris 1972), *Journal of Theological Studies* 25, 190-1

        Patrick Granfield and Josef A. Jungmann (eds.), *Kyriakon: Festschrift Johannes Quasten*, 2 vols. (Münster Westfalen 1970), *Journal of Theological Studies* 25, 509-13

1975   Edwin M. Yamauchi, *Pre-Christian Gnosticism: A Survey of the Proposed Evidences* (London 1973), *Journal of Theological Studies* 26, 187

        E.A.E. Reymond and J.W.B. Barns (eds.), *Four Martyrdoms from the Pierpoint Morgan Coptic Codices* (Oxford 1973), *Theology* 78, 494-5

1976   Rodolphe Kasser (ed.), *Tractatus Tripartitus 1: De Supernis. Codex Jung F. XXVI^r-F. LII^v (p. 51-104)* (Bern 1973), *Journal of Ecclesiastical History* 27, 181-3

1977   Elaine Hiesey Pagels, *The Gnostic Paul: Gnostic Exegesis of the Pauline Letters* (Philadelphia 1975), *Journal of Theological Studies* 28, 176-7

1978   H.A. Drake, *In Praise of Constantine: a Historical Study and New Translation of Eusebius' Tricennial Orations* (Berkeley, Los Angeles, and London 1976), *Journal of Ecclesiastical History* 29, 94-5

1979   Gerhard May, *Schöpfung aus dem Nichts?, Arbeiten zur Kirchengeschichte* 48 (Berlin and New York 1978), *Journal of Theological Studies* 30, 547-8

V. Loi *et. al.*, *Ricerche su Ippolito* (Rome, 1977); Klaus Koschorke, *Hippolyts Ketzerbekämpfung und Polemik gegen die Gnostiker, Göttinger Orientforschungen, VI Reihe: Hellenistica Band 4* (Wiesbaden 1975), *Journal of Theological Studies* 30, 549-53

1981   Rudolf Lorenz, *Arius judaizens? Untersuchungen zur dogmengeschichtlichen Einordnung des Arius, Forschungen zur Kirchen- und Dogmengeschichte* 31 (Göttingen 1979), *Vigiliae Christianae* 35, 299-302

1982   R.C. Gregg and D.E. Groh, *Early Arianism: a View of Salvation* (London 1981), *Journal of Theological Studies* 33, 285-9

Colm Luibheíd, *Eusebius of Caesarea and the Arian Crisis* (Dublin 1978), *Journal of Theological Studies* 33, 346

1983   Gérard Vallée, *A Study in Anti-Gnostic Polemics: Irenaeus, Hippolytus and Epiphanius, Studies in Christianity and Judaism* 1 (Waterloo, Ontario 1981), *Journal of Theological Studies* 34, 285-6

J.N.D. Kelly, *Early Christian Doctrines* (London 1977⁵), *Journal of Theological Studies* 34, 639-40

Colm Lubheíd, *The Council of Nicaea* (Galway 1982), *Journal of Ecclesiastical History* 34, 478

G.R. Evans, *Augustine on Evil* (Cambridge 1982), *Expository Times* 94, 376

Wolfgang A. Bienert, *Dionysius von Alexandrien: Zur Frage des Origenismus im 3. Jahrhundert, Patristische Texte und Studien* 21 (Berlin 1978), *Zeitschrift für Kirchengeschichte* 94, 122-4

1984   Édouard des Places, *Eusèbe de Césarée commentateur: platonisme et écriture sainte, Théologie Historique* 63 (Paris 1982), *Journal of Theological Studies* 35, 230-2

Marie-Josèphe Rondeau, *Les commentaires patristiques du psautier (III-V siècles)*, vol. 1, *Les travaux des pères grecs et latins sur le psautier. Recherches et bilan, Orientalia Christiana Analecta* 219 (Rome 1982), *Journal of Theological Studies* 35, 556-8

F.M. Young, *From Nicaea to Chalcedon: A Guide to the Literature and its Background* (London 1983), *Journal of Ecclesiastical History* 35, 147-9

1985   Charles Kannengiesser, *Athanase d'Alexandrie: évêque et écrivain, Théologie Historique* 70 (Paris 1983), *Journal of Theological Studies* 36, 220-9

1986   Mariette Canévet, *Grégoire de Nysse et l'Herméneutique Biblique. Études des rapports entre le langage et le connaissance de Dieu* (Paris 1983), *Journal of Theological Studies* 37, 223-6

        W.H.C. Frend, *Saints and Sinners in the Early Church* (London 1985), *Journal of Ecclesiastical History* 37, 484

        Joseph Wilson Trigg, *Origen: The Bible and Philosophy in the Third-Century Church* (London 1985), *Theology* 89, 161-3

1987   R.C. Gregg (ed.), *Arianism: Historical and Theological Reassessments, Patristic Monograph Series* 11 (Cambridge, Ma. 1985), *Journal of Theological Studies* 38, 199-205

        André Villey (ed.), *Alexandre de Lycopolis: contre la doctrine de Mani, Sources Gnostiques et Manichéennes* 2 (Paris 1985), *Journal of Theological Studies* 38, 526-7

        Gerald Bonner, *St. Augustine of Hippo: Life and Controversier* (Norwich 1986[2]), *Journal of Ecclesiastical History* 38, 488

1988   George Dion Dragas, *St. Athanasius contra Apollinarem* (Athens 1985), *Journal of Theological Studies* 39, 250-3

        Basil Studer, *Gott und unsere Erlösung im Glauben der alten Kirche* (Düsseldorf 1985), *Journal of Ecclesiastical History* 39, 139

1989   H. Dörrie, *Der Platonismus in der Antike: Grundlagen, System, Entwicklung. I Die Geschichtlichen Wurzelm des Platonismus* (Stuttgart-Bad Cannstadt 1987), *Journal of Theological Studies* 40, 230-2

1990   R.P.C. Hanson, *The Search for the Christian Doctrine of God* (Edinburgh 1988), *Journal of Theological Studies* 41, 668-73

        W.H.C. Frend, *Archaeology and History in the Study of Early Christianity, Collected Studies* 282 (London 1988), *Journal of Ecclesiastical History* 41, 327

1991   Frances M. Young, *The Making of the Creeds* (London 1990), *Theology* 94, 363-4

        Alvyn Pettersen, *Athanasius on the Human Body* (Bedminster 1991), *Journal of Theological Studies* 42, 732-5

INDEX OF BIBLICAL REFERENCES

INDEX OF MODERN AUTHORS AND EDITORS

SUPPLEMENTS TO VIGILIAE CHRISTIANAE

1. TERTULLIANUS. *De idololatria.* Critical Text, Translation and Commentary by J.H. Waszink and J.C.M. van Winden. Partly based on a Manuscript left behind by P.G. van der Nat. 1987. ISBN 90 04 08105 4
2. SPRINGER, C.P.E. *The Gospel as Epic in Late Antiquity.* The *Paschale carmen* of Sedulius. 1988. ISBN 90 04 08691 9
3. HOEK, A. VAN DEN. *Clement of Alexandria and His Use of Philo in the* Stromateis. An Early Christian Reshaping of a Jewish Model. 1988. ISBN 90 04 08756 7
4. NEYMEYR, U. *Die christlichen Lehrer im zweiten Jahrhundert.* Ihre Lehrtätigkeit, ihr Selbstverständnis und ihre Geschichte. 1989. ISBN 90 04 08773 7
5. HELLEMO, G. *Adventus Domini.* Eschatological Thought in 4th-century Apses and Catecheses. 1989. ISBN 90 04 08836 9
6. RUFIN VON AQUILEIA. *De ieiunio I, II.* Zwei Predigten über das Fasten nach Basileios von Kaisareia. Ausgabe mit Einleitung, Übersetzung und Anmerkungen von H. Marti. 1989. ISBN 90 04 08897 0
7. ROUWHORST, G.A.M. *Les hymnes pascales d'Ephrem de Nisibe.* Analyse théologique et recherche sur l'évolution de la fête pascale chrétienne à Nisibe et à Edesse et dans quelques Eglises voisines au quatrième siècle. 2 vols: I, Etude; II, Textes. 1989. ISBN 90 04 08839 3
8. RADICE, R. and D.T. RUNIA. *Philo of Alexandria.* An Annotated Bibliography 1937-1986. In Collaboration with R.A. Bitter, N.G. Cohen, M. Mach, A.P. Runia, D. Satran and D.R. Schwartz. 1988. repr. 1992. ISBN 90 04 08986 1
9. GORDON, B. *The Economic Problem in Biblical and Patristic Thought.* 1989. ISBN 90 04 09048 7
10. PROSPER OF AQUITAINE. *De providentia Dei.* Text, Translation and Commentary by M. Marcovich. 1989. ISBN 90 04 09090 8
11. JEFFORD, C.N. *The Sayings of Jesus in the Teaching of the Twelve Apostles.* 1989. ISBN 90 04 09127 0
12. DROBNER, H.R. and KLOCK, CH. *Studien zur Gregor von Nyssa und der christlichen Spätantike.* 1990. ISBN 90 04 09222 6
13. NORRIS, F.W. *Faith Gives Fullness to Reasoning.* The Five Theological Orations of Gregory Nazianzen. Introduction and Commentary by F.W. Norris and Translation by Lionel Wickham and Frederick Williams. 1990. ISBN 90 04 09253 6
14. OORT, J. VAN. *Jerusalem and Babylon.* A Study into Augustine's *City of God* and the Sources of His Doctrine of the Two Cities. 1991. ISBN 90 04 09323 0
15. LARDET, P. *L'Apologie de Jérôme contre Rufin.* Un commentaire. 1993. ISBN 90 04 09457 1
16. RISCH, F.X. *Pseudo-Basilius: Adversus Eunomium IV-V.* Einleitung, Übersetzung und Kommentar. 1992. ISBN 90 04 09558 6
17. KLIJN, A.F.J. *Jewish-Christian Gospel Tradition.* 1992. ISBN 90 04 09453 9
18. ELANSKAYA, A.I. *The Literary Coptic Manuscripts in the A.S. Pushkin State Fine Arts Museum in Moscow.* ISBN 90 04 09528 4
19. WICKHAM, L.R. and BAMMEL, C.P. (eds.). *Christian Faith and Greek Philosophy in Late Antiquity.* Essays in Honour of Professor Stead's 80th Birthday. 1993. ISBN 90 04 09605 1